From Brezhnev to Gorbachev

Domestic Affairs and Soviet Foreign Policy

From Brezhnev to Gorbachev

Domestic Affairs and Soviet Foreign Policy

Edited by

Hans-Joachim Veen

BERG
Leamington Spa / Hamburg / New York
Distributed exclusively in the US and Canada by
St. Martin's Press New York

Berg Publishers Limited
24 Binswood Avenue, Leamington Spa, CV32 5SQ, UK
Schenefelder Landstr. 14K, 2000 Hamburg 55, W.-Germany
Room 400, 175 Fifth Avenue, New York, NY 10010, USA

The present volume is a revised edition of
*Wohin entwickelt sich die Sowjetunion? Zur aussenpolitischen
Relevanz innenpolitischer Entwicklungen*, Verlag Ernst Knoth,
Melle, 1984.
© Verlag Ernst Knoth GmbH, Melle, and Konrad-Adenauer-Stiftung
e.V., St Augustin, 1984

English publication © H.-J Veen and Berg Publishers 1987

British Library Cataloguing in Publication Data

From Brezhnev to Gorbachev: domestic affairs
   and Soviet foreign policy.
   1. Soviet Union—Social conditions—1945–
   I. Veen, Hans-Joachim
   947.085   HN523.5

   ISBN 0–85496–501–7

Library of Congress Cataloging-in-Publication Data

Deutsch-Amerikanische Konferenz (3rd: 1984:
   Sozialwissenschaftliches Forschungsinstitut der
   Konrad-Adenauer-Stiftung)
   From Brezhnev to Gorbachev.

   'Revised edition of Wohin entwickelt sich die
Sowjetunion?'—T.p. verso.
   Bibliography: p.
   Includes index.
   1. Soviet Union—Economic conditions—1976–   —Con-
gresses.   2. Soviet Union—Politics and government—
1953–   —Congresses.   3. Soviet Union—Social
conditions—1970–   —Congresses.   I. Veen,
Hans-Joachim.   II. Title.
HC336.25.D4953   1984   330.947′085   86–29926
ISBN 0–85496–501–7

Printed in Great Britain by Billings of Worcester

Contents

Preface

Domestic policy and foreign policy are mutually dependent and influence one another. This is as true for the Soviet Union as elsewhere. Nevertheless, one cannot deny the impression that there is little systematic knowledge about those internal developments in the other superpower that do, in various ways, have an impact on Soviet foreign, national security and trade policy, on the USSR's international role in general.

The papers in this collection will address those kinds of questions. They can be seen as a balance-sheet on the domestic situation in the Soviet Union, in its economic and cultural as well as political aspects. This volume represents an attempt to sketch a picture of the Soviet Union in the 1980s in a comprehensive (so far as it is relevant to Moscow's international behaviour) but nevertheless precise and detailed fashion.

The papers were originally presented at a conference sponsored by the Research Institute of the Kondrad-Adenauer-Stiftung in the spring of 1984 under the title: 'The Soviet Union in the 1980s: Foreign Policy and Domestic Affairs'. All papers have been revised for publication. The article on the Kremlin leadership has been expanded to take account of Gorbachev's rise to power.

There are many people who helped make this volume possible and whom I should like to thank. Among them are Professor Wolfgang Pfeiler, responsible for editing, and translators Mrs Eileen Martin, Mr Richard Fulker, Mr P.S. Falla and Mr Dean S. McMurry.

Sankt Augustin bei Bonn,   H.-J. V.
December 1986

Foreword

Our German–American conferences have become a welcome tradition for both sides. At our first symposium we set ourselves the task of taking a closer look at internal developments in the United States. Our analysis concluded that the label 'Neo-Conservatism', used quite commonly in those days, was insufficient in characterizing these developments. This common stock-taking helped enhance our mutual understanding.

Our second conference was devoted to some of the problems in German-American relations. Our question was, where will this relationship lead to? The discussion made it clear that it is not enough to know the internal developments of each others' country but that, for a partnership to last, mutual understanding must also include a common perception and evaluation of the international situation and its problems.

The conference at which these papers were presented dealt with the Soviet Union. It was the first symposium of the Konrad Adenauer Foundation to concentrate exclusively on the USSR. However, it fitted seamlessly into the tradition of previous gatherings. Our aim was to focus on those essential aspects of international politics which have had a decisive impact on the United States and on Europe.

Our subject was: 'Where is the Soviet Union going?'

The change in the Kremlin leadership after the death of Andropov lent this question a new urgency. However, the conference had been planned long before that event and the questions that were raised and answered there, were of a long-term nature. There was much more involved than a new leadership. Essentially, our question was: what are the sources of Soviet power? We are interested in the Soviet economy, its resources and the people who are using these resources for economic purposes. What will the future situation be for the consumer? What are the main trends in economic-industrial development? How dependent is the Soviet Union on Western technology? We are interested in the system of power and its potential dangers. What impact do dissidents and intellectuals have as oppositional forces? Is the military gaining new importance in Soviet politics? What is the impact of ethnic and religious problems on the stability of the system? Finally, we are interested in the possibilities and limitations in reforming the system as a whole.

The former American Deputy Secretary of State, Ken Dam, remarked: 'Despite fifty years of intense preoccupation with our Soviet relationship, we still know and understand far too little about the Soviet Union'.

In addition, the opinions given in the West in answer to these questions often differ widely and are sometimes extremely antagonistic. There are assessments which point to the instability of the Soviet system and insist that these trends will grow stronger. On the other hand, one can always hear voices emphasising how stable the system is. The uncertainty over how to assess developments in the Soviet Union, the stability or instability of the system, is widespread.

Consequently, it is necessary not only to intensify Soviet studies in general. There is also a growing need to discuss the findings of the research in the light of the different perspectives coming from both sides of the Atlantic. And so European and American experts came together at this symposium to discuss and to share both their knowledge and the results of their academic research. Here I would like to take the opportunity to thank Ambassador Staar and the Hoover Institution for its participation. But my very special thanks also go to our co-sponsor, the Center for Strategic and International Studies of the Georgetown University, Washington, DC, for making it possible for Professor Byrnes, together with a number of experts who have recently concluded a more substantial research project on our topic, to present their findings at this conference.

To sum up: The purpose of this conference was to enhance European-American cooperation in the political and academic field. We hope that helped to contribute to the common understanding of a country which sees us above all as its potential military adversary and has never stopped fighting an ideological struggle against liberal democracies under the cover of peaceful coexistence while aggressively denying ideological coexistence. There are, however, signals of change in the Soviet Union which we will not ignore, especially since nobody will prevail on us not to find ways and means to give

Europe a lasting order of peace.

There have always been divergent opinions and different perceptions of the Soviet Union on both sides of the Atlantic, especially over the last few years. Correspondingly, ideas on how to deal with the Soviet Union and how to respond to Soviet policy have quite often differed.

By better knowing each others' perceptions and by studying together the other great world power in order to gain an internationally balanced systematic knowledge of the Soviet Union, we create an essential precondition for coordinating our policy in the alliance of freedom.

The Konrad-Adenauer-Stiftung was happy to bring together such a renowned and in this respect rather extraordinary circle of Soviet experts from the United States, Israel, the Federal Republic of Germany and other West European countries.

Bruno Heck
President of the Konrad-Adenauer-Stiftung

PART I

The Soviet Economy

Introduction to Part I: The Soviet Economy
Wolfgang Pfeiler

Well before Mikhail Gorbachev became the new General Secretary of the Communist Party in March 1985, he made clear that he attached special importance to the development and 'intensification' of the Soviet economy: 'Only an intensive economy, developed on the most up-to-date scientific and technical basis, can constitute a reliable material foundation for increasing the well-being of the working population, consolidating our country's position in the international field and enabling it to embark on the next millenium in a worthy manner, as a great and flourishing power.'[1] In his keynote speech on economic policy, delivered on 11 June 1985 Gorbachev declared that this 'intensification', based on scientific and technical progress, was the 'fundamental question of the Party's economic policy'.[2]

There is nothing surprising in the news that the Soviet economy leaves much to be desired in this respect but the declining growth rates at the beginning of the 1980s revealed what might be a dramatic worsening of the situation. For this reason in particular, the third German-American conference of the Konrad Adenauer Foundation attached primary importance to the subject of the Soviet economy. Experts from the USA and West Germany, as well as from Britain, Israel and Austria, discussed developmental trends, energy problems, the role of modern technology and the importance of foreign trade to the Soviet Union. Close attention was also devoted to the possibilities and likelihood of economic reform.

All these problems were presented and discussed against the background of the most recent crises in the Soviet leadership. While Yurii Andropov's policies had begun to show some initial success, they had not overcome the lethargy of the Brezhnev era, and the succession of Konstantin Chernenko brought about fresh stagnation.

The assessment of the Soviet Union's economic relations with foreign countries is an important factor in determining Western

1. M.S. Gorbachev, speech to ideological functionaries reported in *Pravda*, 11 November 1984, p. 2.
2. Cf. *Pravda*, 16 June 1985, p. 1.

policy towards the USSR. The well-known differences of view between the US and Western Europe concerning East–West trade and the importance of technology transfer were also reflected in a lively discussion.

1

Trends in the Soviet Economy

The Consumer Economy
Maria Elisabeth Ruban

Definition

In scientific and newspaper reports on everyday life in the Soviet Union there is frequent mention of a 'crisis in supply'. Experts produce statistics on production and consumption to show stagnation or decline in a variety of consumer goods, while scarcely a travel report fails to mention the endless queues at food shops. The Western visitor is also put off by the scanty selection, if there is any at all, of meat and vegetables in the state-run shops, making the low subsidised prices for these goods a mockery for most consumers. These reports are not false, they are merely a vivid illustration of the fact that the Soviet Union is still suffering from a shortage of basic essentials, unable to provide what people want and can afford to buy.

The gap between supply and demand, between needs and the goods to satisfy them, varies greatly however, from one item to another. There have also been noticeable changes — mostly improvements — over time, although these have not been consistent. The beginning of the 1980s in fact marked a disappointing phase for the consumer.

This chapter attempts to provide as realistic a description as possible of the present level of supply and consumption by examining three questions:

— What supply targets has the Soviet Union set itself?
— How have supply and consumption developed over the last two decades and what is their present level?
— How should Soviet consumer policy and the way it is implemented be assessed?

'Rational' Norms and 'Reasonable' Needs

Soviet experts distinguish between three kinds of need: minimal (the basic essentials), actually satisfied (annual per capita consumption) and 'potential' ('desirable' consumption by 'reasonable' or 'rational' standards).

It is generally accepted that neither the minimal nor the desirable needs are absolute or objective; they are influenced by a large number of factors, such as regional conditions, traditional consumer habits, fashion and not least the real financial situation of low, middle and high income groups.[1]

The television set is a good illustration of how an item can change from one category to the next: in the 1950s a television set was a 'potential' need, but it has long since moved up into the second category; now that 90 per cent of all households have one it is an actually satisfied need. Soon it will probably be regarded as a basic essential.[2]

To quantify desirable consumption the Soviet Union has developed a system of norms. These are sets of figures on which experts in various fields (economists, medical experts, food specialists, sociologists and so on) are constantly working. It is their task to assemble a kind of 'basket of items' containing all the goods and services a person requires to satisfy his physical, psychological, social and cultural needs to a high level. Work has been proceeding on this system of norms for more than twenty years now and the list has not only been greatly extended (it began with between twenty and thirty foodstuffs but now includes nearly 600 items of every kind), quantity data has also been revised at various times and certain items have been taken off or exchanged for others. The value of the norms, which of course are not in any way binding for the consumer, consists mainly in defining the long-term targets for consumer goods production and the services sector, and so indicating the framework in which the Soviet leaders see the future optimal level of supply for their people and by which real development can be measured. Since this development varies according to the major consumer categories (food, clothing, housing and household goods) these will have to be examined separately.

1. V. Orlov, O. Saenko, 'The Emergence and Development of Needs and Consumption' (in Russian), in: *Voprosy ekonomiki* 10/1982, p. 97.
2. Loc. cit.

Consumer Goods

Food

Quantitatively the food supply can be regarded as having been satisfactory since the 1960s, for since then food consumption in the Soviet Union has been above 3,000 calories a day per person. It has now stabilised at 3,400 calories, just below the European average.[3] However, the choice available is still unsatisfactory, and neither suits the requirements of a modern industrial society nor matches the Soviet Union's own desired norms. Animal products, for instance, are too low, accounting for only a quarter of the Soviet diet but one-third of the average daily intake of calories in Europe (East and West).[4] The development in per capita consumption of the main foodstuffs from 1965 to 1982 can be seen from the following table.

Table 1.1 Per capita consumption of foodstuffs, in kg.

	1965	1970	1975	1980	1982	rational norm	1982 in % of norm
Meat, meat products	41.0	48.0	57.0	58.0	57.0	82.0	69.5
Milk and dairy products[1]	251.0	307.0	316.0	314.0	295.0	434.0	68.0
Fish, fish products	12.6	15.4	16.8	17.6	18.4	18.2	101.0
Eggs[2]	124.0	159.0	216.0	239.0	249.0	292.0	85.3
Sugar	34.2	38.8	40.9	44.4	44.5	36.5	122.0
Vegetable fats	7.1	6.8	7.6	8.8	9.3	—	—
Potatoes	142.0	130.0	120.0	109.0	110.0	97.0	113.0
Vegetables	72.0	82.0	89.0	97.0	101.0	146.0	69.2
Fruit	28.0	35.0	39.0	38.0	42.0	113.0	37.2
Cereal products[3]	156.0	149.0	141.0	138.0	137.0	120.0	114.0

1. Calculated in milk units
2. Number
3. Calculated in flour units
Sources: *Soviet Statistical Yearbook*, various years

Three major developments are revealed here:
— From 1965 to 1975 there was a marked improvement in the food structure. The changes in consumption typical of a rising stan-

3. *FAO Production Yearbook 1982*, p. 262.
4. Loc. cit.

dard of living are evident, namely a rise in the consumption of meat, milk, eggs, fruit and vegetables with a simultaneous decline in the consumption of potatoes and cereal products.

— Since 1975 this trend, especially in meat consumption (a particularly sensitive indicator of prosperity) has halted, and the consumption of milk has actually fallen below the 1970 level.

— The consumption levels indicated are greatly below the norms, which in turn roughly correspond to the Western pattern of consumption; Czechoslovakia and the GDR have also achieved these.

The shortcomings in the level of consumption in the Soviet Union are clearly the result of shortages in supply, and these are the direct consequence of the production crisis which the Soviet grain industry has suffered from since 1979. Extensive imports of grain from Western countries (mainly as animal feed) did prevent the — otherwise inevitable — drop in meat consumption, but were not sufficient to raise per capita consumption as intended. Under the impact of the continuing supply problems, which at times necessitated meat and milk rationing in some areas, the Soviet leaders developed a food programme at the beginning of the 1980s which was unveiled by Brezhnev in May 1982 and subsequently reconfirmed by Andropov and Chernenko. The programme aims to provide a 'radical' solution to the food question by 1990, and at the same time to overcome or at least to reduce the dependence on foreign grain imports. The prospects of meeting the targets in the programme are judged rather sceptically in the West, firstly because the consumption targets per capita of the population for 1990 are still below the scientific norms, so that they would not amount to a 'radical' solution, and secondly because it would be difficult to achieve even these relatively modest aims in the time remaining. In the critical area of meat supply in particular, it is hard to see how per capita consumption could be increased by 13 kg. in eight years (1982–90), namely from 57 to 70 kg. (with an annual population increase of c. 2 million) after a virtual zero rate of increase over the previous seven years (1975–82). All in all the food programme should not be taken as a signpost to a radical solution but as an attempt to find the way back to the path of slow but steady progress which Brezhnev had brought about and was able to maintain for so many years. It must also be borne in mind that the Soviet leaders have put themselves under considerable pressure with their vigorous propagation of the food programme, and considerable dissatisfaction may be anticipated among the population at large if current targets are not met.[5]

Clothing and shoes

The supply situation regarding clothing and shoes is much more a matter of quality and range. While the consumption of meat, milk and fruit (too low by the norms) is a result of the shortage of supply, the stagnation in consumption of clothing and shoes is due to the reluctance of customers to buy old-fashioned, badly made and unattractive goods. Table 1.2 provides a survey of the quantitative development in consumption of these items (new purchases p.a.):

Table 1.2 Consumption of clothing and shoes per inhabitant per year

	Unit	1965	1970	1975	1980	1982	rational norm	1982 in % of norm
Material	sq.m	26.5	30.4	32.5	34.6	34.6	50.0	69
of which[1]								
Cotton	sq.m	19.1	21.2	22.0	23.8	24.1	28.4	85
Wool	sq.m	2.5	2.7	2.8	2.7	2.6	3.8	68
Silk	sq.m	3.6	4.7	5.9	6.6	6.3	9.1	69
Linen	sq.m	1.3	1.8	1.8	1.5	1.4	4.5	31
Knitwear	items	0.9	1.8	2.0	2.1	2.0	4.0	50
Underwear	items	3.3	3.5	3.9	4.4	4.3	9.4	46
Stockings								
and socks	pairs	5.8	6.0	6.1	6.8	6.7	8.3	81
Leather								
shoes	pairs	2.4	3.0	3.2	3.2	3.1	3.6	86

1. Not including material for industrial use
Source: Soviet Statistical Yearbook, various years

The clothing norms, like the food norms, are not orientated to minimal requirements, they describe a desirable standard. However, consumption of silk, wool and cotton goods, as well as shoes and stockings, have now come closer to the norms, at two-thirds to four-fifths. It can be assumed that the greater majority of the

5. Y. Markish, A.F. Malish, 'The Soviet Food Program: Prospects for the 1980s', in: *The Aces Bulletin* 1/1983, p. 64.

population is adequately provided with basic items of clothing and this explains their reluctance to buy more. They can afford to be choosy and wait for the goods they really want. Western imports, together with clothing and shoes from Hungary, the GDR and Czechoslovakia, enjoy high priority over domestic products, large quantities of which accumulate in the shops from year to year. There are no regular summer or winter sales in the Soviet Union but at irregular intervals the shops do try to get rid of stock that has not been sold by drastically reducing prices.

Consumer durables

The astonishingly rapid rise of the television set from a desirable to a *de facto* satisfied need, almost a basic essential, is not a unique case among household goods. On the contrary, in no other consumer area has the standard of supply improved so markedly in the last two decades as in consumer durables. Radio and television sets, fridges, washing machines and vacuum cleaners (see Table 1.3) can be taken as representative here.

Table 1.3 Stock of consumer durables per 100 households

	1965	1970	1975	1980	1982
Radio sets	59	72	79	85	90
Television sets	24	52	74	85	91
Fridges	11	32	61	86	89
Washing machines	21	52	65	70	70
Vacuum cleaners	7	12	18	29	33

Source: *Soviet Statistical Yearbook*, 1982

There are consumption norms for these (and a large number of other items of household equipment), and many of them have been revised upwards. At the beginning of the 1960s, for example, the Standard of Living Section of the Central Planning Agency considered that washing machines and fridges could if necessary be shared by several families, and they assumed that forty-seven washing machines would suffice for 100 families. However, it soon became apparent that families were not prepared to share items of this kind — they wanted their own and were prepared to do without other things to get them. So the Planning Agency raised the norm for washing machines to 100 per cent. The figure for radios and television sets now stands at above 100 per cent, as a growing number of families want these items in their weekend homes as well, or else individual members of a family want their own set.[6]

Private cars

A private car is every Soviet consumer's dream and is second only to an apartment in his list of priorities. This is a wish that is still far from being satisfied, but strong and persistent pressure from people who are in a position to buy a car will certainly have helped to make the planning authorities drop their opposition to the idea of broad sections of the population being motorised. Khrushchev, who wanted the Soviet people to have the highest standard of living in the world and prophesied that they would achieve this goal in the near future, expressly did not want to see private motorisation on the Western scale. An optimal public transport network and efficient taxi system were to make private cars unnecessary. Perhaps it was also the prospect of being able to cream off surplus purchasing power that made the economic planners more prepared to meet the demand for private cars. At any rate, production of private cars trebled during the 1970s, the great leap forward coming with the construction of the Togliatti works from 1970 to 1975. The current annual production of 1.3 million private cars, which is to rise to 1.5 million by 1985, is not nearly enough to meet demand, and the waiting lists are many years long, despite extremely high prices. A small Moskvich car costs nearly 7,500 rubles after the latest price increases in 1981, or forty-three gross months' wages for an average blue or white collar worker.

Altogether, the stock of private cars remains very low and so does the 'motorisation density'. About 6 per cent of all private households can be taken to have their own car, a very low figure even by CMEA standards (40 per cent of all families have a car in the GDR and Czechoslovakia). The Soviet Union will only be able to make up the gap very slowly, and for years the private car will presumably remain an item 'with scarcity value and so a high social prestige'.[7]

6. J.J. Busljakov, 'Das Wohl des Menschen — höchstes Ziel des Sozialismus. Zur langfristigen Planung des Lebensstandards in der Sowjetunion', in: *Die Wirtschaft* 5/1973, pp. 5f.
7. M. Lodahl, 'Private Motorisierung', in: Ruban *et al*, *Wandel der Arbeits- und Lebensbedingungen in der Sowjetunion 1955–1980*, Frankfurt 1983, p. 234.

Housing

In the list of priorities of Soviet families that is occasionally revealed in surveys 'a separate flat with comforts' regularly occupies first place. 'Comforts' amount to a bath, drains and central heating. The average city dweller has to wait many years for these. The situation is relatively satisfactory for persons employed in certain privileged jobs or in one of the major enterprises because they may be able to get an apartment through their boss. In that case a blue- or white-collar worker with a family may have a chance of being allocated a flat after three or four years. Those without these advantages can expect to wait between eight and ten years. In any case applicants have a right to be put on the municipal housing list if they are living under very bad conditions, that is with less than 5 sq.m of living space per family member or without essential amenities such as running water.

New housing

Like agriculture and the consumer industry, housing has been one of the neglected areas of the Soviet economy for decades. Up to the end of the 1950s housing demand was assessed as 'a roof over the head' for every inhabitant, and the great majority were housed in communal or community housing, i.e. each family had one room and shared kitchen and bathroom. It was not until the new housing laws were passed in 1957 and 1959 that two important changes took place:
— Housing construction doubled.
— The new flats are almost all small separate apartments intended for one family. The average size is also growing slowly, having risen from 42 sq.m. in 1960 to 52 sq.m. in 1980.
Housing costs are extremely low to the consumer, since the state meets all building costs from budget funds and the running costs are also heavily subsidised. An average family spends only 1 per cent of its household income on rent, and 4 per cent if all costs for heating, lighting, water etc. are included.

Around two million new housing units (apartments and houses) are built every year. The state share has grown steadily, and now accounts for about 80 per cent of new housing construction. Unlike some of the other CMEA countries (Poland, Hungary, Bulgaria and Czechoslovakia) co-operative housing construction, which enables members to buy their own homes, is only of minor importance in the Soviet Union. In 1982 it accounted for 5 per cent of new housing, the remaining 15 per cent being privately built homes. These were mostly the very simple stone or wooden shacks in which the kolkhoz peasants live with no urban amenities at all.

The housing stock

The Soviet housing policy target is 15–20 sq.m of living space per inhabitant, and if the present tempo is kept up this could be achieved by 1990–2000. On an international level of comparison even this is a very modest goal (present living space per inhabitant in the GDR is 24 sq.m and in the FRG 31 sq.m.).[8] Nevertheless, there has been remarkable progress since 1960, particularly considering the stagnation prevailing over previous decades (Table 1.4).

Table 1.4 Urban housing stock

	Total usable space in mill. sq.m	Usable space per urban inhabitant in mill. sq.m
1913	180	6.3
1917	185	6.4
1940	421	6.7
1950	513	7.0
1960	958	8.9
1965	1,238	10.0
1970	1,529	11.0
1975	1,867	12.3
1980	2,200	13.2
1982	2,343	13.6

Source: Narodnoe Khozyaistvo SSSR, various years

Current data on the expansion of housing per inhabitant was previously published only for the urban population. Since 1980 however, official figures have also been available for the rural population. They reveal that in 1982 the country dweller had on average 14.8 sq.m living space[9], while the urban dweller had to make do with 13.6 sq.m. Data on the quality of housing is sporadic and sketched in rough outline, but from what is available it may be

8. M. Melzer, 'Qualitative Aspekte der regionalen Wohnungsversorgung in der DDR', in: *Deutschland Archiv*, May 1980, p. 154.
9. *Narodnoe Khozyaistvo* 1982, Moscow 1983, p. 394.

concluded that: About half the total number of urban families are now living in flats that are both separate and have the usual amenities, a further quarter are in separate flats which lack these amenities, while the remaining quarter are still in community housing.

The kolkhoz peasants' own homes and those of other rural dwellers do not usually have any amenities (except electric lighting) and they have little more space than city apartments. However, they do have a garden and perhaps some additional facilities (such as a veranda, a shed and so on), which give a bit more scope. The people generally see these as being more important than the amount of living space or urban 'comfort'. Living in a house of your own is not regarded as a sign of higher income, it is part of the rural, specifically peasant, way of life.'[10]

Assessing Soviet Consumer Policy

The Soviet leaders have long recognised that meeting consumer needs more effectively by offering a greater selection and range is a major precondition to achieving higher economic growth (because it acts as an incentive). The concrete targets for the supply of goods are high. However, Soviet planners are clearly inclined to overestimate the productivity of their economy, while the time-scale envisaged for many of the projects is too short. In content the targets describe a level of supply similar to that prevailing in a highly developed Western industrial society. The same applies to the satisfaction of need, which is totally individualistic, from a separate flat for each family with private ownership of all technical durables, to the (still very distant) goal of one car per family. There do not appear to be any particular features of a socialist consumer pattern here. Groups similar to those in some Western societies that are seeking an 'alternative' way of living, in which reducing consumption is one of the determinant factors, are not to be found in the Soviet Union (and their ideas would probably be incomprehensible to people living there).

However, Soviet economists, philosophers and sociologists are now asking how households with above average incomes can be directed to develop a reasonable structure of demand, for the

10. W. Teckenberg, *Die soziale Struktur der sowjetischen Arbeiterklasse im internationalen Vergleich. Auf dem Wege zur industriellen Ständegesellschaft?* Munich/Vienna, 1977, p. 111.

consumer behaviour of the more prosperous groups has not so far been what is looked for. They tend to spend too much on food and drink, particularly alcohol, and too little on services.[11] Reorientating these groups is regarded as important because they will set standards for the others. The problem is how, while recognising the right to individual selection in consumption and leisure pursuits, to implement the claim that raising living standards under socialism also means 'educating people to a reasonable demand structure and a meaningful way of using their leisure'.[12] Solutions are still being sought to that particular problem.

11. Orlov, Saenko, loc. cit., p. 106.
12. T. Dorochina, 'The Economic Aspect of the Socialist Way of Life' (in Russian), in: *Voprosy ekonomiki* 11/1979, p. 17.

Soviet Agriculture
Karl-Eugen Wädekin

Over the medium to long term the production trend in Soviet agriculture has been quite impressive since the death of Stalin: from 1960 to 1980 agricultural production increased by 3 per cent p.a., while the population grew by just 1.3 per cent annually. Incomes also rose markedly, but it must be borne in mind that with growing incomes the share of expenditure on food tends to drop. Nevertheless, even before 1970 growth in incomes, which went beyond the possibilities for increasing agricultural production, led to an accumulated surplus in demand and in 1962 this, together with increasing production costs, brought the only open and considerable increases in consumer prices (for meat and dairy products).

In the last five years, on the other hand, the growth in gross production in Soviet agriculture has been below the growth in population; the average for 1980–3 was only 1.3 per cent above that of 1976–9, and without imports of animal feed it would have been below that level, while the total population increased by 3.33 per cent from 1978 to 1982. The sum of nominal wages (not including kolkhoz members) actually rose by 17.6 per cent during the same period. Since there was already a surplus in demand for food, especially high quality foodstuffs, the critical supply situation is evident even from the official figures.

The main reasons for the demand surplus are the forced industrialisation and urbanisation policies that have taken the number of wage- and salary-earners from 62 million in 1960 to 115 million in 1982 (though this includes more than five million kolkhoz peasants who became workers on co-operative farms), and the wage policy designed to act as an incentive, which raised the average nominal wage from 80.6 rubles to 177.3 rubles a month, though only rather more than half this probably amounted to an increase in real wages.

A similar picture is apparent from the index figures calculated by the Food and Agricultural Organisation of the UN, from which the following table was compiled. They should be compared with the rise in purchasing power that can be deduced from the official figures on average wages and salaries of the non-rural population and the total number of people in this sector. However, this needs to be deflated by the effect of concealed price increases, for which the *CIA Handbook of Economic Statistics* (1983) gives realistic estimates. This shows a rise of 23 per cent in total purchasing power in 1975 over 1970, and a further rise of 25 per cent by 1982. It must be added that the average food price increases in the official shops are very low, but on the legal and illegal free markets they have been much greater. On the other hand, side-earnings presumably also rose more than wages and salaries. So these percentages should rather be seen as the lower threshold for the rise in demand in the food area as a whole.

Table 1.5 The development of per capita food consumption in the USSR 1971–82 (three-year averages, index 1974–6 = 100)

	1971–3	1974–6	1977–9	1980–2
Total (kilo calories)	98.3	100	102.8	95.5
of which animal products	95.8	100	103.4	99.9
Grain production (phys. quantity index)	105.8	100	108.3	91.3

Source: *FAO Production Yearbook 1982*, Rome 1983, Tables 9, 12 and 15

Assuming a coefficient of income elasticity in demand for food of 0.6 — a cautious estimate for Soviet conditions — at least 10 per cent more should have been produced per capita in 1975 than at the beginning of the decade (instead of just on 2 per cent), if only to avoid widening the existing surplus in demand, and at least 6 per cent more in 1982 than the average for 1974–6, instead of 4.5 per cent less, as was actually the case. So the demand surplus has increased, especially during the last six years.

Add to this a weak consumer goods industry and service sector which cannot offer consumers an adequate choice, and a policy of almost unchanged low and increasingly subsidised prices for basic food-stuffs, and the result is a high income elasticity in demand, especially for animal products which need more plant produce (feed) per calorie than direct human consumption. There is not on the whole an absolute, physiological shortage, not even of animal protein (but that does not mean there are no periodic or regional shortages).

A major factor in the years since 1975 has been the huge imports of grain, oil seed (both used mainly as animal feed), butter, meat and sugar. Only thanks to these could per capita consumption of meat (but not of milk) be kept at least to the 1975 level, while that of

sugar has actually increased. The official figure for per capita consumption of meat in 1982 was 57 kg., but by Western statistical
definitions this should at most have been 48 kg. Grain imports again
dropped slightly in 1982 and 1983 (see below, p. 29), partly owing
to greater imports of oil seed which have a higher protein content in
feed. Many Western observers have concentrated too much on the
grain balance and were therefore surprised by the latest recovery in
Soviet livestock farming.

However, although other plant crops are of great importance
there can be no doubt that grain is still the basic foodstuff in the
Soviet economy. It plays an unusually big part in Soviet livestock
production, while 35 per cent of all cattle feed used in 1982 (including pasture, reckoned in oats units) was concentrated feed, 80–90
per cent of which consisted of grain. The 1965 figure was 23 per
cent, appropriate for the low productivity per animal. The grain
harvests were not only below the average target of 205m. tonnes for
1976–80, they actually dropped even further, to an average of
170–80m. tonnes during the period 1981–3 (by Western estimates,
which have in the main proved correct). Even with imports of more
than 30m. tonnes *p.a.* this was not enough to meet the grain
requirements for animal feed. Moscow did not publish any grain
statistics for 1981 and 1982, and it was not until Chernenko took
over that (in his election speech of 2 March 1984) he claimed that
more than 190m. tonnes had been harvested in 1983.

Only Limited Possibilities for Growth in Production

The increase in Soviet agricultural production is due mainly to the
following factors and measures:

Capital

The use of capital for investment and as operating funds can no
longer be increased at the same rate as in the past, since at the level
now reached this would require very much greater sums. These are
not available, because the investment rhythm has slowed down in
the economy as a whole. The share of agriculture was 19.5 per cent
in 1982 and this actually increased to 20.3 per cent over the period
1976–80. In more recent Soviet statements more use is made of the
wider term 'investment to develop the agricultural-industrial com-

plex', which includes related areas and is to account altogether for 30–35 per cent in 1981–5, as compared with 27 per cent in the narrower definition 'capital investment for agricultural development in the whole complex of labour'. In absolute terms the increase during 1981–5 will certainly be only around 10 per cent. It must also be borne in mind that we are talking here of gross investment. The increase in net investment will have been even lower, if there is any at all after allowance has been made for price increases.

Wages and labour

Similar reservations apply to wage rises in agriculture, although these are still far ahead of the economy as a whole. In assessing the figures for both capital input and earned income it must be remembered that the real figures will be much more subject to the effects of inflation today than twenty and more years ago. There is now a labour surplus only in relation to the degree of mechanisation in the sub-regions, and the total numbers in the workforce (excepting the private sector, see below) is still dropping.

Land

No further increases of note can be expected in the acreage of arable land, unlike thirty years ago, unless very costly irrigation projects are carried out (particularly the re-routing of the northern rivers), or unless elaborate recultivation of exhausted or fallow areas of central and northern Russia (programme for the non-black earth zone) takes place.

Reorganisation

No fundamental changes in the planning, steering and administration structures are envisaged, but Soviet agrarian experts are now clearly pinning their hopes on measures to change the use of labour within the enterprise and the wage system ('contract brigades', autonomous work-teams) and to integrate agriculture with related areas (agro-industrial associations, especially at district level). The author has explained in detail elsewhere why he does not expect this to have any noticeable effect in increasing productivity and has no more to add here.[1]

The Private Sector

The subject of much discussion in the Soviet Union, and of considerable interest in the West, are the attempts (greatly stepped up since 1977) to make private subsidiary farming a growth factor in food production. According to Soviet estimates these private plots produce around one-quarter of the gross agricultural value produced. However, there are two undeniable political obstacles and these are also discussed, indirectly and sometimes directly, in the Soviet press and the specialist journals. These are the opposition from lower and middle functionaries and the determination apparent at the top to prevent any surpluses the private farmers may have accumulated from finding their way onto the free market at appropriate prices. This produce is instead to be channelled onto the official market at controlled prices, but the official markets are generally neither efficient nor flexible enough, and their prices do not adequately reflect quality or offer the incentive which the free market offers. A further factor to be considered is the demographic one which, unlike twenty years ago, is having the effect of gradually eliminating the labour reserve, particularly in areas where plots are lying fallow and require this very labour-intensive kind of farming. The total supply of labour in the private sector has increased again in recent years, but this will not alter the situation. So the measures adopted thus far, unless they are very greatly stepped up, may at best achieve a moderate increase in production on the part of the private sector, but not the upswing required to bring about a noticeable and lasting improvement in the supply situation as a whole.

The earlier rapid increase in agricultural production, especially in the mid-1950s and again in the 1960s, resulted mainly from the relaxation in the official attitude to the private sector and especially to private cattle farming (1953–5 and 1964–7), the expansion of arable land (by opening up new farming land and some irrigation), greater capital input and an increase in wages. Since then the policy towards the private sector has been inconsistent, and the natural limits to opening up new farming land have been reached. Taking the five-year average for 1976–80 over 1966–70 the growth rate was

---

1. ''Contract' and 'Normless' Labour on Soviet Farms', and 'Agro-industrial Associations take Root Across the USSR', in: *Radio Liberty Research* 49/84 and 60/84 (8, 13 February 1984).

only around 2.2 per cent. A return to the growth rates of the period before 1975 is not to be expected, certainly not to that of the 1950s. However, a continuation of the near stagnation of the period from 1979 to 1982 is not very likely either. Some additional investment and operating funds will certainly be provided, so the quality of the labour force should gradually improve while the numbers should drop only slowly. Moreover, the private sector is at least now not being actively suppressed. An average growth in gross production terms of between 1 per cent and 2 per cent is therefore likely over several years, and this would amount to between 0.5 and 1 per cent above the natural increase in the population. However, it would not suffice to reduce the huge surplus in demand in the foreseeable future.

Some Chance of a Gradual Improvement

The heavy losses in grain and other feed harvests will probably be reduced, if only very slowly. But if the grain losses could be reduced by only one half percentage point, more than 1m. tonnes more would be available in an average year, and similar improvements would be possible in wet and raw feed.

Adequate quantities of feed are not the only factor in higher livestock production; the intensity of the farming matters as well, as do other factors such as the quality of the herds, stall capacities and quality, the care of the animals (adequate personnel and machinery) and so on. Soviet livestock farming has so much backlog to make up here that it is hard to imagine things going on without any improvement. Progress in one or the other area would have a positive effect on the feed utilisation coefficient. If this improved by only 5 per cent it would mean the same percentage increase in production (or savings in feed) of around 20m. tonnes of oats units, some of which would be directly in grain. Some improvement in both appears to have been achieved in the years 1982–3.

The seed areas, especially the grain areas, have been continuously reduced since 1973 while the fallow black soil area has grown. This should have a favourable effect, not only on yield per hectare, but also in helping to reduce the bottlenecks in labour and machinery at seed time and harvest. Meat and milk yields were increased in a similar way in 1982 and 1983, but mainly by individual animal, not by increasing the number of cows and fatstock. That should reduce the consumption of feed per unit produced, and there have been signs of this also in the last two years.

There can be no doubt that grain production between in 1981 and 1985 was nowhere near the average annual target of 238 to 243m. tonnes, even if there were increases in 1984 and 1985. The target for meat production, which is the main reason for the increase in grain production, is equally Utopian.

Taking the published Soviet statistics up to and including 1982 and the annual report for 1983, together with the plan figures for 1981–5 and the grain import figures, an outline of probable developments over the next few years can be elaborated, and this can be supplemented by the calculations published by the OECD. It is assumed that around 85 per cent of Soviet concentrated feed consists of grain and that 17–18 per cent must be added to the figures for grain imports to make them comparable with Soviet statistics on 'bunker harvests'. The results contain wide fluctuations and numerous uncertainties, so that one hesitates to publish them as a table since this gives the impression that the figures are precise. However, setting them out in tabular form does provide a clear idea of the assumptions and so after due consideration the following table was included. It must be pointed out that, unlike grain, a steady increase in production of 1–2.5 per cent a year has been taken as plausible for other kinds of feed (including pasture) and these, after all, account for around 70 per cent of total feed consumption. The figures are derived from the other calculations. They are in keeping with Soviet declarations of intent since 1978 and the fact that in 1982, despite reductions in grain imports, production here rose by 2 per cent and animal products by 2.6 per cent; according to preliminary data now available this development appears to have continued in 1983. The above figures do show higher grain imports during the five-year period 1981–5 than ever before and these were certainly greater than had been planned. However, on a yearly average this works out at around 30m. tonnes, or around 8m. tonnes a year less than the average for 1981–3; to put it differently, most of this has already been imported, so a reduction for the following two years has been assumed.

For the end year 1985, not the whole Five-Year Plan period, at least 2–3m. tonnes of meat less were probably produced than was intended (target: 19–20m. tonnes for the end of the five-year period). This means that actual demand for feed was about 20–25m. tonnes of oats units less than given in the plan, of which presumably

Table 1.6 Supply of grain, meat and animal feed in the Soviet Union 1976–85, in m.t

	1976–80 (Actual)	1981–5 (Plan)	1981–3 (Actual)	1981–5 (Expected)
Grain production ('Bunker' harvest)	1025	1190–1215	510–530	900–950
Grain imports (standard quality)	115	90–100(??)	114	131–166
Meat production (slaughter weight)	74.2	85–87.5	46.6	78–80
Feed production (oats units)	1550–1700	1900–2000*	—	1700–1850
Feed consumption or demand (oats units)	1979	2170–2200	1200–1220	2000–2050
of which grain (oats units)	570–615	610–660	355–365	560–615

*estimated from the plan figure of 500m.t oats units for the end year 1985 and the lower production at the beginning of the five-year period

Sources: Apart from the figures in the Soviet statistics and plan guidelines and the *FAO Production Yearbook*, calculations in *The Soviet Feed Livestock Sector and the Meat Processing Industry*, OECD, Paris 1984, pp. 66, 68, 71 (for expected meat production and feed demand) and those of the author

8–11m. tonnes was grain. Other factors may have helped to reduce the demand for grain, although they are not so important. These include a greater share of non-grain feed, a reduction in population growth and cut-backs in consumption. Consequently, Soviet grain consumption in 1985 may, at a very rough estimate, be about 12–18m. tonnes less than was planned. Around the middle of the decade or immediately after grain imports by the Soviet Union will probably not amount to more than 10–15m. tonnes in an average year and demand on the world market will be correspondingly less.

Production Costs and their Structure — the Main Problem for the Soviet Food Industry

Taking the long-term view, the main weakness of Soviet agriculture is not the quantitative discrepancy between supply and demand but the costs of the increase in production that must be achieved. The growth in costs can be gleaned now from the volume of investment, which at one-third of total investment for foodstuffs and related areas is a heavy burden on the economy as a whole. However, it is evident from other figures too: the diminishing remainder of kolkhoz gross income after deduction of labour costs, the diminishing return per ruble on investment in fixed assets and especially the constant increases in state producer prices and subsidies. Price subsidies alone were envisaged as costing 47.7 billion rubles in 1983. The other grants to agriculture (investment from the state budget, allocations to state farms, subsidies on running costs and so on) amount to the same again, altogether around 70 per cent of the total value produced by agriculture or as much again as its total sales revenue.

The hope (so often proved vain) that increased mechanisation and modernisation would lower production costs per unit produced and so help to reduce subsidies does not look like being fulfilled in future either. It is also clear that it would only be possible to increase consumer prices enough to eliminate the demand surplus and the subsidies very slowly, over an extended period and in a number of small graded steps. Admittedly the state saves money because it can keep wages lower than would otherwise be possible as long as basic foodstuffs are subsidised, and the state is virtually the only employer outside agriculture. More serious, however, is that subsidies make possible a level of consumption that is above the — very modest level — permitted by the condition of agriculture and the economy as a whole. Moreover, like most subsidies they prevent what is most urgently required: an improvement in enterprise structures and location distribution; in other words, the real reforms that would reduce the pressure of costs and so the need for subsidies.

The Soviet War Economy and Economic Development
Michael Checinski

One of today's most distinguished American Kremlinologists noted in a recently published essay (before Yurii Andropov was succeeded by Konstantin Chernenko): 'If one looks at these three successions [1953, 1964, 1982], they have in common not only deemphasizing the military, but also focusing of attention on agriculture. . . . It must result from a desire of new leadership to win support from the population and provide it with incentives. . . .' It is no wonder, he argues, that despite Marshal Ogarkov's alarmist articles 'which clearly call for higher defense expenditures, his appeals have not been satisfied. It was, to repeat, Gorbachev's Food Programme that has received the significant increment in spending. . . '.[1]

If this observation is correct, we should soon witness in the USSR not only a flourishing agriculture, but also, especially if successions become more frequent, the long-needed adequate provision of food for the Soviet population and the basic consumer goods they have also so sorely lacked; and we should further expect true freedom and democracy to appear and finally be reflected in the transient slogans and promises of the countless newspapers and books published in that country. Yet Soviet citizens know that their living conditions have never been determined by the political platitudes and baseless declarations which are circulated when each new leader comes to power, but by the hard realities of economic programmes outlined in secret sessions of the highest decision-making bodies, namely the Politburo and/or the Defence Council.

A historian writing about the economic development of the Soviet state would at his peril underestimate the importance of Soviet defence policy, particularly armaments policy and its broad and multifarious economic implications. True, Soviet economic planning has seen 'intermediate' periods when specific industrial branches or technologies were preferred to military-industrial programmes. Such temporary preferences, however, should not be

---

1. Jerry F. Hough, 'Andropov's First Year', *Problems of Communism* 32/1983, pp. 50–1.

misread as shifts in economic policy towards civilian needs, but rather as being motivated by the perceived need to build a more stable, broad based and modern arms industry.

This assessment can be borne out by reviewing the development over six-and-a-half decades of Soviet defence policy; the process can be divided into the following stages, according to changes in domestic conditions and economic programmes and the international political–military configuration:

(1) 1921–31: Most of the Soviet resources were channelled to develop a strong industrial base, although emphasis was given to those branches required for building a modern arms industry.

(2) 1932–8: The policy of rapid industrialisation continued, but a growing proportion of newly built plants was devoted exclusively to the production of military equipment. A system of preference for armaments branches in the allocation of resources was developed. The discrimination against agriculture and non-military industrial sectors and preference for quantity over quality became the permanent means of fulfilling the state economic plans, including those relating to armaments production.

(3) 1939–45: A dramatic shift of the majority of available resources to the military sectors occurred. Administrative pressure enforced by terror became the main instrument used to convert the entire national economy into a war economy; even basic civilian needs were abandoned in order to continue the military-industrial build-up and win the war; the result was suffering and starvation for millions of Soviet citizens.

(4) 1946–53: The reconstruction and modernisation of industry was accomplished with the help of resources transferred from occupied Germany and other captured parts of Europe and Asia, including resources from 'liberated' countries (Poland, Czechoslovakia). The USSR began to build a nuclear industry and to develop a modern ICBM technology. Armaments plants slowed down the production of many obsolete weapons; most resources were channelled to develop a more modern industrial base for the arms industry (ICBM, nuclear, new conventional weapons).

(5) 1954–61: New arms enterprises developed quickly and the oldest ones began to be modernised. The continuing discrimination against non-military sectors, including agriculture, was only slightly interrupted, without any serious improvements in the supply of civilian goods. Arms production began to be coordinated with other CMEA countries, whose resources, manpower skills, know-how,

international trade relations and intelligence activity were exploited. Soviet rule in Eastern Europe was stabilised through military intervention and blackmail (Poland, Hungary in 1956).

(6) 1961–71: The Soviet government started to investigate new possibilities for extending its influence and presence in other parts of the globe. Its failures in the Berlin and Cuban crises (1961) revealed the weakness of the Soviet armed forces and their inability to open a new phase of military–political expansion. This experience and the creation of a large number of new, independent states in Africa and Asia became important motivations for planning an unprecedented military build-up. For the first time in its history, the Soviet Union had overcome the constraints imposed on its military and political influence through the possession of sufficient numbers and kinds of military equipment. A large arsenal of nuclear and ICBM weapons, a powerful air-transportation system and a huge navy were all developed, and Soviet presence around the world steadily increased. In Africa and Asia the Soviet Union fomented 'wars of liberation' and created a colonialist world *imperium* in a Communist mould. Massive arms exports enhanced the continuing modernisation of the Soviet military–industrial sector. New conventional weapons were introduced to support the nuclear age war economy doctrine and military strategy, which were based on the conviction that any war, despite tremendous losses and destruction, was winnable. A new economic policy, intended to prepare the entire country to survive a nuclear conflict, began to be implemented. This included the dispersal of many new factories and towns; new transportation and communications networks, including pipelines and specially constructed roads and bridges; the creation of special material reserves and production lines; and many other very costly arrangements. In order to fulfil such an ambitious programme, the non-military sectors continued to be victimised, and the living standards of the population improved only slightly.

(7) 1972–9: This was the decade of *détente*, exploited perfectly by the USSR in order to achieve military–political objectives never before attainable. The importation of Western know-how and technologies aided modernisation and the more rapid development of the entire arms sector, particularly the backward electronics and chemical industries. The flow of Western credits and the unprecedented increase in the price of gold, oil and gas — products freely exported by the Soviet Union — created a chance simultaneously to develop arms production and to increase the living standards of the

population to a significant degree. In addition, many oil-rich countries started to buy, or to finance the purchase by others of Soviet arms on an unprecedented scale, supplying the USSR with a vast amount of much needed hard currency. This new historical phenomenon — the flow of foreign resources to the Soviet Union and its East European allies — provided the major motivation for changing the strategy of military build-up; most new technologies were imported and so did not need to be produced at the expense of non-military sectors or basic industries. For the first time the Soviet Union became one of the biggest importers of Western grain. This enabled both an increase in investment in the non-military sectors (light industry, agriculture, services) and an improvement in the supply of consumer goods, while the military–industrial build-up continued. It was not 'Brezhnev's policy' which partly rescued the domestic market from decades-old infirmity and improved the living standards of the population, it was rather the 'good luck' created by a combination of economic and political factors, the oil and gold boom coupled with growing arms exports, which were shrewdly exploited by the Soviet leaders. These conditions also helped the Soviet armed forces to become equal and, in many spheres, superior to US military power. The Soviet leadership began to believe that the time had come when their 'imperialist' adversaries could be weakened and paralysed step by step by playing the 'domino game' in sensitive areas around the world.

(8) The intervention in Afghanistan at the end of 1979 and the Polish crisis shortly afterwards created new political realities, while the drop in oil and gold prices activated a new stage in East-West relations. The Soviet leaders were forced to change some elements of their defence policy, with many implications for the coming decade.

Even this briefest of surveys of Soviet armaments policy refutes the thesis that changes were closely related to the succession process. On the contrary, a stable, coherent long-term policy with clear cut strategic aims is evident: to become the most powerful state in the world and to be able to act freely in any corner of the globe — using military blackmail, if necessary, against any nation. Such aims can be achieved only if they remain in harmony with the economic development of the Soviet state. Consequently, we must examine more closely the interaction between the defence policy and economic conditions in the past and in coming years. As we shall see, Soviet military production programmes have gained such a preponderance that few real changes can be anticipated in economic planning or defence policy in the foreseeable future.

The Soviet defence industry operates as part of a broader military–industrial complex that encompasses all segments and aspects of Soviet economic, social and administrative activities. We should stress particularly the high official priority of such diverse military–economic programmes as: civil defence; strategic material reserves (including grain); construction and location of stockpiles for wartime; special logistical arrangements with costly transportation systems adapted to war conditions; militarily orientated education programmes and health service establishments; specially organised and costly reserve production lines and militarily adaptable technologies in many industrial enterprises. These and similar defence-related outlays have multifarious and far-reaching consequences for the entire Soviet economy. They are often more expensive than important sections of the 'pure' defence budget. There is no doubt, however, that the part of the Soviet military outlay which most deeply affects the economy as a whole is arms procurement and the overall operation of the defence industry. Both tend to expand rapidly and to absorb the best available technology and manpower. A few figures will illustrate this:

From the era of *détente* in the 1970s until 1982, the USSR spent more than the equivalent of $2 trillion (US) on defence, increasing the cost of the military burden from about $130 billion in 1970 to over $200 billion in 1981 (in 1979 prices).[2] In the last decade, the USSR spent on defence an amount equal to the national NMP (net material product) produced between 1980 and 1983.[3] Despite the fact that (according to Soviet sources) productivity in recent years was only 40 per cent that of the US (55 per cent in industry, 20–25 per cent in agriculture), while the NMP was 65–67 per cent,[4] the Soviet defence outlays were higher than America's.

It is worth noting that in recent years not only have the Soviets outstripped the US in terms of total size of defence expenditure (see Chart 1 and Table 1.7); more impressive is the trend in Soviet defence outlays in per capita terms.

2. *World Military Expenditures and Arms Transfers 1971–1980*, US Arms Control and Disarmament Agency, Washington, DC, March 1983, p. 66 (further quoted as WMEAT); *The Military Balance 1983–1984*, The International Institute for Strategic Studies, London, 1983, pp. 13–14.
3. According to published Soviet figures, the NMP between 1980 and 1983 was as follows (in billions of rubles): 1980 — 462.2, 1981 — 486.7, 1982 — 511.3, 1983 — approximately 550.0. *SSSR v tsifrakh v 1982 godu* (The USSR in figures in 1982), Moscow, 1983, p. 177.
4. *SSSR v tsifrakh . .*, pp. 60 and 62.

35

Table 1.7 Total and per capita military expenditures, ME, and GNP, in US$.

	Total ME		ME per capita		GNP per capita	
Years	USA	USSR	USA	USSR	USA	USSR
1971	128.0	140.9	618	575	8822	3987
1975	117.9	166.0	550	653	9307	4541
1976	122.2	174.0	521	676	9806	5048
1977	117.4	177.0	540	683	10219	5230
1978	117.7	180.0	537	689	10579	4848
1979	122.3	183.0	553	695	10747	4849
1980	130.5	188.0	573	708	10408	4861

WMEAT, *ibid.*, pp. 66–71.

From 1977 to 1980 there was a continuing decrease in the per capita GNP. The per capita defence outlays, on the other hand, increased in the same period from $683 to $708 or at the rate of about 2 per cent per annum. In other words, the average Soviet citizen was not only paying more for the government's defence policy, he had to do it from a smaller portion of per capita GNP. This phenomenon is particularly impressive if compared with the trends in American defence spending (see Table 1.8) during the same period.

During the decade 1971–80, Soviet per capita GNP increased from $3,987 in 1971 to $5,230 in 1977, then dropped to $4,848 in 1978, held at $4,849 in 1979 and rose slightly to $4,861 in 1980, or to about 7 per cent less than in 1977. In comparison, the US per capita GNP increased steadily from $8,822 in 1971 to $10,408 in 1980. In the same years the per capita US defence outlays decreased from $618 in 1971 to $521 in 1976 and increased only slowly in the following years, reaching $573 in 1980. The per capita Soviet defence outlays, as noted above, increased steadily and without interruption despite the negative trend in GNP growth. In 1971, Soviet per capita GNP stood at about 45.2 per cent, in 1977 — 51.2 per cent and in 1980 only 46 per cent of that of the US. Over a similar period Soviet per capita ME was, in comparison with that of the US, as follows: 1971 — 93.0 per cent, 1977 — 126.5 per cent, 1980 — 123.6 per cent.

Many may justifiably argue that such a comparison between Soviet and US defence spending involves questionable methodology and is not adequately precise. More attention should indeed be devoted to original Soviet statistics. A detailed investigation, based

Table 1.8 Changes in Soviet GNP and ME in comparison with the USA (1971–80 per capita)

	1971	1975	1976	1977	1978	1979	1980
GNP USSR USA	45.2	48.8	51.1	51.2	45.8	45.1	46.7
ME USSR USA	93.0	118.7	129.8	126.5	128.3	125.7	123.6

Calculated from Table 1.7

on published data, of the size of the Soviet defence industry and its annual output in comparison with industry as a whole is especially illuminating.

According to various estimates, the total output of the defence industry, including the manufacture for military purposes of clothing, food, housing materials, etc. comprises about 40 per cent of the entire output of all Soviet industry. Out of about 500 of the largest Soviet industrial plants, approximately 150 work exclusively for the military and these are supported by an additional 4,000 assembly factories. It should be noted that the total number of medium-size industrial enterprises is less than 4,000. Altogether, some 36–37 million people work in industry, and of these 15–18 million are engaged in producing goods and in services for the defence sector.[5] 'Military representatives' alone (i.e. military buyers — 'voenpredy') could be estimated to number half a million, including both military and civilian experts. Together with the Soviet armed forces, border guard and internal security units, the defence sector of the USSR employs a work-force of approximately 25 million of the most highly skilled, best educated and best trained people in the Soviet state. In the current decade this number was equal to that employed in the entire non-defence sector, and comprised about 22 per cent of total Soviet manpower.[6] It is therefore no exaggeration to state that not a single significant aspect of the Soviet economy can be properly examined without considering the impact of the defence sector, and particularly the armaments sector, in the coming years.

5. For a detailed method of calculating these figures, see Michael Checinski, 'An Estimate of Current Soviet Military–Industrial Output and of the Development of the Soviet Arms Industry in the Eighties', *Osteuropa-Wirtschaft* 2/1984.
6. Total Soviet manpower in 1982 was 115.2 million. *SSSR v tsifrakh* . . ., p. 163.

In the 1980s, the Soviet Union will confront the following developmental problems created by the interaction of new military-political and economic conditions:

(1) The challenge posed by the faster modernisation of NATO, particularly of the American armed forces.

(2) A very slow rate of growth and productivity in the Soviet economy.

(3) A decline in innovation and in capital investment in industry, together with a growing perceived need for faster modernisation in the arms sector.

(4) An increasing shortage of labour and energy.

(5) A deteriorating ability to improve the domestic economy by relying on the resources of other CMEA members or the world market (credits, international trade, technology transfer, etc.).

(6) The economic and political implications for the Warsaw Pact of the Polish crisis.

(7) The need to respond to uncontrolled and unexpected changes among Third World nations (the Iran–Iraq war, events in African countries etc.).

Moreover, in the coming years the Soviet armed forces will begin a new procurement cycle leading to new designs in major weapons systems. According to Western observers, the weapons and equipment replacement cycle will include sophisticated and highly costly procurements such as: new short and long-range missiles, new naval weapons, surface ships and submarines, a new generation of front line tanks and self-propelled artillery, long-range bombers and new fighter aircraft, a large and very expensive space programme and new electronic systems.[7] Such extensive arms modernisation will obviously increase the military burden and will absorb the most efficient capacities of Soviet industry and the best part of its manpower; all major branches of the national economy will be affected.

Where will the new reserves be found to accomplish the new armaments programme and why is it necessary? The paradox of the Soviet economy is that, precisely because it is not efficient, it accumulates production reserves. This is why Soviet leaders are less pessimistic than Western experts about the long-term consequences of the current difficulties. The slowdown in many indicators does not necessarily produce the kind of results that would follow in a

---

7. David Fewtrell, 'The Soviet Economic Crisis: Prospects for the Military and the Consumer', *Adelphi Papers*, The International Institute for Strategic Studies, London, 1983, pp. 12–13.

democratic society and free market economy. Some phenomena in the Soviet economy will illustrate this point:

A. Many believe that the difficulties in supplying the market with necessary goods and services may force Soviet leaders to slow the continuing growth of arms production. Past experience shows, however, that the opposite may be true. In Soviet practice, a poorly supplied market compels people to work better for less pay, decreasing the total cost input for the same units produced and improving the efficiency of work. In a free market economy, increasing incentives for faster and harder work usually results in higher cost inputs as a result of higher salaries. In a Soviet-style economy, precisely because of the lack of many basic products and services, the employer can offer different incentives without increasing the salaries of workers. Even the promise of improved housing conditions, access to more quality furniture, food or clothing, a car, use of a kindergarten, a summer vacation and the like, is enough to motivate employees to work harder. Therefore, Soviet leaders and managers are not troubled by the flow of resources primarily to the military sector.

B. It is an oversimplification to believe that the 'second economy,' including bribery and the black market, poses an obstacle to the more efficient operation of the Soviet economy, or that it works against the interests of the majority of the population. Most Soviet citizens would in fact find it difficult to live and work without it. Millions profit, and their professional activity would be impossible and personal benefits unattainable without these 'negative' aspects of Soviet reality.[8] Again, there is no compelling reason for Soviet leaders to be upset by the continuing growth of the arms sector and the slowness of the increase in civilian goods and services which it causes.

C. The Soviet military–industrial sector is part of an autarkic economy, and while defence planning is based on the financial resources of the state, it relies primarily on the industrial and

8. For a brief sketch of the problems of the Soviet 'second economy', see Gregory Grossman, 'The "Shadow Economy" in the Socialist Sector of the USSR'; Peter Wiles, 'What We Still Don't Know about the Soviet Economy'; A. Kroncher, 'CMEA Productive and Service Sector in the 1980s: Plan and Non-Plan', in: *The CMEA Five-Year Plans (1981–1985) in a New Perspective, Planned and Non-Planned Economies*, NATO Economic Colloquium 1982, Brussels, 31 March–2 April 1982, Bonner Universitäts-Buchdruckerei, 1983, pp. 99–138 and 195–208; Friedrich Haffner, 'Legale und illegale Märkte in der UdSSR', in: *Sowjetunion 1982/83. Ereignisse, Probleme, Perspektiven*, Carl Hanser Verlag, Munich/Vienna, 1983, pp. 169–80.

technological capacities of the defence establishments. The current arms technology is developed in 8–12 year cycles. No single Soviet leader can undermine the industrial basis of the continuing modernisation of the Soviet armed forces. Neither international agreements nor domestic economic difficulties will therefore change the intentions of the Soviet decision makers to keep the military–industrial sector in full operation and constantly modernised.

D. In a centralised and state-owned economy, it is very difficult to change the existing economic structure of large, well-established industrial branches. Even if the Soviet government had domestic or international political reasons to 'victimise' the defence industry and to reallocate resources to the civilian sector of the economy it would not be able to do so, not only because of the interests of the Party–military bureaucracy, but also because of the internal mechanics of such a huge industrial sector. Equipped with all the necessary machinery and technologies and supplied with the best manpower, the defence industry is self-sufficient both in its operation and need for growth. To change this would require not only a reorientated economic plan imposed by the central decision-making bodies, but also highly costly additional investment to absorb the resources and manpower reallocated from the giant military–industrial sector. It is simpler and less expensive to continue a policy of economic growth based on the existing production capacities than to invest in a hazardous reconstruction of well-established military–industrial branches.

E. An additional barrier to decreasing the size of Soviet defence production is the large export trade in arms. More than fifty states around the world, including Communist countries, are customers of the Soviet arms industry. If we exclude oil, gas and gold sales, the arms industry has, for more than a decade, been the biggest single earner of hard currency: from 1971 to 1981 the annual value of arms exports in current dollar terms doubled from more than $5 billion to over $10 billion.[9] With this money alone, the Soviet Union can easily pay for its total grain imports from the West, and also for a large portion of imported Western technology. Consequently, it would be impossible for the USSR to modify the scale of its arms production in the foreseeable future, because the country does not have the capacity to offer any other substitute to its foreign customers.

9. WMEAT . . ., p. 108.

To sum up: Despite the economic difficulties which are anticipated in the 1980s, the Soviet defence industry will continue to grow and to accelerate production. However, that growth will most probably be accomplished by the use of more sophisticated methods than in the past. We can predict that the simplistic policy of allocating resources from non-military branches will be halted. More and more efforts will be made to improve the efficiency of the arms industry itself, as well as many defence-related industrial branches, thus releasing their large hidden production capacities for increasing arms production. Upgrading management, faster modernisation of production facilities, better exploitation of building and factory space, improving work discipline and the quality of labour, and other similar steps will be achieved primarily by using administrative pressure. In many respects this will replace the former extensive method of simply increasing arms production, but in the coming decade, and probably beyond, the ambitious Soviet arms build-up will not cease.

2

Energy and Raw Materials

Energy as a Factor of Soviet Power
Wolfgang Pfeiler

The Soviet Union is the only country on earth that is 'practically independent in energy'.[1] The Soviets themselves clearly assume that this will remain the case for at least the next two decades. The USSR has 97 per cent of the energy resources in CMEA,[2] which makes the East European CMEA countries particularly dependent on the Soviet contribution. About 20 per cent of Soviet oil production is exported and this accounts for nearly two-thirds of total foreign exchange earnings. Energy is still, therefore, the most important export commodity.[3]

Production of all five major sources of energy (gas, oil, coal, nuclear and hydroelectric power) has been increased in recent years. The targets have been met and, in gas particularly, where the increase in production in 1983 was 6 per cent, exceeded. Gas has also shown the greatest rise in labour productivity. The more difficult extraction conditions for coal and oil have meant that targets have only just been met while labour productivity has stagnated.[4]

1. W. Gumpel, 'Entspannungspolitik und wirtschaftliche Entwicklung. Die Grenzen des internationalen Aktionsradius der UdSSR', in: *Beiträge zur Konfliktforschung* 2/1982, p. 77.
2. J. Bethkenhagen, 'Die Nuklearpolitik der RGW-Staaten', in: K. Kaiser, F.J. Klein (eds.): *Kernenergie ohne Atomwaffen (Schriften des Forschungsinstitutes der Deutschen Gesellschaft für Auswärtige Politik)*, Bonn 1982, p. 247.
3. W. Gumpel, loc. cit. (note 1), p. 66; see also V. Asow, *Der Handel — ein Faktor des Friedens und der guten Beziehungen*, Moscow 1982, p. 38 and W. Beitel, 'Das sowjetische Interesse an Aussenwirtschaftsbeziehungen mit dem Westen', in: *Europa-Archiv* 8/1983, p. 254.
4. Report by the Statistical Administration, *Pravda*, 29 January 1984, p. 1.

How the Soviet energy sector will develop has always been a matter for speculation, estimates and prognoses in the West. Considerable uncertainty regarding the Soviet oil potential was caused by the forecast in a CIA study of 1977 that the Soviet Union would be a net importer of oil by the end of the 1980s. This was taken to have considerable implications for future foreign policy. The forecast has now proven to be mistaken and the CIA has revised it, admitting that future prospects are very much better than was once believed.[5] M. Goldman has shown just what led to this error by the CIA.[6]

Probably the main reason for the Western failure to judge the Soviet energy situation correctly is that the priorities of Soviet energy policy were not adequately observed, while the priorities themselves changed several times over the last fifteen years. It was assumed, for instance, that the Soviet Union would maximise its oil production. In fact, Soviet investment policy is directed to a kind of optimal 'energy mix',[7] with 'optimal' meaning that clear priorities are set according to certain political and economic factors.

However, the Soviet leaders have several times changed these priorities fundamentally since 1975, and it is these changes that have largely contributed to Western errors in forecasting. We could take as a point of departure the energy mix of 1976: 53.6 per cent oil, 28.1 per cent coal, 22.3 per cent gas, 2.7 per cent hydroelectric power, 0.5 per cent nuclear power. At the XXV Party Congress Brezhnev was still arguing that efforts should be concentrated on producing energy from water, nuclear power and coal, with coal accounting for the major share in volume.[8] In December 1977 this orientation was changed, with gas and oil replacing coal. This priority was not retained either, however, and at the XXVI Party Congress (February 1981) oil moved down to bottom place on the list while natural gas moved to the top.[9] So by 1981 the Soviet energy mix was as follows: 37 per cent oil, 28.5 per cent coal, 24.9

5. H. Smith, 'Soviet Military Spending Grew More Slowly Than Estimated', in: *International Herald Tribune*, 21 November 1983, p. 5; see also *New York Times*, 19 May 1981, p. 1 and D. Fewtrell, 'The Soviet Economic Crisis: Prospects for the Military and the Consumer', in: *Adelphi Paper* 186, London, Winter 1983, p. 5.

6. M.I. Goldman, *The Enigma of Soviet Petroleum. Half-Full or Half-Empty?* London 1980, pp. 90f.

7. T. Gustafson, 'Soviet Energy Policy: From Big Coal to Big Gas', in: S. Bialer and T. Gustafson (eds.), *Russia at the Crossroads. The 26th Congress of the CPSU*, London 1982, p. 131.

8. *Pravda*, 2 March 1976, p. 5.

9. T. Gustafson, loc. cit. (note 7), pp. 121 and 130 and *Pravda*, 24 February 1981, pp. 4f.

per cent gas, 4 per cent hydroelectric power and 1.1 per cent nuclear power.[10] Now the share of gas will be approaching 30 per cent.[11]

The Priorities

The following can be said of the priorities in Soviet energy policy:
(1) Altogether the energy sector occupies a high place in Soviet economic and investment policy. In April 1983 the Politburo approved a long-term energy programme of major structural, technical and organisational change to force intensive growth in this sector and also to save energy. Yurii Andropov compared the new energy programme with Lenin's plan for state electrification, GOELRO.[12] The significance of the programme was stressed at the annual conference of the Academy of Sciences that opened on 14 March 1984, when the main direction and proportions of the new development were laid down up to the year 2000, in conjunction with the State Committee for Science and Technology, Gosplan and the energy ministries. An indication of the high value placed on science and research in this context is the fact that the President of the Academy of Sciences is the head of the programme. Both the internal and external economic situation suggest that the energy industry will retain its major importance in future as well.[13]
(2) Oil has now dropped to bottom place on the energy list. Although we can only make assumptions and deductions on the Soviet decision-making process in this respect, it is possible to give some economic and political reasons for the decision. The rise in the cost of oil exploration and oil extraction is certainly a factor, while investment in other energy sources brings an earlier return. Moreover, the oil extraction technology is still underdeveloped. But the following consideration was certainly a major factor and indeed may have been the decisive one: in the longer term it would doubtless be advantageous to the Soviet state and its people not to exhaust the oil reserves too soon. It would be better, as one Soviet oil minister has argued, to keep the oil for later generations.[14]

10. M. Czakainski, 'Die Sowjetunion an einer energiepolitischen Wegscheide. Die Schlüsselrolle des Erdöls', in: *Neue Zürcher Zeitung*, 18 July 1983, p. 7.
11. Leading article 'Gazovaya Industriya', *Pravda*, 28 March 1983, p. 1.
12. *Pravda*, 29 December 1983, p. 4.
13. 'Rychagi Tekhnicheskogo Progressa', *Pravda*, 15 March 1984, p. 3.
14. R.X. Larkin and E.M. Collins, *DIA Statement before the Joint Committee*,

Voslenskii actually goes so far as to see this as a deliberate long-term political decision. The Soviet leaders may have decided, not to increase oil production further so that in twenty years, when the other oil reserves in the world will be greatly depleted, the USSR will have something approaching a monopoly on the oil market.[15]

It is not clear exactly what the motive was. However, there is evidence that the Soviet Union is deliberately keeping its oil production lower than might be necessary.[16] It has also cut down its deliveries to other CMEA states and almost ceased exporting oil to Third World countries altogether. At present it looks as if production is to be limited to existing operational fields.[17] The oil wells here are to be improved and production made more efficient.

Consequently, it is not possible to make precise statements on the Soviet oil industry — unlike the gas sector — because it is still very largely a secret area.[18]

(3) Coal has also lost some of its importance as a source of energy. The main reason for this is the disproportionate rise in mining costs. In the European part of the Soviet Union the coal has to be mined from greater and greater depths and some of it is no longer of the same quality. The transport costs are then hardly justifiable. Coal transport even now takes up nearly half the capacity of the Soviet railways, and for that reason a large part of the coal that is mined is used at the pit head to fire power-stations.[19] Some easing of the situation in coal transport may now be expected, however, as the new Baikal-Amur line is operating along its full length.[20]

Coal is of little significance in exports. There was an increase in

---

Subcommittee on International Trade, Finance and Security Economics: Allocations of Resources in the Soviet Union and China — 1981, July 1981, pp. 44 and 50. This may be a reflection of Solzhenitsyn's warning that the Russians should preserve their raw materials and not sell them to other countries; M.I. Goldman, 'Autarchy or Integration?' in: *Soviet Economy in a New Perspective. A Compendium of Papers submitted to the Joint Economic Committee, Congress of the United States*, October 1976, p. 84.

15. W. Pfeiler, *Aussenpolitische Relevanz der Ressourcen der Sowjetunion*, Sankt Augustin 1982, p. 32.

16. Larkin/Collins, loc. cit. (note 14), p. 126.

17. A.F.G. Scanlan, 'Die künftige Rolle von Öl und Erdgas in der UdSSR, MS of a paper read to the Gesellschaft für Energiewissenschaft und Energiepolitik on 11 March 1983 in Bonn, p. 6.

18. A.A. Meyerhoff, 'Soviet Petroleum: Technology, Geology, Reserves, Potential and Policy', in: R.G. Jensen, T. Shabad and A.W. Wright (eds.), *Soviet Natural Resources in the World Economy*, Chicago and London 1983, p. 327.

19. A. Scanlan (note 17), p. 7 and 'Foreign and Commonwealth Office London, Soviet Energy Prospects', in: *Background Brief*, June 1983, p. 2.

20. Report by the Central Committee of the CPSU, *Pravda*, 24 March 1984, p. 1.

coal exports to Japan in 1983, but the total share of coal in all Soviet exports has dropped during the last decade from 4 per cent to 2 per cent.[21]

(4) The Soviet Union is carrying out an urgent programme to develop nuclear energy. Apart from France it is the only industrial country to have initiated such a rigorous programme of nuclear development. Nuclear power is to reach a capacity of 90 gigawatts by 1990.[22] However, so far the results have been far less than was expected. A few years ago, eight new nuclear power-stations a year were to be built, but later on, the same number became the target for the entire period of the Eleventh Five-Year Plan.[23] In some cases the delays were such that they had internal political consequences.[24] At present the share of nuclear power in total electricity production is over 30 per cent.[25] However, if the ambitious targets have been lowered the programme itself will go on, despite the Chernobyl accident.

The Soviet Union clearly has several reasons for forcing the development of nuclear energy. One important factor is that the six East European CMEA states without nuclear power are proving a growing burden, and by 1990 roughly one-quarter of their electricity requirements are to be met by nuclear power. Also, there is now scarcely any other way of increasing the energy supply to the European part of the country and it is significant that all the new Soviet nuclear power-stations have been built west of the Urals, most of them near densely populated areas.[26] This provides additional energy at low transport cost as well as heating for the central long-distance heating systems.

Research on what is to be the biggest nuclear reactor in the world, with a capacity of 1.5 million kW, has recently been concluded.[27]

21. T. Shabad, 'The Soviet Potential in Natural Resources: An Overview', in: R.G. Jensen *et al.*, loc. cit. (note 18), pp. 254f.
22. T. Gustafson, 'Energy and the Soviet Bloc', in: *International Security*, Winter 1981/1982, p. 77; W.C. Potter, *Nuclear Power and Proliferation. An Interdisciplinary Perspective*, Cambridge/Mass. 1982, p. 99. These figures do not take into account the development of the fast breeder reactor, which is still uncertain; otherwise they would be even higher. See 'U.S. Study Predicts Tenfold Jump in Soviet Nuclear Capacity by 2000', in: *International Herald Tribune*, 8 July 1982.
23. M. Czakainski, loc. cit. (note 10), p. 7.
24. T. Shabad, 'Brezhnev Construction Chief Retires, Apparently a Dismissal by Andropov', in: *International Herald Tribune*, 1 August 1983, p. 4.
25. N.V. Talyzin (Chairman of Gosplan), in: *Pravda*, 27, November 1985, p. 2.
26. L. Dienes and T. Shabad, *The Soviet Energy System: Resource Use and Policies*, Washington 1979, p. 159.
27. *Pravda* loc. cit. (note 13), p. 3.

It should also be mentioned that nuclear power provides the Soviet Union with further export opportunities, for since 1979 it has been exporting the only two small reactor types on the world market, mainly to Third World countries. So it has been able to step into the breach left by the Western nuclear states.[28] The final point that needs to be made in this context is that estimated Soviet uranium production should suffice over the longer term for a programme of this nature. The Soviet Union is not in any way dependent on the Western world for this. 'The nuclear energy industry in the Socialist countries can develop on its own base, it is not dependent on the capitalist market.'[29]

(5) Natural gas now occupies first place in the list of priorities, although its importance only became clear during the last ten years. Up to and including 1975 the Soviet Union was still a net importer of natural gas but in recent years its gas production has shown the highest growth rates in the economy. Gas is also expected to be the most profitable sector in the future, with investment here showing the fastest returns in usable energy. Natural gas is therefore regarded as the most important factor in the Soviet domestic energy supply in the longer term, and in supplies to 'fraternal states', while it is also expected to prove a profitable export commodity to the West. It is also economically suitable for the production of a number of chemical products and fertilisers.

The Soviet Union has huge known gas reserves — not much less than half of all the known natural gas reserves in the world are on Soviet territory.[30] Therefore, there is everything to suggest that by 1990 natural gas will have surpassed all other energy sources in importance, while the Soviet Union will try to replace as much of its oil exports as possible with natural gas.[31] Investment in gas production has assumed priority, although the costs of transporting gas by pipeline are roughly five times those of transporting oil. That is not what mattered to the Soviet leaders, however, and they are now constructing a uniform system for the continuous production, processing and delivery of gas to all economic regions of the country as well as for export. The network now extends over

28. J. Bethkenhagen, loc. cit. (note 2), p. 257 and G. Duffy, 'The Soviet Union and Nuclear Drift', in: W.R. Duncan, *Soviet Policy in the Third World*, New York 1980, p. 30.
29. A. Troitskii, 'Energiya sotsializma', *Pravda*, 13 June 1983, p. 4.
30. J.P. Stern, 'Soviet Natural Gas in the World Economy', in: R.G. Jensen *et al.*, loc. cit. (note 18), pp. 363f.
31. Ibid., p. 381.

150,000 km. with a system of subterranean gas tanks.[32] The pipeline system is something of an equivalent to the Western tanker fleets.[33]

(6) To complete the picture we should also mention that the Soviet Union is still investing in hydroelectric power, but in percentage terms this is only of minor importance compared with other sources of energy. Wood and peat play a tiny marginal role as energy sources and some research projects have been started on renewable energy sources such as geothermal, solar, tide and wind energy. A few pilot projects have already been constructed.[34]

The Problems

In view of the situation outlined above it could be argued that the Soviet Union has solved its energy problems. That is not the case, even if it occupies a unique position where resources are concerned. The shift in production from the Western to the Eastern parts of the country is causing a rapid rise in extraction costs, as well as environmental problems, transport costs and not least social problems, for the climate in the areas where most of the resources are located is not such as to encourage workers to move there.[35] However, already more than half of oil and gas production is now located in Western Siberia, and this is expected to rise to about two-thirds by 1990.[36] The possibilities are being considered of exploiting the other resources of these areas as well over the longer term, so as to locate processing near the energy sources. But most of these projects are still at the exploration stage and largely dependent on the assessments of geologists.[37] The Soviet Union is believed by Western observers to have very highly trained and qualified geologists, but their number remains small, and difficulties are also being encountered in putting the results of their research into practice.[38]

Regionally, Western Siberia is the focal point for gas production. It is hoped that oil production there can be maintained at the present level until the end of the century, while gas output is to be

32. Leading article 'Gazovaya Industriya', *Pravda*, 28 March 1983, p. 1.
33. A. Scanlan, loc. cit. (note 17), p. 4.
34. 'Foreign and Commonwealth Office', loc. cit. (note 19), p. 3.
35. W. Kortunow, 'Reichen die Ressourcen?', *Horizont* 19/20/1983, p. 661.
36. 'Foreign and Commonwealth Office', loc. cit. (note 17), p. 1 and A. Scanlan, loc. cit. (note 17), p. 3.
37. Leading article 'Geologi — Narodnomu Khozyaistvu', *Pravda*, 10 June 1983, p. 1.
38. A.A. Meyerhoff, loc. cit. (note 18), p. 316.

trebled at least. It must also be assumed that there are still a large number of as yet undiscovered gas fields. About two dozen large fields are known to exist which have yet to be opened up. Consequently, it is hoped that by the year 2000 Western Siberian stocks will be providing a secure basis for domestic supply. Considerable reserves may also be anticipated in Eastern Siberia and exploration for natural gas and oil deposits has already started between the Yenisei and Lena rivers. So all the expected increase in fuel production will come from Siberia, and this means that for the present about three-quarters of the volume produced will have to be transported into the European part of the country and other regions.[39]

In other words, the Soviet Union will have to move into increasingly remote and inhospitable areas in order to exploit its raw material and energy resources. In addition, like industry and agriculture, the energy industry has not so far succeeded in moving from extensive to intensive growth. What Robert Campbell saw as particularly characteristic of Soviet energy production as early as 1960, namely extremely low labour productivity both in drilling, and in exploration, is still the case, even if to a lesser extent.[40] What effect the system of contract brigades will have in the future remains unclear.

In Moscow at any rate it is hoped that the situation can be mastered, and the scientists are expected to play a major part. The first successes are apparent in that it is now possible to bore down to 12 km.[41] Another way of increasing the energy supply, namely conserving energy, has been rather neglected in the Soviet Union so far. Until recently initiatives in this direction were limited to non-binding recommendations,[42] but these are now more concrete. The present Five-Year Plan provides for energy savings of 10–13 per cent over 1980. About half of this is to be achieved in production and transport and the remainder by the consumers, who are now constantly being urged to save energy.[43] The first major step in this direction was an increase of more than 40 per cent in the price of

39. For more details see A. Aganbegyan, 'Toplivo Sibiri', *Pravda*, 1 August 1983, p. 2 and L. Dienes, 'Soviet Energy Policy and the Fossil Fuels', in: R.G. Jensen *et al.* (note 18), p. 285.

40. R.W. Campbell, *Soviet Economic Power: Its Organization, Growth and Challenge*, Cambridge/Mass. 1960, pp. 64f.; see also *The Russian Review* 1/1982, p. 90.

41. *Pravda* loc. cit. (note 13) and A.A. Meyerhoff, loc. cit. (note 18), p. 318.

42. For example, *Pravda*, 4 July 1981, 17 November 1981, 9 April 1983, 29 October 1983 and 26 January 1982, p. 2.

43. 'Foreign and Commonwealth Office', loc. cit. (note 19), p. 3.

coal and gas that came into force in January 1982. The desired effect was to be achieved mainly in that the price increases were not to be passed on to the customers. As in the West, car engines are to be fitted with fuel-saving devices, and it is hoped that this will conserve between 30 and 40 per cent.[44] Much is also expected from a completely new carrot and stick approach: anyone who uses more fuel than envisaged will have to pay all the costs of the difference from his own pocket, while savings in petrol and diesel fuel are to be rewarded with payment of 95 per cent of the saving as a bonus.[45]

In Moscow it has been estimated that the potential for saving energy is 100m. tonnes of oil equivalent a year.[46] Energy wastage of this magnitude is probably due to the fact that up to now there have been no real incentives to save energy and no sanctions for wasting it. In the mid-1970s Soviet primary energy consumption was 69 per cent above that of Western Europe and even 13 per cent above that of the United States. These figures have now shifted further to the disadvantage of the Soviet Union as Western countries have adopted energy-saving policies.[47]

The Soviet Union will also presumably have to introduce a more stringent energy-saving policy towards the end of the present decade. Whether it can come even approximately close to the huge potential for saving oil in the shorter term is doubtful. However this would entail fundamental changes in energy policy, for so far the end consumer in the Soviet Union has virtually no incentive to save energy at all. The costs of domestic heating are subsidised and account for only a tiny fraction of income, so there is no financial incentive to cut back. In any case, many of the apartments on the long-distance heating systems have no regulatory equipment, so the consumer can do little. 'This means that Soviet energy policy will have to concentrate on the supply side, for with the indolence of a centrally planned economy it is easier to change the structure of energy supply than to introduce economy measures.'[48] Nevertheless, there is a big potential for energy saving and this can be utilised over the longer term. That is becoming increasingly clear in

44. Leading article 'Berech' Goryuchee', *Pravda*, 16 November 1983, p. 1; leading article 'Uluchshat' Rabotu Avtotransporta', *Pravda*, 12 December 1983, p. 1.
45. Decision by the Central Committee of the CPSU and the Council of Ministers of the USSR, *Pravda*, 7 December 1983, p. 1.
46. On Radio Moscow, according to A. Scanlan, loc. cit. (note 17), p. 16.
47. M Czakainski, 'Energieversorgung des Comecon-Stand, Probleme und Perspektiven', in: *Osteuropa* 6/1984, MS p. 8.
48. Ibid., pp. 9f.

Moscow. The former President of the Academy of Sciences, A.P. Aleksandrov, has stressed the enormous importance of introducing energy-saving technologies. It was, he asserted, three to four times more efficient to invest in energy saving than in energy production.[49]

The Outlook

So the energy outlook is very positive for the Soviet Union, even after 1990. Geological exploration may be expected to make further finds and as technology improves the existing stocks will be better utilised in future too.[50] The energy sector is therefore the main asset in long-term Soviet economic development and the Soviet Union is likely to remain independent in the five main sources of energy (as with most other raw materials). 'The Soviet Union will not be dependent on imports up to 1990, either for energy as a whole or for any of the individual sources of energy.'[51] It will remain the biggest producer of oil and gas in the world, and it looks as if it could also become the largest coal producer in the world by the end of the decade.[52]

The Political Implications

Self-sufficiency in energy gives the Soviet Union a very high degree of independence in foreign trade. This is also a power lever, and the political leaders will want to make use of it, particularly in the longer term. They are clearly trying to optimise the chances for doing this by the priorities they set in their energy policy.

Firstly, there is everything to suggest that they will be able to provide the quantities of oil and gas needed to acquire the foreign exchange they want.[53] If a recovery in the world economy leads to a higher demand for energy this will also strengthen the Soviet position.

49. *Pravda*, loc. cit. (note 13), p. 3.
50. W. Kortunov, loc. cit. (note 35), p. 8; see also Dienes/Shabad, loc. cit. (note 26), p. 257; Larkins/Collins, loc. cit. (note 14), p. 41; W.P. Moshin, Sibirien und der Ferne Osten der Sowjetunion; Probleme und Perspektiven der Entwicklung', in: *Einheit* 5/1982, p. 526.
51. F. Müller, 'Ost-West-Beziehungen und Energiesicherung', in: *Deutsche Studien*, June 1982, p. 223.
52. A. Scanlan, loc. cit. (note 17), p. 15.
53. Ibid., p. 18.

The Soviet Union will be able to make use of the dependence of its partners in CMEA, economically and politically, to an even greater degree than before. It is certainly ready and willing to go on meeting their energy needs, but it expects adjustment and energy-saving measures from them. These include substituting gas for oil. The construction of gas pipelines to Western Europe will also enable gas supplies to Eastern Europe to be improved.[54] One of the adjustment measures the Soviet Union is demanding is that the East European countries should orientate more to Soviet needs. 'We are well aware of the CMEA countries' interest in deliveries of energy and raw materials from the Soviet Union. We will make efforts to continue these deliveries as far as possible in future too. But under-standably our position will largely depend on to what extent the other countries can supply what the Soviet economy needs.'[55]

Thus, Soviet policy is to use trade with its CMEA partners to cement the bloc as a whole and to make these countries more dependent on Soviet policy. A favourite phrase now is 'the closer proximity of the fraternal states'[56] and this is to bring not only greater political control over these countries but also greater contributions from them to investment in the Soviet Union.

Everything suggests therefore that the dependence of the East European states will increase because they cannot manage without Soviet energy in the longer term. The Western countries cannot offer an alternative because they themselves have to import energy. So in addition to the political and military dependence of these countries there is an economic dependence in the energy sector.

In the future too the energy situation offers very favourable prospects to the Soviet leaders. It gives them additional means of binding their East European allies more closely, and as world demand for energy rises again the rest of the world may well have to accept that the Soviet Union is more than just a military power. Autarky with respect to energy and raw materials signifies a high degree of defensive power.[57]

54. 'Deutsche Welle', *Monitor Osteuropa*, 20 January 1984, p. 9.
55. *Pravda*, 19 October 1983, p. 4.
56. M.S. Gorbachev, Speech at the X Congress of the Portuguese Communist Party, quoted in from *Pravda*, 17 December 1983, p. 4.
57. See also R.G. Jensen, T. Shabad and A.W. Wright, 'The Implications of Soviet Raw Materials for the World Economy', in: *Soviet Natural Resources in the World Economy*, p. 680 (see note 18).

Soviet Energy Policy and Plans
Robert Campbell

Soviet energy policy is one of the most important domestic areas for Soviet international relations. Energy exports are extremely important in overall Soviet trade policy, and its dependence on energy sector technologies imported from Western countries plays a major role in the Soviet Union's trade and foreign policy.

Against the background outlined by Wolfgang Pfeiler, this article concentrates on some recent developments in energy policy that are, in my view, important for the Soviet Union's international economic relations and foreign policy. This is an opportune time to think over again what the Soviet choices may be, because recently guidelines for resolving long-term energy problems to the year 2000 were published by the Soviet leaders. Last summer the Politburo approved this energy plan, then nothing was heard about it for practically a year. Out of the blue, a fairly lengthy document outlining the plans appeared, and I would like briefly to review some of the elements in the perspective revealed in this plan that I think are important in any assessment of East-West relations over the next couple of decades.

One of the biggest issues, of course, is what is going to happen to oil output. This has been a controversial question for a long time now, with many diverse forecasts. It is quite clear from this statement of the energy plan that the Soviet planners do not count on oil output growing. They give no actual output target, but there are numerous ways in which they express their pessimism about the ability to maintain oil output. There are phrases like 'we hope to maintain a stable level of output at a high level' and 'oil will have a reduced share in the overall energy balance'. It is made clear in the plans for coal that one of the major motivations for coal expansion is to produce synthetic fuel. Similarly, fairly explicit statements about oil shale appear in this energy programme and the real rationale for the oil shale programme is to provide another source of liquid fuel to make up for the loss of oil. Perhaps the most telling indication of the plans for oil is the statement that 'we hope to maintain oil output at something like the current level until 1990', with no indication whatever as to what the prospects are likely to be beyond that date. It is also clear that to maintain oil output at this level, or even to retard its fall will require a very expensive effort. There is talk of doubling drilling capacity between 1980 and 1990. Given the investment burden drilling already imposes, this implies a big increase in the burden. Even with capacity doubled, the expectation is to meet these targets only by greatly increasing rig productivity, both in development and exploratory drilling.

My general reaction to these clues is that they reveal a pessimistic, but nonetheless ambitious target for oil. The hope to keep oil output even as high as this plan suggests is a somewhat fragile one, however, depending, as it does, on optimistic productivity increases and major increases in the allocation of resources to oil production.

The second energy source of interest is gas. What do the Soviets anticipate in this area? Here the plan is explicit, stating that gas output is expected to peak in about 1995 and thereafter remain stable. Not a great deal is said about what will happen to gas exports, but it is clear that gas will continue to play an important role, both domestically and with regard to exports. However, I think it is quite remarkable that the experts do not see it continuing to rise beyond 1995.

The third big fossil fuel is coal. This has not recently been given much attention and output has stagnated. The perspective outlined in the plan is that after 1990 there will be a considerable expansion of coal output. Between now and then, however, the planners expect to set the stage for that expansion by creating the technological base — doing the R&D work to make transport possible (work on slurry pipeline technology is essential) and processing it into liquid fuel.

It is also clear that in order to meet current energy need projections there will have to be a heavy dependence on non-fossil fuel sources, nuclear power, renewable sources and conservation. This forecast is thin in terms of numbers, but by injecting into the calculations some figures from other sources, it is possible to make a prediction as to what total consumption of energy will be and what each of the sources will contribute. One then sees that there will be no fossil fuel growth at all between the present time and the end of the century. All of the projected growth in energy needs is to be covered by two sources, about half and half, — conservation (reduction of input per unit of output) and substitution of new energy sources for fossil fuel. This is really quite remarkable, since it implies that there will have to be a great deal of technological change. It has important implications for continued Soviet dependence on or at least interest in Western technology to achieve these goals.

Another point that emerges quite clearly in the guidelines is that the Soviet energy planners see virtually no relief in the great burden that energy expansion will impose on investment resources, and this is one place where the forecast is explicit. During these two decades the share of the energy sector in total investment in the economy is expected to remain at between 20 and 22 per cent. According to my calculations it is about 21 per cent in the current Eleventh Five-Year Plan period. So, given all the changes in structure and having canvassed all their possibilities, the leaders do not see any way of getting out from under the very heavy investment burden they are now experiencing. There is not the space here to go into this in detail, but I think many economists would say that many of the problems in the Soviet economy today flow from an investment crunch, and much of this investment crunch comes from the increase in allocation to the energy sector required by the changing conditions that Wolfgang Pfeiler describes.

To come to the implications; as I said earlier, energy is especially interesting because it has an impact on the Soviet Union's trade position, and through it on foreign policy in general. It is quite clear that the Soviets will continue to need transfers of energy-sector technology from more advanced countries. 'This is the case in refinery technology, in coal processing and in coal transport. They have also experienced a great many difficulties recently in the nuclear power sector and these may inspire nuclear equipment imports. In a number of places the forecast spells out what kind of equipment the Soviets hope to obtain from abroad. One interesting theme is that it is hoped to produce more of some kinds of energy equipment domestically, and some specific tasks are laid down for the machine-building industries. But not all the need can be met in this way. Secondly, there is an emphatic message contained in the forecast: more help is expected from Eastern Europe. Some of the new technologies are to be developed in co-operation with East European countries, but there is an explicit statement about continued scientific technical co-operation (which I think means technology imports) from Western Europe. One of the most interesting features of the document is a conspicuous absence of any mention of imports of energy technology from the United States. One associated point in connection with import policy concerns equipment for offshore development. Last summer, a couple of months after the Politburo had approved the energy programme, a special offshore development programme was approved. The Politburo summaries in the national press say very little about this, however, and little move was indicated than that the offshore plan had been approved. As with the energy programme there was little additional discussion in the press. These guidelines say very little about offshore prospects. The main place where offshore plans are mentioned is in the section relating to the demands on the machine industries for new equipment to meet the goals of the energy plan. There is quite a long passage in which the ship-building ministry is called on to provide a great deal of new equipment for these efforts, and this raises in my mind some interesting questions. I do not know why so little is said in the forecast about the offshore programme but it may be that this part of the overall energy problem is the most technologically demanding, where there is the least possibility of getting help from Eastern Europe or of the Soviets meeting the need on their own. It may be that the leadership has decided that this is the area where they should take most care to protect themselves against foreign dependence. This is only a guess, and it will be very interesting over the next year or so to see if they come forward with a more clear cut explanation of offshore development plans.

The other external implication (export prospects) is very difficult to assess in the context of the plan. Exports of the order of 300m. tons of standard fuel are about the amount that can be lost in the imprecisions of the different elements contained in the forecast. No mention is made of the volume of exports intended. Nevertheless, I believe the leadership is counting on exports. There are a number of hints to this effect in the document.

To conclude: what is the political significance, what can be read into the fact that after such a long silence a detailed exposition of energy plans has been revealed? I think this is especially intriguing as perhaps an indication that the leaders have at long last reconciled themselves to the fact that energy will not be an engine of growth as it was in the 1960s and 1970s. From now until the end of the century, energy will present much more in the way of problems, much more in the way of investment demands, much more in the way of technological requirements that will burden the economy, than it will present in terms of opportunities for economic growth and expansion of trade.

The Soviet Union in World Trade: Energy and Raw Materials
Jochen Bethkenhagen

The Soviet Union is one of the few industrial states in the world that can meet its need for energy and raw materials from its own resources (autarky capability). With very few exceptions (such as bauxite or clay to produce aluminium) it is not dependent on foreign trade for raw materials supplies. Indirectly, however, foreign trade is important, for the Soviet Union buys capital goods on the world market, some of which are used to exploit its raw material deposits. The natural gas pipeline contracts with West European firms are only one example of this.

So raw materials, and particularly energy, are an asset in Soviet foreign trade. Since the USSR produces few industrial goods that could be sold on world markets its future potential in foreign trade will largely depend on the ability to export energy. This analysis therefore concentrates on the present and future importance of these goods, but a section is also devoted to a brief outline of the importance of Western technology in the exploitation of Soviet deposits.

Soviet Exports — A Monoculture

In the last few years the structure of Soviet exports to OECD countries has assumed something of the character of a monoculture. In 1982 the Soviet Union earned 80 per cent of its foreign exchange income from sales of oil (64 per cent) and natural gas. Thus, energy exports have become the decisive factor in the Soviet Union's trade with the West[1]; the other raw materials are of minor significance and do not need to be discussed here.

The dominant share of oil and gas in Soviet exports is primarily the result of price increases. As a 'free rider' on the OPEC cartel the Soviet Union has enjoyed considerable 'windfall profits', with

---

1. J. Bethkenhagen, 'Erdöl und Erdgas im Ost-West-Handel', in: *Vierteljahrshefte des DIW*, 4/1983, p. 345.

Table 2.1 Soviet energy exports to OECD countries

| | in mill. tr | | in mill. t[1] | | Index 1982 (1973 = 100) | |
	1973	1982	1973	1982	Value	Quantity
Oil[2]	1176	12085	46.4	66.3	1028	143
Natural gas	22	2739	2.0	25.1	12450	1255
Coal[3]	124	192	9.3	3.4	155	36
Total	1322	15016	75.9	127.3	1136	168

1. Natural gas in bill.cu.m.; total in mill. t coal eq.
2. Oil and petroleum products
3. Incl. coke

Sources: Soviet Statistical Yearbooks on Foreign Trade, DIW estimates

earnings on sales of oil and gas to the West rising from 1973 to 1983 from 1.3 billion to 13 billion tr (transfer rubles), although the quantities exported did not even double over that period.

Exports of oil to the West have remained fairly stable and over the period reviewed here they correlate fairly closely with production. At 11 per cent of the quantity produced sales were, relatively, as important in 1982 as in 1973 and the thesis repeatedly put forward since the beginning of the 1970s that the Soviet Union or CMEA would be net importers of oil by the beginning of the 1980s has proved to be incorrect.[2] If only for strategic reasons the Soviet Union may be expected to do everything possible to avoid dependence in the energy sector.

Over the same period, however, Soviet exports of natural gas have changed remarkably. In 1973 only 2 billion cu.m. was exported to the West but this had risen to 27 billion cu.m. by 1982. The decision taken at the end of the 1960s to begin exporting natural gas is now proving very advantageous, for gas prices have followed oil prices and the Soviet Union has made further windfall profits with a second commodity. Average earnings on 1 cu.m. of gas have increased tenfold, and export earnings on gas have risen from 22 million tr in 1973 to 2.7 billion tr in 1982.

2. W. Gumpel, 'Sowjetunion: Erdöl und Nahostpolitik', in: *Aussenpolitik*, 11/1971, p. 676; I. Dobozi, 'Energy Sources in the CMEA Economies' (in Hungarian), in: *Valóság*, Budapest, 1/1973, pp. 18ff; Central Intelligence Agency, *Prospects for Soviet Oil Production*, Washington, DC, July 1977. The author has always doubted these arguments; see J. Bethkenhagen, 'Bedeutung und Möglichkeiten des Ost-Welt-Handels mit Energierohstoffen', *Sonderheft des DIW*, 104/1975, pp. 252f; 'UdSSR vor Erdöldefizit?' (ed. J. Bethkenhagen), in: *Wochenbericht des DIW*, 50/1977.

So the Soviet Union has become more important as a supplier on Western energy markets. Its share of OECD countries' oil imports rose from 3.6 per cent in 1973 to 7 per cent ten years later. The Soviet Union only began exporting gas to three EEC countries in 1973 but by 1983 already accounted for the following shares of their gross gas consumption:

Federal Republic of Germany	21%
Italy	28%
France	13%

The Soviet Union probably owes its growing shares of the now shrinking energy markets mainly to the following factors:
— its prices are rather below the average so they help to provide a cheaper source of energy;
— energy supplies from the Soviet Union have been regarded as a way of making the energy supply more reliable through diversification;
— natural gas has no known pollution effects so it serves the goal of environmental protection.
However, the Soviet Union owes its growing weight in East-West trade exclusively to the rise in energy prices. In 1973 it accounted for only about one-third of exports to the West by all CMEA countries, but now the figure is clearly over 50 per cent. The Soviet share of OECD imports has actually nearly doubled over the same period, although it is still low at just on 2 per cent.

Altogether, the Soviet Union's foreign exchange earnings have become highly dependent on price and quantity developments on world energy markets. The favourable conditions for exports of energy sources have concealed the weaknesses of the Soviet export industry, while the lack of a broad competitive range of industrial export goods has not had a negative effect on export earnings. However, this will make itself felt in times of stagnating energy markets and could hamper the growth of Soviet exports to the West.

Substitution Plans in Exports to the West not Realised

At present, the situation on the world energy market is characterised by a low rise in consumption and falling real prices, and this has also affected Soviet trade with the West. The Soviet Union already had to take a loss of earnings on oil exports in 1982–3. At the existing level of exports to the West of around 500 m. barrels, a drop in price by one dollar a barrel will cause a loss in earnings of half a billion dollars. However, this effect will be reduced if the trade is invoiced in currencies that have lost value against the dollar, like the D-Mark,[3] and this is presumably one reason for the 22 per cent increase in Soviet supplies of oil to the Federal Republic of Germany in 1983.[4] However, the drop in demand also had repercussions on Soviet export plans. At the beginning of the 1980s the Soviet Union was planning new contracts for gas deliveries to the tune of 40 billion cu.m. So far, however, only 20 billion cu.m. has been signed up (FRG 11.5 billion cu.m., France 8 billion cu.m. and Switzerland 0.4 billion cu.m.). Belgium and the Netherlands have now turned down Soviet offers and Italy is clearly still hesitating to ratify a delivery contract for 8 billion cu.m. The reserve on the part of Western gas importers is motivated not by political but by economic considerations, as current forecasts are for consumption of natural gas to rise less than originally planned over the next ten years.

The reluctance of Western purchasers to buy, means that the Soviet Union will not be able to realise all its plans to substitute natural gas for at least some of its oil exports. The production targets for the Eleventh Five-Year Plan give some indication of what was in mind, for they provide for an average increase in the production of gas by 7 per cent p.a. from 1981 to 1985, while oil production is only to rise by less than 1 per cent. The figures mark a clear change in Soviet economic policy, the end of the expansion phase in oil and a new priority: not to increase supply but to make better use of the available reserves.

The Soviet Union has been forced into this policy mainly by the rise in costs. It increasingly has to shift its oil production, like its coal and gas production, to the remoter and climatically inhospitable areas of Siberia, and this entails costly investment simply to provide the necessary infrastructure. At present, the fuel industry takes around 25 per cent of total industrial investment (18 per cent in 1973) and half of this is in the oil industry alone. The following relations show how the financial burden has grown: in 1973 110

---

3. The average border price for Soviet oil dropped in 1983 over 1981 by 6 per cent in D-Mark, but by 22 per cent in dollars.
4. J. Bethkenhagen and H. Wessels, 'Der Osthandel der Bundesrepublik und seine Beschäftigungseffekte', in: *Wochenbericht des DIW*, 11/1984.
5. Th. Shabad, 'News Notes', in: *Soviet Geography*, November 1983, p. 703.

Table 2.2 The development in Soviet oil production: average annual growth

	in m.t	in %
1971–5	27.6	6.8
1976–80	22.4	4.2
1981–3 (actual)	4.3	0.7
1981–5 (plan)	5.4	0.9

rubles investment was needed to increase oil production by 1 tonne, but by 1980 this had risen to 400 rubles and by 1982, to 2,300 rubles. Natural gas production is still one of the success stories of Soviet economic policy, however, and in the current plan period alone gas production is to rise by around 200 billion cu.m. (7 per cent p.a.). The whole increase is to be in the Urengoi field in North-West Siberia. There are two main reasons for substituting gas for oil: firstly, the gas stocks, which are put at 34,000 cu.m. or one-third of total world stocks, are presumably greater than the oil reserves, which are kept secret. Secondly, the costs of exploration and production are said to be between 33 and 50 per cent lower.

The Soviet Union's Future Foreign Exchange Needs

Since the drop in demand from the West has meant that the plans for substituting gas for oil could not all be realised the question now arises of how the Soviets will react. Soviet planners will have to answer the following questions: how will the demand for imports from Western countries develop, say up to 1990? What possibilities are there for exports to meet the cost of these imports?

Globally, world imports can be seen as dependent on expected economic growth, and the relations in the 1970s were:

	1970–5	1976–80
Economic growth (real)	5.7% p.a.	4.1% p.a.
Growth in Western imports (real)	17.1% p.a.	6.4% p.a.
Western import elasticity	3	1.6

Prognoses are now required for economic growth for the period 1983–90 and Western import elasticity. Two projections are to be made, assuming an average growth of 3.5 per cent and 3 per cent *p.a.*

Table 2.3 Model calculation of Soviet oil and gas exports to OECD countries with alternative assumptions on economic growth and western imports

	Actual 1982 Western imports	Model Calculation for 1990			
		Variant 3.5%/1.3 = 27.2 bill. tr[1]		Variant 3%/0.8 = 23.0 bill. tr[2]	
		Share of oil and gas in exports to the West			
	81%	80%	60%	80%	60%
		in bill. tr			
Energy earnings of which:	14.8	21.8	16.3	18.4	13.8
gas	2.7	5.8	5.8	5.8	5.8
oil	12.1	16.0	10.5	12.6	8.0
		in bill. cu.m. or m.t			
Quantity exported[3]					
gas	27	57	57	57	57
oil	66	87	57	69	44

1. Growth in national income 1983–90: 3.5% *p.a.*; Western import elasticity 1.3; this gives 27.2 bill. tr worth of imports for 1990 at 1982 prices
2. Growth in national income 1983–90: 3% *p.a.*; Western import elasticity 0.8 = 23.0 bill. tr worth of imports for 1990 at 1982 prices
3. Average prices in 1982: natural gas 102 tr/1000 cu.m.; oil 183 tr/t
Source: DIW

and a Western import elasticity of only 1.3 per cent and 0.8 per cent respectively. The expected reduction in elasticities is due to the expected low foreign exchange earnings.

The assumptions result in a clear drop in growth in Soviet imports from the West for the period 1983–90. Clearly the Soviet Union had already reacted to the change in the situation in 1982, for its imports from Western industrial countries did drop slightly (–1 per cent). The significance of this for exports of oil and gas is evident from the following table:

Since the amount of natural gas exports is largely fixed in long-term contracts, a constant quantity of 57 cu.m. could be used for all the alternatives. This also assumes higher deliveries to Italy, but only of 5 billion cu.m. It is not certain that exports will be at this level, as consumers could make use of the appropriate clause in the contract if demand drops and so cut their imports by up to 20 per cent. The Soviet Union suffered from this back in 1982, when exports of gas to Western Europe dropped for the first time (by around 9 per cent), and Soviet earnings fell by 7 per cent.[6]

There is more uncertainty regarding future exports of oil by the Soviet Union. While gas exports are limited at present due to lack of demand, the volume of oil exports will primarily be restricted by factors on the supply side. These include production, domestic consumption and exports to CMEA countries. However, in the short term it is possible that one of these areas will be subordinated to balance of payments considerations.

The Export Potential

As far as oil production is concerned, this is not expected to rise further after 1985, owing mainly to the cost factors outlined above. Two-thirds of the investment in the fuel industry is already in oil (1973: 50 per cent), but it will only be possible to maintain production at the present level by moving into increasingly inhospitable areas such as North-west Siberia and (later) Eastern Siberia and the Barents Sea. Since the same applies to the other fuels (gas and coal) and the possibilities for expanding investment in the civilian area are shrinking, no further notable increases in production are to be expected. However, a drastic decline (as forecast by the CIA in 1977 for the beginning of the 1980s) is equally unlikely.[7] On the contrary, it is striking that the Soviet Union has been the biggest oil producer in the world since 1973 and its share since then has grown steadily, from 16 to 23 per cent.

Domestic consumption will probably have a decisive influence on future export potential. Generally, it may be said that consumption of primary energy in the Soviet Union is disproportionally high, largely as a result of the economic system. Although the social product per inhabitant is more than 50 per cent lower than that of the FRG, energy consumption per capita in the Soviet Union in 1982 was 10 per cent higher. These figures show the huge potential for saving oil, although it is doubtful whether it can be even approximately utilised. A strategy of this kind would require far-reaching changes in economic policy. Inadequate material incentives, old plant, a shortage of capital and lack of interest in innovation all stand in the way of energy saving in the Soviet Union.

6. 'Der Brennstoff- und Energiekomplex der UdSSR', in: *Die Wirtschaft*, East Berlin, 11/1982, p. 25.
7. Central Intelligence Agency, loc. cit.

However, in a centrally directed economy it is easier to change the structure of consumption than to achieve savings. The main possibilities for substituting gas for oil in domestic consumption are in power-stations, and around one-third of thermal power-stations are still oil fired.[8] Therefore, if the Soviet Union cannot implement its substitution plans in exports to the West because there is insufficient demand for gas, it may well be able to do so in its domestic economy.

The energy and oil supplies envisaged for the other CMEA countries are now a problem area in these countries' bilateral trade. The divergence in interests became clear at the thirty-seventh CMEA Congress, held in East Berlin in October 1983, when the Soviet Chairman of the Council of Ministers (Tikhonov) pointed out that the possibilities for further energy supplies 'depend in many respects on the extent to which the other CMEA countries can produce what the Soviet economy needs',[9] while his the Romanian equivalent affirmed that adequate supplies of energy to member states were no longer guaranteed.[10]

In 1980 the Soviet Union informed its partner countries (excluding Romania)[11] that it did not intend to increase its energy supplies further; contrary to the original agreement, it also reduced oil supplies in 1982 by around 10 per cent to 70m. tonnes. The Soviet Union was no doubt glad to have this extra quantity available for export to the West, but ultimately the cuts in supplies announced in 1981, can be attributed to the financial difficulties experienced by the smaller CMEA states. From 1975 to 1983 these countries accumulated a trade deficit with the Soviet Union of around 14 billion tr. If one also bears in mind that as a result of the price fixing system for trade within CMEA (by average prices over the previous five years),[12] Soviet oil prices were up to 50 per cent below world market prices, it becomes clear that:

— The East European countries are a growing burden to the Soviet economy and the thesis that they are being economically exploited by their huge neighbour is difficult to maintain.

8. L. Dienes and Th. Shabad, *The Soviet Energy System*, New York, 1979, p. 37.
9. *Izvestia*, 20 October 1983.
10. *Neuer Weg*, Bucharest, 21 October 1983.
11. Romania only imports a small part of its energy needs from the Soviet Union (1981: 3 m.t; 1982: 0.3 m.t of oil). It had to pay world market prices in convertible currency.
12. This principle may have been changed in practice for oil and gas. Since 1981 the prices have been nearer to a three-year average. See J. Bethkenhagen, 'Erdöl und Erdgas im RGW-Intrablockhandel', *Wochenbericht des DIW*, 51–2/1983.

65

— The East European countries are not very viable. Although oil accounts for only a small share of their energy consumption (21 per cent in 1982, except for Romania) and although most of this came from the Soviet Union at reduced prices,[13] they were not able to cover the rising cost of their oil imports with higher exports of goods. However, their weakness is also a result of the economic system which the Soviet Union is responsible for.

— It will hardly be possible to reduce oil exports to the CMEA countries further without destabilising their economies, which would be contrary to the Soviet Union's hegemonial interests. Martin Kohn has argued in this context that 'Eastern Europe enjoys the leverage of weakness *vis-à-vis* the Soviet Union'.[14]

Against this background it may be assumed that in all probability Soviet oil exports to the CMEA countries will hardly change in quantity over the next few years. Since the same applies to production, the main factor that will affect export potential is the development in domestic consumption. Even if progress can certainly be expected in oil conservation, it is unlikely that with overall economic growth rates of between 3 and 3.5% oil consumption will drop in absolute terms. A slight rise is considered likely, but this would mean:

— Soviet oil exports would drop to at least the extent of the additional gas supplies (17m. tonnes coal equivalent).

— There will be no overall increase in Western energy dependency on the Soviet Union.

— The Soviet Union is unlikely to have a 'flood of foreign exchange earnings' from its additional gas sales.

— The growth in Soviet trade with the West will be much lower in the 1980s than in the previous decade.

13. The savings to the East European countries resulting from the differences between the world market prices and CMEA trade prices (except Romania) were just on 25 billion tr for the period 1975–82, which is the value of Soviet exports to these countries for 1982. However, this was a gross effect, and the loss in earnings to the CMEA countries from their exports to the Soviet Union, which are also calculated at prices based on the average for the past five years, need to be deducted from this, although they were very much lower.
14. Quoted from A. Wright, 'Soviet Natural Resource Exports and the World Market', in: R.G. Jensen (ed.), *Soviet Natural Resources in the World Economy*, Chicago, 1983, p. 619.
15. W. Obst, 'Russland schwimmt in West-Devisen', in: *Die Welt*, 28 July 1982.

Energy Production and Western Technology

Imports from the West do not play a significant part in the exploitation of Soviet oil and gas fields, apart from transport equipment such as pipelines, compressor stations, pipeline laying equipment and so on.[16] It is not possible precisely to calculate the import dependence because no exchange rate is published for the transfer ruble and for domestic currency, but assuming a rate of 1:2 (although it seems more likely that it is nearer to 1:1)[17] we can at least give approximate figures, and a comparison of investment and imports of equipment for the oil and gas industry would look like this:

	1971–5	1976–80
Investment (bill. rubles)	23.49	36.70
Imports from the West (bill. tr)	0.16	0.69
Import ratio	0.7–1.4	1.9–3.8

Altogether, then, the dependence on Western technology is slight. A study by the Office of Technology Assessment reaches the same conclusion. It set out to assess the actual and possible contribution which Western technology can make to the development of the Soviet oil and gas industry and concluded that 'whether for lack of hard currency, a lack of perceived need, or a fear of dependence on the West, the USSR has never imported massive amounts of oil field equipment'.[18]

Thus, if the Soviet Union has become the biggest producer of oil and natural gas in the world without relying on extensive imports from the West, the question arises as to what effects selective bans on exports of equipment would have on the Soviet oil and gas industries. They could certainly cause losses in productivity or delays in implementing production plans but they would not have serious effects on the Soviet economy. Therefore, Western imports

16. See E.A. Hewett, 'Near-Term Prospects for the Soviet Natural Gas Industry, and the Implications for East-West Trade', in: *Joint Economic Committee, Congress of the United States* (ed.), *Soviet Economy in the 1980s: Problems and Prospects,* loc. cit., pp. 408ff.

17. J. Bethkenhagen and H. Machowski, 'Entwicklung und Struktur des deutsch-sowjetischen Handels — Seine Bedeutung für die Volkswirtschaften der Bundesrepublik Deutschland und der Sowjetunion', *Sonderhefte des DIW*, 132/1982, p. 41.

18. Office of Technology Assessment (ed.): *Technology and Soviet Energy Availability*, Washington, DC, 1981, p. 10.

play too small a role to be used as a political lever and the same applies — as we have recently seen with the latest pipeline embargo — to transport equipment. Here too Soviet dependence on imports from the West is frequently overestimated. The Soviet Union is now the biggest pipeline producer in the world, probably as a result of the 1963 embargo. It produces both large-bore pipes and compressor stations. The export pipeline from Urengoi to the Soviet border is only one of six that will link this field with the centres of consumption in the European part of the Soviet Union. Altogether the Eleventh Five-Year Plan provides for 48,000 km. of gas pipes to be laid and only a small proportion of these will have Western parts.

Conclusion

Unlike the East European countries the Soviet Union was able to increase its trade with the West from 1973 to 1982. On the export side this was mainly due to price increases for raw energy sources, i.e. the effect was nominal. On the import side, windfall profits enabled the Soviet Union to import large quantities of goods, so here there was also a strong increase in real terms.

In future the trend is likely to be the reverse, for at present no gains in the terms of trade are to be expected from energy exports. An expansion of the quantity exported will only be possible in gas, and this is limited at present by lack of demand from the West. It is unlikely that the energy dependence of Western Europe on the Soviet Union will as a whole increase through the additional gas supplies because a drop in oil exports is to be expected in the course of the next few years.

The Soviet Union has neglected to develop competitive export goods and this will soon be making itself felt. Against this background it can be anticipated that its share in OECD trade will fall again.

If the West does not want to contribute to a shortage of energy on the world market and to a drop in its exports to the Soviet Union, it must not take a negative stance on East-West co-operation in exploiting Soviet energy sources. The main areas where co-operation might be possible are in energy saving and oil and coal production or processing, although the question of how profitable coal processing can be will rear its head again if oil prices stagnate.

3

Technology

Industrial Development and Technology
Jürgen Nötzold

Structural Change in Industry through Technical Progress

The use of new technological knowledge in industry leads to the development of new production processes and new goods. That is how the share of individual sectors in total industrial production changes in the course of industrial development. If one traces this structural change in industry over time one sees that it moves in the same direction in the Western market economies and in the East European centrally planned states. However, there is one major difference, namely the speed with which new technological knowledge is fed into production and the share of the most modern technological production areas in total industrial production. Soviet industry is years behind corresponding developments in Western industrial societies and in its adjustment to the rapid changes in world technological standards.

The next few years will bring very rapid technical change. We need only mention the increases in productivity to be expected from the many different applications of micro-electronics, communications technology, biotechnology, the development of new materials and new energy techniques. Soviet industry is faced with the task of changing the production structure in line with the new technical knowledge fast enough to reduce the gap now opening up in so many civilian technical areas *vis-à-vis* the Western industrial states, and increasingly now to a number of newly developed countries.

The Existing Condition of Soviet Industry

In the 1970s Soviet industrial policy concentrated more strongly than before on modernisation. However, it is evident that the investment policy which should have brought new production processes did not have the desired effect. There are the following indications of this: the average age of the stock of machinery and production facilities in Soviet industry increased further, from 12.2 years in 1960 to 14.2 years in 1980.[1] This was because the new machines that were produced were assigned mainly to new plant, rather than to replace obsolete or ageing stock in existing plant. Consequently, it was not possible in the 1970s to change the familiar 'traditional' pattern of investment policy in Soviet industry in either. Investment was used mainly to expand industrial fixed assets, not for rationalisation. However, if rationalisation in existing plant is inadequate, the increase in labour productivity is correspondingly low. Soviet industry is therefore working with technically obsolete machinery and its production facilities are used for a disproportionately long time.

To enable productivity to be increased through new production processes Soviet industry must also provide an adequate number of technologically new products. In the 1970s, however, the development of new types of machinery and production facilities appears to have declined as well. The Soviet machine-building sector is still apparently producing machines that are out of date; in other words, it is not concentrating on the most technologically advanced processes or goods. Clearly, the industrial production apparatus in the Soviet Union is still directed to extensive growth; the lifetime of the existing plant has not been shortened, nor has more technical progress, i.e. the production of new goods and processes, been implemented.

The Potential for Technical Progress

The continuing trend towards extensive development in Soviet industry cannot be explained by inadequate expenditure on research and development. New technological knowledge is the basis for the

1. E. Böhm, S. Reymann, 'Entwicklungsprobleme der Sowjetwirtschaft an der Schwelle der 80er Jahre', *HWWA-Report 63*, HWWA-Institut für Wirtschaftsforschung, Hamburg, September 1983, pp. 23ff.

production of new machinery and production processes, and this depends on research. Progress in research is achieved with the appropriate expenditure of money and staff. Here, however, the Soviet Union is at the top of the world list; ahead of Japan, the USA and West Germany in the share of staff in R&D in the total population, in the absolute number of scientists, engineers and technicians and in the share of expenditure on research and development in the national product. Nonetheless, we must remember a factor that is particularly important in a centrally planned economy: the quality of research and development does not depend exclusively on how much money is being spent on it. The productivity of R&D is more important. It is frequently assumed that central planning of R&D, as in the Soviet Union, brings particularly good results. On the contrary, central planning hampers productivity in Soviet R&D, since it creates a strongly formalised structure, particularly in applied research. The heavy expenditures on organisation wastes time that could be better spent in finding solutions to research problems. A random example from the Soviet literature will illustrate this: the task of increasing the speed of drilling in oil and natural gas exploration within the Soviet Union entailed the co-operation and coordination of nearly ninety research and construction organisations and industrial enterprises under the control of fifteen different ministries and offices.[2]

The productivity of research is also negatively affected because some research institutions are inadequately equipped with scientific apparatus and instruments. The equipment used in R&D needs constantly to be adjusted in line with new developments, requirements and targets. However, this is generally acquired in individual items or very small lots. The technological level and general flexibility, both of the machine building sector and the supply system, substantially affect the equipping of the R&D sector.

Industrial production in the Soviet Union is geared towards mass production for specific purposes. And the rigidity of the supply system is well known. Many experts therefore believe that equipment is the main reason for the backlog in Soviet applied research.[3] B.E. Paton, a member of the Soviet Academy of Sciences, has

2. E. Prochorenko, 'Wissenschaft für die Produktion in der UdSSR', *Marxistische Blätter*, 17/1979, p. 52.
3. Th. Gustafson, '*Why Does the Soviet Union Lag behind the United States in Basic Science?*', Center for Science and International Affairs, Kennedy School of Government, Harvard University, September 1978, p. 47.

admitted that: 'In the quality of our scientific instruments we are far behind the USA and some other countries. Even our best institutes urgently need new equipment.'

So it is possible to identify factors that are mutually intensifying and which make it very difficult to provide a general solution to this problem. These include inadequate production of parts and instruments, a backlog in the appropriate technologies, such as microprocessors, over rigid planning of supply, communication problems between producers and users of apparatus and, finally, coordination problems between the various industrial ministries responsible for developing the equipment, depending on the materials it consists of.

Innovation research has in fact been carried out on the best way to organise the construction of scientific instruments, and this showed that the laboratory users play a big part in the development of new types of instruments and in making improvements to existing ones. In the Soviet Union too there are channels of communication between the users and producers of scientific instruments, mainly in the form of contracts between academic institutions and specialised construction bureaux in the Ministry for Machine-Building, Apparatus and Instrument Construction. It would be erroneous to generalise on the organisational weaknesses of Soviet research, for if a project is accorded high priority by the central planners then the contacts between the users and producers of the equipment will also bring the desired results. However, if equipment is needed for a low priority project the system does not work so well, problems characteristic of the supply situation in Soviet industry arise and the reaction to unplanned or unforeseen technical progress is too slow.

Soviet industry is concentrated on certain focal points and the lack of competition means that technological differences between plants are not levelled out. It may be assumed that the situation is similar in R&D. It is probable that the differences in performance between various research institutes within the Soviet Union itself are greater than those between the Soviet Union and Western industrial countries. Generalisations on the level and efficiency of Soviet research would also lead to erroneous conclusions. The Soviet Union has achieved immense successes in basic research. The research institutions of the Academy of Sciences can be regarded as first class. Indeed, in many fields the Academy has the best Soviet researchers and theoreticians.

Soviet research is particularly strong in areas that are less dependent on the supply of instruments and equipment. Where experiments do not depend on new instruments but rather on inventiveness in theoretical work the development of Soviet science is far from sluggish. The best example of this is in mathematics.

Basic Soviet research tends to become weaker the further one moves from the abstract to the experimental. It is less successful in areas where there have been rapid developments in scientific instruments and apparatus, and where technical progress is necessary for progress in research. However, the Soviet Union can also achieve first-class results by concentrating funds and staff, as a centrally planned economy can. Nuclear physics and laser technology are examples of this. Soviet research is an international leader in areas requiring large-scale capital-intensive equipment, like plasma physics.

The Soviet Union has about 5,500 research institutes. Many of them are engaged in applied research. All are under the control of the appropriate industrial ministry and it may be assumed that a few hundred of them are first-rate.

Central Planning of Industrial Structural Change and Technical Achievement

When all is said and done, however, the Soviet Union had this research and development policy in the 1970s and it still failed to achieve the investment needed to modernise its industry. Consequently, it must also be said that the sum of expenditure on research and the number of scientists and engineers is only one factor in the flow of technological progress into production. The technological level of an economy depends to a decisive extent on how rapidly the results of research can be used in the production process. In a planned economy it is the job of the central planning organs and the production enterprises they direct to integrate research findings into the production process. However, precisely this form of organisation means that structural change, i.e. the creation of more productive areas in industry, is not fast enough.

The biggest problem regarding central planning and the implementation of technical progress lies in the modernisation of the many existing plants. It is hardly possible to plan from the centre the huge range of changes that might be possible in the utilisation of means of production or in production itself for the individual enterprise. Planning bureaucracies cannot take account of all the

73

need for change or recognise all the possibilities for new production processes. The real dilemma of the centrally directed socialist economy lies in finding and implementing the numerous small technical advances within the entire spectrum of industrial production, since technical progress does not depend exclusively on major industrial techniques but also on their application in the form of many small individual innovations.

It is urgently necessary to make better use of the results of research and development. Not long ago a memorandum by the Economic Institute of the Siberian Department of the Soviet Academy of Sciences drew attention to the need for change in Soviet economic organisation, but at the same time affirmed: 'The fundamental need to change the system of state control of the economy has long been recognised by the Party and it is to be found in a number of decisions; . . . but the problem has not been solved, and the existing system of economic administration stubbornly retains those features the Party documents regard it as so necessary to overcome.'

Why have the necessary changes not been made? There are many possible answers. One might be that the leadership sees advantages in the present system of focal point administration. We have already shown that there are differences in the quality of various R&D institutes, as well as in the utilisation of research, both between various sectors and individual plants. The achievements of the armaments industry, the result of concentrating on focal points, are a particularly impressive example of this, and one must remember that the Soviet Union sells licences to Western industrial countries; in other words, it is technologically competitive in this area.

Increasing Industrial Efficiency by Changing Economic Organisation

The discussion of problems standing in the way of rapid structural change in Soviet industry in favour of more modern technology has focused attention on the need to change economic organisation, and the question arises whether changes of this nature might be possible in the 1980s in order to increase the efficiency of Soviet industry. So far it is evident that the traditional method of using administrative measures to increase efficiency will be retained and no changes are envisaged which would expose plants to greater competition.

At the plenary session of the CPSU Central Committee in November 1982, changes were announced to increase technological efficiency, while in August 1983 both the Central Committee and the Council of Ministers issued a decree containing the following measures:

(a) Complexes were to be formed grouping together research and construction units and plants;
(b) Direct supplies to plants were to be stepped up;
(c) Meeting the plan targets for 'Science and Technology' was to become one of the main targets for plant activity;
(d) Reserves were to be made available for the development and production of new goods and processes.

How should these measures be assessed? The complexes described above are on the lines of the Research and Production Associations of the 1970s, which did generally succeed in accelerating the flow of research results into production. However, it also became apparent that the plants were still inadequately motivated to take on new products and production processes. The innovation risk may be too high for the plant, for the results of research can generally only be used in the production process after some adjustment, and this may prevent the plant from meeting its target data. The Soviet specialist press is always drawing attention to cases where plants fail to adopt innovations because these would not facilitate implementation of the plan.

For this reason, the other measures in the decree of August 1983 are important. The provision of reserves for technological innovation — in other words, capacities for research and development and production facilities, could improve the innovation process. Shifting the weight of the plan targets for plant activity is an attempt to adjust the data so as to further the implementation of the new aims. However, this does not eliminate the problem of revaluing target data: if more weight is put on 'Science and Technology', other areas will have to be neglected.

Evidently, new mechanisms are to be incorporated into a planning system that remains basically unchanged. The measures will bring improvements and there may well be an acceleration in the flow of research into the economy. Nevertheless, the forming of focal points and consequently the imbalance in industrial performance will continue. This is not the way to achieve a lasting breakthrough to greater technological efficiency across the entire breadth of industrial production.

4. B.E. Paton, member of the Academy of Sciences, in: *Ekonomika i Organizatsiya promyshlennogo proizdvodstva*, 5/1973, p. 6.

Technology Transfer and Economic Development
Claus-Dieter Kernig

Technology Transfer and the Superpowers

Technology transfer is nowadays discussed mainly in the context of military and defence policy and I shall do the same. It is evident that the Soviet Union uses all the appropriate technological knowledge to build up its political and military strength. One can go much further and assert that the Soviet Union uses every foreign trade advantage it can get to stabilise its system. Technology transfer is only one component in this use of comparative cost advantages.

That in itself is not unusual. The nations of Europe have rarely acted otherwise since industrialisation began. They have all tried to turn the advantages of world markets to bolster national strength. However, the conditions used to be different. In the past a whole series of nations were engaged in a pluralist power race. The disadvantages were felt less by the competitors themselves than by others, the former colonial nations.

The situation today is different. The superpowers are imposing a heavy burden on themselves and on their allies. Moreover, the arms race entails an incalculable risk which makes it rationally indefensible.

For these reasons, opinions in the West differ on economic relations with Eastern Europe. Some say that trade and the transfer of technology is a dangerous game to play for a slight economic advantage and could lead to a defence sell-out. Others believe that since one cannot in any case prevent the Soviet Union from building up arms, then trade and technology transfer will not only bring some trading advantages but will also help to build confidence; it will lead to mutual dependence and might possibly help pacify the Soviet Union. In the wake of the disillusionment with *détente* this latter argument no longer sounds convincing. Since no one knows how to stop the Soviet Union or any other country from obtaining access to Western technology, the best solution is held to be to advance so far and so fast as to confront the Soviet Union with weaponry so sophisticated that it will yield and come to reason.

I regard both these viewpoints with scepticism. I also suspect that here in the West two partly erroneous assessments are being combined to form quite the wrong conclusion. Let me explain this.

Technology Transfer and Development

There are three different methods of technological development: the Western, the Soviet and the Japanese.

(1) The Western method consists of letting companies develop technology in response to market considerations and cyclical mechanisms; i.e. firms either pay licence fees or invest in research and development.

This method causes a continuous diffusion of technology, mainly through civilian consumer markets.

(2) The Soviet method is to take up foreign technology (as far as possible without paying for it) and allow it to be used or maybe even further developed by a privileged technological *élite* which, as the broad mass is deprived of consumption, works extremely effectively towards attaining the strategic objectives of the political leadership.

This method does not lead to any noteworthy diffusion of technology beyond the strategically important *élite* sectors. The most striking feature of the Soviet economy is the singular lack of technological diffusion into agriculture, which still absorbs more than one-fifth of the total labour force.

(3) The Japanese method consists of the concentrated further development of the technical product, from the sophisticated individual part to the end product which should as far as possible be beyond reach of competitors, with a broad mass of core workers in kohai-sempai relations subsidised by the MITI.

The Japanese method leads to high technology in certain sectors with a steady and deliberate diffusion into others that are not necessarily related (from the piano industry, for instance, to electronics and from the motor industry to photo technology).

In assessing technology transfer, too little attention is generally paid to the significance of the particular path of development pursued by the Soviet Union. The Soviet system makes it impossible to use imported technology other than at a strategically important point. The planning system, the singular nature of enterprise management and the organisation of research ensure that everything moves in the same direction.

The more strategic importance is attached to weapons (instead of the railways, for instance, or building harbours and merchant fleets, as in the Europe of old) the more politics and the economy will become militarised. The tension which the Soviet Union constantly transmits is re-processed at home in a self-affirmatory cycle, so helping to cement the system.

All the debates on disarmament and technology transfer are therefore nothing more than discussion on the modalities of a given situation which they will not be able to change.

Technology Transfer and its Segmentation

Seven stages of technological knowledge can be identified:

I. Basic knowledge	V. Knowledge of maintenance and repairs
II. Research knowledge	
III. Development knowledge	VI. Production knowledge
IV. Innovation knowledge	VII. Product knowledge

The basic knowledge (I) is documented in school books and textbooks, teaching materials, handbooks, monographs and so on; it is available to the public.

Research knowledge (II) is documented in special periodicals, company news-sheets, internal reports and laboratory reports; some of it is public but some remains confidential or secret.

Development knowledge (III) is documented in technical drawings, file notes, instructions, minutes of meetings and other reports; it is virtually never available to the public although some of it is reconstructed in company histories, biographies and memoirs; the results are available in patent form.

Innovation knowledge (IV) is documented in technical drawings, assembly instructions and descriptions of processes; generally it is accessible only through delivery contracts.

Maintenance and repair knowledge (V) is documented in service instructions; it is either accessible to those who buy the plant or available after the purchase in a maintenance agreement for outside staff.

Production knowledge (VI) is documented in trade journals and congress reports and is stored in the skills of company work-forces; it is accessible by acquiring these workers, through instructions on delivery or by training.

Product knowledge (VII) is documented in advertisements and instructions for use, and is supplemented by user know-how; it is generally available.

The industrial pioneer nations built up their modern economies by repeatedly moving from Stage I through to Stage VII. There was also what is called a constant technological feed-back effect (Fig. 3.1 below).

Fig. 3.1

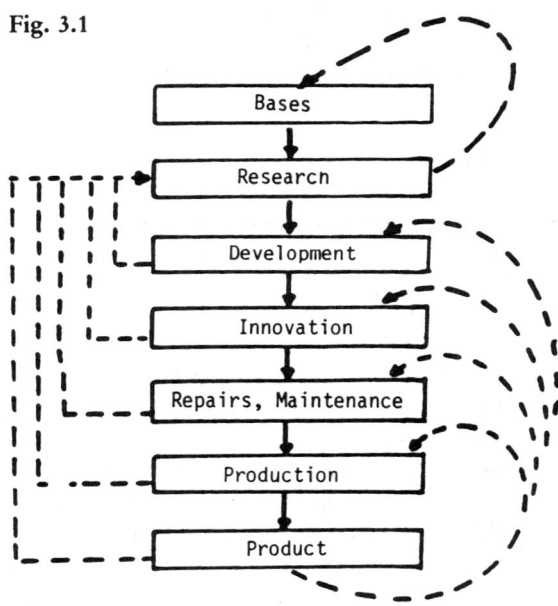

This creates its own development dynamic. As the basic knowledge is extended, more and more educational assets are created. The workers become more highly qualified. Their capabilities grow. This in turn leads to product innovations and production process innovation, both of which increase the level of supply and the level of demand in a society. The dynamic will increase the more modern technology affects consumer goods markets, and the system will acquire the force typically inherent in a capitalist structure. This subsequently leads to high growth rates and is reflected in a correspondingly high tax revenue, which in turn enables the state to promote education (I), research (II) and development (III) and creates a demand for high technology goods (VII, e.g. armaments, or goods to expand the infrastructure).

79

The Soviet Union is not one of the industrial pioneer nations. Nevertheless, it could have trodden the path taken by most of the late developers and which the threshold countries today have chosen: they are exporting raw materials or processed products to pay for imports of plant to build up their own industries. This mechanism develops Stages VII, VI and V before the earlier stages (Fig. 3.2 below).

Fig. 3.2

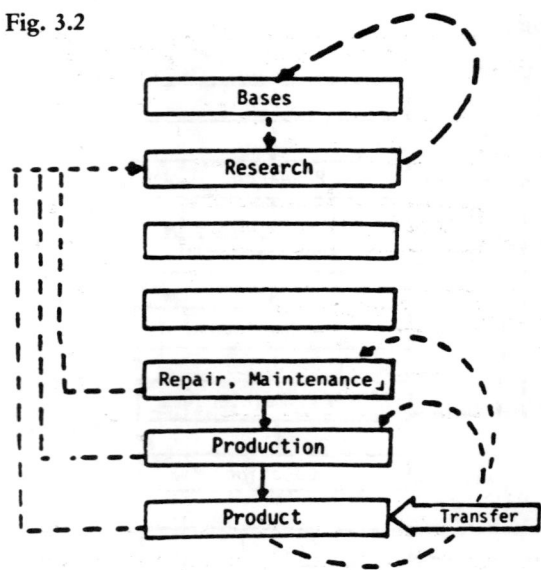

This pattern of development makes a nation a threshold country. It can then develop Stages II, III and IV independently (and provide the necessary capital from raw materials or from cheap labour export goods).

For historical and political reasons the Soviet Union has not been able to develop along these lines. War Communism had destroyed the basis of the export industry by 1922. The New Economic Policy (NEP) made some corrections but the collectivisation of agriculture completed the destruction. The forced labour camp period of the great purges also prevented the Soviet Union from moving back on to the path chosen by the threshold countries and funding its development from export earnings. Since NEP the Soviet Union has therefore concentrated on technology transfer and the acquisition of experts (Fig. 3.3, p. 81).

Figure 3.3

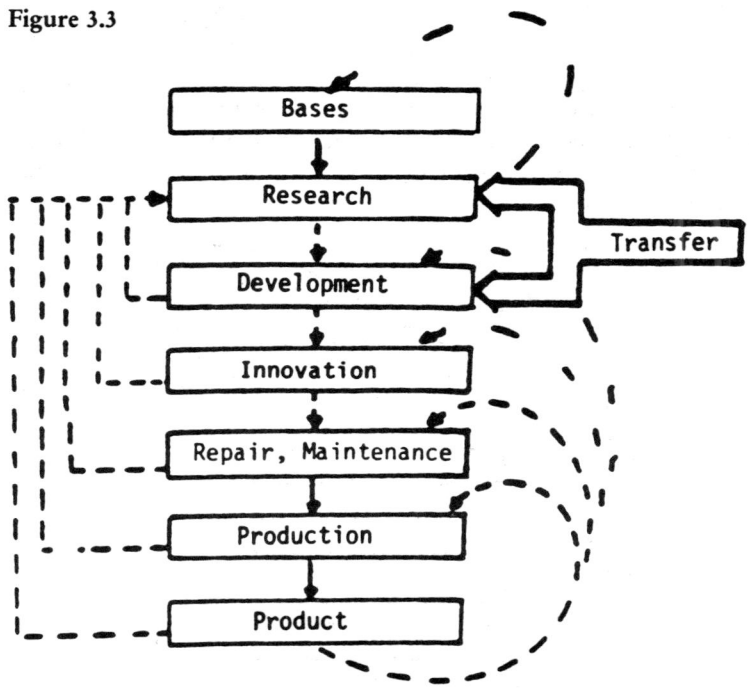

This path was combined with what is known as the strategy of 'Outstripping growth by Sector I', i.e. a one-sided concentration on promoting heavy industry. With this decision the Soviet Union finally left the path of orientation towards the West and Stalin did not diverge from the traditional economic policy even after 1945; on the contrary, he strengthened it during his 'autarky period'. The challenge of the cold war and the arms race cemented the economic structure of the Soviet Union, resulting in a one-sided orientation of advanced technology in the service of strategic aims. Although the Soviet Union now benefits from the same technological feed-back effect as the West and Japan this only affects a very narrow range of its products (Fig. 3.4, p. 82).

If one takes a closer look at the limited range of high quality products in the Soviet Union, one fact emerges which is of crucial importance in assessing technology transfer into that country: The Soviet Union has no notable production plant that could mass produce high technology goods. This means that there can be no

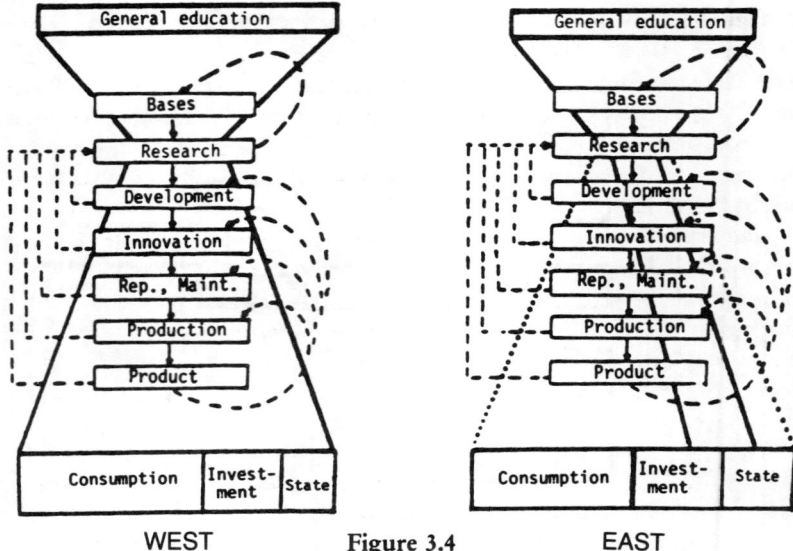

WEST   **Figure 3.4**   EAST

broad technology feed-back effect through greater mass consumption. The nation remains technologically undynamic. The workers' qualification level remains as low as the level of supply.

Nor is there any mass production of high quality equipment (office products, process control equipment, industrial computer installations). The Soviet Union has not even reached the starting line in the latest technology round, namely micro-processor production. Yet these are the most far-reaching innovations of our century. And the Soviet Union should have a greater interest than any other nation in rationalising administration, since it has the greatest bureaucracy on earth.

While the Soviet Union competes with the West for advantages in the military–strategic sphere and in a war theatre that can probably never again be entered with any hope of success, it has long since lost the race for the advantage in non-military development.

The burden of armaments and the potential for destruction repeatedly focus the attention of politicians and analysts on the military–strategic confrontation. However, it is worth while asking if this does not itself keep the pot boiling. The superpowers are giving priority to something that may perhaps already have lost some of its significance because it is now an effect rather than a cause.

Technology Transfer and Soviet Internal Stability

The Western approach to technology transfer to the Soviet Union is very largely 'tit for tat'. As long as the Soviet Union causes us defence problems (the argument goes) we shall cause it as many economic difficulties as we can. That is what is said, but is it perhaps counter-productive?

The arms race forces the Soviet Union to use the latest and most highly developed technology in the strategic field. This is enormously expensive for a nation whose per capita GNP in 1982 was 45 per cent that of the United States, or 56 per cent in absolute terms. However, since private consumption in the Soviet Union cannot be forced down below 50 per cent of total GNP the arms race has to be financed from what is in fact far too small a budget.

The arms race has greatly hampered economic growth in the Soviet Union. The transition from quantitative to qualitative growth is being delayed more and more. The service sector (which includes education, culture, research and development) has not notably increased its share of GNP since 1965, as it should have done. The appropriate share of agriculture has not dropped below 14 per cent. Industry and construction are still rising slightly. In short, in comparison with Western nations the Soviet Union has an antiquated development profile.

The capital absorbed by the arms industry reduces the possibilities for modernising the economy. The resultant backwardness of agriculture and certain industries makes it necessary to import agricultural products and industrial plant. For the most part these imports can only be paid for with export earnings from (a) raw materials, (b) gold and (c) weapons. However, as exports of raw materials cannot be increased freely because of the difficulties of extracting them and gold exports are limited by world market prices, weapons exports remain an economic necessity. The Soviet Union thus has an essential interest in exporting weaponry for internal economic reasons and this constantly refuels the global potential for conflict.

These problems are likely to worsen in future. The latest technological revolution in the West and Japan will bring a new growth thrust and the share of the Soviet Union and the Eastern bloc in the world national product will shrink further. The burden on the people of the Eastern bloc will grow.

Is there a corrective to these developments? I do not see any possibility of a significant change over the next decade and a half, for it will not be possible for the Soviet Union to move on to a Western pattern of development, with its broad technological feedback effect, within that period, despite it being the path adopted by the other threshold and developing countries. For this the Soviet Union lacks the necessary capital. For sociological reasons, however, it cannot follow the Japanese model. So it will remain structurally bound by its faults. Ultimately, this means that as a superpower the Soviet Union will reach the point of relatively greatest weakness in the economic sphere at the same moment as it finds itself at the peak of its military strength. To put it even more simply: economic crises and military strength will synchronise and peak together. The present political course steered by the West will intensify both, helping to promote a crisis in the Soviet economy, while at the same time inciting it to a peak in military build-up.

There is no sign that the current Western strategy will resolve this problem. In the eventuality of open hostilities the civilised world will be destroyed. This is no solution. If the Soviet Union were to suffer an internal crisis that shook the system at its roots; that is if the power of the ruling Party were to be jeopardised, it is unclear whether that would affect the outside world and if so, how.

Any discussion with the Soviet leaders that might in any way help to ease the symptoms of the synchronised crisis-power syndrome are essential for survival and in that sense formal and informal discussion can only be whole-heartedly supported. However, if the opinion takes hold that this will cure more than the symptoms, it will be implying an error of judgement that is as tragic as it is fantastic. Historically and culturally the Soviet system is a variant and branch, not to say a deformation, of the capitalist economic and social system. If we cannot understand that the problem will dominate us, we will not dominate it.

Since the distinctions drawn here — and they could be extended by a whole range of parallel considerations — are not common to the general literature on technology transfer, nor form part of the discussion on technology transfer to the Soviet Union, those who have now to decide on that transfer are taking only a limited view of the symptomatic perspectives. The means aids they have available to arrive at a judgement are out of proportion to the object. It is rather like hunting butterflies with a hammer — one either misses or destroys what one is trying to catch.

Military Aspects of Technology Transfer
Miles M. Costick

I would like to begin by stating something that is very obvious, but too often neglected. The world finds itself at a critical juncture of human history; that is, in the midst of a process which can best be described as a protracted systemic conflict. The Soviet understanding of the German strategist von Clausewitz is total; in fact, they have built upon his ideas. It is not just that they regard class conflict as an extension of foreign policy by other means (that is, they view Communist aggressions as legitimate wars and legitimate acts of foreign policy), but that they actually view foreign policy itself as nothing but the conduct of warfare by other means. This outlook also encompasses the foreign economic relationship.

At this point it would be rather instructive to scrutinise the nature of the Soviet economy. I propose that from the very onset of Bolshevik rule the Soviet economy was built with the intention of creating a war economy rather than a consumer-orientated one. According to the seasoned perception of economic development — that is, from the Western perspective — the Bolsheviks chose the wrong path of economic development. Instead of developing their agriculture, infrastructure, and light industries and building upon these, they opted from the beginning for heavy industry, which in the practical language of the time translates into a military or war-orientated economy. If one examines the Soviet economy today one can see that about 80 per cent of the total economic activity of the USSR is (more or less) related to military needs. Similarly, if one looks at the activities of the Soviet Academy of Sciences one will discover that about 80 per cent of the work done in the thousands of scientific institutes and research and development organisations is performed on behalf of the Soviet military machine. As a result, the economic relationship between the Western entities and the Soviet state is not normal commerce, but a form of systemic struggle. The trade between ideological blocs is of a politico-strategic nature, rather than that what we in the West perceive as 'business as usual'. Consequently, the terms of trade are not acceptable because so far the trade process has fuelled the Soviet war machine. It has provided the Soviet Union with solutions for their industrial and scientific problems, and has especially helped to alleviate some important problems within the military–industrial complex. The economic exchanges with the West have also reduced the cost of Soviet military production and provided the Soviets with solutions for things which were conceived, but which could not be translated from the designing draft boards of inventors into concrete mass production.

It should be emphasised that from its very beginnings the Soviet Union depended on the inflow of Western technology. At the outset Germany and the United States especially played the leading role in that process. After World War II the situation gradually changed and, practically speaking, we were all competing and tripping over each others' feet 'to sell the rope to the hangman'. What has been accomplished? In the Soviet perspective there certainly has been a very significant achievement. For example, the USSR's fourth generation of strategic weapons is based on Western technology: the technology of the US, and that of Japan, Germany, France and the United Kingdom. Let me demonstrate this simply by pointing to the SS-18, the most lethal strategic weapon in the world (it carries between twelve and eighteen nuclear warheads, each three times the size of the largest US nuclear warhead). It is true that the Soviets have a tendency to go for huge systems. At the same time, if one combines the concept of the huge with the quality to be found in American technology, one has the two most important elements of the Soviet strategic weapons systems. Let us examine both the SS-18 and the SS-20. The SS-20 is a weapon for which we have all jointly provided assistance; yet in providing this assistance we may have inadvertently spelled the end of the Atlantic Alliance.

The SS-18 and the SS-20 both belong to the fourth generation of the Soviet strategic arsenal. Everything from the skeleton to the metallurgical parts, from the technology of the electronic sub-systems to the inertial guidance systems, MIRV-ing mechanism and so on, originated in the West. It originated in the West as a concept, a patent, a technology of production, as tools used in manufacturing or instruments used in quality control and testing in the production process. The missile itself represents very much what has been achieved with the third generation of American missiles, although they are not as mobile as the SS-20. Nevertheless, this missile basically follows the developmental path of American strategic weaponry.

One of the basic problems we have today is the tremendous

leakage of American technology via Japan, France and West Germany. For example, in the case of the SS-20 and the SS-18 the nose cone, the technology of the nose cone and the compounds which are on the nose cone (which reduce the impact of high temperatures in outer space) were transferred from the United States to our ally, France. And the French manufacturer illegally sold the cone technology and the compound technology to the Soviet Union. The computer controlled or digitally controlled machine-tools developed in Germany with US assistance for the American aerospace programme, used in the manufacture of equipment such as rocket and space vehicles for the Apollo programme — equipment of critical importance — has been advertised in Soviet engineering journals by stressing the contribution they made to the Apollo programme. And, of course, the Soviets bought it. Today they use these machine-tools (which can perform ten simultaneous operations and measure 30 m in diameter) to machine titanium, one of the hardest strategic alloys. With the assistance of these machines the Soviets are building the titanium monster hulls of submarines, which can dive deeper and out-run American submarines (we are talking here of the Alpha and Taifun class of submarine). The SS-20 and SS-18 missiles, whose first stage is made of titanium, are being built with the same machine-tools from West Germany. The Soviets could not weld titanium until they perfected the technology with the assistance of Japanese metallurgical experts. The contemporary Soviet space effort would be nowhere without the joint programmes they had carried out with the United States. Some of the most important technologies — coupling technology, micro-electronics, computers, inertial navigation guidance systems, space antennas to name just a few — are of American origin. There are a lot of stories about the so-called precision miniature ball-bearings which the Soviets acquired from the United States. These are to be found in many Soviet systems, such as MIG aircraft (in the firing control mechanism), missile guidance mechanisms, automatic pilots of all kinds of guided missiles, Soviet spacecraft, the automatic antennas of satellites (these operate by using gimbals which contain the precision miniature ball-bearings) and so on.

There is also a case of significant technology leakage by way of Sweden. Generally speaking, these leaks have been going on for some forty years. The wind-tunnels for testing jet engines and rocket engines, which have been bought by Sweden, are a case in point. Later Sweden re-exported this equipment to the Soviet

Union in clear violation of the contractual obligation undertaken *vis-à-vis* the United States. Perhaps one of the worst incidents in this respect is the DATASAAB affair: illegally, the Swedes transferred the primary and secondary radars to the USSR. This gave the Soviets the capability to track a low flying penetration B-1 bomber (which has a low radar profile) as well as cruise missiles.

The Soviets manufacture chemical warfare agents in chemical factories bought from Germany and France. And, if one follows on a case by case basis the T-70, T-80 and T-64 Soviet tanks, one finds that they integrate the technology of the German Panther-I and Panther-II tanks, as well as British Chobham armour. There is hardly any type in the Soviet conventional or strategic weapons systems which did not, in one way or another, benefit from the proceeds of Western technology imported into the Soviet Union. It is my calculation that over the last twelve years the Soviet Union has saved itself about a $100 billion of efficiently used research and development by importing, via overt or covert channels, technology from the West.

What is the answer? Simply that we cannot conduct our economic relationship with the Soviet Union as if they were another free-market partner, subscribing to multinational arrangements such as GATT. The Soviets do not view the conduct of economic affairs from that perspective, but rather as the conduct of economic warfare by a variety of means. In the face of this, sanctions are a cosmetic proposition since they do not achieve the objectives they should have. It is time that we treat the entire matter from a strategic, that is from a long-term adversarial perspective. This suggests that we should have clear objectives, and in my judgement the principal one should be to retard Soviet scientific, technological and industrial development. Only when we agree on this objective can we speak about having an alliance which promises a brighter future for all of us in the free world.

4

Economic Interdependence

International Debts and Proxy Costs
Klaus Schröder

The discussion on the indebtedness of the Soviet Union to the West, its credit worthiness and ability to meet its repayment obligations punctually, has at times given rise to speculation, firstly, that the USSR might have difficulty in repaying credits as agreed and in maintaining the required interest payments, and secondly, that its standing as an international borrower has dropped so low that no new credits will be forthcoming. The subject of Soviet international indebtedness must be seen in connection with the events in Afghanistan and Poland, the debate on rearmament and the deployment of missiles, and the complexity of these issues has caused it to be overweighted. If we take a closer look at the real situation we can see that the picture is in fact very clear, though it deviates from many assumptions and does not offer subject for speculation.

The Soviet Union has been and will remain cautious and conservative in its finance policy, and particularly under the 'linkage philosophy' will not expose itself to excessive indebtedness, for this could make it dangerously dependent on Western capital markets and so perhaps on Western politicians. It is not, in fact, financially dependent and there is no sign of any serious increase in its need to borrow on Western capital markets. The Soviet Union will adjust its borrowing to its supply of foreign exchange and will not force trade with the West to step up domestic growth. To put it another way, the Soviet Union derives its demand for imports, not from its domestic investment opportunities but from the ability of its export industry to earn Western currency. So, understandably, its indebtedness has never given any particular cause for concern thus far.

A difficult obstacle at times, both for Western creditors and for the Soviet Union itself, is the uncertainty concerning the actual level of Soviet holdings of foreign exchange and indebtedness. The USSR has always maintained silence on its assets, its existing repayment obligations and intended borrowing. What we know is based on Western estimates, some of which differ markedly, and not on official Soviet figures.

With this reservation, it has always been said that the Soviet Union's gross indebtedness to the West is low, at around US $18 billion (end of 1983). Deducting from this the extremely high deposits with Western banks of US $9.7 billion, we have a net indebtedness of only US $8.3 billion.

This estimate needs correcting as far as the level of indebtedness is concerned. The statistics on borrowing published by the OECD, together with the Bank for International Settlements in April 1984 show a Soviet volume of borrowing of $28.6 billion for the end of 1982. If the credits to the two CMEA banks (the International Bank for Economic Co-operation and the International Investment Bank, both in Moscow) to the tune of c. $4 billion are deducted from this, and if one remembers that the new statistics do not give a complete list of all Soviet borrowing in the West, we may take it that Soviet indebtedness is at least $25 billion. The latest estimate is exactly 25 per cent above other figures that are frequently used, by banks as well, and this clearly shows how justifiable it is to ask for clear information from borrowers. Since the *de facto* illiquidity of Poland in 1981 the Soviet Union has been even more cautious than usual on Western capital markets. It has built up clear current account surpluses in trade with Western industrial and developing countries (US $4 billion in 1982 and more than US $5 billion in 1983), and has been able to reduce its Western indebtedness even without recourse to its gold holdings. Borrowing from banks dropped between the end of 1981 and the end of 1983 by US $1 billion, to US $14.9 billion, and at the same time deposits with Western banks were increased by US $1.2 billion to US $9.7 billion, so net indebtedness dropped by US $2.2 billion.

All the economic indicators used by the banks to assess Soviet credit worthiness speak for positive decisions. The main factor, apart from the high foreign exchange balances in the West, are the gold reserves. All the data on gold production, gold exports and gold reserves are a carefully kept state secret in the Soviet Union. However, by Western estimates the gold reserves amount to about

Table 4.1 The Soviet Union's balance of payments with the West in US $ billions

	1979	1980	1981	1982	1983
Exports to the West	19.4	23.6	23.8	26.2[a]	
Imports from the West	21.4	26.2	27.8	27.5[a]	
Trade balance	-2.0	-2.5	-4.0	-1.3[a]	
Net interest burden[a]	-0.8	-0.7	-1.3	-1.5	
Balance on current account[a]	2.2	1.9	-0.1	4.2	
Revenue from gold sales[a]	1.5	1.6	2.7	1.1	
Revenue from weapons exports[a]	3.9	4.2	4.2	5.9	
Revenue from exports of goods, gold and weapons	24.8	29.4	30.7	33.2	
Borrowing[a]	4.5	2.9	6.2	2.7	
of which on the Euro-market[b]	0.3	0.1	0.0	0.2	0.0
Repayments	2.8	3.1	3.2	3.4	
Gross indebtedness[a]	18.1	17.6	20.9	20.1	18.0[1]
(Gross indebtedness acc. to OECD/BIS				24.6[2]	
of which: to Western banks[c]	12.9	13.4	15.9	14.2	14.9
to FRG banks in DM bill.[d]	4.3	4.1	3.8	3.4	4.9
Deposits with Western banks	8.6	8.6	8.4	10.0	9.7

Sources: Joan Parpart Zoeter, 'USSR: Hard Currency Trade and Payments', in: *Joint Economic Committee, Soviet Economy in the 1980s*, part 2, Washington 1983, pp. 479ff.

a. *US Department of Commerce, Staff Report, Statistical Abstract of East-West Trade Finance*, December 1983.
b. OECD, *Financial Statistics Monthly*, International Markets, Paris 11/1982.
c. Bank for International Settlements, International Banking Developments, Basle, various quarterly reports.
1. Own estimate.
2. OECD/BIS, *Statistics on External Indebtedness: Bank and Trade-Related Non-Bank External Claims on Individual Borrowing Countries and Territories at End-December 1982 and End-June 1983*, Paris/Basle, April 1984. This report gives Soviet indebtedness at US $28.6 billion, from which credits totalling US $4 billion to the two CMEA banks were deducted.
d. *Statistical supplements to the Monthly Reports of the Deutsche Bundesbank*, Series 3, 5/1984.

US $20 billion, or roughly total gross indebtedness. In estimating Soviet gold reserves it is always assumed — whether correctly or not — that the Soviet Union would use these if it was prevented from maintaining its contractual repayments. But Soviet policy on gold exports is not transparent; it appears to be orientated firstly to the gold price and essential imports from the West and only secondly to credit repayments policy. There have been very few sales actions without regard for the gold price and gold appears to play an important role in Soviet policy: firstly, it is used cautiously after careful consideration of the price situation and how urgently the imports the sales are to pay for are needed and secondly, great importance is attached to maintaining high reserves of gold.

Leaving aside these factors, the Soviet Union's repayment profile is unblemished and this also speaks for its creditworthiness. There have been no cases of peak demand to suggest that the financial planners in Moscow were having to struggle with any particular liquidity problems. These indicators suggest that the Soviet Union does not constitute a particular credit risk, either for individual banks or the Western capital markets as a whole. No basic changes derived from economic causes may be expected in this.

Consequently the Soviet Union's economic creditworthiness, if not its creditworthiness as a whole, can be confirmed unreservedly. That is also the view of every bank that is strongly engaged in trade with Eastern Europe, even American banks. Problems with repayments turn out to be mere rumours and in reality there have never been any serious difficulties. That the Soviets, when negotiating a loan, always try to get the interest rates down and prolong the term of the loan — in other words, cut the costs of borrowing as far as possible — is not a sign of weakness or the beginnings of liquidity problems, but a sign of strength in negotiation and good standing. It may seem contradictory that the Soviet Union, despite its confirmed economic creditworthiness, received hardly any new credits from 1981 to 1984, certainly not international syndicate loans. For it was not until the spring of 1984 that another Euro-loan was signed between the Soviet Union and Western banks, and this was a sign of a change in the attitude of Western banks to credit risks with the Soviet Union, indeed East European countries altogether. It is possible that the Soviet Union did not negotiate any new loans with the West in the last few years because its foreign trade plans did not necessitate recourse to Western financial markets.

The true reason, however, is that the banks refused to increase their lending to the Soviet Union because they doubted its political creditworthiness. Political factors caused its general standing as a

The Soviet Economy

Table 4.2 Soviet gold production, exports and reserves

	1970	1975	1978	1979	1980	1981	1982	1983
Gold production in tonnes[1]	217	258	294	307	316	326		
Gold exports in tonnes[2]	3	147	401	220	80	200		
in US $ bill.	—	0.7	2.5	1.5	1.6	2.7	2.2[a]	0.8[a]
Gold reserves[1] in tonnes	1620	1900	15200	1580	1800	1880		

Sources:
1. Directorate of Intelligence, *Handbook of Economic Statistics 1982*
2. Joan Parpart Zoeter, 'USSR: Hard-Currency Trade and Payments', in: *Joint Economic Committee, Soviet Economy in the 1980s*, part 2, Washington 1983.
   a. Wharton Econometric Forecasting Associates, *Recent Developments in Soviet Gross Hard-Currency Debt and Assets*, vol. IV, no. 18, Washington, DC, March 1984.
   b. US Department of Commerce, *Statistical Abstract of East-West Trade Finance*, Washington, DC, December 1983.

borrower to be called into question, in complete contrast to its economic creditworthiness, which is always affirmed. The good standing as a borrower which the Soviet Union enjoys on the strength of the financial indicators became of secondary importance as soon as it was overlaid by political factors. These first came to the fore after Afghanistan and worsened after the events in Poland. For the banks these political events were surprise factors and they were 'caught on the hop'. During the *détente* phase, which directly affected the credit policy of Western banks, Western credits worked at times like intoxicants on both the Eastern and the Western side, and at no time in the 1970s did political factors play a part in the banks' calculations of lending risks.

Consequently, Western financiers were all the more surprised by Afghanistan and Poland and the ensuing credit policy wrangle,[1] and when they suddenly had to take political risks into account they may have over-reacted somewhat. In a kind of autonomous sanctions policy[2] they greatly reduced their engagement, not only with

1. K. Schröder, 'Die Ost-West-Finanzbeziehungen', in: H.D. Jacobsen/R. Rode (eds.), *Wirtschaftskrieg oder Entspannung*, Bonn 1984.
2. K. Schröder, 'Wirkungen monetärer Sanktionen gegenüber den RGW-Ländern', in: F. Müller *et al.*, *Zur Frage von Wirtschaftssanktionen in den Ost-West-Beziehungen: Rahmenbedingungen und Modalitäten*, Baden-Baden 1983.

the Soviet Union but with the whole of Eastern Europe, and with the smaller CMEA countries this went so far that these countries had to repay around US $5 billion at short notice to the banks.[3] The Soviet Union was spared a loss of liquidity from a withdrawal of capital by Western banks but was not able to negotiate further loans. The reserve on the part of Western creditors increased after their awareness of the political risks was reawakened as the Americans began discussing monetary sanctions against the Soviet Union in reaction to the events in Afghanistan and Poland and some of the sanctions were imposed. The whole complex of sanctions made the banks even more nervous; it strengthened their reserve and the result was an almost complete stop on lending.

However, recently this phase has been increasingly giving way to a more objective assessment, the main feature of which is that Western creditors are differentiating more strongly than ever between the individual CMEA countries. The banks are giving very thorough reconsideration to their lending policy over the past decade and are now well on the way to reorganising their East European strategy. This involves establishing tougher rules that are more suited to the present situation. It has long become apparent that it is not Eastern Europe as a whole that is broke, only Poland, and that the Soviet Union, like the other East European countries, is a good credit partner in economic terms. A further indication that lending relations with Eastern Europe are gradually returning to normal is that many creditors have now accepted that the Soviet Union cannot be made responsible for the fact that the 'umbrella theory', evolved in the West, led to false estimates in the banks. The word has also gone round that a credit stop, other things being equal, will only cause a deterioration in their stock of claims as a whole, and for that reason it is necessary to find a more cautious policy that more correctly reflects the real circumstances. Finally, it is particularly important to recognise that in this phase, when the situation is being reassessed, the political risk factors, which have been of such determinant weight so far, lose some of their significance.

One lesson remains for the Soviet Union from the last three years: it must accept that it is not only important to appear as a reliable business partner with few financial risks, but that the

---

3. K. Schröder, 'Die Umschuldungen mit den Ländern des RGW — Ursachen, Ziele, Modalitäten, Stiftung Wissenschaft und Politik', *SWP-AP 2353*, Ebenhausen 1983.

political risk component must also be kept low and acceptable.

In the monetary sphere one of the main recognitions of the past three crisis years (if one wishes to call them that) for the West, especially for the USA, is that the Soviet Union, intended as the main target for Western sanctions, was the country that suffered least from the Western reaction, and of all CMEA countries was best able to react flexibly to it.

In conclusion we can say that the *de facto* insolvency of Poland caused a phase of over-reaction and overvaluation in the West, which is now giving way to a new phase of objective differentiation and less emotional reactions. West European and American banks are looking for good borrowers in Eastern Europe. The Soviet Union is one of them; it tested the Euro-market again in the spring of 1984 for the first time for some years and obtained a major loan. The banks are also ready to lend to the Soviet Union beyond this.

However, it looks as if the negotiations over credit conditions are gaining in importance, both on the supply and the demand side. As far as can be foreseen the Soviet Union will use the better standing it has regained as a borrower by international standards to choose from among prospective lenders those that offer the best conditions. It will not have to beg for money, and will be able to make major import contracts dependent on favourable finance conditions.

The interest premiums that tend to drop from pressure of supply could be compensated on the demand side by a relative rise in demand from the Soviet Union. There are good arguments to suggest that credits will become a more important competitive factor in trade with the Soviet Union and that the planners in Moscow will have to return more frequently to Western credit markets, if only because of the cessation of the windfall profits which, after all, made up the grand sum of c. US $60 billion[4] between 1973 and 1982. Moreover, in the 1980s there will be neither price nor quantity effects to increase Soviet earnings from energy exports to the same extent as in the previous decade. It will also be more difficult to export goods and weapons to developing countries in return for foreign exchange. No particular increases are to be expected in exports of Soviet industrial goods. This means that the main supports of the Soviet foreign exchange balance will be less

4. E.A. Hewett, 'Response to External Shocks, USSR and Hungary', paper presented at the meeting of the American Economic Association, San Francisco, December 28–30, 1983, table 6, p. 25.

secure than in the past decade, unless gold exports play a growing role as a stop-gap.

Soviet foreign exchange borrowing to cover 'empire costs' in Poland, Afghanistan, Cuba and so on, are of virtually no significance in comparison with annual foreign exchange earnings (US $28 billion a year from 1979 to 1981). However, goods credits to all CMEA countries are a very considerable burden on the Soviet economy and the Soviet trade surplus with these countries amounted to around 20 billion tr between 1976 and 1983.[5] But since these balances cannot be used as assets for international payments, which is certainly a major fault in the East European system, the possibility cannot be excluded that the growing CMEA surpluses will cause the Soviet planners to finance these by borrowing in the West, in order to acquire the imports which the other CMEA countries cannot supply.

All these details should not be allowed to obscure the fact that, as already stressed, Soviet demand for credit will essentially remain dependent on planned foreign exchange earnings. Favourable conditions on Western capital markets may increase Soviet demand, but not so strongly as to lead to financial dependence. The demand for credit is determined by the need for technology imports to industrialise Soviet agriculture and Siberia and for imports of grain and feed.

In each decision on loans to East European countries the fundamental differences between the market economy system and the centrally planned economies have to be taken into account. Neither the hegemonial position of the Soviet Union nor the national capabilities and responsibilities of the other CMEA states should be overlooked. The Soviet Union is certainly interested in stable economic development and monetary discipline within the CMEA region, and it may certainly be expected that after the financial collapse of Poland and Romania it will make its influence felt to prevent reversals and repetitions of this in future. The Moscow leaders may be aiming for a Soviet financial 'supreme command', for this would probably lead to more conventional borrowing with a greater balance in the flows of foreign exchange earnings and expenditure. The loss in growth from more cautious borrowing would be denied (in Moscow, not in the other CMEA capitals) or reckoned as the costs of less dependence on Western capital mar-

5. 'Zur Lage der sowjetischen Wirtschaft', *Wochenbericht des DIW*, 1983/1984, 25/1984, p. 307.

kets. This Soviet option is bound to appear enticing to those Western banks that are mainly interested in cash flow.

However much this may look as if a powerful damper has been put on the more exciting future prospects which the 1970s seemed to hold for the smaller CMEA countries and that a new phase of 'backward-looking' relations is about to begin, the limits to what Moscow can do should not be overlooked. The existing economic systems of the CMEA countries all have their own stamp and the various steering and controlling mechanisms cannot be restandardised at the touch of a switch. Moreover, the Soviet Union does not have the necessary financial umbrella to take on the repayment obligations of the smaller CMEA countries and still offer incentives to a forced integration in CMEA.

A further need for new financial relations can also be seen in the need to remove the reasons for the over-reaction on Western markets. In addition to a stronger national orientation of the loan decision, an important factor, for instance, is that the CMEA countries now have to take more account of matching maturities in their financing than formerly. On the highly sensitive money markets, on which money is lent between banks at short term without security, the participation of East European banks is destabilising if they use short-term credits to finance long-term projects. and with as fast a turnover in credit conditions as possible, are not in a position to make the necessary repayments without taking up new funds. Cases of this kind are known; they not only affect the standing of the borrower but also the stability of the whole market.

The banks' Western credit policy and the state system of credit insurance always had a procyclical effect in the past. The danger of excess, both in the expansive and contractive phase of lending, is evident and should be cause to consider whether the budget rule that no new guarantees may be given if there has been default is still relevant and whether this does not in fact also force the banks to make sudden draconian cut-backs in their lending, or in some cases reduce an engagement to zero.

Procyclical behaviour furthers instability because credit concepts are neither (clearly) formulated nor explained and coordinated between lenders. During an expansive phase these open points may not be very important; but if there are signs of markets becoming tighter or of an actual crisis emerging, the hidden objectives and lack of adequate information may cause short-term loans to be recalled and a run on debtor balances. If at the same time the system of credit guarantees (as in the case of Poland and Romania) ceases to operate, it will be virtually impossible to prevent a growing deflationary trend in the debtor country, and this will be all the more serious the more significant the political role which the debtor country has played for the creditor country, the longer the credit expansion phase lasted and the higher the state of indebtedness.

For banks that are orientated to the market economy and working in a competitive environment the idea of revealing their own strategy and providing mutual information may be unacceptable.

However, if this is set not only in the East European context but also considering the (possibly explosive) pressure latent under the lid of world-wide indebtedness, it becomes clear that not only the Western governments, who have considerable amounts of tax revenue involved, but the banks, too, must have a growing interest in the mutual exchange of information. At any rate they should have, when (at regular intervals) the indebtedness piles up and the banks' capacities are no longer sufficient to ensure the stability of the Western finance and currency system. On these occasions, then only the united efforts of all the groups of creditors are enough to prevent financial, economic and political chaos.

East–West financial relations also need to be reshaped on the Eastern side. The monetary discipline of the state planners has clearly taken a knock. Events like the financial collapse of Poland, which will occupy us for a long time to come, and the Romanian payments difficulties, which are due to quite different causes and should be resolved relatively quickly, must not be the standard for the next few years. The image of financial responsibility must be reactivated in Eastern Europe and this can only be restored if the CMEA countries build up their credit policy with a greater orientation to projects and at the same time take more account of balance of payments constraints. The confidence of Western creditors has not merely been scratched on the surface. The deep uncertainty is the result not only of objective difficulties like those experienced by Poland and Romania but also the lack of candour concerning the extent of the indebtedness, the use to which the credit is to be put, the extent and scope of the resources available for repayment and uncertainty in the political sphere. These are all holding the Western banks back and damaging the standing of East European countries as borrowers.

Greater transparency has always paid off for those countries that had to reschedule, with the exception of Hungary, which more or less voluntarily offered figures and information. The principle of only making the information available in the negotiations on rescheduling must be reversed. Openness and transparency must be preconditions if difficult liquidity or even insolvency phases are jointly to be overcome.

However, the conditions of East–West financial relations should also include Western capital markets offering themselves to the Soviet Union as stable and reliable partners. Moscow's foreign exchange position will no longer be as comfortable as in the 1970s, and the Soviet need for credit could increase and then be satisfied. If Moscow has that security, it will again be easier for the smaller CMEA countries to get their slice of the Western credit cake. The demand for credit in Moscow (and the rest of Eastern Europe) will, in accordance with our initial thesis, remain modest; spectacular changes that might suggest the Soviet Union becoming a major borrower like Mexico and so perhaps contributing to market instability are not to be expected.

Economic Co-operation within the CMEA
Friedrich Levcik

The Beginnings

The beginnings of the CMEA, the foundation of which was announced in a communiqué of 25 January 1949, were modest. Between 1950 and 1954 no meetings of the Council took place at all and for a long time the understanding of its work and of the means of implementing it were unclear. In fact, it was not until ten years after the CMEA was founded that the first statutes were approved. During this initial phase the East European countries, after the establishment of Communist rule, adopted the Soviet system of directive and quantity planning and the strategy of 'socialist industrialisation' which had been developed under different conditions in the closed and huge economic expanse of the Soviet Union. Since absolute priority was accorded to the basic materials and mechanical engineering industries in all the national economies, parallel rather than complementary industrial structures evolved. Foreign trade played only a minor and passive role, its main function being the acquisition of goods that could not be produced at home.

All the East European countries needed raw materials for their new material-intensive industries and they imported most of these from the Soviet Union. In return they provided finished products, generally simpler machinery and equipment which were difficult to sell outside the CMEA region. In such a situation the role of the Soviet Union, already incontestably the senior partner in terms of size, as well as political and economic weight, increased and a mainly radial system of trade evolved. The share of intra-CMEA trade was growing but the system consisted mainly of trade between the individual member states and the Soviet Union. Some things have changed since then, but the basic pattern of growing ties between each individual member state and the Soviet Union, without the satisfactory development of a uniform, integrated economic region has remained.

After lengthy discussion, principles were established for price formation for intra-CMEA trade, according to which prices were negotiated bilaterally on the basis of world market prices 'adjusted for cyclical and speculative fluctuations'. These principles remain in force today, with some modifications, since it has not proved possible to agree on a uniform price system for foreign trade with the autonomous and arbitrary price-fixing systems in each individual country.

The 1960s were taken up with the first attempts at international production specialisation, but again these produced few tangible results owing to the unsatisfactory coordination of the national economic plans. The establishment of the International Bank for Economic Co-operation in Moscow in 1963 was to replace the existing system of payment for foreign trade flows through a clearing system by means of multilateral offsetting in transfer rubles. However, the change-over remained a formality and in practice foreign trade accounting is still on a strictly bilateral basis.

The Complex Programme as a Basis for Co-operation Today

In 1971 the 'Complex Programme for the Further Intensification and Perfection of Co-operation and the Development of the Socialist Economic Integration of the CMEA Member States' was accepted. This was to introduce a new and higher phase of co-operation for the period up to 1990. Before it was accepted, lengthy discussions were held between the individual member states. There was agreement that co-operation within the socialist community of states must be put on a better footing, and that ideally a unified economic area should be built up; however, there were two basic notions of how this should be done. The first was to achieve integration through co-operation in planning, i.e. to make use of planning instruments, the second was to use functional economic mechanisms, i.e. real prices, credits, exchange rates and so on. The Programme, which may be regarded as a compromise, combines the two methods. The coordination of the national Five-Year Plans is the most important item of integration and this has been supplemented by joint prognoses and planning in selected areas. The Programme also includes economic and financial measures, such as the improvement of price formation for intra-CMEA trade, the expansion of multilateral accounting and greater use of credits between member states, but it must be said that this has largely remained on paper. Real progress has been achieved only in planning co-operation (including production and specialisation). It would, in my view, be an over-simplification to claim that the second part of the Programme was not

101

realised because the Soviet Union did not wish it. Apart from the Soviet Union, other East European states were not in a position to co-operate in any other way than through the traditional means of planning coordination. The major error, and it is actually inherent in the Programme, is that instruments cannot be used in international co-operation that are not being used in the national economy at home. In other words, where the domestic economy is run by directive and quantity planning one cannot assume that instruments like real prices, exchange rates or credits will work at CMEA level.

Consequently it has only proved possible to make some progress in the planning sphere, and here two measures must be mentioned. In 1976 an 'agreed plan for multilateral integration measures' was accepted at the thirtieth Council meeting. This *inter alia* obliged member states to engage in joint major projects, mainly in raw materials, fuel and energy extraction, most of which were located in the Soviet Union. However, the plan also included measures for multilateral co-operation and for specialisation on a larger scale. This was a change from the normal coordination envisaged in the Five-Year Plans, in that individual parts of the agreed plan were integrated into national economic plans. One of the most important projects in the first 'agreed plan' was the well-known Soyuz project for the longest gas pipeline in Europe, stretching from Orenburg to the Soviet border with the West. Altogether nine or ten of these large-scale projects have been realised and it is assumed that the costs amounted to between 9 and 10 billion transfer rubles between 1976 and 1980. The 'Long-term Target Programmmes for Co-operation for the Period up to 1990' point in the same direction. They were agreed in 1975 for the following areas: raw materials, fuel and energy; agriculture and foodstuffs; mechanical engineering, where this serves the first of these areas; industrial consumer goods and transport. The target programmes are no more than declarations of intent and they subsequently have to be given concrete form in multilateral and then bilateral agreements. During negotiations and even more in the implementation phase the original intentions, which are pretty ambitious, have to be adapted to real circumstances. There is never any mention now of the original figure of 80 billion rubles envisaged for the target programme projects up to 1990. The objectives in the long-term programme will be changed slightly in the course of the present decade, giving more emphasis to the economical and rational use of the available resources than to expanding the raw materials, fuel and energy base.

The mechanical engineering programme demands an acceleration of the introduction of modern processes and machinery. Under the impact of Western restrictions on exports of high technology the new focal points are the development of robot technology, the use of micro-processors, uniform parts for the electronics industry and colour television.

The Weak Points in CMEA Co-operation

While there have been some notable successes, mostly in individual large-scale projects, like the Orenburg gas pipeline, or in specific structure reforms such as unifying the CMEA energy systems with a central dispatcher organisation, attempts at co-operation within the CMEA still suffer from the lack of effective economic mechanisms that will function internationally. Trade within the CMEA is still strictly bilateral, on the basis of five-year trade agreements between two member states, with annual protocols negotiated by delegations from the two countries. The directive planning means that quantities and prices for imports and exports have to be fixed in advance in these bilateral agreements, depending on the domestic economic plans. It has, moreover, become apparent that the CMEA cannot develop its own autonomous price system for international trade, and as a result world market prices, which are so to speak imposed from outside on the domestic production conditions, lead to an additional structural bilateralism because of the distorted domestic price structures. The exports and imports that are valued at world market prices and the official $/tr rate are not only to be balanced globally between the two partners; individual groups of goods are also identified and 'directly' balanced with each other as far as possible. Naturally, there are different scales of preference here — most important being the saleability of certain kinds of goods on the hard currency markets — and these then find expression in the linking of 'hard' and 'soft' goods, as they are called, for bilateral compensation. In addition to balancing hard against hard and soft against soft the negotiations also cover a system of deviations, premiums and price reductions to achieve a global balance as far as possible. Accordingly, one and the same item may be differently priced in various bilateral agreements and the transfer ruble has a different purchasing power in different transactions.

A further weakness of this bilateral system is the lack of a meaningful exchange rate, i.e. one formed on an economic basis and verified by the market, or convertibility for the transfer ruble, if only within the CMEA area and against the national currencies. For this reason most of the CMEA countries use internal conversion coefficients, at least for accounting purposes. Some actually use different coefficients for individual goods which may differ greatly from the official exchange rates. The system is so complicated that it is quite impossible to tell whether a certain transaction is ever economically meaningful or efficient at the prices negotiated, even though these are derived from world market prices.

Since the second half of the 1970s certain quantities of goods have actually been traded not in transfer rubles but in convertible Western currencies. These are mainly quantities of 'hard' goods which go beyond the agreed quota, or exports of goods for which the pre-products had to be bought in the West for hard currency. There is a tendency here too to balance hard currency liabilities for imports and claims for exports bilaterally, but Hungary at least has been able to book larger surpluses of hard currencies in its trade with the Soviet Union over the last few years.

For the world market prices used in intra-CMEA trade the 'Moscow price formula' has been in use since 1975. This lays down that contract prices are to be fixed each year on the basis of the average of world market prices over the preceding five years. This sliding five-year average for prices was accepted as a compromise on the insistence of the Soviet Union, since the previous method of using the average price over the previous five-year period unchanged throughout the current five-year plan period was no longer viable after the first rise in oil prices.

The introduction of the Moscow price formula has had far-reaching consequences and these have not yet been fully analysed. All that is clear is that the terms of trade shifted in favour of the Soviet Union. According to a recent study, by Dr Dietz of the WIIW, an improvement of altogether 76 per cent in the terms of trade for the Soviet Union over Eastern Europe may be expected by 1985 over 1972. This is because energy prices will rise very much faster than the prices of finished industrial products, and it also results from the structural differences between Soviet exports to Eastern Europe and its imports from that source. Energy and raw materials predominate in Soviet exports, while its imports from other East European countries consist mainly of finished products.

The actual accrual in revenue can be deduced from improvements in the terms of trade. If Soviet terms of trade profits are accumulated for the period 1973–85, we have a real transfer from Eastern Europe to the Soviet Union resulting from price changes of 71 billion tr, roughly the value of Soviet exports to Eastern Europe from 1979 to 1982. However, the Soviet Union would have earned more and the East European deficit would have been greater had the CMEA prices been adjusted to world market prices straightaway and without a time-lag.

A further effect of the Moscow price formula, which is not so well known, is its negative impact on directive economic planning. Since this depends on quantity, planning aggregation is only possible for the whole five-year period at constant planning prices. Earlier, the five-year plans were hampered by the uncertainty factor of price trends on capitalist markets, but the small percentage of trade with non-socialist countries meant that this problem was not so acute. Now, however, the Moscow price formula brings that 'disruption' into CMEA trade as well. Since prices currently change every year, moreover to an unforeseeable extent, it is very difficult to integrate foreign trade plans into the national plan. This strengthens the tendency to plan in physical quantities, which in turn undermines the possibility of using economic instruments like prices, interest and credits to stimulate enterprises.

Then there is the problem of maintaining the real value of trade claims and liabilities. For, as the terms of trade shift the Soviet Union acquires a more or less permanent trade surplus with its CMEA partners. As contract prices move upwards each year, following world inflation but with a time-lag, the value of Soviet claims drops. On the initiative of the Soviet Union this problem was put on the agenda of the CMEA Standing Commission for Foreign Exchange and Finance, but no solution has yet been found. Equally complicated and also unresolved is the question of the mutual accounting of deliveries for joint projects (investment participations) which last several years.

So far it has been increasingly evident that a restriction on the methods of directive planning and organisational measures agreed between member states without a functioning mechanism of economically meaningful prices means that currencies and credits will only be successful in isolated areas. However, this will not achieve economic efficiency or a stronger integration within the CMEA. Ultimately, the still unresolved problems will make themselves felt in slower economic growth and an unsatisfactory supply to the population at large.

So the oft postponed summit conference of Party leaders is awaited with interest. This, it is supposed will 'deepen the integration process, perfect the economic mechanisms within the CMEA and provide new initiatives for the development of the integration process'. But whatever can be gleaned from the fragments of available information and from the use of the word 'perfect' in the above statement suggests that, especially as regards the economic cohesion of this region no real progress is to be expected towards a functioning price, currency, interest and credit system.

5

Reforming the Economic System

Economic Reform: Soviet Style
John P. Hardt and Donna L. Gold

The initial speeches of Konstantin Chernenko — his acceptance address of 13 February 1984 and his election speech of 2 March 1984 — indicated that 'increasing the effectiveness of production and accelerating the effectiveness of the country's economic development'[1] were high priorities for the new General Secretary. Stressing continuity as 'a live and real cause'[2] Chernenko pledged to carry on and advance the policies and programmes of his predecessor. However, the 'essence of continuity', he maintained, 'is down primarily to moving forward without stopping'.[3] In his view: 'The system of economic management, the whole of our economic machinery, needs a serious restructuring. Work in this direction has only been started.'[4] His speech at the plenary session of the Party Central Committee on 10 April again supported this theme but did not carry it further. Chernenko's caution here is especially important as it was his first real opportunity to express his own personal strategy: 'We have now set about improving all aspects of the system of management of the national economy and we are looking for new forms and structures of economic activity. But the necessary quest for the new must not be allowed, of course, to distract us from a more effective use of the existing institutions of management.'[5] Chernenko appeared to want to go further than Andropov in im-

1. *Pravda*, 14 February 1984.
2. Ibid.
3. Ibid.
4. Ibid.
5. *Pravda*, 11 April 1984.

plementing changes in the Soviet economic mechanism (i.e., the Soviet economy). Although the new leader seemed open to new ideas, the pressures for institutional change appeared to be rooted in a growing consensus. Discussions in the Soviet press subsequent to the death of Brezhnev in November 1982 highlighted the inadequacies of the Soviet economic performance, and a feeling that 'something must be done' now seemed to be shared by the whole of Soviet society, as well as by the Party rank and file, Chernenko and the younger members of the Senior Party hierarchy — Mikhail Gorbachev (responsible for agriculture and light industry), Geidar Aliev (transport), Vladimir Dolgikh (energy and heavy industry) and Grigorii Romanov (machine-building and defence industries) — appear to have reached a degree of consensus on moving ahead with some form of economic change. Although Romanov may not be dedicated to technical progress through institutional change, his responsibility for the results may incline him pragmatically to follow the 'technocrats.' The replacement of Dolgikh as head of the Central Committee's heavy industry and energy department by his long-time deputy Ivan Yastrebov will probably not diminish Dolgikh's influence, for he still appears to be the most senior official responsible for those key economic sectors.

If one accepts the step by step approach to change and improved performance, then even the current modest movement may produce results; significant improvements do not have to await the full transformation of the economy. Likewise, important as personnel changes are to enhancing performance, bringing in a new, technocratic team of economic ministers, and from Tikhonov and Baibakov down to enterprise level, is not a necessary condition for correcting the economic mechanism. In fact, Chernenko stressed the importance of reducing the numbers of ineffective personnel in his speech of 10 April 1984: 'Once we are on the subject of management, I cannot but mention the problem of reduction of the administrative apparatus. The work of reducing ministerial staffs should be carried out not only at lower and middle levels but also at its summits, so to say, whether people like it or not, such is the need.'[6] Are there reasons to believe that the post-Brezhnev leadership is indeed serious about economic change and will proceed in that direction? This paper looks at the issue by addressing a few fundamental questions: Why would the Party (CPSU) be willing to

6. Ibid.

initiate changes within the economy now when under Brezhnev it would not? What has been done since Brezhnev's death to indicate that the Party is planning to make significant adjustments in the Soviet economic mechanism? What could such adjustments mean for the performance of the Soviet economy?

I. Why would Yurii Andropov and Konstantin Chernenko be willing to introduce measures in the Soviet economy that their predecessors considered but never implemented?[7]

The answer to this first question has two parts: one relates to Brezhnev himself and the other to the post-Brezhnev Party. Firstly, there had been substantial growth during the three completed Five-Year Plans of the Brezhnev era (1965–80). From 1964 to the late 1970s it appears that the leadership felt that all key resource claimants, i.e. investment, consumption and defence were adequately served and that the economy could 'muddle through' without major change, Peter need not be robbed to pay Paul, or in Russian metaphor, Trishka's Kaftan covered the priority needs.

This temporary success appears to have encouraged a policy of equivocation and consensus. Problems were deferred instead of addressed, especially in the areas of food and agriculture, transportation and metallurgy. The substitution of short-term adjustments for long-term solutions became the norm instead of the exception, and the bottlenecks in the key economic sectors were left unresolved. The consequences of this inaction became evident during the last few years of Brezhnev's tenure, when Soviet economic growth began seriously to decline. The economy, which had grown at an average rate of 5.4 per cent p.a. during Brezhnev's first (the Soviet Eighth) Five-Year Plan (1966–70) grew at only 2.7 per cent in his last (the Soviet Tenth) (1976–80).

Turning now to Brezhnev's successors, Andropov and Chernenko, neither had ever been directly involved in economic affairs, foreign or domestic. Although their records were untarnished when they assumed power, they were also lacking in substance. The Party consensus may now hold that the series of economic down-turns have reached a point where deferment of change is more costly

7. See John P. Hardt and Donna L. Gold, 'Andropov's Economic Future', *ORBIS*, Spring 1983, pp. 11–20.

politically and economically than unsettling change. Specifically, a minimum 'threshold' of growth in national income of between 3 and 4 per cent may be politically and economically necessary to meet investment, consumption and defence needs: investment must expand not contract; the gap in consumption between purchasing power created and absorbed must be closed and necessary defence needs must be served. Slow growth below the minimum threshold would force unhappy choices among priority claimants.

Furthermore, in order to consolidate power during the succession period, the new leadership may be required to address the economic issues as seriously as did Stalin and his rivals during the industrialisation debate of the 1920s and as Khrushchev did in his economic de-Stalinisation programme of the late 1950s. Staying in power may well require success in managing the economy. Although Chernenko is no longer young, he will need to establish and retain his placemen in power and strike a positive note for his regime. His period in office may, therefore, see the changing of the guard in economic assignments, as well as at other levels of leadership. Where Brezhnev seems to have staked everything on the struggle for improved economic performance, the new cadres not only of Chernenko but also of Gorbachev, Romanov and Aliev too may sally forth to battle on all economic fronts to establish themselves in power and to ensure their longevity.

II. What has been said and done by the post-Brezhnev leadership to indicate a willingness to implement a programme of economic change?

Yurii Andropov publicly stressed the critical need for improvement in the Soviet economy throughout his brief tenure in power. He was quite outspoken about the problems that hamper the efficiency and productivity of Soviet industry and agriculture.

Beginning in November 1982 — not long after the death of Brezhnev — Andropov outlined the draft Twelfth Five-Year Plan (1986–90) at the CPSU Central Committee plenum. At that time, he was quick to focus on the inadequacy of past performances:

> . . . . I would like emphatically to draw your attention to the fact that by a number of indicators the planned targets of the first two years of the Five-Year Plan period turned out to be unfulfilled . . .

The chief indicator of the economy's efficiency — labor productivity — grows at a rate that cannot satisfy us. . . .

Plan targets continue to be met at a price of large outlays and production costs. . . .

Apparently, the strength of inertia and adherence to old ways are still at work . . .[8]

In January 1983 Andropov made an unusual appearance at the Ordzhonikidze machine-tool factory. There he made an extremely candid speech to the workers focusing on the existing gap between wages and production. While suggesting that this disparity could be corrected by increasing prices, Andropov pointed to more efficient productivity as the key to the problem: 'You yourselves understand that the government can only give as many goods as are produced.'[9] This visit was soon followed by an article authored by Andropov and appearing in *Kommunist*, the journal of the CPSU Central Committee, in which he once again discussed the 'tasks before the Soviet economy'.[10]

In June 1983 Andropov went so far as to call for a new Party programme.[11] In this, the third such programme since the founding of the Soviet state, he signalled changes in the Party guidelines that would affect economic performance:

. . . To ensure the smooth and uninterrupted work of the entire economic mechanism is both a requirement of today and a programme task for the future. This is a component part of the general process of perfecting our social system.

The main road to a qualitative shift in the productive forces is, of course, the transition to intensive development . . . this direction of the activity of the Party and people should be worthily reflected in the new edition of the Party programme of perfecting our social system.[12]

Later, on 15 August 1983, Andropov told his audience at a Party veterans meeting that the preparations underway for the next Plan, the Twelfth (1986–90), included changes in all facets of the Soviet economic mechanism:

8. *Pravda*, 23 November 1983.
9. Serge Schmemann, 'Andropov on Plant Tour, Tells Workers to Produce', *New York Times*, 1 February 1983.
10. See Yurii Andropov, 'The Teaching of Karl Marx and Some Questions of Building Socialism in the U.S.S.R.', *Kommunist* 3/1983.
11. Chernenko endorsed this new Party programme in his 13 February 1984 speech and in his speech on 10 April 1984 he indicated that the new Party programme will be discussed at the XXVII CPSU Congress; see *Pravda*, 11 April 1984.
12. *Pravda*, 16 June 1983.

.... We have often taken half measures, and have been unable to overcome the accumulated inertia with sufficient speed. We must now make up for omissions. This apart from anything else, demands changes in planning, management and in the economic mechanism, and it is our duty to carry out these changes so as to enter the new Five-Year Plan, as the saying goes, 'fully armed.'[13]

Chernenko thus far seems to be reiterating the basic tenets of Andropov's economic strategy. In his speech of 2 March 1984 he stated that:

I have mentioned the need for a drastic restructuring of the economic management system. It is apparent, however that improvement of this system is in no way limited to eliminating shortcomings in the work of the, so to say, professional managers. Another thing is no less important: conditions should be created for enhancing all the initiative and creative spirit of the broadest sections of the working masses.[14]

Earlier, on 13 February 1984 he had also discussed such Andropovian themes as: the need for boldness and risk in striving for economic efficiency; the central role of the workers' collectives in the economy and the need for 'social justice' in salaries and bonuses. One might therefore say that Andropov's policies and pronouncements have provided the basis for what seems to have evolved into a Party position on how to adjust the Soviet economic mechanism. However, Chernenko, in contrast to Andropov, appears to feel that economic change requires less deliberation and more action — less 'looking before you leap'. At the same time, however, there appears to be a greater reluctance on the part of Chernenko to replace cadres, presumably because they represent his support base. In his view: 'Neither their frequent replacement nor any ossification of the cadres' composition are admissible.'[15]

Turning from words to actions, the measures introduced over the last sixteen months to stimulate improved economic performance can be divided into three categories: measures to increase discipline, measures to stimulate worker initiative and measures to improve management and administration.

13. *Pravda*, 16 August 1983.
14. *Pravda*, 3 March 1984.
15. *Pravda*, 11 April 1984.

Measures to increase discipline

Almost immediately after coming to power Andropov embarked on his well-known discipline campaign. Police were sent to check public places, e.g. restaurants, cinemas, shops and markets in search of truant workers. Reprimands and warnings for lateness, absenteeism and drunkenness were issued to workers and managers alike. Andropov also made personnel changes aimed at ridding the economy of 'corrupt and incompetent' managers. Two examples of such dismissals were the removal of Ivan Pavlovskii as the minister for railways, and Stephan Knitrov, the minister for rural development, in December 1982. Although this was an auspicious beginning for a policy of matching criteria with administrative action, it should be acknowledged that no major purge of the economic apparatus followed. Andropov's failing health, which some speculate as becoming an issue for the Party leadership as early as February 1983, was probably a major factor.

During the first month of Chernenko's tenure, two significant personnel changes took place: the promotions of Vladimir Chirstkov to the post of minister for petroleum and gas installation enterprises and of Yurii Solovyev to the post of minister for industrial construction. The former is particularly of interest because of the high priority accorded to the energy sector by the leadership in recent years. Both changes may turn out to be important, both in substance and symbolic terms, as many observers have argued that changes in the management of construction would be a key test of the seriousness of leadership aims to get the best administrators into the economic mechanism.

Measures to stimulate worker initiative

Both in industry and agriculture new laws have been introduced giving workers more say in the day to day functioning of the factory and farm. In industry, worker collectives have been delegated more authority: '. . . it (the new law) widened the questions that the working collective was empowered to discuss and gave the collective some rights to decide and supervise the implementation of decisions.'[16] [17] In agriculture, a contract system has been introduced

16. Philip Hanson, 'Soviet Economic Policy under the Andropov Leadership', RFE/RL Research no. 283/83, 27 July 1983, p. 6. See *Pravda*, 19 June 1983. See also *Sovershenstvovanie Khoziaistvennogo Mekhanizma: Sbornik Dokumentov*, 2nd

whereby the workers 'contract' voluntarily for a portion of the work and are given land and equipment. Wages, based on performance and effort, are guaranteed.

Chernenko has emphasised the importance of both positive and negative incentives and, in keeping with his past concern for popular needs, seems to want to move decisively and quickly in this area:

> Our chief concern is that the socialist principle of distribution according to one's work be put into effect everywhere once and for all. Those who work with complete devotion should by all means have better pay. Some may say: But we can, even today, punish slackers financially and award bonuses to conscientious workers. This is so. But it seems the penalties still lack strictness, while material incentives lack the proper fairness and sometimes, I would say, generosity. This question should be thoroughly dealt with, and without delay either.[18]

Measures to improve management and administration

On 25 July 1983 the Soviet Government announced its programme of planning and management experiments in five selected industries. The relevant ministries include the Ministry of Heavy and Transport Machine-Building, the Ministry of Electrical Equipment, the Lithuanian Ministry of Local Industry, the Belorussian Ministry of Light Industry and the Ukranian Ministry of Food. This modest development, covering only five pilot industries should not lead immediately to the conclusion that the experiments are too limited to be considered significant. Rather, the importance of these five lies precisely in the nature of the ministries chosen. Each of them is a prototype of a specific class of ministries: for example an all-Union consumer goods ministry, an all-Union heavy industry ministry. Moreover, the Lithuanian experiment seems to be patterned on the East German model. So, if these experiments are successful they may subsequently be introduced throughout their respective ministerial groupings.

The five pilot experiments were implemented as scheduled in January 1984, giving plant managers 'wider authority over their budgets with discretion in matters of investment, wages, bonuses

---

edit., Moscow, Publishers 1982.
17. In his 10 April speech, Chernenko announced that the law on workers' collectives was passed by the government.
18. *Pravda*, 3 March 1984.

and profit retention'.[19] Specific measures provide for the retention of a fixed share of profits for the wage fund and for coordinated plant investment. In addition, factory performance is being rated on the basis of a reduced number of indicators with increased importance being given to the marketability of goods based on world market standards; hence, managers will have to pay close attention to demand instead of fulfilling quotas.[20]

Many of these same measures had in fact been included in the 1965 and 1979 decrees on planning and management, but were offset by continuing ministerial control and by specific countermeasures taken especially by the Ministry of Finance. Now, in 1983 and 1984 a series of centralising measures suggest a new dimension that may assure introduction of as well as adherence to the new rules:

(1) Revival of the division of responsibility for industrial and transport performance among individual Politburo members: Dolgikh (energy), Aliev (transport), Romanov (heavy and defence industries) and Gorbachev (agriculture);

(2) Establishment of a new economic unit within the Secretariat of the Central Committee under Nikolai Ryzhkov (this Committee appears to be staffing up to about fifty persons);

(3) Granting new statutory administrative powers to the State Planning Commission (Gosplan). Establishment of 'super ministry' units within Gosplan to supervise the ministries of various functional areas, e.g. energy, metal-working and machine-building;

(4) Establishment of a number of governmental commissions, such as one for agriculture, to oversee ministerial coordination and planning.

The centralisation of planning and coordination above the ministerial level may lead to more balanced planning overall, especially in investment. Moreover, these superior organs may provide the clout necessary to assure adherence to the decentralisation decrees on enterprise autonomy. In the past, managers seem to have been left without a court of higher appeal if the ministries undercut the decrees for changes in the economic mechanism by issuing offsetting regulations or by inaction. The new superior organs may even encourage changes within the ministries themselves.

19. John F. Burns, 'Moscow Will Try Again to Widen the Powers of Factory Managers', *New York Times*, 27 July 1983.
20. Ibid.

III. 1983 Soviet economic performance: improved but by how much?

The Soviet economy performed better in 1983 than it did in 1982: industrial output grew cumulatively by 5 per cent,[21] the harvest was reported at about 190m. metric tons by Chernenko himself[22] and the energy sector performed well — oil output was stable while gas output was in excess of planned demand.[23] (Two brief comments on the performance of the energy sector are in order here: (1) Although oil output has declined in the early months of 1984, it is too early to make any long-term assessment. (2) Gas supplies are in excess because the Soviets have to date only contracted for just 20 of the 40 billion cu.m. of gas that will be available from the new export gas pipeline, the Urengoi–Uzhgorod pipeline, in 1984. However, the apparent pro-French tilt of Soviet policy, including the cordial meetings between Chernenko and Mitterrand, may provide an economic bonus in increased French gas orders.)

What is behind this improved economic report card is still un-clear. Limited disclosure and inconsistencies in the Soviet data have made it difficult for Western students of the Soviet economy to identify changes in Soviet economic policy. Investment remains particularly puzzling. In September 1983 the CIA reported that 'state capital investment increased by 6 per cent, compared with the first half of 1982'.[24] However, at the year's end, investment seemed to drop to a level equal or possibly below that of 1982.[25] If Andropov did, in fact, deviate from Brezhnev's policy to hold down annual investment to 2 per cent throughout 1985, this would represent a significant shift in policy. Although price changes during 1982–3 may account for some inconsistencies, until better data is available and more study is possible, using the 1982 and 1983 data, one can say only that: 'Comparing the first four years of the 11th FYP

21. Philip Hanson, 'How Good A Year Was 1983 for the Soviet Economy?', RFE/RL Research, 71/84, 14 February 1984, p. 1. See also N.K. Baibakov, 'O gosudarstvennom plane ekonomicheskogo i sotsial'nogo razvitiya SSSR na 1984 god i vypolnenii plana v 1983 godu', Moscow, 1984.
22. *Pravda*, 3 March 1984.
23. *Hearings on the Allocation of Resources in the Soviet Union and China — 1983. CIA Testimony, before the Subcommittee on International Trade, Finance, and Security Economics of the Joint Economic Committee*, Congress, 20 September 1983.
24. Ibid, p. 12.
25. Herbert Levine, 'Current Issues in the Soviet Economy', *Current Analysis*, Wharton EFA, Inc., IV/2, 11 January 1984, p. 3.
For a discussion of data problems, see Jan Vanous, 'Soviet Economic Performance in 1983', *Current Analysis*, IV/8–9, 14 February 1984.

(including the plan for 1984 with the first four years of the 10th FYP) investment appears to be growing at the rate of 2.8 per cent per year, which is at the top of the range indicated in the original guidelines to the 11th FYP.'[26] Consumption continued to rise during 1983.[27] This increase was largely the result of organisational restructuring and some additional investment in agriculture and the other industries included in the agro-industrial sector.[28] Together, this sector accounts for over 27 per cent of all investment. While there is no doubt that the production of consumer goods exceeded that of capital goods in 1983, the question remains at what cost. Some suspect that the increase in the availability of consumer goods 'reflects a purely quantitative advance to the detriment of the quality of the goods produced'.[29]

Meanwhile, according to the CIA, defence expenditures have only been rising by 2 per cent annually between 1976 and 1981, indicating that defence seems not to have regained the priority position it held in the early 1970s when military spending grew by 4 per cent a year.[30] Since 1976, defence expenditures have not increased in relative terms, that is, relative to GNP growth: 'The rate of growth in overall defence costs is lower because procurement of military hardware — the largest component of defence spending — was almost flat in 1976–81.'[31]

If the new leadership continues to moderate the military's claim on resources, this would be quite significant, both in terms of economics and politics. What only time can reveal is whether a new leader can hold down defence spending and still retain the support of the military for his regime. This may be particularly interesting in the case of Chernenko, who has already indicated that in current circumstances the welfare of the people should not be sacrificed for the sake of national security concerns:

During the past five years, the complexities of international life com-

26. Ibid., p. 3.
27. See Douglas Whitehouse, 'Consumer Policy under the Andropov Regime', unpublished manuscript presented at the Southern Slavic Conference, October 1983.
28. Soviet agricultural investment policy for 1983 is not clear. See Yuri Markish and Anton Malish on the Soviet food programm: 'Prospects for the 1980s', *ACES Bulletin*, Spring 1983; Newsletter for Research on Soviet and East European Agriculture, 5/4, December 1983, p. 2.
29. Allan Kroncher, 'Anomalies in the Economic Results for 1983', RFE/RL Research, 50/84, 1 February 1984.
30. CIA Testimony, pp. 7–11, 45–9.
31. Ibid. p. 13.

pelled us to divert considerable resources to the need connected with the consolidation of the country's security. *But we did not even think of curtailing social programmes*, since the ultimate goal of all our work is improving the well-being of the Soviet people. And our approach to this task is broad. We want the people not only to be better off materially, but also healthy physically, developed spiritually and active in social life. (Emphasis added).[32]

IV. What might adjustments mean for future Soviet economic performance?

There is one body of thought that maintains that incremental changes in the Soviet economic mechanism, such as those described above, and others which Chernenko may introduce over the next two and a half years before the Twelfth Five-Year Plan is implemented, will not have a significant nor lasting impact on the performance of the Soviet economy.[33] In this view, the nature of the Soviet economic system, a centrally planned economy, mitigates against efficient performance. Previous Soviet efforts to institute change, e.g. the 1965 Kosygin and 1979 Brezhnev reforms, are generally regarded as having been inconsequential, and any similar changes that might be introduced in the future are thought to be destined for the same type of disappointing results. The implication of this line of argument is that the only way to improve the economy by any significant degree is to transform it into something more similar to a market economy, i.e. to introduce changes more along the lines of market socialism. However, in order for the leaders to move in that direction, they must first overcome political and institutional resistance, which is not easily surmounted.

There is another body of thought which argues that it is both possible and probable that the Soviets can and will make further changes within the existing political and economic structures that prove to be both meaningful and effective. Supporters of this view accept the argument that no Soviet leader — especially one who has not yet consolidated his power base — is likely to follow the phoenix approach; that is, destroy the old system of control confident that something desirable (in the form of market socialism)

32. *Pravda*, 3 March 1984.
33. CIA Testimony, pp. 41–43. See also Marshall Goldman, *The U.S.S.R. in Crisis: The Failure of an Economic System*, New York, 1983.

would arise from its remains. They maintain that the Leninist system is the most likely framework within which economic change will be attempted, and that the near-term engines of change will likely be planning and management measures designed to relieve pressing bottlenecks in troubled industrial and agricultural areas, and a shifting of the institutional power of the ministerial system to higher central organs for planning and to enterprises for management.

In this view, the potential for change hinges on tapping what might be termed 'reserves of unleased efficiency'.[34] If the barriers erected by the current planning and management system were removed, these reserves may be drawn upon. Consider the following illustrations drawn from the energy sector:

If extraction and transmission of oil, gas, and coal approached world levels of efficiency.

If the time and quality of civilian projects in Siberia were comparable to that of American or Korean construction complexes in comparably hostile climes.

The Soviets are now following an energy programme that is aimed at securing a fuel-energy balance. Increased investment has been allocated to the energy sector for the development of oil, gas, coal, electric, and nuclear resources. (Investment in the energy sector accounts for 42–47 per cent of industrial investment or 21–23 per cent of total investment.) In addition, conservation measures have been introduced; for example, the installation of energy-conserving equipment.

Proven gas supplies are clearly not a short-term constraint; proven gas reserves rival the equivalent of the Saudi oil fields. The efficiency of Soviet gas transmission, however, now stands at about two-thirds that of the United States. However, considerably more could be transported and exported without the construction of any additional transmission lines.

Nikolai Tikhonov, in his election speech of 1 March 1984 stressed this material-saving aspect of Party policy: 'Already in the current

---

34. The term 'unleased' may be defined as those efficiency measures persistently below Western norms that Soviet leaders have specifically identified as focal points for improvement. There are other examples of 'reserves of unleased' efficiency to consider. In the Automotive Industry: If the quality of output were comparable to German, Japanese, Italian processes that much of the Soviet imported equipment emulates. In Industrial and Transport Manpower: If materials handling requirements, in general, were similar to American and European standards: if transport, e.g. railroad, labor productivity and passenger services were equivalent to comparable German, French, of Japanese levels.

year, the planned 3.1 per cent increase in the national income is to be ensured with a 2.5 per cent cut in metal intensity and 1.5 per cent cut in energy intensity.'[35] In agriculture, as in industry, there are 'reserves of unleased efficiency'. Once again, consider these illustrations:

If bread-quality wheat in the Soviet mills were regularly equivalent to what would be available under similar weather conditions in comparable Canadian acreage.

If the feed grain conversion ratios of corn and other high protein feed for hogs were equivalent in Soviet agriculture to American levels.

If farm to market facilities and the food supply system in the Soviet Union were as effective as similar East European systems using agricultural infrastructure; for example, the corn production project at Babolna in Hungary that uses US agricultural technology.

In May 1982 Leonid Brezhnev outlined the contents of the new long-term 'food programme' intended to provide the basis for improved agricultural planning and performance by increased efficiency and output through to 1990. The main components of the programme included: more incentives for farm workers and managers, the shifting of more responsibility from ministry to *raion* (district) level by means of agro-industrial complexes (RAPOs), the allocation of a greater share of investment to agriculture — more than 27 per cent — in the Twelfth Five-Year Plan (1986–90), and increased domestic livestock production.

Although the Programme might have been delayed with the death of Brezhnev in early November 1982, Andropov was quick to make it a top priority of his leadership. In his speech of 22 November, delivered to the Party plenum, he stressed the importance of continuing the Brezhnev food programme and pledged to implement its provisions. Over the course of his first year in power, Andropov set up a significant number of RAPOs and issued major decrees on the planning and functioning of the Soviet agricultural sector:[36] 'The new planning arrangements are intended to make plans for industrial supplies to agriculture dependent on orders from the farms, following review by the local agro-industrial associations.'[37] Furthermore, the contract system was introduced on the collective farms.

35. *Pravda*, 2 March 1984. See also N.A. Tikhonov, *Sovetskaya Ekonomika: Dostizhenia, Problemy, Perspektivy*, Moscow, 1984.
36. See *Pravda*, 10 April and 26 June 1983.
37. Hanson, see note 21; RFE/RL Research 283/83, p. 5.

Although these agro-industrial associations have shown results individually, they have not generally been throughout the agricultural sector. Therefore, their overall value has yet to be demonstrated. If the principles of reward based on performance and of management based on technical training (i.e. comprehension of the full supply and delivery process) become common practice, there may be more widespread success in the future. Chernenko argued that it was improvements in the organisation of agriculture, in spite of continued poor weather, that accounted for the increased yield in 1983.[38]

In line with the food programme, Andropov also stressed the need 'to preserve the gathered harvest',[39] that is, to reduce the losses that occur during and after harvesting, and to invest more in transport and storage facilities. Current Soviet post harvest losses amount to as much as 20 per cent from inefficient grain storage alone. Adjusting the quality of wheat in the silos (bunker weight) to Western standards of cleanliness and moisture content indicates an additional 10 per cent loss. The Soviets do, however, have the natural resources for self-sufficiency in wheat: good fertile soil land and a suitable, albeit changeable, climate. Already the world's largest wheat producer, any modest improvement in harvesting would show substantial returns, presumably enough to make the Soviets self-sufficient in cereal grains during normal weather years, such as 1983.

Conclusion

Judging from the recent statements and actions of both Andropov and Chernenko, the potential for introducing lasting and meaningful changes within the established economic system mechanism should not be underestimated. Several factors suggests that the post-Brezhnev leadership may be determined enough to make a difference:

(1) A consensus on 'perfecting' or adjusting the economic mechanism seems to exist within the Party. Members have been un-

38. *Pravda*, 3 March 1984. See also F.I. Bogomolov and A.A. Kosynkin, *APK: Organizatsiia, Planirovanie, Upravlenie*, Moscow, 1983. For a discussion of recent changes in the structure of labor organization in agriculture, see Karl-Eugen Wädekin, '"Contract" and "Normless" Labor on Soviet Farms: An Interpretation and Prognosis', RFE/RL Research, 49/84, 8 February 1984.
39. *Pravda*, 23 November 1983.

usually critical and candid about the failures of the past. While a consensus for change seems clear, however, there is not yet clear agreement on the direction of change. The 'technocratic' solution stresses both the centralisation of planning and the decentralisation of management as well as emphasising improvements in input-output relations in key areas of production. This approach would probably lead to significant personnel changes at all Party and government levels of the economy. The ideological view appears to accept the need for institutional and technical change while avoiding a purge of the economic cadres.

(2) There are indications of an ongoing economic debate taking place within the Soviet ranks. One report from an academy in Novosibirsk was leaked to the West in early August 1983.[40] Other sources provide further evidence of differing opinions on economic change. What is significant is that change, either from a reformist technocratic or conservative ideological viewpoint, is being discussed and steps towards implementation taken.

(3) It seems reasonable to expect some increase in material and labour efficiency from the incremental changes in planning and management. Moreover, there is reason to believe that such incremental change will have an accelerating effect and that a process of institutional change towards eventual marketisation of the economy and a transition from physical to financial planning may be attained. For example, the full staffing and functioning of the super ministerial planning organs, together with the extension of the ministerial decentralisation experiments throughout the economy, may eventually change the existing system of management at all levels.

(4) There has, in fact, been some improvement both in industrial and agricultural output. In 1983 industrial production grew by 5 per cent over the previous year's figures. In addition, the harvest was over 190m. metric tons, the best in over four years. There were undoubtedly many factors that led to this improvement but the introduction of changes in the economic mechanism and the enhanced priority accorded to energy and agriculture appear to have shown results.

(5) Finally, it seems prudent not to make over-hasty judgements about the possible effects of the economic changes being considered and introduced in the Soviet Union. In fact, as Professor Herbert

40. Dusko Doder, 'Soviet Study Urges Economic Changes', *Washington Post*, 3 August 1983.

Levine, Soviet expert and economist, recently wrote: ' . . . the potential impact of the changes announced and under discussion should not be weighed individually but together, for the total impact is the sum of individual impacts, and furthermore they promise to have interactive, synergistic effects.'[41]

Highlights from discussions of John P. Hardt with visiting Soviet economists and planners as reported at the Bonn meeting

Since preparing this paper, I have had the opportunity to discuss the subject of change in the Soviet system with a group of leading Soviet economists and planners during their visit to the US. The following points represent the highlights of these discussions.

The first point is that the Soviet leaders are serious about the need for economic change. Slow growth is not acceptable. One might characterise this in terms of a minimum threshold of economic performance. In terms of Soviet national income I would place this threshold at about 3.5–4 per cent p.a. in Net National Product [NNP]. The Soviet leadership's political imperative is that there must be more investment, both in absolute and relative terms. At the same time, there must also be a continuous allocation of resources to defence. An economic slow-down in growth below the threshold would mean a relative decrease in the resources available for investment, defence and consumption; consequently, the leadership will not accept slow growth.

Increases in consumption in terms of quantity and quality are required to close the gap between purchasing power created and purchasing power absorbed. Hence, positive incentives are needed. Some measurable increases in living standards need to be resumed; increases have been stalled since the mid-1970s.

The second point deals with the effectiveness of incremental institutional changes in planning and management. Incremental change should be viewed in two ways. The first is in terms of decentralisation, that is, in looking at the five ministries whose enterprises are getting more power in terms of their labour management prerogatives and control of wage funds, control of production and contracting, etc. The second way is through centralisation; that

41. Levine, p. 7.

is, in looking at the increasing central power of the leadership at the Politburo level, the expanded responsibility of the staff of the Central Committee Secretariat and the increasing role of the State Planning Commission and specialised commissions at governmental level. The related question is: Why should one assume that these planning and management changes might now be successful, even modestly, when before, in the reforms of 1965 and 1979, they were not? From these discussions, I think the key to answering this question lies in the current move towards the centralisation of planning, reinforcing the decentralisation of management — in both cases away from the ministerial locus of economic authority.

At the core of current economic change is the modification of the ministerial system; here I am referring to several things: (1) The responsibility for various key sectors of the economy is now being assumed by individual Politburo members, e.g. Gorbachev for agriculture, Aliev for transportation, Romanov for the heavy industries and, perhaps, for the defence-related industries and Dolgikh for energy. (2) The new economics section of the Secretariat under Ryzhkov is slowly adding to its staff, which may eventually number as many as fifty people. This new division is in a position to effect changes in planning and management while bypassing the authority of the ministries. (3) If the changes within Gosplan continue along the present lines, that is, the establishment of 'super ministry' sections responsible not just for steel but for metallurgy, not just for oil and gas but for energy, then the power of the ministries in planning might be reduced. (4) Centralisation is also evident in the case of commissions, e.g., the Agricultural Commission at Council of Ministers Level. These devolutions and evolutions of power below and above the ministerial system may overcome the known ministerial resistance to institutional change.

The third point deals with the impact of technical incremental change on overall economic performance. The question is whether or not changes in terms of input-output relationships can be effective in improving performance; for example, can technical coefficients be improved if cast in physical terms and cast in terms of directives to conserve energy and metals. In a recent speech, Nikolai Tikhonov highlighted the importance of improvement in the 'intensity' of use of energy and metals and reported on progress in each of these areas. Is it possible to move towards more overall efficiency by reducing the kilocalories of energy used per unit of output of metals? And is it possible that by moving along a technical spectrum, step by step approaches may in time lead not only to improved input-output coefficients, but to a shift from financing to planning? It is possible. By international standards the Soviet Union has an enormous potential for improved efficiency, so this kind of incremental change in the economy may make a difference. I suggest that we take seriously the possibility that it will.

Although there is a consensus within the leadership on the need for change, these discussions with Soviet economists indicate that significant differences exist between the so-called 'ideologues' and the 'technocrats.' The ideologues agree that there should be change, but without personnel changes requiring the replacement of cadres. Nikolai Tikhonov, Chairman of the Council of Ministers, might be a leader in this kind of thinking. The 'technocrats' would certainly include Gorbachev. He and others in this group are interested in fostering change through decentralisation, professionalisation and improvement in technical performance, and many of them are, in fact, responsible for cadre selection.

In sum, I would suggest that incremental institutional and technical changes may make a difference in Soviet economic performance. However, the question as to whether or not these kinds of change would make a difference that might be called progressive — that is, successful change to foster more change, remains open. Further insight into the views and inclinations of Konstantin Chernenko would be needed to hazard even a tentative answer to that question. The new Party leader's speech of 10 April 1984[42] provided some indication as to where he stands. Certainly the person occupying the position of General Secretary of the Party makes a difference in the types of economic policies introduced within the Soviet Union. But more pointedly, will the 'technocrat' view of change pull Chernenko along lines that his past record as an 'ideologue' argues against?

42. *Pravda*, 11 April 1984.

Soviet Economic Policy
Hans-Hermann Höhmann

At the end of the Brezhnev era the Soviet economy was in a critical phase with chronic systemic malfunction, unfavourable trends in factors affecting production, structural change that was counter-productive and acute problems of disproportion. The massive disequilibria that appeared at the end of the 1970s in particular brought a major slump in growth, and this can truly be called a 'crisis of disproportion'.

When Andropov took over from Brezhnev in November 1982 he left in no doubt his conviction that extensive action was needed in the economic sphere.[1] However, there were two key restrictions affecting the measures that could be taken and these will continue to impose themselves on Soviet leaders in future; they are the lack of funding for deep-rooted sectoral and regional redistribution and the impossibility of effectively changing the basic institutions or the way the planned economy works in the foreseeable future, i.e. of inaugurating systematic reform of a transformatory nature.

What remains after these restrictions is a collection of measures of limited scope orientated to targets, resources and productivity. Andropov had too little time to establish his own course in economic policy and some months before his death he was probably no longer in active control of the economy. However, his first speeches and measures indicate a number of approaches that could be described as 'turning muddling through into a strategy'. Andropov was probably aware that, particularly when far-reaching alternatives and the *élan* necessary to change system and structures are not available, what is needed is a well-adjusted mosaic of measures coordinated with a firm hand.

Four areas of the strategy can be identified: economic policy in the narrow sense (decisions on the speed and proportions of growth together with the allocation of production factors), labour and cadre policy (discipline at work, worker motivation, changes in the wage system), economic policy reforms (changes in policy instruments, the institutions of planning and control, and the functional mech-

1. H.H. Höhmann, 'Von Breschew zu Andropov: Bilanz und Perspektiven sowjetischer Wirtschaftsentwicklung', in: *Sowjetunion* 1982/83, Bundesinstitut für ostwissenschaftliche und internationale Studien, Cologne, Munich, 1983, pp. 113–23.

anisms) and foreign trade policy (decisions on CMEA integration, East-West relations and relations with the Third World).

The reorientation and tightening of economic policy needed by Andropov to tackle the defects in the way the system functions was taken over in principle by Chernenko.[2] What focal points he will choose to set for the policy, however, and with what consistency he will be able to act remain to be seen. The main determinant will be his ability to realise, the consensus and ability to act of the leadership as a whole. Finally, success will not least depend on whether it proves possible to use the Party apparatus as an instrument to increase economic efficiency and to stop it from developing into a parasitic feudal class. Chernenko's clientelist approach has raised doubts here.[3]

Economic Policy

In economic policy the watchwords have been consolidation at a reduced level and a shift in emphasis in the structure of use or input. The plan targets for 1983 and 1984 did involve an acceleration of economic growth over the unfavourable preceding years, but for the Eleventh Five-Year Plan (with some exceptions) there was a considerable correction of the plan targets downwards. The intention was probably to ease the pressure, to create more scope and reserves in order to stop enterprises from hoarding, which in turn would help to overcome disproportions, restore consistency in planning and finally point to new possibilities for growth.

As far as the utilisation of the national product is concerned, it is particularly significant that investment growth has again been accelerated, unlike the original concept for the Eleventh Five-Year Plan. This is expected to ease bottlenecks, close gaps in capacities and modernise the production structure. The main focuses of this policy are the energy sector, agriculture (or the 'agro-industrial complex'), transport and sections of industry.

2. *Pravda*, 2 March 1984.
3. R.W. Campbell, 'The Economy', in: R.F. Byrnes (ed.): *After Brezhnev, Sources of Soviet Conduct in the 1980s*, London 1983, p. 120.

Labour Policy

Labour policy encompasses Andropov's attempts to improve discipline at work, achieve a better adjustment between wages and performance and tackle corruption. In August 1983, after the mass work discipline campaign of the previous winter and spring, two resolutions were published by Party and government,[4] to the effect that action was to be taken against various groups disrupting work and that the labour legislation law would be sharpened (but without a return to Stalinism). After he took over Chernenko announced that the discipline campaign was to be a permanent, not a temporary measure. However, much of the original momentum has since disappeared. It also remains to be seen whether the Decree on Works Councils, also passed in 1983, with its limited element of worker participation, will not have a neutralising effect on discipline. Chernenko appears to prefer a leadership style which would enable the jeopardised social consensus to be restored through more confidence in the Party. His populist approach is hard to reconcile with a continued stress on discipline, as might have been expected from Andropov's more élitist approach.

Reform Policy

Andropov was also hoping for reforms, even if these were necessarily to be of a limited kind, and Chernenko appears to be following the same road. In 1983 a number of measures of a general or regional nature were announced to promote technical progress, save energy and material, make wages better orientated to performance and so on.

In agricultural policy, apart from the continuation of the 'food programme' and a few organisational changes (under the slogan RAPO), special emphasis has been given to the system of group contracts. This takes up the old idea of loosening the agricultural enterprise structure by allowing more scope in production for small groups and it has now been implemented on a broad front.

Most important, however, was an experiment begun on 1 January 1984 by five industrial ministries which, if it proves successful, is to be applied throughout industry.[5] Much of what is to form part of

4. *Pravda*, 7 August 1983.

the experiment is familiar from the reforms of 1965, 1973 and 1979, and a certain reorientation *vis-à-vis* to the Kosygin–Liberman reforms of the late 1960s is undeniable. The main planks of the experiment are:

— The planning framework is to be redrawn to allow planning in good time that will be stable over the medium term (an old idea that has never been realised);

— An extension of the scope for decision-making for the production associations and enterprises through participation in planning, a reduction of the binding target data, interchangeability of target figures, an expansion of normative methods and more stress on contracts between enterprises;

— Wider financial scope for production associations and enterprises through more decision-making on their own funds, wider borrowing powers and a transition from profit transfer to the 'normative method', i.e. a kind of profit steering;

— A reorganisation of the incentive system by 'perfecting and simplifying' the bonus system, setting new 'figures for fund-building' and more elasticity for wage formation within the enterprise.

Whether this experiment, on the progress of which both negative and positive reports have appeared in the Soviet press, will be chosen as model for a general reform, remains to be seen. Chernenko and other members of the Politburo have certainly spoken in favour of continuing it. Moreover, the beginning of the Twelfth Five-Year Plan period (1986–90) is approaching. Experience has shown that a change from one plan period to another often involves changes in the planning system. A new reform following the principles of the experiment, however, would not mean a change in the basic institutions and functional mechanisms of Soviet planning and to that extent it would again be encumbered by the functional problems inherent in all administrative planning. Nevertheless, on principle improvement should be possible 'within the system'. There is nothing to say that the 'social technique of small steps' cannot be used in a socialist planned economy as well. But for this three basic conditions should be better fulfilled than they have been in the past:

5. *Pravda*, 26 July 1983; H.H. Höhmann, 'Richtung und Grenzen neuer Wirtschaftsreformen in der UdSSR', in: *Berichte des Bundesinstituts für ostwissenschaftliche und internationale Studien*, 44/1983 (Cologne).

— a reform concept more consistent than its predecessors;
— a leadership that can take decisions and is more consistent in realising the concept;
— a reform policy better attuned to plan behaviour (reducing the 'plan pressure') and a structural policy more orientated to overcoming disproportions than the reform policy of the past.

No doubt these conditions are on the whole too 'heroic' to be fulfilled under Chernenko's leadership. However, after many years' experience with improving the quality of 'human capital' through planning, administration and management some progress should be possible. Moreover, it must be borne in mind that a large number of factors outside the system contributed to the decline in growth between 1979 and 1981 and so it might be hoped that factors outside the system might help improve things now.

Foreign Trade Policy

This foreign trade policy, finally, this has always been one of the areas in which the main trends have at best been vague and difficult to quantify. This is due to the loose relations between the domestic and external economies in the Soviet Union, the lack of transparency in world markets and the effects of the often unstable external situation. Whereas the climate in East–West relations (especially between the Soviet Union and the United States) has been very bad, the course of economic relations with Western industrial countries could still be regarded as favourable. Soviet foreign trade statistics in current (1983) prices did show a shift to the CMEA area but, taking the price developments in Soviet foreign trade into account, economic ties with the West did strengthen in real terms.[6]

Since this development will in any case be limited by economic factors one can hardly say that foreign policy has been a restraining force. On the contrary, the trend is more a reflection of the efforts made by the Soviet Union to disengage foreign trade from foreign policy somewhat, and this has found a counterpart in the behaviour of most Western states.

---

6. *Soviet Foreign Trade Performance in 1983*, Wharton EFA, Centrally Planned Economies Current Analysis 22/23/1984.

Conclusion

In conclusion we can say that the Soviet economy has again achieved a rather impressive rate of growth after the drop between 1979 and 1981, which was unparalleled in Soviet economic history. The new growth rate would appear to be stabilising in the medium term. However, in addition to a number of consolidating factors there are still major obstacles. It is hardly to be expected that the Soviet economy will return to the 4 per cent growth rate in GNP of before 1978, but rates of between 2.5 and 3 per cent would appear possible in the next few years. Growth on that scale would ease the worst worries of the Soviet leaders. In view of the many claims on their resources (consumption, armaments, capital formation) they will, however, still be looking for further stimulus to growth. In addition to the traditional structural policy and process measures, better economic policy instruments to achieve limited 'reforms within the system' will play a lasting part. However, anything beyond that is unlikely within the foreseeable future. The risks of far-reaching reforms are too great, the traditional structure of interests in society too firmly fixed and the situation in the economy still too good to induce a leadership that is not traditionally orientated to reform to pursue real alternatives.

Political Obstacles to Economic Reform
Ronald Amann

In the course of studying Soviet industrial research and development over many years one issue has come to seem more interesting and relevant than any other. It is not whether much of Soviet non-military technology is backward in comparison with equivalent sectors in the major Western countries: with some notable exceptions, it is.[1] Nor does the main point of interest lie any longer in the reasons for this relative backwardness: these are already widely understood, not least by the Soviet leaders themselves. The main puzzle is why, given a full and longstanding appreciation of the problem, nothing decisive has been done to put it right beyond the incrementalism of the last decade.

As a citizen of a country which has also been on a 'treadmill of reform' for many years one should not be too surprised by the way in which the momentum of reform can dissipate in the face of institutional resistance. Successive British governments have wrestled with systemic problems which the country's economic and social history has bequeathed:[2] inflexible working practices, unprofessional management, amateurish civil servants and, even, unworldly university teachers! Yet the desired policy objectives have not always been achieved. One is therefore familiar in a general way with the politics of institutional inertia. In comparison even with British experience, however, the Soviet government's lack of impact breaks new ground.

This continued hesitancy seems all the more remarkable when we remind ourselves of the general economic context in which reform is being contemplated in the Soviet Union. Firstly, it is one in which the rate of economic growth has declined continuously over the past two decades. Since the USSR still lags substantially behind the leading Western countries in per capita output and the technological sophistication of its manufactured products and processes it is not plausible to view this slow-down as an inevitable consequence of advanced development and close proximity to the international technology frontier. Moreover, as a number of analysts have

1. R. Amann, J.M. Cooper and R.W. Davies, *The Technological Level of Soviet Industry*, Yale University Press 1979.
2. Martin Wiener, *English Culture and the Decline of the Industrial Spirit 1850–1980*, Cambridge University Press 1981.

observed,[3] this slow-down poses a number of serious political problems and is becoming ever more difficult to arrest by the traditional engines of growth; the pool of surplus labour is drying up, energy growth has slowed down and deposits of raw materials are becoming more inaccessible and expensive to extract.[4] Secondly, the rate of technological progress is insufficient to compensate for the growing relative scarcity of these other factors of production. In recent years we have witnessed an appreciable fall in the annual average growth of labour productivity, now running at around 2–3 per cent per annum, which is to a considerable extent influenced by sluggish technical progress. The failure to achieve a significant reduction in the material intensity (*materialoemkost'*) of industrial manufacture is further evidence of technological inertia. Coupled with this are the widespread criticisms of the real quality and novelty of new products and processes in the USSR in contrast to the optimistic (and largely fictitious) estimates of those who create them. On the basis of official figures, one Soviet economist has pointed out that the real economic return on equipment produced by the machine-building ministries during the 1980s has been on average only 44 per cent of the predicted return[5] — and this estimate is over-generous because customers are reluctant to disclose the full discrepancy between theory and practice for fear of antagonising their monopoly suppliers. It is ironic but not accidental that this discrepancy has coincided with a massive general increase in bonuses for new technology since the late 1970s. Unreal estimates of the future impact of new technologies and unreal prices, which are based upon these estimates, are a major source of concealed inflation; the latter masks a sharper slow-down in the rate of economic growth than the official figures show. Indeed, some Western specialists, notably Professor Peter Wiles, believe that the USSR may now have entered a phase of zero growth[6] and this inevitably restricts the diffusion throughout the economy of new

3. P. Hanson, 'Economic Constraints on Soviet Policies in the 1980s', *International Affairs*, Winter 1980–1981, pp. 21ff.; S. Bialer, part v, *Stalin's Successors: Leadership, Stability and Change in the Soviet Union*, Cambridge University Press 1980.
4. R. Campbell, in R.F. Byrnes (ed.), *After Brezhnev*, London 1983, pp. 81f.
5. V. Fel'zenbaum, 'Upravlenie nauchno-technicheskim progressom, *Voprosy Ekonomiki* 11/1983, p. 16.
6. P. Wiles, 'Has Soviet Economic Growth Ceased?' Paper presented to the general seminar, CREES, University of Birmingham, 8 March 1984; see also 'Soviet Consumption and Investment Prices and the Meaningfulness of Real Investment', *Soviet Studies*, 2/1982, pp. 289ff.

technology, which is embodied in new plant and equipment. G. Marchuk,[7] Chairman of the USSR State Committee for Science and Technology, has acknowledged that in the last ten years the economic impact of one ruble spent on the creation of new technology in the Soviet Union has fallen, largely because of slow diffusion and only secondarily because of higher development costs. Thus, through these indicators one begins to catch glimpses of the vicious circle which seems to have the Soviet economy in its grip. The slower real growth of capital investment holds back the diffusion of new technology and strengthens the unwillingness of industrial ministries to withdraw resources from normal production in order to provide experimental and testing facilities. These factors in their turn inhibit the accumulation of practical know-how and adversely affect the morale of R&D personnel, who take refuge in formalistic and ivory tower attitudes. The even more intense desire of the central authorities for technical advance (and the political obligation of the lower levels to respond) continues to be met by spurious claims about new items of equipment, which turn out later to be poorly proven and over priced. This, of course, undermines the quality of future investment and technical progress — and so the spiral continues.

Experience over the last two decades would suggest strongly that the Soviet economy, forged in the era of Stalinist industrialisation, is impervious to incremental reform and that despite repeated attempts to break into the vicious circle the same familiar tendencies persist: ineffective incentives and departmental barriers to innovation which, apparently, affect even the 170 priority programmes under the formal supervision of the State Committee for Science and Technology. We return, therefore, to the question posed earlier. Why, given the persistence of these economic problems, are there no stronger signs that a bolder (more market-orientated) reform is being contemplated which would address itself to the core influences on the economic system (centralised supplies, prices, absence of direct relations with customers and lack of real rewards for success and penalties for failure)? At a time when one might have anticipated bold change, we have, instead, the cautious 'mini-reform' of July 1983.[8]

7. G. Marćuk, 'Nauchno-technicheskii progress i effektivnost' proizvodstva', *Pravda*, 9 December 1983.
8. *Pravda*, 26 July 1983.

The answer to this paradox, it seems to me, lies primarily in the political domain. The Soviet leadership is caught between two conflicting tendencies: a pressing economic need for institutional reform and a political reluctance to carry it through. Up to the present time, the outcome of this dialectical process has been hesitation, incrementalism and compromise. What, then, are the political obstacles to economic reform?

(a) Vested interests of institutions. Reform of the traditional central planning mechanism would remove or dilute several of the most important sources of power of the party apparatus: control over resource allocation and the placement of personnel. It would run counter to the well-established priority access to supplies of the defence industries. Above all, however, it would transgress the most fundamental principle of Soviet-style socialism — the claim of a class-conscious *élite* to express the 'real' social interest. Such a view has been argued vigorously by P. Ignatovskii, editor of the leading Soviet planning journal *Planovoe Khozyaistvo* in a recent article in the party theoretical journal *Kommunist*.[9] Ignatovskii contends that 'commodity relations' in the Soviet economy have already gone too far and have to be reined in by selective Party controls; only in this way can corrosive selfishness and the predominance of narrow departmental interests be avoided. From a theoretical point of view, this is perhaps the crucial conservative argument against a far-reaching quasi-market reform.

(b) The introduction of a market element would produce economic distortions such as regional imbalances and unemployment, which could only be overcome by forms of control which are unfamiliar (and, perhaps, culturally alien) to the Soviet leadership. The alternative of retaining the traditional planning mechanism while tolerating the marginalisation of private enterprise[10] carries with it the danger of sapping the long run vitality of major investment schemes in the state sector.

(c) A far-reaching economic reform could heighten social tensions by (i) increasing income differentials in a general context of decreasing working-class social mobility and (ii) alleviating the problem of labour shortage and, hence, undermining the main bargaining power of workers to bid up their wages.[11]

9. P. Ignatovskii, 'O politicheskom podkhode k ekonomike', in: *Kommunist*, 12/1983, pp. 60ff.
10. J. Berliner, in: *Problems of Communism*, January–February 1983.
11. V. Zaslavsky, *The Neo-Stalinist State*, M.E. Sharpe, 1982, pp. 44ff.

(d) Political leaders would only contemplate reform if they had confidence in the ability of officials at all levels of the system to carry it out. However, there is some evidence that Soviet leaders are mistrustful of both the technical competence and the moral qualities of these officials. Moreover, as Zaslavskaya has suggested in the so-called 'Novosibirsk Paper', which was leaked to the Western press,[12] the desire for reform among central planners and enterprise staff is in any case weak.

(e) Even if they decided to go ahead with reform, Soviet leaders would almost certainly recognise that the economic benefits could only be enjoyed in the long term, whereas the political costs summarised above would be experienced in the short run. This perspective would be bound to make them err on the side of caution.

What are the future implications of this political response?

In some ways the present answers we have to this crucial question are unsatisfactory because the arguments have not been pressed to their logical conclusion. The most immediately plausible answer is to conclude that a balance will be struck between economic imperatives and political inhibitions. Thus, there will be a modest reform (perhaps involving a reduction in the powers of branch ministries, some greater rights to industrial managers, a better system of material incentives, etc.) but the essential mechanism of central planning will remain. However, this line of reasoning probably does not give sufficient weight to the poor track record of incremental reform and the capacity of the system to overwhelm partial change, much as a body might reject a transplanted organism. Nor does it pursue the argument that as the rate of economic growth decreases and the 'politics of scarcity' increases it becomes progressively more difficult to introduce a major institutional reform. The time to do it is when a government, perhaps capitalising on reformist sentiment among certain segments of the intelligentsia after a long period of political stagnation, still has some room for manoeuvre. 'Muddling through' is a political concept which is usually applied to countries with a fundamentally dynamic economy; it relates to an unsatisfactory process of allocating resources, not generating them. The main Soviet problem, on the other hand, lies in the creation of wealth, not in its distribution. Thus, the real choice confronting the Soviet leadership may be between bold reform with uncertain political

12. First in: *The Washington Post*, 3 August 1983.

side-effects or long-term economic decline, which beyond a certain point may be very difficult to stave off by reform. If the Soviet leadership chooses the line of least resistance and opts for yet another incremental reform, they could find that the illusion of muddling through could well become the reality of muddling down. A tentative but paradoxical conclusion to be drawn from this analysis is that the present impetus for reform in the USSR may be greater than we think it is from the visible evidence.

Summary of Discussion: Part I

The discussion centred mainly on agriculture, energy, defence expenditure and technology transfer.

It was noted that the poor performance of Soviet agriculture was above all due to faults in the economic system. There was no proper proportion between investment and profit and agricultural workers did not have sufficient incentive to improve production. This basic problem could not — as Maria-Elisabeth Ruban pointed out — be resolved by importing either grain or technology.

Reference was made to the qualitative decline of Soviet farming. Persons of mobile, adaptable character, with a taste for responsibility, were leaving the countryside. According to Karl-Eugen Wädekin, a reversal of this trend was scarcely to be expected. Private production was likely even to decrease as an element in the total yield. It could not yet be foreseen whether the government would encourage the private sector at a future date; in any case the middle and lower administrative cadres were hostile to it. Improvements in state production would only be possible if production units were made smaller and the heads of departments enjoyed some freedom of decision.

Karl-Eugen Wädekin thought there might in future be a shift towards increased imports of farm technology. To the question whether high investment in technology made sense in view of the low quality of agricultural labour, he replied that a certain degree of technology absorption could not be ruled out, though it clearly had its limits.

It was pointed out that US exporters had a strong interest in selling not only wheat but farming technology to the Soviet Union.

The discussion revealed differing views as to the importance of the energy sector to the Soviet economy and to foreign policy. Some speakers regarded Soviet autarky and the ability to export energy as a source of strength, others as a limitation. Wolfgang Pfeiler observed that it made a considerable difference whether a state had to import energy, was self-sufficient or had an export surplus. Autarky in respect of energy signified a high degree of defensive power. In any case the current position regarding energy was far more favourable from the Soviet leaders' point of view than it had been ten years ago.

John P. Hardt laid stress on the change from oil to gas in the

Soviet consumption of energy. He believed that gas would also be of increasing importance as a source of energy in the West. It was even possible that the Soviet Union would achieve a monopoly position with regard to gas supplies in the 1990s. Soviet credit prospects for the future were good, so that he expected to see intensified industrial co-operation, especially with Germany.

Those speakers, on the other hand, who were more impressed by the limitations of the Soviet energy sector laid stress on the demand aspect.

Robert Campbell saw the importance of energy as an element in national power, primarily in terms of the net profit to be gained from it. Soviet returns from this source would not be so high in future as in the past.

Jochen Bethkenhagen observed that the market for natural gas was very limited on the demand side. West Germany's requirements had settled at 15 per cent of total energy consumption. The Soviet share might come to exceed 35 per cent of total gas supplies. At the same time, Soviet oil export possibilities were limited. Altogether, the Soviet share in the foreign trade of the OECD countries would probably tend to diminish. Since the dependence was mutual, he warned against exaggeration and did not himself believe that the Soviet Union would become a major power in respect of energy in the 1990s.

Friedemann Müller emphasized the domestic limitations of the Soviet energy sector. He pointed to the ever increasing investment costs, especially in oil production, and the limited possibility of replacing oil by gas. He also doubted the feasibility of substantial energy savings. If there was a choice, Soviet capital investment would be devoted to expansion rather than rationalisation.

A number of questions arose with regard to Soviet defence expenditure. There was an acute need of information concerning variations in the rate of increase, their causes and the share of the GNP assigned to the military budget. Another important question was the ratio of Soviet to American defence expenditure and that between Soviet military and non-military production.

Michael Checinski referred to the varying estimates by the CIA and DIA as to the rate of increase of the Soviet military budget. He assumed that the dollar figures of Soviet defence expenditure published in the US were intended for domestic purposes rather than for scientific comparison. The CIA experts were highly professional, but they had to conform to the wishes of Congress, which, if only to save time, insisted on estimates in dollars rather than rubles.

Amnon Sella also stressed the political aspects of the CIA report. He pointed out that the report which had overestimated Soviet military investment dated from the time of Ford and Carter, whereas the latest one, in which that investment was underrated, was produced under President Reagan. In general, the CIA and DIA estimates were now in agreement.

Robert Campbell defended the CIA figures. They might often be used for political purposes, but they represented the best information available. He also wished to point out that the relationship between the military and the non-military sector of the Soviet economy had not as yet been adequately investigated from the scientific point of view.

Michael Checinski observed that the effect of the armaments industry on the Soviet economy as a whole was by no means entirely negative: for instance, much benefit accrued to the economy from technological developments in the arms field. Nor did he believe that defence took away many resources from the civilian sector. The defence industry already accounted for about 40 per cent of all capital investment, and it would be difficult to expand it further by taking away resources from another sector. Instead, it was to be expected that in the next decade the Soviet leaders would, in the first place, make use of concealed resources. Such resources would come, first and foremost, from rectifying the economic inefficiency that had hitherto prevailed in the defence industry itself: there was a usable potential here.

Jürgen Nötzold expressed the view that in the coming years the Soviet Union would not be able to keep up with the West in civilian technology, but that it would be able to do so in the defence sector. The assessment of productivity in research and development involved considerable basic difficulties: there was really no exact method.

Supplementing Dr Nötzold's remarks, Ronald Amann observed that, while several of the research institutes attached to the Academy of Sciences were of high quality, the position regarding technical progress and innovation was much less impressive in the branch research institutes.

The fourth and last section of the discussion was concerned with West-East technology transfer, where a lively argument took place with particular reference to Miles Costick's paper.

Criticism focused on the question of the cost to the West of introducing controls as advocated in the paper. In Jerry Hough's opinion three strategies were open to the West. Firstly, they could build a wall and eliminate the Soviet problem completely. Secondly, they could stop the leaks, but unfortunately such leaks were part and parcel of the democratic system, which involved the free exchange and circulation of ideas. If ideas were prevented from flowing outward, it would stifle democracy at home as well. The third possibility was to intensify the dialogue with the Soviet Union in respect of, among other things, technology transfer from West to East.

German experts considered that Dr Costick's picture of the situation was over-dramatic. Heinrich Vogel spoke of an 'overkill' of information policy, meaning a generalisation from particular cases to fit a chosen interpretation.

German participants also criticised the term 'illegally exported': this implied criminal action, and was not an adequate basis for discussion. It was doubtful whether, for example, the export of a chemical plant to Eastern Europe should be represented as a bad thing. The poison gas used by Iran had been produced in a pesticide factory, but no one would say that on that account the export of pesticides should be prohibited.

Ronald Amann said that the share of Western components in Soviet weapon systems was an insufficient basis for an evaluation of the whole situation. To begin with, Soviet imports of technology were small in extent, about 4–5 per cent of domestic investment. Secondly, the Soviets had generally taken delivery of turnkey projects, so that they would not have been able to further develop the technology in question. Thirdly, there had clearly been no macro-effects on the economy as a whole. He referred to estimates that imported technology was less productive than Soviet technology. There were widespread complaints in the Soviet literature of the inefficiency of Western technology. Finally, such technology was not used on any large scale in the Soviet economy, because the adaptation of Western technology gave rise to the same problems as innovation in the Soviet Union itself.

Claus-Dieter Kernig, referring to the example of IBM computers, said that the Soviet problem was not one of copying hardware or stealing software, but of mass-producing both. This problem was far from being resolved. The Soviet Union was not an advanced technological society: it was necessary to distinguish between an

141

élite which, under certain conditions, could handle the most advanced technology, and the mass of the population, with a very low GNP per head. The development of the Soviet system was planned in such a way as to acquire technology as cheaply as possible, which meant using every source of information in the world. This being the nature of the system, it was no use complaining that the Soviets acted accordingly.

The Soviets were and had always been able to procure from somewhere or other what they needed for strategic purposes. To introduce the controls demanded by Dr Costick would be contrary to the nature of the Western system.

Another German critic of Dr Costick's paper observed that not every technical innovation in the Soviet Union was derived from Western sources. In the strategic field, at least, the USSR had made sufficient technological progress on its own account. Thus, according to Heinrich Vogel, the transfer of an American licence had advanced by only six months the implementation of the precision control of Soviet MIRVs.

Dr Vogel also doubted whether the efforts of some sections of the American government in connection with the Export Administration Act would have the right effect, or whether they would do severe damage to Western co-operation in the fields of technology, weapon techniques and the civilian economy. The object should at all times be to take advantage of Soviet technological backwardness for the purposes of Western policy.

In reply to all these remarks and objections, Miles Costick once again expressed his concern over technological leaks. A tightening of controls was a matter of survival, not an economic but a political question. Referring to a speech by CIA director William Casey, he gave further examples of Western components being discovered in Soviet weapon systems. From conversations with former Soviet citizens belonging to the military-industrial-scientific complex he knew that there had been a directive by Kosygin instructing Soviet scientists not to use their own technological discoveries because they had no idea as to their cost-effectiveness.

Asked if he really thought that strategic export controls could ever be a substitute for arms control agreements, Dr Costick said that in his view shortages were the deciding economic factor. The more the Soviet Union was aided in particular spheres, the more economic reserves could be transferred to sectors to which the Soviets gave priority, i.e. the defence sector. If they were provided with the credit and technology for a gas pipeline, then they had less reason to develop their own capacity for that purpose and could devote it to the military-industrial complex. The end result was to push up American defence costs.

Jeremy Azrael warned Europeans not to misunderstand the US position in regard to East-West trade. The Reagan administration was in favour of mutually profitable trade with the Soviet Union on a commercial basis, but it had always reserved the right to control its own foreign trade policy. Economic sanctions would be used if they appeared more effective than military or other means. The US wished to co-operate with its allies in this, but would act unilaterally if necessary.

The US attached great importance to security controls in the case of defence-related transfers, but there were many grey areas in the definition of this term. None the less, it had been possible to stop a substantial number of leaks in co-operation with the COCOM governments.

PART II

Culture and Society

Introduction to Part II: Culture and Society
Wolfgang Pfeiler

The second part of the conference was concerned, in the widest sense, with the peoples of the Soviet Union. On the one hand, attention was devoted to quantitative changes and the available demographic data were discussed from various angles. Notice was taken of the age composition of the Soviet population and, more particularly, of the basic alterations in numbers as between the different Soviet nationalities. What long-term consequences were to be expected from the fact that the Slav and Baltic populations remained static while those of the Central Asian Republics were increasing at a significant rate?

Still more important than the interpretation of demographic data was the qualitative aspect of the problem: the outlook and way of thinking of the Soviet people, both the *élite* and the masses. The influence of Russian, non-Russian and specifically Soviet traditions was discussed, as well as the picture presented by current Soviet literature and the unhappy situation of dissidents. Attention was given to the function and structure of the Churches and the educational system, and above all the revival of religious ideas and traditions. Much interest was taken in the various manifestations of Russian, non-Russian and anti-Russian national sentiment.

The final contributions to this part of the conference were concerned with the state of Marxist-Leninist ideology. In addition to an expert analysis of the propaganda apparatus with which the CPSU continues to instil its ideology into the minds of the population, special attention was devoted to the changes discernible over the past two decades in the content and credibility of that ideology. The discussion centred here on the miscalculations in the CPSU programme of 1961, which is for the first time to be replaced by a new programme at the XXVII Party Congress in February 1986. Meanwhile, the promises of a Marxist Utopia have been reduced to absurdity by practical developments, a fact clear to all Soviet citizens including Party members. The main point for discussion here was the extent to which the Soviet people has taken this state of affairs to heart, and how the Party leadership is reacting to it.

6

The Soviet Citizen

The Soviet Citizen and his State: A Split Relationship
Reinhard Meier

The broad masses of the Soviet population are not in basic political opposition to Communist rule. The system as such is fundamentally questioned only by a few scattered and isolated minorities. The 'silent majority' perceives the political state of affairs, its mechanisms and rituals, as a sort of normality bestowed by nature and with which one must come to terms one way or another. The average citizen tends to be politically apathetic and gives hardly any thought to possible alternative social orders. In any event, the political conformity of the masses *vis-à-vis* state authority is wider and more deeply rooted in the Soviet Union than in most of the Communist-ruled East European countries.

Nonetheless, in everyday life the Soviet citizen's relationship to his society is not devoid of tension. More than anything else, the daily struggle for existence, with the accompanying frustrations resulting from a lack of material goods, frequently gives rise to annoyance, dissatisfaction and resignation. On this non-political level of everyday life and of personal material concerns, the harmony between the average Soviet citizen and the conditions of Communist reality is much more unstable and burdened with conflict. Such tensions find their expression in the many forms of passive resistance — withdrawal into one's own private niche, apathy, corruption, and the devising of skilful ways of cheating the state authority and its demands.

For this reason, most of the people in the Soviet Union, either

149

consciously or unconsciously, live in some sort of dichotomous relationship to the realities of the system. In broad sectors of the population one finds a diffuse emotional concordance with the basic tenets of the proclaimed ideology, with its ideals and its myths, especially when patriotic sentiments are awakened. Here I define 'patriotism' in a very wide sense, ranging from a non-political love of the homeland through the various levels of Russian and Soviet national sentiments, all the way to crude chauvinism. On the other hand, almost nothing remains of the genuine Communist enthusiasm, much less the mood of revolutionary renewal, which was once prevalent among wide sections of the population. In practical day to day behaviour, a person's attitude towards the system is characterised to a great extent by cynicism and by a nerve-racking small-scale war which he is forced to wage in order to secure his personal material needs.

To date, however, practically no ideologically conscious opposition to the system has developed among the politically weary masses. Nothing has grown from the isolated criticism and dissatisfaction over the insufficiencies of everyday life. Therefore, although one is able to recognise a few partial elements of conflict, it is impossible to ascertain any general or acute crisis between the normal Soviet citizen and the regime.

Of course, this is only a crude simplification of the relations between citizens and government. These relations are just as complex and diversified in the Soviet Union as they are in any society. In treating such a general and broad subject one can do no more than point out a few basic tendencies, which, moreover, do not lend themselves to precise verification. For we all know that in Communist countries there are no publicly accessible opinion polls conducted on such politically explosive subjects. I would also like to emphasise that my comments mainly concern the 'average Soviet citizen', whom I regard to be poorly informed and uninterested in political affairs. I am, therefore, excluding intellectuals and active supporters of the system, such as Party members and functionaries. This general assessment also does not take into account the specific problems of the various nationalities in the Soviet Union. However, I believe that the 'average citizen' and his attitude towards the system, as described in this article, are certainly no exception in the non-Russian Soviet republics.

Raissa Orlova, who together with her husband Lev Kopelev has been an involuntary exile in the West since 1981, recently wrote a book entitled *The Doors Open Slowly*. In it she compares the living conditions in her Russian homeland with the experiences she has had in the open societies of the West. In view of the many political demonstrations and protest activities she has witnessed, for example in West Germany, she poses the question: 'Why doesn't anyone in our country demonstrate on behalf of Sakharov?' The answer follows: a great many people never come to fight against the injustices of the system or for their personal political convictions 'because they have the feeling that others will not offer them any support'.

I believe that this insight is especially applicable with regard to foreign, national security and military policies. These areas are relatively abstract and difficult for individual persons to analyse. Here Soviet rulers can rely on a particularly wide, naïve and spontaneous support from among the general population. And so there is hardly any doubt that the majority of Russians saw the Soviet invasion of Czechoslovakia in 1968 as a necessary and timely measure — if not greeted with satisfaction, at least accepted without question. Similarly, the war in Afghanistan, if not popular, is at least most likely widely approved as a legitimate representation of Soviet interests. This probably also applies to the shooting down of the South Korean jumbo airliner in 1983. It can also be assumed that in the power struggle in Poland between the Communist regime and the independent workers' union, sympathies were by no means on the side of Solidarity. And in the broad East-West controversy over intermediate-range missiles in Europe, we believe that only a weak minority of Soviet citizens critically questioned the view taken by the Kremlin leadership.

What, then, are the conditions and driving forces behind this mass conformity? Here are three factors which I believe to play an essential role:

Firstly, the power of propaganda. In the West one generally tends to underestimate how effective the Kremlin's permanent indoctrination of Soviet citizenry, with its radically one-sided world perspective really is. As seen from the outside, the Communist mass media's portrayal of the international situation and of the Soviet Union's role therein may seem all too crude and transparent. However, this estimation does not do justice to the effect which the propaganda has domestically on the average citizen. A young Moscow acquaintance of the present writer, someone who is critical of the system, confessed that he was forced to expend a great deal of intellectual energy simply in forming his own opinion independently of the comprehensive barrage of views emanating from the official propaganda machine. Of course, not even the great mass of Soviet people believe everything which is propagated by the system's megaphone, but a great deal of the basic drone which is focused on a person from the cradle to the grave does remain in his consciousness. I have often noticed, particularly with average Soviet citizens, that despite the personal disappointments they have experienced, a certain basic trust in the advantages and the security of the Soviet social system as seen against the background of 'Capitalist conditions' has remained intact. And knowing how vigorously the Western problem of unemployment is thrust into Soviet propaganda, this is not at all surprising.

Gaining access to information which contradicts the official tune requires substantial effort and the average citizen has very little opportunity for this — partly due to the time required simply to see to his or her own basic material needs. And it is well known that the system does a great deal to impair a person's access to critical information. During and after the Polish crisis, the Soviet government resumed its jamming of Western radio broadcasts. In the 1970s the West had made considerable inroads on the Soviet information monopoly, but now this access has once again been drastically reduced.

A second factor is the persistent persecution or elimination of all domestic influences and voices which might possibly frustrate the Party apparatus's total claim to power and opinion-building, thereby endangering the conformity of the masses. Harsh oppression is effective here, but more subtle means are equally efficient, such as threatening to withdraw material or professional advantages if a person's loyalty is found to be inadequate.

A third factor working towards an uncritical, naïve identification of the Soviet citizen with the system, perhaps the most significant factor of all, is the way in which the concept of the Communist empire is progressively embedded within the idea of the continuity of Russian history. The result of this is an extensive fusion of Russian and Soviet sentiments. The regime has been highly successful in mobilising the traditional patriotism of the Russian people and in using it to form a binding commitment to the system. World War II left a deep impression on the national consciousness, and this meant a decisive breakthrough for the system. Stalin dispensed with all of the previous ideological reservations against using Russian-national slogans. Instead, he intentionally invoked the greatness of Russian history and the love of 'Mother Russia' and thus stimulated popular resistance to the enemy invaders. Since then, memories of World War II have been inexhaustibly kept alive; this is achieved thanks partly to the greatest possible propagandistic efforts. Along with the October Revolution and the figure of Lenin, victory in the 'Great Patriotic War' is today one of the central elements of Communist mythology.

It is interesting to note that immediately after the October Revolution, the religious philosopher Berdyayev predicted that the Soviet regime would take on Russian tradition and its sentimental values and use these for its own purposes. He wrote then:

> In its fall, Old Holy Russia has made room for an empire which is also holy, a theocracy in the wrong sense. Marxism is neither of Russian origin nor does it have Russian features. Yet, this ideology will pick up the old style and gradually take on the characteristics of Slavophilism. Red Communism will bring the old dream of the Slavophiles to reality: to make Moscow the nation's capital city instead of St. Petersburg. Communism will claim the motto of the Slavophiles and of Dostoevsky for its own: Ex Oriente Lux.

It is particularly these Russian-Messianic aspects of the Soviet regime — perhaps to be interpreted psychologically as compensation for a certain national inferiority complex — which still find considerable resonance among broad sections of the population. Indeed, the attractiveness and fascination of this mythical view of Russia as the saviour of the world is also evidenced by the fact that its dedicated adherents include a number of dissidents — I mention only Solzhenitsyn here — even though they espouse these ideals in anti-Communist tones.

The lack of deeply-rooted democratic traditions in Russian history has also favoured the process of adaptation and conformity to the Soviet system. As people, Russians possess a number of endearing qualities, but during my stay in Moscow I did not often encounter a genuine understanding for the democratic practice of showing tolerance for people of differing political persuasions — even among critics of the regime. A remark which I find to be typically Russian came from Bukovskii's mother, the brave Nina Ivanovna. After emigrating from the Soviet Union and arriving in Zurich, she was confronted with the constant pluralistic conflict of Western public opinion. Disappointed and uncomprehending, she

153

cried: '*U vas net edinstva* — Here in your country there's no unity!'

The identification of patriotic feelings with the Soviet regime, a phenomenon which presents relatively few problems to many Russians, is beyond doubt quite different from the situation in most of the other countries in Eastern Europe, where the Communist system of rule is perceived as something imposed upon them and bolstered through external pressure, as a factor which impairs the development of their own national identity. The Soviet citizen may, it is true, be worse off in many respects than the average citizen in East Germany or in Hungary. However, from the point of view of the internal legitimation of the system and of psychological harmony between the people and the regime, a significant difference probably rests on the question of whether the country occupies the status of a dominating power or that of a satellite. In other words: the Soviet Union's role as hegemonic superpower supports the common man in Russia in his national pride, whereas in the so-called fraternal countries there is little reason for such subjective harmony; quite the contrary.

Now, it would be a mistake to imagine that the average citizen in the Soviet Union is an impassioned political activist or even an observer following domestic and world political events with an eager interest. A much more accurate assessment would be that, generally speaking, he is apathetic to these things. The system's mass political rituals, such as the First of May or the annual celebration of the Revolution, are hardly perceived as manifestations of active politics, but instead as ingredients of national folklore. Of course, this only serves to promote the popularity of such celebrations. People are moved much more by problems and interests within their own personal spheres than they are by high-level politics, which offer them no opportunities for participation anyway. This is the area in which the average apolitical citizen's dull and passive consensus of feeling with the Soviet government is subject to the greatest amount of stress. The most explosive and vulnerable points here are at the level of the satisfaction of material needs. Here, even the politically apathetic person is directly confronted with the contradiction between the beautiful world proclaimed by official propaganda and the enervating insufficiencies of profane reality. These burdens are powerfully depicted by the Russian author Yurii Trifonov in his novel *The Exchange*. (The plot deals with the exhausting struggle of a small family living in Moscow who want to exchange their single-room flat in a communal apartment complex for a modest apartment located separately.) Still, I do not see any reason to believe that such disillusionments could one day be transformed into conscious political opposition to the Communist system. At least this doesn't seem likely among the broad masses of the Soviet population.

With everything we know of the efforts involved in acquiring material goods and of the usually very constraining limits placed on personal development, it would still be grossly inaccurate to think that all the people in the Soviet empire continually perceive the conditions of their everyday life as an unendurable hell. A variety of individual and private niches blossom within the framework of the system, and within these people manage to create a quality of life in a peculiarly Russian way. And the cramped material conditions undoubtedly foster more intense inter-human relations; these are often missed in prosperous Western societies, with their hectic pace of life. The American journalist Lois Fisher-Ruge, in her recently published book *Everyday Life in Moscow* quotes a Russian acquaintance of hers as follows:

> Don't write about our country so that one is led to believe that everyone is unhappy. That is simply not true. Just like in any country, there are people here who are happy and others who aren't. In order to be happy in our country, you have to observe the rules of life which apply here. Those who do so are successful. But those who know the rules but don't live according to them or who try to change them live in fear and perhaps get into trouble.

This is not to make light of the problems existing between citizens and the regime. Apparently the basic consensus of conformity to the system is much less to be taken for granted among today's youth, who are known to be very materialistically orientated. This is in contrast to the middle-aged and older generations, who were still marked by the optimistic mood of renewal in the early years of the Soviet Union and by the binding experience of the 'Great Patriotic War'. Beyond any doubt, the intelligentsia's relationship to the system is utterly broken and inconsistent. In sum, I still maintain the validity of my thesis: internal political pressure is presently much less a burden to the Soviet system than other dangers, such as the coherence of the empire in Eastern Europe, the power rivalry with the United States or acute economic and structural problems.

Generational Change: In Search of a Post-Stalinist Identity
James H. Billington

The concept of a generation is notoriously vague and elusive in social science, but there are times when the mere physical fact of a difference in age makes an important psychological difference and is likely to have a profound effect on politics and on everything else. Such is the nature of the split between the Stalinist and the post-Stalinist generations in the Soviet Union. The fact that the USSR has experienced nearly two decades of political immobilism and has been in the habit of choosing ever older leaders has served merely to delay — and probably make more potentially disruptive — the transition to the post-war, post-Stalinist generation in the Party.

Even if the problems of deferred maintenance at home and of overextension abroad were not serious, the problem of moving to the new generation would itself pose enormous problems. From Malenkov to Chernenko, the USSR has been led for more than thirty-one years by protégés of Stalin who brought violent collectivisation to the peasantry, terror to everyone, and blood purges to their colleagues before sharing, with the population they had brutalised, the suffering and eventual victory of the Second World War. It was an age of big deeds on a large scale, of horror as well as heroism, which created a clear sense of identity as well an instinct for self-preservation and the endless rationalisation of atrocity and deception in the name of remote goals.

Such are the workings of the cunning of reason, however, that the surviving Stalinists have created an altogether new mentality by giving to the post-war Soviet Union a period of unprecedented and sustained peace, relative prosperity, improved education and extraordinary dullness — leading to a taste for small deeds and a hostility to remote goals. The Stalinist establishment that has ruled Russia since the war represents a kind of peasant mentality, miming both the tsarist aristocracy and the old intelligentsia — with Marxism-Leninism as a sort of intellectual labour-saving device. Their children now represent a kind of spoiled privileged class within a new generation formed by radically different influences.

There are, I believe, two controlling impulses within this generation. The first is the search for efficiency — something which attracts at a simple human level all types of people from ordinary workers to sophisticated scientists: a search not just for more consumer satisfaction but for more private autonomy, more common sense and simple integrity in the workplace. The regime has tried to co-opt and control this 'creeping pragmatism' in a Soviet society under the ideological rubric of the 'Scientific and Technical Revolution', but this simple, post-ideological search for efficiency cannot be satisfied by any abstract, state-sponsored campaign, let alone remote ideals or slogans.

Far more important, both emotionally and politically, is the search for identity among the young. As nationalism comes increasingly to replace communism as the glue holding the Soviet empire together, and as national consciousness grows among so many minority nationalities, the classical question of Russian national identity has assumed renewed importance and taken the form of a search for a post-Stalinist Russian identity within the post-Stalinist generation. This search has its political origins in Khrushchev's 'secret speech', which denounced Stalin's intra-Party crimes and thereby destroyed the key Stalinist myths of Kremlin infallibility and apostolic succession.

By the late Khrushchev era, however, it had become clear that no serious explanation was to be provided of Stalin's crimes, no restitution made to the victims and no structural guarantees provided against a recurrence. Many thinking people concluded (and a few publicly proclaimed) that the Soviet system was neither self-corrective nor capable of defining a worthy identity for a post-Stalinist Russia. The cutting edge in this important task thus moved beyond official channels into the 'second literature' and the 'second academies'.

Within the new, better educated generation, the old Russian tradition of a truth-seeking intelligentsia quietly revived and acquired new importance by taking over the process of de-Stalinization that Brezhnev had artificially arrested. Unable to play a political role in the present, they sought to recover the past as a means of preparing for the future. In the course of the 1960s they systematically restored vital links with three of the roots of Russian culture that had been all but destroyed during the Stalin era: literature, religion and rural life.

Older writers who had returned from the camps (Solzhenitsyn, Shalamov) or from forced exile (Pasternak, Nadezhda Mandelstam)

157

provided models for the young and exposure to a literary tradition of authentic moral passion. The discovery by many young people of their half-obliterated, thousand-year legacy of Orthodox Christianity (often through unorthodox sects or antiquarian curiosity) reminded many Russians that there was an indigenous alternative to socialist realism in the arts and to Party expediency in morality. And the rediscovery of rural Russia by students and writers was a kind of act of restitution to the forgotten peasantry on whose backs Stalinist collectivisation and industrialisation had been so brutally accomplished.

By seeking links with the countryside, urban intellectuals also moved beyond narcissistic preoccupations to broader social concerns — often via societies for the preservation of the environment or historical antiquities. In the late 1960s and early 1970s, there was a perceptible move towards greater social relevance, though not towards politics. The centre of literary gravity moved from histrionic poetry readings to the more biting and contemporary medium of satirical plays. An oral counter-culture developed around protest songs on the guitar, while cheap tape recorders kept alive alternative versions of history and folklore through *magnitizdat*. Finally, there came a kind of civil rights movement — seeking evolutionary reform rather than foredoomed revolutionary protest, trying to overcome isolation by forming small groups, building on the Helsinki agreement of 1975 and infusing the cause of human rights with a moral passion and idealistic purity that is perhaps only possible among those who know what it is like to have lost them.

'Cursed be the land that must live without heroes', Galileo's young follower cries out to his young audience after his idol had recanted before the Inquisition in the great production of Brecht's *Galileo* which played at the Taganka theatre back in the Brezhnev era. Galileo, played by the dissident folksinger Vysotskii, slowly replies in a moment of electric silence: 'Cursed be the land that always has *need* of heroes.' For a while, a small group of heroes seemed to be exorcising that curse — and moving beyond the fear that had been so all-pervasive in the Stalinist past.

In the final lines of *Filming a Movie*, another popular play of the period performed in the Komsomol theatre just off Red Square, an old historian reflects on the humiliation of having constantly to change his writings to suit the authorities and concludes: 'The most awful thing is not that evil people are so powerful, but that others are so afraid of them.' One seemed almost to detect the outline of a new ideal in the change from 1963 to 1973 of the professions most admired by the graduating class of a high school in Novosibirsk: from soldiers, astronauts and physicists to doctors, writers and historians.

However, in the late years of the Brezhnev era the plays were taken off and the dissidents destroyed, while most of the leading figures in the quest for identity either died or were driven into emigration, exile, or silence. If Brezhnev halted de-Stalinisation, then Andropov introduced new elements of surgical sophistication into the repression — reviving terror as a credible instrument of domestic policy without returning to the numbing effects of Stalin's indiscriminate state terrorism. No one should ever have underestimated the power or the resourcefulness of Soviet leaders in dealing with dissent using a wide spectrum of techniques: crush and confine, disorient and divide and even, selectively, co-opt and adopt.

A repressive reaction to dissent (and a political hard line generally) is usually to be expected when there is a period of relatively weak, committee-type leadership. In systems where the transmission of authority is not legitimised by popular elections, there is a tendency to rally round the tomb and to present a stern face to the outside world. And the possibility of a chauvinistic, autarkic answer to the search for identity cannot be ruled out.

Two crucial questions must be answered, however, before one can dismiss the possibility that the new ideas within the coming generation may not produce some real changes in the Soviet system.

The first question is: Did the dissident phenomenon represent only the tip of the iceberg, the more important part of which may still be frozen and invisible within the system — beneath the surface? I believe the answer is a guarded yes. The growing interest in religion and in rural life (witness the controversy over the *derevenshchiki* in literature) show that even the supposedly archaic elements in Russian culture may have modern appeal in the context of the drab urban environment and spiritual emptiness of the Soviet 'new class'.

The even more important and elusive second question is: Will a new generation of leaders, once in power, identify solely with the semi-Stalinist political system through which it will have to emerge? Or will it come to identify, at least in part, with the higher moral aspirations and de-Stalinising quest that has been so important to its own generation?

One reason for assigning no enduring significance to the ferment of the late Brezhnev era is the undoubted cynicism of much of this new generation, particularly of those with access to power. There may, however, be the ghost of a once and future morality behind much of this cynicism. The original cynics were the most moral of men in pre-Christian antiquity, as they may prove to be in post-Christian modernity. For cynicism is morality in search of a home: Diogenes in search of an honest man; and the example of honest men in the recent Soviet past may have more to say to the future — even to those in power — than we can presently imagine for three fundamental reasons.

(1) If for no other reason than to sustain the economic basis of its military power, the Soviet leadership must before long cope with its own peculiar form of energy crisis: the *human* energy crisis. A new generation of rulers, lacking the authority born of wartime memories, will almost certainly have to find new ways to motivate an increasingly frustrated and better informed population.

(2) To elicit fresh effort and sacrifice from their own generation new leaders will have to satisfy the thirst for identity as well as for efficiency. This search for identity is no longer exclusively the preoccupation of an 'intelligentsia' *élite*, the wider concern of a better educated population as a whole (at least in the urban centres). The search for identity is pursued by those who also seek efficiency within (and with support from) the new technological culture; and the ferment is now so rich that it seems likely to outgrow the bounds of old-fashioned anti-urbanism or Slavophile chauvinism within which Western observers have often tried to confine it.

(3) Finally, and most importantly, there is the simple psychological need to make some sense of all their suffering. Untold millions (forty million at least) of their fathers and mothers, uncles and aunts, have been killed by unnatural means (wars, purges, collectivisation etc.) in the Stalin era. There is a profound, long-suppressed desire for a fuller accounting than has yet been offered — as well as for some measure of restitution and a guarantee against recurrence. The more the surviving Stalinists try to revive repressive methods, the more powerful and extensive the demands for renewed de-Stalinisation are likely to be when they finally surface within the new generation of leaders.

This pent-up desire to find an identity beyond Stalinism is unlikely to lead to movements or institutions that will follow Western models precisely, and the ability of the outside world to affect the process is very limited. However, I would argue that the trauma has been so great and the emerging situation so unprecedented that future developments are unlikely to follow any traditional models. The major changes almost certain to come in the next decade could simply be changes for the worse; but there could also be changes for the good. These changes will probably vindicate neither Sakharov nor Solzhenitsyn, but they could surprise those in the West who automatically assume that the ideals of these two are irreconcilable and even irrelevant to the future of Russia.

7

Intellectuals

Literature Between State and Opposition
Wolfgang Kasack

The relationship between the Soviet state and Soviet authors is a controversial one, and opposition is a necessary outcome of this relationship. The state is totalitarian; its guiding principle lies in binding the people to Party opinion, or *'Partiinost'*. This official line, anti-religious, anti-transcendental and non-creative, confines and constrains all intellectual activity. The author, on the other hand, is a priori creative; his ethos consists in expressing his own opinion, his personal view. He illuminates his experiences and searches out all types of phenomena, including the transcendental. Metaphysical matters lie at the core of all art, and often the author's most crucial desire is to investigate the metaphysical. In his works he sets out a number of points of view; after all, the use of contrast is an intrinsic method of creating art. On principle, however, the Soviet ideological system does not tolerate multiple points of view. In consequence, the author is opposed to the state. This phenomenon cannot be eradicated, since it is built into the system.

Of course, not every professional writer in the Soviet Union is opposed to the state. On the contrary, authors such as Markov, Mikhalkov, Dolmatovskii and Chakovskii turn out a certain kind of routine work which espouses the state ideology. In their wake is a virtual army of thousands of comparable writers; my own estimate puts them at about 8,500 currently. However, the contemporary Russian literature which is recognised internationally, in as far as it originates in the Soviet Union today, is not represented by such authors, but instead by others such as Rasputin, Trifonov, Mozhaev, Bitov, Soloukhin, Iskander, Kaverin, Tendryakov and Ait-

163

matov. These literary figures constitute a kind of latent opposition. They have adapted to the system externally while portraying situations in their works in a way which more or less deviates from state propaganda.

Open opposition is a stance which has been taken at one time or another by all those authors forced to live away from their homeland today. I mention first of all a few world-famous figures once hailed by the state as outstanding representatives of Soviet power and who — compelled to make a break with the system — are now rejected: authors such as Aksionov, Nekrassov, Solzhenitsyn, Voinovich, Vladimov; film directors like Lyubimov and Tarkovskii; conductors and musicians such as Rostropovich and Barshai.

I would like to take up Paul Roth's idea: from the state's point of view, if literature is objectively of high quality it must necessarily contain 'false' information. The state must therefore perceive such literature as a basic threat, always scrutinising it closely and considering to what extent it might be more convenient to suppress it. In order to deal with such matters a censorship agency, 'Glavlit', was formed as early as 1922. Today Glavlit is a secret organisation. It subjects every printed work to a triple preliminary censorship and to unlimited censorship after printing. By definition, the censor is opposed to the author. The struggle between the two is a permanent one.[1]

Let us take a brief look at some of the more important Russian authors who are currently living here in Germany. I am thinking of such writers as Georgii Vladimov, Lev Druskin, Fridrikh Gorenshtein, Lev Kopelev, Vladimir Voinovich, Igor Burikhin and Boris Shapiro. Shapiro, incidentally, is one of the few Soviet authors living abroad who is bilingual. He writes in German as well as Russian, just as Jossif Brodskii (who has been living in the United States since 1972) also writes in English.

I would like to concentrate on the question: when and how did these authors come to break their allegiance to the Soviet state? In

1. The Soviet Union's supreme censorship authority is the Central Committee of the Communist Party of the Soviet Union, in particular its ideology and propaganda division. After the Revolution, the state censorship authority was established by the 'Press Act' of 1 November 1917. The special authority 'Glavlit' was created on 6 June 1922 and still exists today. Glavlit is an abbreviation for *'Glavnoe upravlenie po delam literaturi i izdatel'stv'* ('Main Administration for Literature and Publishing Affairs'). This abbreviation has remained customary, although the institution's name has changed. It is now called *'Glavnoe upravlenie po okhrane voennikh i gosudarstvennikh tain v pechati'* ('Main Administration for the Preservation of Military and State Secrets in the Press'). This secret agency is formally a subdivision of the State Committe for Press Affairs of the Council of Ministers of the USSR.

other words; when did their opposition begin, or wher did it become open?

Take, for example, Lev Kopelev. We know he was a convinced Communist who welcomed the 'thaw' in the wake of de-Stalinisation, believing it to be an achievement of the Party. When his era expired in the mid-1960s, he began to take a critical view of life in his country. He published his letter 'Is it Possible to Reha bilitate Stalin?' in Vienna in 1968. After this foreign publication he still made efforts to reconcile his personal convictions with Party opinion. But the gap was already too wide. When he took a stand in support of other 'dissidents' and 'oppositional persons' such as Siniavskii and Daniel (1966) and Galanskov and Ginsburg (1968), and when he continued to adhere to the Party line of the years 1956–61 which acknowledged Stalin to have been a dictator and a tyrant, this led to a break with the system. Kopelev lost both his job and his Party card in 1968. His publications were banned in the Soviet Union, while his treatises on German language and literature, as well as his autobiographical works, were published abroad. In 1977 he was expelled from the Writers' Association, and finally emigrated in 1980.[2]

The present writer spoke with him after his arrival in Cologne. At that time he continued to think in terms of perhaps being allowed to return home. He refused to see himself as an outcast, just as in the thirty-five years since his first arrest at the end of the war, he still thought it might be possible to bridge the gap between his oppositional attitude and the Soviet system. He was unable to understand why he should be subjected to the same treatment which had been meted out to all his predecessors during the third wave of emigration.

Boris Shapiro, born in 1944, is a contrasting example. This poet, who lives today in the cities of Tübingen and Regensburg, studied physics, logic and stylistics at the University of Moscow from 1961 to 1968. Together with a few other students of the natural sciences, all about twenty years old, he organised a circle of lyrical poets

2. Lev Zinovievich Kopelev, born on 9 April 1912 in Kiev. Scholar of German language and literature. As a Communist Party member, he worked during the war in the propaganda division and was imprisoned from 1945–55. His popular scholarly books on Goethe's *Faust* (1962) and on Bertolt Brecht (1966) were criticised by conservatives. Publications in the USA include *Khranit'vechno*, 1975, in German: *Aufbewahren für alle Zeit*, 1976 (*Save for All Time*); *I sotvoril sebe kumira*, 1978 in German: *Und schuf mir einen Götzen*, 1979 (*And Created for Me a False God*); *Utoli moya pechali* 1978, in German; *Tröste meine Trauer*, 1981 (*Console My Sadness*); *Ein Dichter kam vom Rhein* (*A Poet Came from the Rhine* — biography of Heinrich Heine), 1981.

there. They called themselves '*Klenovii List*' — 'The Maple Leaf'. This wholly non-political group existed for two years. They hosted a number of events, including two poetry festivals lasting three days each. During these festivals, poets alternated in reciting their pieces for about ten hours each day. The poets were all science students who wished to share what they had written with other young people before it had been seen by any censor. They hoped for recognition and were willing to listen to criticism. These poetry festivals were not organised by the state and had not been previously cleared by the Party. 'The Maple Leaf' also established a poetry theatre, somewhat in the tradition set by Kharms, a non-futurist poet active in the 1920s. Unlike Kharms, though, they did not venture into the absurd. The theatre was a straightforward symposium of various poetry readings. There were four highly successful performances. However, in 1966 either the Party or the KGB intervened and forbade this activity. How could these young people, with their artistic enthusiasm, have not been disappointed by this strong rebuff? How could they have helped but be driven into opposition to the state? Shapiro himself had written his poems, as it were, without the 'internal censor' and had therefore not published a single work in the Soviet Union. He rejected Boris Polevoi's offer to write a couple of lines of topical political poetry which would have served as introductions to the poems (that is, in Yevtushenko's words, to hitch them to a 'locomotive engine'.)[3] In 1971 the authorities prevented him from defending his doctoral thesis; this drove him further into opposition. A Jew, he finally emigrated from the Soviet Union in 1975. Here, too, we see a case in which a person gradually grew away from the system, forced to do so because of state measures directed against poetic and literary activities. In Shapiro, however, one does not see the tendency towards self-deception typical of the older generation.[4]

3. See Yevgenii Yevtushenko, *Wo die Beeren reifen* (*Where the Berries Ripen*), Vienna, 1982, p. 220: 'You need a locomotive engine.' 'What sort of locomotive engine?' Krivtsov was quite honestly astonished. 'Any sort of short poem with ideological content which pulls along everything else in its tow . . .'
4. Boris Israilievich Shapiro, born on 21 April 1944 in Moscow. After emigrating to West Germany in 1975, Shapiro earned his doctorate in physics at the University of Tübingen. Shapiro was first made known to the German readership in 1981 with a volume in German: *Metamorphosenkorn* (*Grain of Metamorphoses*). In addition to translated poems, this collection includes poems which Shapiro wrote in the German language after having come to Germany. In *Solo na flete*, Munich, 1984 (*Flötensolo* — *Flute Solo*), Shapiro compiled his most important Russian poems from a period of over two decades. The manuscript of a volume of new German poems, *Ein Tropfen Wort* (*A Drop of Word*), was finished in 1984.

The next two Soviet authors to claim our attention are perhaps already known from press reports. Although quite different from one another, they have become equally famous; they are Vladimir Voinovich and Georgii Vladimov. At one time, both were respected Soviet authors. The former now lives near Munich, the latter in the Frankfurt area.

Voinovich discovered his own unique style in his satirical novel *The Memorable Adventures of the Soldier Ivan Chonkin*. This was around the year 1963, when the novel was published in samizdat form.[5] After some time, parts of the work appeared in the Frankfurt magazine *Grani*, and in 1975 the entire book was published in Paris. In 1974 Voinovich was banned from the Writers' Association. As we can see from his autobiographical story *An Incident in the Hotel Metropol* (among other works) the state made repeated efforts to persuade him to relinquish his oppositional stance and to attract him back into the fold of obedient Soviet writers. The authorities subjected him to massive pressure and made attractive offers. But none of the authors mentioned here sold out. Voinovich fought for his right to remain in the country. Although he took an energetic stand in support of oppressed authors, he tended to avoid the most severe confrontations. By 1980 he had completely exhausted his options. He was forced to emigrate (or allowed to; both formulations are equally accurate).[6]

Georgii Vladimov's story, with regard to his position as an author *vis-à-vis* the state authority, is a similar one. A young man of twenty-five, he worked as a prose editor for the Soviet magazine

5. Samizdat literally means 'self-publisher'. The term is linguistically analogous to gosizdat ('state publisher'), and originated in the mid-1970s to signify private literary and publication-related production and distribution in the Soviet Union as a substitute for publications of books or magazines which are suppressed by the state censor. A number of significant works of modern Russian literature have reached the West via samizdat. See W. Kasack, *Lexikon der russischen Literatur ab 1917 (Dictionary of Russian Literature after 1917)*. Stuttgart, Kröner 1976, pp. 331–2.

6. Vladimir Nikolaevich Voinovich, born on 26 September 1932 in Stalinabad. His first story 'Mi zdes' zhivem' ('Wir leben hier' — 'We Live Here') appeared in 1961 in the magazine *Novi mir*. The novel he began to write in 1963, *Zhizn' i neobichainye priklyucheniya soldata Ivana Chonkina*, in German: *Die denkwürdigen Abenteuer des Soldaten Iwan Tschonkin*, 1975 (*The Memorable Adventures of the Soldier Ivan Chonkin*), was just as unfit for publication in the Soviet Union as was the satire *Ivan'kiada*, 1976 (German: *Iwankiade*, 1979), a work of documentary prose concerning Voinovich's struggle to obtain his apartment in Moscow. Another documentary story characterised by ironic detachment is his meeting with the KGB, described in 'Proisshestvie v Metropole' (printed in: *Kontinent*, Paris 5.1975 — German: in: *Kontinent*, deutsch 3. 1975). A sequel to the Chonkin novel appeared under the title *Pretendent na prestol. Novye priklucheniya soldata Ivana Chonkina* in 1978; in German: *Iwan Tschonkin Thronanwärter*, 1983 (*Ivan Chonkin, Successor to the Throne*).

Novyi mir and to became acquainted for the first time with genuine literature. *Novyi mir* was then the country's most important literary publication and was relatively liberal by Soviet standards. There, he saw the manuscript of Pasternak's novel *Doctor Zhivago*, and also had access to Vladimir Dudintsev's *Man Does Not Live by Bread Alone*. As editor of this book, Vladimov was forced to reconcile the conflicting authorities of censor (Glavlit), Party officials, editors and the author. As a result, Vladimov, as a young man, was thrust into the forefront of the struggle between author's truth and Party lies. He saw the false promises which the state authorities made in their efforts to prevent Dudintsev from moving into open opposition. The course of developments befalling Vladimov's most significant and best-known book *The Story of the Faithful Dog Ruslan* reflect the process of his own gradual detachment from the state and his move into 'opposition'. This novel originally existed as a short story. Tvardovskii agreed to print it, but suggested that it was actually the stuff of a *'povest'*, a short novel. Vladimov then withdrew it for reworking, and the story circulated as a samizdat.

Three years passed. In 1964 Khrushchev was toppled from power and the Party line changed. By the time *Ruslan* was finished as a novel, it was no longer eligible for publication. Then, in 1977, when the authorities failed even to inform Vladimov that he had been invited to Frankfurt, he withdrew in protest from the Writers' Association. This was something new in the Soviet Union, an unprecedented form of opposition. Vladimov then joined Amnesty International — an organisation which was not, of course, approved by the state — and led its Moscow chapter, also leading a struggle against the authorities on behalf of a number of persecuted individuals. In 1983, with German assistance, he and his wife narrowly escaped arrest and were allowed to emigrate. Vladimov is thus one more author who underwent a gradual process of alienation (over a period of about twenty years) characterised by a continuous growth in tension and culminating finally in emigration.[7]

7. Georgii Nikolaevich Vladimov, born on 19 February 1931 in Kharkov, became known in the Soviet Union through his novels *Bol'shaya ruda*, 1961, and *Tri minuti molchaniya*, 1969, in German: *Das große Erz* and *Drei Minuten Schweigen* (*The Great Ore* and *Three Minutes of Silence*); the latter was strongly criticised by the official press and publication as a book was not possible until 1976. (Uncensored version, Frankfurt, 1982). *Vernyi Ruslan* appeared in the West in 1975, in German: *Die Geschichte vom treuen Hund Ruslan*, 1975 (*The Story of the Faithful Dog Ruslan*). Shortly before emigrating he published a realistic, satirical story, also in the

As far as other authors are concerned, I will confine myself to brief descriptions: Fridrikh Gorenshtein, now living in Berlin, had written in the underground for about two decades. He had been able to publish only one story in the Soviet Union. That was in 1964; after that, not a single line of his was allowed to appear in print. He then became a film writer. Eventually, he was no longer able to endure writing only for himself and for the desk drawer. He released his works for publication in the West, and they have been appearing here since 1977. With his short novel *Steps*, which because of its religious character did not get past the censor, Gorenshtein was one of the authors represented in the famous collective edition *Metropol*. That was in 1979. He emigrated one year later.[8]

Lev Druskin wrote poems which were not objectionable to anyone. He was allowed to publish seven volumes of poetry. This tolerance was based in part perhaps on sympathy for his handicapped condition: he is severely paralysed. But in his diary he wrote the truth — the fates of fellow authors, the machinations of functionaries, realistic scenes from everyday life in the Soviet Union and poems based on his own personal experiences. A police informer who had deceived him and gained his trust prepared for a search of his home by the KGB. They confiscated the diary and part of his library, everything in past which was regarded as 'oppositional material'. In the same year, 1980, Druskin was allowed to leave the country under humiliating circumstances (none of the civil employees present were allowed to assist the wheelchair-bound man when he boarded the plane.[9])

West, about the KGB's spying on a satirical author: 'Ne obrashchaite vnimaniya, maestro', 1983 (German: 'Schenken Sie dem keine Beachtung, Maestro — Don't Pay Any Attention, Maestro').

8. Fridrikh Naumovich Gorenshtein, born on 18 March 1932 in Kiev, published only the story 'Dom s bashenkoi' (German: 'Das Haus mit dem Türmchen — The House with the Little Tower') in the magazine *Yunost'* in 1964. The novel *Iskuplenie*, in German: *Die Sühne (Atonement)* appeared complete in 1979 in German and in a shortened version in the Jerusalem magazine *Vremya i my*. The drama *Berdichev* also appeared in the same publication in 1980 (nos. 50–1). In the Salzburg almanac *Neue russische Literatur*, nos. 2–3 (1979–80) the stories 'Kontrrevolyutsioner' (German: 'Der Konterrevolutionär' — 'The Counterrevolutionary') and 'Tri vstrechi s Lermontovim' ('Drei Begegnungen mit Lermontow — 'Three Meetings with Lermontov') were published in German and in Russian. Two larger novels *Psalom* (German: *Der Psalm — The Psalm*), written in 1974–5 and *Mesto (Der Platz — The City Square*), written in 1969–76, have not yet been published.

9. Lev Savelevich Druskin, born on 8 February 1921 in Petrograd. Books of his poetry appeared in the Soviet Union, for example in the years 1961, 1964, 1967, 1970 and 1974. After emigrating Druskin published various single poems in the magazines *Kontinent, Vremya i my* and *Grani*. Poems translated into German appeared in 1983

Igor Burikhin came from Leningrad. He became known in the West through Shemyakin's collective edition *Appollon '77*, which included his poems and a commentary by Maramsin. His religious poetry has never been released in the Soviet Union. During the 1964 Brodskii trial, which drew world attention, he was forced into opposition when his interpretation of Brodskii's poems circulated as a samizdat.

Like Shapiro, Burikhin was not allowed to defend his doctoral thesis. Also like Shapiro, he never deluded himself as to the system's true face. His knowledge of religion matured over the years, but for a long time he failed to recognise that it was impossible to reconcile independent intellectual activity with the practices of the Soviet state. He was permitted to leave his homeland in 1979.[10]

Despite their varying ages, all of these authors have one thing in common. In each case, love of literature, high regard for the integrity of the writer and self-respect in maintaining and standing up for one's own opinions led to conflict with the state. The end of the 'thaw', around 1963–4, certainly played a role in each of these authors' personal developments, but other political events also had their effect.

As regards the older authors who had already earned respect in their homeland, the break with the system was based in part on their declarations of solidarity with other persecuted persons. This form of protest, often collective, first emerged after the Pasternak affair. This was when Soviet intellectuals began to realise that they had more in common with Pasternak than with the state which was persecuting him.

My descriptions have been confined to Russian *émigré* writers currently living in Germany. This is an arbitrary selection, yet it offers general insights. If these individuals are compared to important writers currently living in the USSR, such as those mentioned at

---

under the title *Mein Garten ist zerstört* (*My Garden Has Been Destroyed*). His autobiography appeared in 1984 in London under the title *Spasennaya kniga. Vospominaniya Leningradskogo poeta* (in German: *Das gerettete Buch. Erinnerungen eines Leningrader Dichters* — *The Book That Was Saved. Memoirs of a Leningrad Poet.*

10. Igor Nikolaevich Burikhin, born on 3 October 1943 in Troizkoe, in the Vologda region, completed his studies of German Language and Literature at the Institute of Theatrical Sciences in Leningrad. His first published poems appeared in the anthology '*Appollon '77*' in Paris. Poems have been printed in the magazines *Kontinent, Grani, Vremya i my* and others. His first published book was the cycle of poems *Moi dom slovo* (German: *Mein Haus ist das Wort* — *My House is the Word*), Paris, 1978.

the beginning, then the two groups differ from one another only in the degree of their detachment from the state. Censorship prohibits those who have remained in their country from writing the full truth, and yet they have found literary methods and forms which contain a great deal of truth about life in the Soviet Union and which penetrate the true depths of human existence. These writers occupy a position somewhere 'between opposition and the state'.

Is the term 'opposition' an appropriate one? Certainly, seen from our political point of view. For the attitude of these authors is contrary to that of the state, which insists on acquiescence to the Party line. But democratic ideas such as these do not exist in the USSR. I have often noticed that Russian authors, when they are in the West, refuse to speak of themselves as 'oppositional forces' or even as dissidents or nonconformists. If one offers them a different term, *inakomyslyashchii*, (one who thinks differently) after some hesitation they reject this too. People who think differently? No — we are *myslyashchie* — thinking people.

This thinking opposition cannot therefore be eliminated. It is true that the state has rid itself today of many of its most prominent writers. They either live abroad or are under arrest — but tomorrow there will be others to take their place. They already think independently, they write in a way which does not conform to the wishes of the primitive functionaries and their censors who have no appreciation of art; these authors already occupy an oppositionist stance. The intellectual process cannot be stopped. It is even strong enough to be able to derive its nourishment from the opposition. The Soviet Union has existed long enough for us to have forgotten many former holders of state power. But those authors who were pressured into opposition or even murdered live on in their works.

Dissidents
Cornelia I. Gerstenmaier

The scope and severity of oppression in the Soviet Union have reached the highest level in decades. Tracing this development, one is aware that the current situation began to take shape years ago. A closer examination, however, reveals that the elimination of human rights movements in the USSR began in the mid-1970s, precisely the period following the signing of the final accords on European security and co-operation in Helsinki.

Yurii Andropov, as former director of the KGB, had already proven his organisational talents. Compared to his predecessors, he worked with more differentiated methods and greater flexibility. The so-called provisional solution to the Sakharov case, in which the scientist was banned to Gorky, was probably worked out in the KGB under Andropov's aegis. In his capacity as chief of the security police, Andropov was bound to the directives of the Kremlin leadership, to which he himself belonged, having been a member of the Politburo since 1973. As such, he was obliged to orientate his activities to the framework of *détente*, in so far as the Soviet leadership chose to make a few meagre contributions to this for a time.

These contributions included issuing emigration permits for several hundred thousand Jewish Soviet citizens, a concession the United States had achieved via negotiations. In the wake of these emigrations, a number of non-Jewish critics of the regime were also permitted to leave the Soviet Union. Thus, several aims were achieved with one stroke. Firstly, the USSR, in exchange for technology, most-favoured-nation status in trade and other measures of essential importance to the country, rid itself of several thousand citizens who represented a partly acute, partly potential irritant to the state. Moreover, in taking this step, which at first was heatedly disputed within the Kremlin, the regime created the impression in the West of a certain liberalisation in its outlook, perhaps even a new respect for human rights. It seemed to imply that 'the Soviet Union is now letting its critics emigrate (whereas it used to arrest them), and is therefore showing political generosity'. No one noticed that at the same time countless opponents of the regime were arrested and that a large proportion of the Jews who wished to emigrate were not allowed to. Moreover, this was a measure by which the Soviet authorities successfully weakened the human rights movement in their country. If this movement had been quite cohesive in the 1960s, it began to fragment during the 1970s. When the option of emigration was made available to these individuals, the group promptly split into two factions: those willing to emigrate and those who believed they could work effectively only in their homeland.

In retrospect it is clear that as a result of this temporary option, the human rights movement changed its profile and was, in the final analysis, weakened — partly through the decimation of its membership through emigration, and partly by the change of emphasis: one was compelled to choose between emigrating or holding out. The authorities had presented a number of those emigrating during the 1970s with the option either of leaving their homeland or going to jail. At the very least, they would have been permanently prohibited from working and would have been subject to material deprivations and administrative pressures.

During the 1970s political trials continued to be held in rapid succession, and by the beginning of the 1980s it was evident that human rights activists were by no means the sole targets of persecution: members of the wider critical intelligentsia were subjected to pressure. These included academics (for the most part scholars in the humanities) who took a differing point of view from the Party line, as well as artists. Some of those persecuted had at first been completely apolitical. It was necessary merely to belong to a group which practised yoga or was involved in parapsychology, feminism, unofficial Marxism or the anthroposophic movement. A Lithuanian anti-alcoholism group was persecuted and driven into the underground, and the Committee for the Protection of Invalids, an association which worked in complete conformity with the system, suffered the same fate.

In recent years, nearly all the highly disparate groups which once constituted the loosely federated democratic movement of the 1960s and 1970s have either been destroyed or driven underground. Take, for example, 'SMOT' ('Free Inter-professional Association of Working Persons'), a workers' union founded in 1978. Like its predecessors, this association was never allowed to grow into a mass organisation. Many of its members were sentenced to long prison terms. In 1983 the twenty-nine-year-old physicist and poet Irina Ratushinskaya and the mathematician Valerii Senderov each received twelve-year prison sentences.

Now, the 'Group for the Building of Trust Between the USSR and the USA', an association formed in 1982 by scientists, artists and physicians, has been placed under severe pressure. This unofficial peace movement had organised cells in several Soviet cities, collected hundreds of signatures, conducted private seminars in which questions of peace were discussed and had published a number of pertinent articles in samizdat form. However, as a result of their demand for disarmament *on both sides*, members of this association were soon dismissed from their jobs or subjected to house arrest, compulsory psychiatric treatment or imprisonment.

The Helsinki groups, formed in 1976 and 1977 in the five Soviet Republics of the RSFSR, Ukraine, Lithuania, Georgia and Armenia, were put out of action through the arrest or expatriation of their members. The best known of these, the Moscow Helsinki group, having lost nearly all of its members through persecution, discontinued its activities in September 1982, under pressure from the authorities.

Altogether, nearly fifty members of the Soviet Helsinki groups, whose goal it had been to examine the enforcement of human rights provisions contained in part 3 of the Helsinki Final Agreement, were subjected to severe restrictions on their personal freedom during the 1970s: the sentences imposed on them total 220 years of prison camp and 125 years of banishment.

Emigration movements, including Jewish, German, and to a lesser degree Armenian emigration, were radically reduced, not least through the arrest of their protagonists. In 1983 the number of emigrants of German ancestry declined to 1,447 — the lowest number in twelve years (in 1976 the figure was 10,000). Jewish emigration, at a quota of 1,307 in 1983, was at its lowest level in twenty years. In 1979 alone 51,320 Jews had been allowed to leave the USSR.

Since the autumn of 1979, the number of imprisoned critics of the regime and persons wishing to emigrate has nearly doubled. Since then there have been around 200 known arrests each year, although the actual number is unquestionably much higher. As a result of the ever decreasing transmission of information, little news on this subject ever reaches the West. Professor Sakharov's deportation to Gorky in January 1980 dealt a severe blow to the human rights movement.

Freedom movements in the USSR have always been subjected to

persecution. However, during certain periods this persecution was noticeably less severe than it is today, both with regard to the number of imprisonments and to the severity of the sentences imposed. The upshot is that Soviet citizens are today condemned for 'offences' for which they would not have been indicted during the late 1960s and for almost all of the 1970s.

For almost ten years, until 1973, the KGB leadership and the Politburo seem to have underestimated the strength and significance of the entire dissident phenomenon. In the early autumn of that year a massive campaign, including propaganda, was initiated against human rights activists. There had already been a heavy wave of arrests in the Ukraine in 1972. For a number of reasons, having to do not least with the country's image abroad, this campaign was not as successful as the Soviet authorities had wished. At that time the reaction in the West was a great deal more one of outrage, both in the media and at the political level.

The Soviet leadership showed itself willing to make concessions. This was not only in the area of Jewish emigration, but doubtless also had something to do with the Conference on Security and Co-operation in Europe, which the USSR had long been preparing for and by which the government hoped to realise specific interests and goals.

Punishment, at least for political prisoners, has grown continually more severe since the Helsinki agreements were signed. During Andropov's rule all sorts of human rights activities were denounced as the product of conspiracies instigated by American or Western intelligence agencies. It is true that this had already been claimed in 1978 in the trial against the Jewish activist Anatolii Shcharanskii, but it was not until Andropov that Soviet human rights activists were branded *en bloc* as CIA agents. One of the leading and most fervent proponents of this argument is the historian Nikolai Yakovlev; his book *CIA Against the USSR* has a circulation totalling several million. Yakovlev has also seen it as his special responsibility regularly to denounce Andrei Sakharov and his wife. With unusual openness, he also propagates the thesis that the dissident movement in the USSR is a direct outgrowth of the de-Stalinisation process of the late 1950s and early 1960s.

Beginning in the autumn of 1979, renewed massive clean-up activities were instigated against the dissidents, apparently in connection with the approaching Olympic games in Moscow and Andropov's preparation for seizing the party's highest office. This met with relatively mild criticism in the West and since then Moscow has continually stepped up the severity of domestic repression. A myth had sprung up in the West to the effect that Andropov was something of a liberal and a reformer. In actual fact, during his short rule the wheel of history in the human rights field was turned back by several decades. Within fifteen months, the now deceased Party boss had not only succeeded in placing individuals from the security apparatus in key positions and in leading areas of the administrative bureaucracy. He is also to be credited with a number of legal extensions and amendments, particularly in the area of penal law, which restrict the Soviet citizen's right more than ever before. The Decree on the Borders of the USSR, which aimed to make them impenetrable, and the Decree on the Workers' Collective were both approved. The latter is directed, not least against any incipient signs of self-management among workers and seeks to prohibit groupings such as those which led to the Solidarity movement in Poland.

Even more serious, however, is the addition of two paragraphs to Soviet law, or to the penal code of the union Republics. These permanently establish a system of terror which, although already practised under Stalin, was at that time illegal, since no such provision had been made in penal law. Article 188, paragraph 3 of the Penal Code of the RSFSR came into effect in October 1983. It allows for imprisoned persons to be punished for so-called malicious disobedience and given additional prison sentences of up to five years. It is of course an easy matter for the prison camp administration to provoke any type of disobedience. With this new law, prisoners are left almost completely at the mercy of the prison governors.

On 1 February 1984 an additional law came into effect which flagrantly violates the Helsinki agreements. With the introduction of Article 75, paragraph 1 to the Penal Code of the RSFSR, it is unlawful to pass on official secrets to foreign organisations. For this offence the law provides for prison terms of up to three, and in special cases, eight years. It has not been clarified what is meant here by official secrets. In any event, it is absolutely certain that this most recent law permits even greater state despotism than before, for a totalitarian system can classify almost any piece of information as an official secret, regardless of whom it is given to. Therefore, any economic or statistical data which are not published in the USSR could be defined as secret information. This might also apply to other information, such as news of natural of environmental disasters.

Finally, paragraph 70 (concerning anti-Soviet agitation and propaganda), under which countless critics of the regime have already been condemned, has been given greater scope. The new version gives a legal basis to the practice of prosecuting acts of charity, that is charitable assistance accorded to political prisoners and their dependents.

These and a number of other extensions and changes clearly demonstrate that criminal prosecutions can be expected to increase. Prison terms will be lengthened and categories of so-called crimes against the state' will be given broader definition. However, the fact that various human rights groups — national, religious and other freedom associations which for a time were allowed to operate openly, are today, as in the 1950s, forced into the underground, does not mean that dissident activity has ceased to exist in the USSR.

As always, considerable amounts of samizdat materials of varying types reach the West, although the flow of periodicals, such as the famous *Chronicle of Current Events*, has nearly dried up. The era of collective protest letters has also practically ended. Nonetheless, the 'dissident' phenomenon will continue to exist, especially in light of the fact that certain taboos have been broken for the first time during the past two decades. There will be dissidents as long as the regime fails to eliminate the causes of potential unrest. However, it is not possible at this time to make a prognosis as to the extent and forms of possible future dissident movements.

8

Churches and Religion

Religious Revival
Donald W. Treadgold

In discussing religion and the role of the churches in the Soviet Union one might refer to at least three inter-related topics. Firstly, the condition of religious belief and practice in the various faiths concerned. Secondly, the situation of religious dissent or dissent with a religious component and thirdly, Soviet governmental policy towards religion.

I shall concentrate on the third area with some references to the other two. The former General Secretary, Konstantin Chernenko, addressing a plenum of the Central Committee in June 1983, stated: 'Our constitution guarantees freedom of conscience. Communists are steadfast atheists, but do not thrust their views on others.' Furthermore, he admitted that religion was influential among what he called 'a not insignificant part' of the Soviet population. And in a pamphlet and book issued in his name in 1978 and 1982 he seems to suggest that the fight is against religion rather than against believers, that the spread or atheism is to be awaited from 'drawing believers into an active social life' and that 'any violations of believers' feelings will only lead to the strengthening of religious fanaticism'. Now I do not hold that Chernenko was a closet consumer of racy Western novels, Scotch whisky or rock music, or was any kind of lib-eral, as was unsuccessfully argued by some with regard to Andropov. Nevertheless, these positions were sufficient to lead Keston College on 23 February 1984 to express a cautious hope not that religious discrimination or persecution would come to an end in the Soviet Union but at least that it would level off.

In the 1977 Constitution, Article 52 reads: 'Freedom of conscience, that is, the right to profess any religion and perform religious rites, or not to profess any religion and to conduct atheist propaganda, shall be recognised for all citizens of the USSR.' Thus, there is no right to conduct religious propaganda and none is permitted; and this of course has been true for a long time in the Soviet Union. And the Reverend Trevor Beeson in the updated version of his book puzzlingly entitled *Discretion and Valour*, the standard manual on the subject of religion in the Soviet Union and Eastern Europe, in English at least, writes: 'There may well be secret laws or instructions which are more specific on this point . . .', that is on the conduct of religious propaganda and on what that phrase is construed to mean. In general, we need to remember that the Soviet regime may choose not to send the police to impede the right to perform religious worship by a given person but may nevertheless discriminate against that person in ways that do not involve trial or sentencing or any kind of legal or indeed formal punishment. Some of the most important aspects of anti-religious policy in the Soviet Union are extra-legal. They are often subtle, so subtle that visitors such as Billy Graham for example, are unable to perceive any religious oppression at all.

There have been several periods of severe, even savage oppression of religion and of direct attacks on religious persons and institutions — under Lenin, under Stalin and under Khrushchev, though there was also a milder period with regard to religious policy under all these. Khruschchev's persecution, the most recent one, lasting from 1959 to 1964, saw for example a reduction in the number of Russian Orthodox churches, from 11,500 to 7,500 according to one estimate. When the persecution ended, there were only two ecclesiastical academies, three Orthodox seminaries, six monasteries and twelve convents remaining in the entire Soviet Union. And from the little we know about the institutional basis of other religions in the Soviet Union, we can certainly affirm that religious practice generally rests on very fragile foundations.

For Jewish rabbis there is of course no training institution in the Soviet Union; in fact, there is only one in the entire Communist world and that is in Budapest.

For over forty million Muslims, among whom, as we know religion and ethnicity are very closely tied and mixed, there are two training institutions for mullahs, both in Central Asia. There is a centre for Buddhism at a site near Ulan-Ude, though exactly what kind of training goes on there seems unclear. For Roman Catholics, strongest in Lithuania of course, there is one seminary for the entire Church. The Lithuanians are a people in whom national feeling and religion are almost as closely intertwined as in Poland. And it is rumoured that in recognition of this fact it was Bishop Steponavicius who was the secret cardinal created *in pectore* by Pope John Paul II in 1980. The Evangelical Christians and Baptists have no seminary, but one is planned; a Lutheran seminary exists in Riga. The Uniats of course have been suppressed entirely so they survive only in the underground, in conditions obscure to the outsider.

Without doubt there has recently been a religious revival. A journalist writing in *Izvestia* in October 1982 stated that the majority of the Soviet people were not influenced by religion, but that in a number of churches — and several are enumerated — 'one may see young people at services. It has become stylish to marry in church, baptise one's children, and to wear a cross'. He denies that a religious renaissance is taking place, perhaps partly because that phrase has been used by Christian activists, but admits the growth of interest in religion and the Church and tries to explain this as being due not to any desire for religious consolation, but to the need to understand the role of religion in the past and its role in contemporary ideological struggles. Nevertheless, he adds, fashion is fashion, acknowledging by implication that he, as a militant atheist, doesn't like it.

So, there clearly is a revival. It may in turn create pressure to sharpen the entire religious policy of the government. Since the 1960s there has been a rise in religious dissent. In the 1970s a number of committees were formed for the defence of the rights of believers, concentrating on legal and constitutional questions. A series of discussion groups, focusing on the substance of theology and religious doctrine were also organised. Some of these groups were formed by specific churches, notably that organised by Father Dmitri Dudko, who was subsequently arrested, publicly recanted — and privately recanted his recantation, or so I'm told. Some of these discussion groups, however, were independent of any institution — the 1978 Christian Seminar on the Problems of Religious Renaissance, led by Alexander Ogoradnikov being a case in point. Ogorodnikov reputedly began his conversion from unbelief to Christianity by seeing a film while studying at the Institute of Cinematography. The film was Pasolini's *The Gospel According to Saint Matthew*. After hearing about this fellow named Jesus, one thing led to another. There is no doubt that the works of foreign Christians have become much coveted on the black market. C.S. Lewis and G.K. Chesterton are doing quite well in Russian samizdat translation, it seems, and a second-hand Bible may fetch a month's salary on the black market.

For those who remember the initial pages of *Das Kapital* where Marx gleefully speaks at length about the Bible as a commodity, one is indeed tempted to speculate as to what he would make of it if he knew that in the Marxist Soviet Union the Bible is now doing quite as well as a commodity.

A general crackdown on dissenters, including religious dissenters, began in 1979 and 1980 and the number of Christian prisoners today is estimated at just over 300. Some of those prisoners include people who have appealed to foreign religious agencies. Since 1961, of course, the Russian Orthodox Church has belonged to the World Council of Churches. One has to say that the Soviet regime has got a certain amount of mileage out of permitting the Orthodox Church and other Churches in the Soviet Union to join this body, as we saw at the Nairobi assembly in 1975 and the Vancouver assembly in 1983, when the WCC refused to discuss religious persecution in the USSR.

Let me sum up: There remain, of course, many convinced atheists in the contemporary Soviet Union. Other unbelievers are curious about belief or attracted to belief; one may cite an answer given to a Soviet sociologist studying this, from his standpoint, terrible phenomenon. He asked of someone: 'Do you believe in God?', to which the response was — '*Boga net, a chto-to takoe tam est*', that is: 'There is no God, but something or other is out there.' This kind of view, of course, troubles zealous atheist propagandists and agitators no end. As for the believers, they are enjoying the taste of what Jacques Maritain has called 'the great spiritual fruitfulness of the abyss', and have experienced the advantages of persecution which the early Christians learned about many centuries ago.

Religion and the Role of the Churches
Otto Luchterhandt

If one investigates the significance of religion and the role the Churches play within Soviet society, one quickly encounters the thesis that a rebirth, renewal or renaissance of religion is currently taking place in the Soviet Union. There are a number of questions which emerge:

(1) Does such a 'rebirth' — whatever that might mean — actually exist? If so,

(2) What are its most important features?

(3) Where are its causes and driving forces to be found?

(4) What significance should we ascribe to this phenomenon within the context of the post-revolutionary evolution of Soviet society? What perspectives result?

(5) In particular: what effects is the religious renewal having on already-existing religious communities?

(6) How is the state reacting to these tendencies?

In the short space allotted to me I can of course address only a few remarks to these questions.

Is there really such a thing as a current rebirth of religion in the USSR?

This question can be answered in quite different ways by the individuals affected, both in the West and in the USSR. There are those voices who speak almost euphorically of a renewal, of a broad religious awakening. Others, and here I do not mean steadfast atheists, reject the claim that religion is currently growing in strength and significance. They discard those indications which seem to support the idea as superficial manifestations of a passing fashion. Still others arrive at more or less differentiated points of view. Here, too, the truth may lie somewhere in the middle.

Judging from outward appearances, indications of a religious renaissance in the Soviet Union are scarce. Despite documented new admissions of places of worship, the total number of churches declined further during the 1970s. The network of churches today has become extremely fragmented, particularly within the RSFSR. The Russian Orthodox Church's façade-like presentation in Moscow, once described by Ernst Benz as a sort of 'religious open air museum', is certainly no yardstick to measure current conditions in the Church. A side note: the church specially constructed in Talinn for the Olympic games has meanwhile been converted into a lighthouse!

And yet it is accurate to say — and I intentionally express it in general terms — that for some time now religion has enjoyed a renewal of interest among some sectors of the Soviet population. Of course, this applies only to minorities. The picture becomes clear only when a number of events and developments are combined like stones in a mosaic. The renewal is revealed, for example, in the fact that religious subjects are currently being treated in the writings of several Soviet authors. Moreover, sacred art and music exert a strong attraction, the wearing of religious symbols has become fashionable and the level of participation in religious services has risen sharply (particularly among the youth). Most importantly, there is now widespread interest in religious information, theological literature and the Bible. Questions of religion and religious ethics are being discussed more frequently, and a broad thematic spread of sacred subjects is emerging in religious samizdat. Finally, and not least, one must mention the religious resistance which emerged in the period 1965–75.

If the characteristics of this growing openness towards religion are examined from a sociological perspective, one observes — at least with regard to those parts of the country with a predominantly Christian background — that this openness is greater among young people than in the middle-aged generation, much stronger among the intelligentsia than among workers and the rural population, focused more in the large cities and heavily-populated areas than in the countryside. Furthermore, the overall phenomenon is composed of a number of highly varying developments and events and is therefore closely associated with equally diverse aspects of 'the socialist way of life'. Finally, it is essential to note that the growing interest in the religious dimension is unanimously documented not only in the Christian parts of the country, but also in areas where Islam and even Buddhism predominate. In other words, one finds this phenomenon at least in the larger nationalities of the USSR.

These structural characteristics lead one to conclude that the developments observed do not merely indicate a few transient phenomena which have been randomly associated with one another. Instead, they are to be seen as signs of a comprehensive, far-reaching social and intellectual process of fermentation within modern Soviet society. This brings me to a description of the causes of the so-called religious revival.

The fact that some elements of the population are now turning to religion is, in my view, based on a number of highly diverse causes. Not least, it must certainly have to do with man's eternal search for God and for the meaning of the world and his personal place therein. At the same time, the newly emerging interest in religion and in religious values, artifacts, communal forms and a specific brand of intellectualism is also and quite essentially part of a cultural reorientation and search for identity currently taking place among the country's intellectual *élite*. It cannot be considered separately from the general course of developments now affecting the various nationalities living within the Soviet state. One may thus analyse and interpret the religious renewal as being a manifestation of each nationality's strengthened consciousness of its own socio-cultural identity and of the search for a deeper and unique historical dimension. And it is equally valid to regard the turn to religion as being one of many positive reactions to the substantial deficits and weaknesses evidenced by official Soviet culture, its ideological machinery and aesthetics. In short, a reaction to the Soviet 'way of life' as it actually exists. I might briefly summarise the causes and motivating forces of the religious 'rebirth' as follows:

(1) Marxism-Leninism has reached its demise as a world view. It subsists on the dead, unproductive material of social and institutional mechanisms which serve only to reinforce the regime's authority. Those who benefit from the system — ideological functionaries, power politicians and careerists — publically propagate the emptiness of these ideas through their uninterrupted exploitation and devastation of intellectual life, thus making their society's moral crisis more severe.

(2) Many people have been left unsatisfied in their search for answers to the essential question of the meaning of life. This creates a need for a secure moral orientation which the Party, with its moral relativism, cannot provide.

(3) Soviet society has taken on an increasingly dichotomous, even schizophrenic character. On the one hand, there is the façade, the outward public approval of the system. However, this approval goes hand in hand with the proliferation of a number of unofficial alternative cultural forms, a dual economy and widespread private escapism and nonconformity. As a consequence, people in the Soviet Union have grown accustomed to swinging back and forth

between public conformity and inner rebellion; indeed, this behaviour has long been second nature to Soviet citizens.

(4) The various peoples which constitute the USSR are observed to be ever more conscious of their respective national identities. This is understandable, especially in view of the standardisation of life styles brought about by technological and industrial development and by the processes of Sovietisation and Russification. The concern for national identity seems to be rooted among the new *élite* of the national minorities, and this *élite* is mobilising forces of resistance.

(5) Soviet society is becoming increasingly diversified and stratified. Life styles and attitudes are becoming more 'bourgeois', more 'individualised', especially among the privileged social classes. This applies particularly (in an extended sense) to the intelligentsia living in heavily populated urban areas.

In summary, it can be said that the turn to religion is based on internal factors which are related to specific social conditions — quite unlike the resurgence of religious sentiments and needs during the Second World War.

Considering the importance of the 'renewal' of religion and, in particular, its relationship to established religious communities, I find it highly important to make a careful distinction between the spontaneous social movement towards religion and the religious communities themselves. Although the two cannot be completely separated from one another, not least because they are both bound to the question of nationality, they are indeed distinct phenomena with regard to their social consequences. To describe it graphically, the two circles intersect.

Thus, it cannot be surprising that the government will react to all of this with increasingly repressive official policies, in particular religious policies. This is all the more likely against a backround of growing nationalism — with its political implications — which goes hand in hand with the religious renewal.

In conclusion, I would describe the role of the Church in the Soviet state in the following terms:

(1) Religious communities currently exercise an ambivalent influence on Soviet society. On the one hand, they serve to integrate the individual into the Soviet system and are thus forces of stabilisation. However, because they encourage sub-systemic social diversification, they also serve to promote change within and even disintegration of the system.

(2) It can be established that religious communities, most importantly those of the Russian Orthodox Church, are firmly integrated into the system. In fulfilling their cultural function, which is recognised, supervised and controlled by the state, they serve as instruments of Soviet foreign policy and mobilise patriotic feelings. Therefore, in many respects they adhere to state ideology, both theologically and in their world view.

(3) The churches function, in part, as integrating factors in Soviet society. This is because they provide individualistic spiritual relief for the many forms of schizophrenic ambivalence and alienation — an outgrowth of the Soviet 'way of life' — from which many suffer.

(4) On the other hand, religious communities are motors of social diversification, since they also encourage forms of national resistance. A case in point is the Catholic Church in Lithuania. In part, these communities call for a closer association with 'Western' values and offer many individuals an independent intellectual basis of behaviour. These persons are thus able to take up a personal struggle against the system and to work actively for basic change.

9

Nationality

The Nationality Question and the Soviet System
Gail W. Lapidus

The fundamental challenge which the nationality question poses for the Soviet system is not so much the potential threat of political disintegration but the ways in which it constrains and complicates the management of a series of key problems. This essay will briefly survey seven key areas in which the multinational character of the Soviet Union and particularly the superimposing of political-administrative boundaries on ethnic ones, creates major dilemmas for current Soviet institutions and policies.

The Problem of Legitimation

In no aspect of Soviet life today does the national question raise more critical problems than in that crucial realm involving the legitimation of the Soviet system itself. The rise of both Russian and non-Russian nationalism, coinciding with a decline in the vitality and relevance of the official ideology, exacerbates what has been a long-standing and fundamental problem in Soviet political culture; namely, the tension between the internationalist ideology of Marxism-Leninism, which validates key features of the Soviet multinational state, and the unifying force of Soviet patriotism, which derives much of its power and appeal from its association with selected strands of Russian nationalism.

Despite the apparent contradiction between the two, it is precisely the fusion of Marxist-Leninist ideology with its powerful sense of historical mission and its universalist perspective, with selective elements of traditional Russian political and cultural nationalism, reinforced by the global aspirations and satisfactions of superpower status, that form the core of Soviet civic culture and endow it with both dynamism and mass appeal. The inherent and inescapable tension between these orientations is simultaneously an asset and a liability for the Soviet system. It makes it possible to elicit the support of Russian and non-Russian political *élites* alike, but also risks provoking the dissatisfaction and alienation of both. The fine-tuning required to negotiate the necessary but delicate balance is made exceptionally difficult by the atmosphere of political uncertainty and competition that accompanies a political succession, particularly one involving generational change at the apex of the Soviet leadership.

The Problem of Political Control

The nationality problem creates additional difficulties in maintaining a pattern of political rule that combines the centralisation of power with responsiveness to local demands. The Soviet federal system simultaneously promoted the centralisation of power in the hands of a largely Slavic *élite* while providing a framework for, and legitimation of, the assertion of local demands and the opportunity for indigenous *élites* to play important roles in governing their regions. The efforts of these *élites* to enhance the power and the resources available to them produces a pattern of 'crypto-politics' barely visible to the outside observer, involving efforts to expand the power and autonomy of republic governments, to gain greater access by republics to central decision-making organs, particularly Gosplan, to acquire greater influence over these decisions, and to expand the share of indigenous cadres in republic, state and Party institutions — efforts which have provoked growing concern at the centre.

The Problem of Economic Reform

The multinational and federal Soviet system also complicates the optimal management of current economic problems. It is a serious obstacle to centralised planning and management and to the treatment of the USSR as a single economic entity: the republics cut across natural economic regions, they enhance the leverage — however limited — of local national *élites* in promoting local interests, and they add an affective dimension to the interregional competition for resources and power.

Yet the very potency of the symbiosis between regional and ethno-national interests is itself a barrier to the decentralising economic reforms which would give the Soviet system a much needed flexibility in deploying resources. The costly experiment with economic decentralisation under Khrushchev, as well as the experience of Yugoslavia in the 1970s undoubtedly reinforced the conviction of the Soviet economic and political *élite* that any dispersal of decision-making, however essential to elicit initiative and make more effective use of hidden reserves at the local level, would only compound the endemic problems of localism and subvert central economic priorities.

Regional demographic trends further compound these economic dilemmas. Rapid population growth in Central Asia, coinciding with stable or declining birth-rates in the more developed European regions of the country, increase the pressure for a reallocation of resources to the southern regions to maintain living standards and social infrastructure at existing levels, to expand the irrigation system needed to sustain its agriculture, and to soak up a growing labour surplus. However, the 'ethnic factor' also undercuts the operation of conventional economic levers in producing an optimal allocation of labour resources among regions, sharply raising the economic and social costs of policies designed to increase labour mobility.

Language and Cultural Policy

The status and recognition accorded various nationalities, whether in the treatment of their languages, histories, cultural monuments, or customs and traditions, is yet a further source of policy problems for the current Soviet leadership. Language policy is a particularly sensitive issue, demanding a delicate balance between the need for Russian language competence as an instrument of national integration and scientific-technological development, and a realistic assessment of the durability of, and attachment to, national languages.

191

Nationality and the Armed Forces

The 'national problem' impinges most directly on the core security concerns of the Soviet state in its consequences for the efficacy and the reliability of the armed forces. Soviet management of the ethnic dimension of military policy reveals a high sensitivity to its impact on military performance. The presence of ethnic friction and tension within the armed forces has evoked explicit calls in Soviet military publications for more decisive measures to curb discriminatory attitudes and practices and to expand 'internationalist and patriotic' education within the armed forces. The inadequate knowledge of the Russian language by non-Russian conscripts, particularly those from Central Asia, and their poorer educational and technical qualifications, have prompted a current campaign to expand and intensify Russian language instruction in Central Asia. Finally, ethnic stratification within the Soviet military, and the prevalence of units in which non-Slavic troops are commanded by Slavic Officers, are recognised to be a built-in source of tensions. There is a clear effort underway to step up the recruitment and training of officers of non-Russian nationalities and to combat attitudes prejudicial to their promotion.

National Identity and the Policy Process

The unexpected durability of national identities not only creates obstacles to the realisation of important goals but also vastly complicates the entire Soviet policy-making process. Recent research by Soviet ethnographers has called into question the assumption that economic development in a socialist society would automatically produce fundamental behavioural and attitudinal changes leading to the erosion of national differences. It is increasingly clear that national identity is not merely a 'dependent variable' in the modernisation process but has an independent and reciprocal impact on economic and social behaviour and on attitudes, a finding which has far-reaching ramifications for Soviet policy-making. As a distinguished Soviet ethnographer has suggested: 'If this conclusion is true, it means that there can be no universally valid means of improving ethnic relationships. A given technique may lead to different and sometimes even directly opposite results in different social groups.'

The Nationality Question and Domestic/Foreign Policy Linkages

Throughout its history, the Soviet regime has been highly sensitive to the double-edged nature of the linkages between domestic security concerns and foreign policy objectives created by the multinational character of the Soviet state and by the strategic position of minority nationalities on the Soviet borders. Soviet nationalities and foreign minorities have in the past been an important asset in expanding Soviet influence and power beyond its frontiers. At the same time, their presence is also a source of vulnerability: at a minimum, a constraint on domestic policy; at a maximum, a channel for outside penetration. Under these circumstances, Soviet policy makers face a real challenge in maximising the exploitation of these assets while at the same time insulating the Soviet system from contagion from abroad.

Thus, even if the Soviet system retains its considerable capacity to seal off domestic developments from external influences, and even if the emergence of ethno-national movements with separatist goals remains a highly unlikely prospect — whether in Central Asia or in other regions of the USSR — the nationality issue will raise increasingly difficult problems of management for the Soviet leadership in the decade ahead. It will constrain and complicate the resolution of many of the key problems which the Soviet system faces in the 1980s and will compel the Soviet leadership to make difficult, costly, and even unwelcome choices among a limited range of policy options.

Nationality problems
Gerhard Simon

Today, one no longer asks the questions: 'Does the fact that the Soviet Union is a state of many peoples mean that there is a potential for crisis!' — or 'Do nationality problems place a burden on domestic stability?' Instead, the pertinent questions now are: 'How severe is the crisis potential which is rooted in the USSR's multinational character? How serious are multinational conflicts with regard to the stability or instability of that society?' The second question is: 'What measures has the Soviet leadership developed to manage these conflicts?' And the third question: 'Will political measures developed in the past continue to be adequate to guarantee the existence of state and society in their present forms?'

Firstly, how severe is the crisis potential? The nationality question is one of the central problems of contemporary Soviet society. The stability of that society as a whole depends essentially on the Soviet leadership's ability to manage such conflicts. These conflicts cannot be resolved. The problems which result from the fact that one-half of the Soviet population is non-Russian pose a threat to stability which is just as serious as the reduction of economic growth and the ideological crisis. The Soviet leadership is forced to respond to and become politically active in each of these areas. If it fails to do so, it will become passive and developments will take their own course. This would mean loss of power.

Political leaders and social scientists alike are well aware of the situation. One of the leading Soviet ethnographers, Kozlov, notes 'with great concern' *(ser'eznaya trevoga)* that in the year 2000 the Islamic peoples will constitute over 20 per cent of the entire population, whereas in 1959 the figure was only 11 per cent. Even more serious is the fact that according to these peoples' demographic potential, i.e. the numbers of their children born alive, they will then outnumber the Ukranians. This will place them next in line to become the second largest nationality in the Soviet Union. Kozlov then cites an additional statistic. He predicts that in the year 2000 there will probably be more Kazaks and Azerbaijanis than Belorussians. Beginning in the late 1980s, the increase in the work-force will be concentrated in central Asia, Kazakhstan and Transcaucasia alone. By the 1990s, between one-quarter and one-third of Red

194

Army recruits will belong to the Islamic nationalities. These estimates are not merely statistical games of passing interest. On the contrary, they are imbued with political significance. This was confirmed by none other than Yurii Andropov. In a speech of December 1982, on the occasion of the Soviet Union's sixtieth anniversary celebrations, he said: 'It is an experience of life that the economic and cultural progress of all nations and peoples is accompanied by an increase in their feeling of national importance. This is a regular process and an objective law.'

Of course, the 'feeling of national importance' is 'growing' among the various peoples in the USSR at differing rates. There is no 'national question' in the Soviet Union, but instead a large number of problems resulting from the fact that many nationalities are forced to live together. These problems vary greatly and depend in part on the options available for resolving the conflicts. The Russians themselves are rapidly acquiring a raised national consciousness. Among a substantial portion of the Russian intelligentsia today, the condition of being Russian, Russian history and the Russian intellectual-cultural tradition are more meaningful than they were one or two generations ago. Although dampened by censorship and other coercive measures, Russian nationalism is equipped with a wide spectrum of means of expression in the areas of art, literature and, in part, publishing. This Russian-national world view includes differentiated and extraordinarily sensitive village prose and 'historical painting' (such as that of Glazunov) and extends all the way to the chauvinistic depths of uninhibited Russian messianism and talk of a Russian God. On the one hand, the Party leadership is concerned about this. However, the holders of power cannot and do not wish to dispense with Russian nationalism. It has become indispensable after the collapse of Marxism-Leninism as an ideology of integration. There are advocates of Russianism within the establishment, even in the highest cadres. This makes the selection of a non-Russian General Secretary absolutely unthinkable today, quite unlike the situation in 1922.

With respect to the relationship between the centre and the periphery, one finds conflicts and problems of varying severity. I mention here (a) potential conflicts which, in my estimation, are relatively insignificant; (b) conflicts which can still be managed today; (c) examples of open conflicts of loyalty and national resistance.

(a) The Belorussian people, large in number, and the small Finnish peoples living in the Volga region and the European north have developed only a limited national consciousness. They show a substantial readiness to assimilate themselves into the Russian culture.

(b) In the nations of Central Asia an ambitious intelligentsia has emerged for the first time in the post-Stalin era. Today, this class is in the process of taking the national republics into its own hands and thus, after a delay of several decades, quietly bringing about the '*korenizatsiya*'. The loyalty of these new Asiatic *élites* of Islamic tradition is not yet open to question. Here I take a stand which differs from that of a number of Western experts who regard this conflict as much more severe.

(c) By way of contrast, there are a number of open national conflicts in which the demand for national self-determination is associated with criticism of socialism in its existing form. These are to be found in the Baltic states, the Western Ukraine, Georgia and Armenia. If these peoples were allowed to do so, they would vote to secede from the USSR. A possible exception might be the Armenians, who are dependent on a strong defence against Turkey.

Now, my second question: 'What measures has the Soviet leadership developed in order to manage these conflicts?' There are a number of political instruments which have enabled the Russian Empire, as the only European colonial power of the nineteenth century, to survive until today. Beyond a doubt, the Soviet leadership employed military and political force without ethical considerations and thereby suppressed separatist and autonomy movements, beginning with the civil war and including the post-World War II era, when entire peoples were deported. I would like to emphasise, however, that it has also made certain concessions and thus prevented unsatisfied nationalist sentiments from destroying the Soviet system. These concessions include equal legal treatment of persons of every nationality, linguistic autonomy and the prestige symbol of Soviet federalism. Moreover, the Soviet leadership has systematically employed the 'revolution from above' to reduce social differences between the peoples, to physically obliterate pre-Soviet *élites* and to nurture new national *élites* which are in any case more homogeneous than the pre-Soviet *élites*. The Soviet leadership is co-opting a substantial portion of these new *élites*, thus allowing them to participate in the differentiated Soviet system of privilege. During the period between the two world wars, Soviet nationality policies were superior to the minority policies of most East European countries, notably those of Poland. And the Soviet peoples today have greater opportunities for independent cultural development than do the national minorities in, for example, Afghanistan or Iran.

Third question: 'Are the political measures developed in the past still adequate?' Some of the Soviet instruments of power which were developed in the past in order to integrate the many peoples are no longer applicable today, or are at least of limited usefulness. The current political leadership no longer regards it as advantageous to regulate problems of nationality by force, as was done for several decades. An example: the peoples of Central Asia are extremely reluctant to migrate, and as a result, approximately 2 million people here, mostly young, have no appropriate jobs. At present, they could be motivated to take on work in the European part of the USSR or in Siberia only by means of deportation, or at least through the application of massive administrative pressure. The Soviet leadership is afraid to employ such measures. One other measure which was very effective until the 1950s has since become blunted; namely, the migration of Russians to the national republics. In earlier decades, the Russians stabilised their rule by migrating to the national territories. Today, in contrast, one observes a trend in which Russians are leaving Transcaucasia and several areas of Central Asia. The Russians who remain have to compete with the new local elites for privileged jobs and positions.

The leadership's policy is for the Russian language to replace Russians as an instrument of integration. Language policies have become more aggressive since the second half of the 1970s. However, the forced use of Russian as the language of instruction at universities and in other areas of public life provokes resistance. This cancels out the integrative effect which is to be achieved by expanding the use of the Russian language in public life. The literary, artistic and even pedagogical intelligentsia do not support the increased use of Russian, and the resistance to Russification is also observable within the Party apparatuses of the national republics themselves. The co-opting of non-Russian *élites* — that classical instrument of rule which has been used for centuries in many multinational empires — is, of course, a policy which can be employed in the future as well. Even more so, since the Soviet leadership has no other choice but to assimilate the non-Russian nationalities into the leading social classes. However, the political cost of these policies will increase because the non-Russian *élites* can

197

be expected to make increased demands for a better consideration of their own economic, cultural and personnel interests.

This brief survey has shown that many of the measures which have been used until now to manage national problems will not be as successful in the future. The leadership faces the task of developing new policies to integrate the Soviet peoples. Otherwise, it will have to prepare to pay the increased political costs of ruling the former colonial territories at the end of the twentieth century. New political measures are not yet in sight. It is therefore to be expected that in coming decades the Soviet leadership will have to give stronger consideration to the specific concerns of the non-Russian peoples. At the same time, the opposing national feelings will grow more pronounced, since Russians perceive this development, which can no longer be halted, as 'colonial ingratitude'.

10

Ideology and Propaganda

Soviet Ideology: From the End of Utopia to 'Real Socialism'
Jacques Rupnik

It is not easy to speak about a vanishing subject. The Kremlin's suppression in August 1968 of the most far-reaching attempt at reform carried out in the name of a 'rejuvenated' or 'humanised' Marxism has, according to L. Kolakowski, killed off not just any 'revisionist' hopes, but the official Marxist ideology itself. From then on, Kolakowski argues, communism ceased to be an intellectual or ideological problem and remained merely a problem of government power.[1] Though the long-heralded 'end of ideology' has definitely taken place in East-Central Europe, one should perhaps remain more cautious as far as the Soviet Union itself is concerned. However, there is perhaps another way of reconciling Kolakowski's assessment with the Soviet bloc 'realities' of the 1980s: ideology has indeed ceased to be an intellectual problem but it has remained an essential instrument of Communist power at least in three respects:

(1) Intellectual sterility does not prevent the official ideology from remaining the prime *source of legitimacy* of Communist rule.

(2) An essential function of the ideology is to *hold together the ruling Party elite*. And since it embodies the only available discourse it can also provide keys to the internal political debates within that elite.

(3) The ideological discourse remains the prime form of com-

1. L. Kolakowski, *Main Currents of Marxism*, Oxford 1978, III, p. 467.

199

munication between rulers and ruled. Hence the double dimension
of ideology as a *ritual* and as an instrument of *social control*.

What then are the contours of the ideology of 'real socialism'
today? What are some of its functions and what are some of the
ideological worries of the present leadership?

The Ideology of 'Real Socialism'

Instead of the 'end of ideology' it might be more appropriate to talk
about the exhaustion of the Utopian and mobilising dimensions of
Communist ideology which were dominant not only in the Stalinist
period but also (and perhaps mainly) under Khrushchev. It is
enough here to recall Khrushchev's programme, adopted at the
XXII Congress of the CPSU in 1961, planning not only 'to catch up
and overtake' the capitalist West, but to achieve communism itself
by 1980 (with all the accompanying consequences that such a
forecast entailed, i.e. the 'dictatorship of the proletariat' loses its
raison d'être and the 'withering away of the state' should shortly
follow). As Yurii Andropov put it at the ideological meeting of the
Central Committee in June 1983, some of these propositions 'have
not fully withstood the test of time in as much as they contained
elements of separation from reality'. In other words, the Utopian
elements of the Party programme must be done away with; reality
should prevail over eschatology in the ideological discourse while at
the same time becoming less specific and detailed. Hence the importance of the concepts of 'real' and 'developed' socialism as key
elements in this move from Utopia which characterised both the
Brezhnev and the Andropov legacy.

The concept of 'developed socialism' has thus discreetly removed
the prospect of communism from the Soviet ideological horizon. It
is not the projection of a new society but merely a preparatory
phase for the construction of communism. The reality itself becomes the project. The Soviet Union has, according to Chernenko,
entered 'the historically *prolonged stage* of developed (*razvitoi*)
socialism'.[2] For Soviet ideologists, communism seems to get further
and further removed the closer one tries to get to it.

'Developed socialism', according to R.I. Kosolapov, the editor of
Kommunist and a Central Committee member, is a '*qualitative*

2. K.V. Chernenko, in *Pravda*, 15 June 1983.

organic totality' which submits to its laws of development new spheres of social life, thus eliminating remnants of the past, i.e. non-socialist elements. This 'organic totality' is characterised by the growing homogeneity of its components. In Andropov's words, 'life suggests that a classless social structure will form itself in its main general features already in the phase of mature socialism'.[3] However, such a homogenisation of society is possible only if the political system leaves no vacuum for 'usurpers seeking to assume the role of spokesmen of the working class' (more on the spectre of the 'Polish syndrome' later).

The concept of 'developed socialism' has a double 'advantage' over the Khrushchevian Utopia. It removes the possibility of questioning policies by contrasting them with ideals. By not creating illusions one prevents the occurrence of disillusions, which was one of the main ingredients of the pressure for change within the Party in the 'de-Stalinisation' era in Eastern Europe. This trend was carried one step further with the concept of so-called 'real socialism', launched in the 1970s as a Soviet response to any alternative concept of socialism, be it that of the 'Prague Spring' of 1968 or that of the 'Eurocommunist' parties in the West. This double concern seemed to prevail particularly at the Sofia conference in 1978, chaired by Ponomarev. The ideological unity of the Soviet bloc was to be cemented precisely through the concept of 'real' or 'actually existing' socialism, which came to mean both the *only existing* and the *only genuine* kind of socialism.

Within the context of Marxist theory the concept of 'real socialism' is a dubious one; it is rather reminiscent of the well-known Hegelian formula: 'What is rational is real, what is real is rational.' For Soviet ideologists the line seems to be: 'What is socialist is real and what is real is socialist.' From the exhaustion of Utopia to the mere preservation of the status quo, the concept of 'real socialism' is the ideological monument to the deep-seated conservatism of the ruling Soviet *nomenklatura*.[4] If socialism is totally identified with the present Soviet reality, then virtually any policy of the leadership can be justified even if it also implies that tomorrow the same concern for such current realities require the rejection of these policies. Conversely, if what exists is by definition 'socialist' and 'rational' then any action or view deviating from or challenging that

3. Y. Andropov, loc. cit.
4. Cf. L. Sochor, *Les Traits conservateurs de l'idéologie du 'socialisme réel'*, Paris 1984.

reality is automatically considered 'anti-socialist' and 'irrational' and therefore warrants either 'security' or 'psychiatric' treatment.

The Functions of Soviet Ideology

Thus, the prime function of the ideology of so-called 'real socialism' is both a legitimating and a repressive one. However, besides this preservation of immobilism, the evolution towards the ideology of 'real socialism' has another important dimension which can be seen, for instance, in the new Soviet Constitution. Whereas the Stalin Constitution of 1936 had a purely declaratory ideological function, the Brezhnev Constitution attempts to bridge the gulf between the ideology and the reality. On the other hand, it incorporates some of the ideological foundations of the Soviet system into the Constitution. The preamble, for instance, states that the 'construction of developed socialism has been completed', a statement which, among other things, is meant to justify the Soviet Communists' leading role among East European states. At the same time however, some of the key political features of so-called 'real socialism' have also been incorporated into the Constitution which thus, besides its ideological function, is also actually meant to codify the relations between state and society. The most significant case is, of course, that of what is euphemistically called the 'leading role' of the Party. Whereas the 1936 Constitution merely referred to the Party as the 'vanguard of the workers', the 1977 'real socialist' Constitution defines the CPSU as the 'guiding and directing force of Soviet society, the nucleus of its political system and of its state and public organisations'. This way, certain 'realities' of the Soviet system are incorporated into, or sometimes substituted for, the ideology. A similar attempt (at about the same time) to include realities such as the 'leading role' of the Party (or the ties with the Soviet Union) in the Polish Constitution met with strong opposition: paradoxically, the Polish human rights movement then resolutely defended the Stalinist Constitution of 1952 which, according to the authorities, was obsolete compared to the allegedly more 'rational' and 're-alistic' one proposed by the Gierek regime. The opposition answered that the best way to bridge the gulf betwen the old constitution and the new realities was to start actually implementing the former.

Another significant feature of current Soviet ideology is its increasing ritualisation. Whereas under Stalin the ritual and the ceremonial elements were intended merely to accompany the ideological mobilisation, nowadays the ideology itself tends to become absorbed by ritual. In the relationship between rulers and ruled the Marxist-Leninist liturgy is combined with a whole range of new Soviet ceremonies and rituals. While this could be a new field of investigation for anthropologists rather than for students of Soviet ideology, in the Soviet Union it has turned into an important component of 'ideological work'.

A recent Soviet publication entitled: *Our celebrations. Soviet state, labour, military, youth and family celebrations, ceremonies and rituals* (Moscow, 1977) indicates the scope of this phenomenon. In it the authors state clearly the purpose of this kind of para-ideological activity: 'The characteristic feature of ceremonials as instruments of Communist education lie in that they have an influence on man's conscience, on the rational as well as on the emotional level' (pp. 1–2). These ceremonials and rituals are, according to the authors, 'an effective means of educating people in the spirit of Marxist-Leninist ideology' (p. 13).

An essential element in this ritualisation of ideology is a use of language which has reached almost Orwellian dimensions. Two books published in 1982 give a detailed exposition of the problem: 'the great task of the mass media in the socialist society is to develop and perfect, in the desired direction, the conscience of everyone'. The Soviet language allows one to realise 'that his optimal place is to be an infinitesimal cell within the social organism'.[5] As Michael Heller points out, the goal is clearly 'to give a political nuance to every work' and thus reach one of the prime goals of Soviet ideology which is 'to politicise all spheres of life'.

In this perspective, the goal of Soviet ideologists is a dictatorship of language through the MacLuhan method. As Heller puts it:

The state has rationalised the language and the means of information; it became both the medium and the message. It speaks of itself. It says that the state is the most important thing, of which the citizens are merely minute components. So it is necessary to retain power. The ideology of yesterday was debatable. On the contrary this magnificent technique of power which the rationalisation of language is, does not allow any answer.[6]

5. A.N. Vasilieva, *Journalistic and Publicistic Discourse*, Moscow 1982, p. 18. See also *Language in Soviet Society*, Moscow 1982, p. 75.
6. Michael Heller, in : *Esprit*, 2/1983, p. 43.

Cracks in the Soviet Ideology

Whatever the purpose of ideological 'newspeak' may be, under slowly maturing 'real socialism' the Soviet leaders have shown growing signs of concern about the vulnerability of the population to adverse ideological influences. These vulnerabilities were listed by K. Rusakov at an ideological conference,[7] when he accused the West of fanning nationalism, religious prejudices (he mentioned Catholics, Muslims, Jews in particular), trade union freedoms, private farming, artistic freedom and 'apolitical' attitudes among youth. These influences are attributed to three sources: Western ideology, rival ideologies in Soviet society, and crisis at the periphery of the Empire (Poland being the latest case after Czechoslovakia in 1968).

(1) Western influence is the most common official worry. This is the familiar theme of the 'sharpening of ideological struggle on the world scene'. 'Ideological workers' are exhorted to combat the 'psychological war' launched against the USSR by the Reagan administration. The only interesting point here is the growing reliance on the army (or the Party organisations within the armed forces) as the ultimate guarantor of ideological purity, an institution which could stamp ideological conformity on Soviet youth of all nationalities.

The 'peace' campaign is the other side of the same coin, though there is a growing awareness, at least in Eastern Europe, that the campaign could backfire in the current context of the deployment of Soviet missiles there (G.D.R., Czechoslovakia).

(2) The rival ideologies which seem to worry the authorities most are religion and nationalism. Hence Chernenko's insistence in his June 1983 speech on the fact that 'a part of our people still remains under the influence of religion and, to put it plainly, it is no small part either. Innumerable ideological centres of imperialism (he went on) are attempting not only to support but also to cultivate religiosity and to give it an anti-Soviet, nationalistic tinge'.[8] As for resolving the nationality question Chernenko recommended the more widespread use of the Russian language as a means of access to what is described as 'Soviet civilisation'.

(3) Finally, the Polish crisis has brought into the open differences concerning the urgency of reforms within the Communist system.

---

7. K. Rusakov, in: *Sovetskaya Estoniya*, 13 October 1982.
8. Chernenko, loc. cit.

In a major article published in *Pravda* in March 1983,[9] the editor in chief of *Kommunist*, R.I. Kosolapov, criticised those Soviet ideologists who have used the Polish crisis to argue that, unless certain reforms are undertaken, unresolved problems could lead to a similar crisis in the Soviet Union itself. Kosolapov argued that contradictions can continue to exist under socialism but these are only 'non-antagonistic' in character. Poland, unlike the Soviet Union, he went on, has not yet reached the stage of 'developed socialism' (private agriculture, the Catholic Church). Kosolapov's criticism of contradictions under socialism was aimed at a series of articles devoted to this subject which appeared in Soviet journals. For instance, the editor of *Voprosy Filosofii*, V.S. Semenov had argued in September 1982[10] that the Polish events showed that, if allowed to develop, 'non-antagonistic' contradictions could develop into 'antagonistic' ones. In the following issue, Anatolii Butenko argued that reforms were necessary in order to avoid such contradictions turning into a political crisis. Butenko asserted that the Polish party had neglected democracy and ignored conflict, which alienated the workers from the system. From a more general perspective, argued Butenko, the Polish case merely highlighted the fact that 'under socialism there is a real contradiction between the necessary development of democracy and the need to develop centralism'. This, he concluded, can be resolved through 'gradual decentralisation of power, bringing it closer and closer to the masses'.

By May, however, the ideological debate about the implications of the Polish crisis brought in the Poles themselves. Ryzhov, in *New Times* (6 May 1983), attacked Polish Vice-Premier Rakowski's paper *Polityka* for promoting 'downright anti-socialist concepts'. The bulk of the Soviet attack, however, concentrated on J. Wiatr, director of the Institute of Marxism-Leninism in Warsaw, who suggested that a new model of socialism was needed if a repetition of the crisis was to be avoided; a crisis which, according to him had arisen from the 'imposition' on Poland of an alien model of socialism that did not conform to its specific conditions. So we are back to the 1968 question about different models of socialism. Such views, the *New Times* article concluded, amounted to stating that future political crises are inevitable, which was a *de facto* criticism of socialism itself.

9. R.I. Kosolapov, in: *Pravda*, 4 March 1983.
10. V.S. Semenov, in: *Voprosy Filosofii*, September 1982.

Thus, the debate about the Polish crisis revealed not only a clash between Soviet and Polish ideologists but a political conflict concerning the reform of the system in the Soviet Union itself. It is not quite clear, however, what the leadership implications were in this debate. Andropov's article, in the February 1983 number of *Kommunist*[11] seemed to endorse Kosolapov's assertion that antagonisms disappear under socialism. But he also added that if not addressed, such contradictions can provoke 'serious collisions' in socialist societies and that the process of correcting such contradictions is one of the sources of progress under socialism. While not endorsing the word reform Andropov implicitly admitted (and confirmed in his speech of June 1983) that differences in the development of socialist countries are a 'natural' phenomenon ('This is natural, even if in the past it seemed to us that it would be more uniform . . . The time comes when dues have to be paid for mistakes in politics').

As for Chernenko, he remained curiously absent from the most interesting phase of the debate under Andropov (autumn 1982 to spring 1983). His earlier pronouncements on the subject ('we should listen more to people, even the unions, now that we've reached such an advanced stage of mature socialism') led some observers (L. Teague, for example) to suggest that he was rather flexible on ideological issues. But his return to the forefront in June 1983 and after seemed marked by a concern for ideological orthodoxy which suggested that conservatism rather than pragmatism had become the order of the day in Moscow.

Conclusion

Three main points to conclude on the changing role of Soviet ideology:

(1) Since the late 1960s there has been a steady decline in Marxist-Leninist ideology as a source of legitimacy and a growing reliance instead on 'Soviet patriotism'. The latter tends to become identified with nationalism on the one hand and on the other with the growing ability of the Soviet system to project its power (legitimacy identified with what H. Carrère d' Encausse called a *'projèt de puissance'* in *Le pouvoir confisqué*, Paris, 1981). For some

11. Y. Andropov in *Kommunist*, 3/1983.

authors (C. Castoriadis, *Devant la guerre*, Paris, 1981) this evolution is closely associated with the rise of the military within the Communist apparatus. The problem with this kind of nationalist legitimacy is that it can appeal only to the Russians; and, that when nationalist ideology rather than Marxism-Leninism is utilised — at the periphery (namely by General Jaruzelski in Poland, as by Ceausescu in Romania), it is perceived in Moscow as entailing, in the long run, counter-productive effects on the stability and homogeneity of the Soviet empire.

(2) Secondly, the crises in Czechoslovakia (1968) and in Poland (1980–1) have both had a serious impact on the ideological debate in the Soviet union itself.

(3) Finally, whether dead or not, the Soviet ideology or rather the ideological debates, remain the privileged forum for raising the issue of the reform of the political system on which all the other reformist plans, including those for the economy, in the last instance depend.

The Educational System: Potential for Crisis or Stability?

Oskar Anweiler

On 4 January 1984 a draft proposal of 'Basic Reform Guidelines for General Education and Trade Schools' was published in the Soviet press. The proposal criticised certain inadequacies of the Soviet educational system — long known and most recently formulated during the plenary session of the Communist Party Central Committee in June 1983 — and set out a number of proposed reforms. This drew fresh attention to the overall social role which training and education play in the Soviet Union, both in politics and ideology and in the economy. In the past decade — in contrast to the 1950s and 1960s — this concentration on education has received much less attention in the West. On 10 April 1984, the Central Committee passed a decree on educational reform which corresponded to the draft proposal, and this was adopted by the Supreme Soviet of the USSR on 12 April. The final document of the 'Basic Reform Guidelines for General Education and Trade Schools', which was approved by both houses, contains relatively few changes from the draft proposal, although these are not uninteresting when examined individually.[1] This laid the groundwork for several decrees passed by the Central Committee in conjunction with the Council of Ministers of the USSR. These decrees dealt with general education schools, worker training and professional orientation as well as with teacher training and trade education. They classify the goals and means of reform in the various areas affected, set planning dates and specify more concrete steps to be taken.[2] The union Republics are then to initiate the school reform in their respective regions by means of further legislative and administrative measures. Finally, it is left primarily to teachers and local school

---

1. The draft proposal appeared, among other places, in *Pravda*, 4 January 1984. The final version was published in *Pravda* on 14 April 1984.

2. The general decrees of the Party and government decision-making bodies mentioned here were publicised — in the order given here — in the *Pravda* editions of 29 April, 4 May, 11 May and 15 May 1984. In addition to this, the Council of Ministers of the USSR issued a regulation dealing with pre-school education; this appeared in *Izvestiya* on 19 May 1984.

administrations — but also to factories and plants — to decide how to shape and execute the reforms.

Criticism of the schools has long been an important feature of Soviet life — among parents, academics, authors, plant managers and teachers. Various problems of everyday school life are discussed quite frequently and often heatedly. Dissatisfaction with schools seems to be an international phenomenon, even though the points of criticism and the recipes for change differ according to interest and conviction.

The reform plan concentrates on two main areas:

(1) The contribution of education in resolving the problems of training young people for work and equipping them with the necessary qualifications.

(2) Regaining lost ground in the political and ideological training of youth.

If one examines the situation of the Soviet educational system in the mid-1980s in the light of the planned reforms, the following problem areas emerge. It is possible to address only the most important questions here. These are questions which, beyond their narrower pedagogical significance, are of general — and political — importance.[3]

(1) General education schools in the Soviet Union, as seen within the context of the entire educational system, exercise a twofold function. They consist of only ten grades, with the exception of schools in the three Baltic republics, which have eleven. Upon graduation, the student attains an 'intermediate certificate' (secondary school diploma). The twofold function lies in the fact that nearly all students are to receive the same standardised basic education, after which specialised vocational education follows. At the same time, however, the school is to provide the student with the knowledge and proper learning attitudes required for university studies. Basically, this double function is more than the 'unitarian school' is able to fulfil. The pedagogical problem is overshadowed by a problem of workers' politics. Having graduated from the ten-year general education school, the student is formally qualified to study at an institution of higher learning. However, substantial discrepancies have always existed between the aspirations of most

3. A comparative overview dealing with the Soviet Union, East Germany and other European countries under Communist rule is found in the volume *Bildungssysteme in Osteuropa — Reform oder Krise?* (*Educational Systems in Eastern Europe — Reform or Crisis?*), published by O. Anweiler and F. Kuebart, Berlin, 1983 (*Osteuropaforschung*, volume 12, published by the German Society for East European Studies).

school graduates, who wish to go on to university, and the numbers of workers which are required in the 'mass occupations'. These discrepancies are due partly to structural problems within the Soviet educational system and partly to still inadequate measures for orientation and guidance into the channels of work which have been established by labour and economic planners.

The new reform is supposed to bring basic improvement to this problem. Firstly, by lowering the minimum age for school attendance by one year to six years of age, general education schools will have eleven grades (and thus schools in the Baltic Republics will have twelve). After ninth grade at least one-half of the young people are to enter an intermediate technical or vocational school. But even those students who remain within the general education secondary school, now in grades 10 and 11 (or 12), are to receive substantially reinforced work training on a polytechnical basis as well. This will supposedly help them to be integrated more quickly and smoothly into the labour economy upon finishing school. One proposed solution was rejected. This would have changed grades 10 and 11 into a selective stage for the college bound (such an arrangement now exists in East Germany). The result of the approved proposal is that the upper grades of secondary school will retain their double function. That is, they are to create the prerequisites of university study and also — most importantly — prepare students to take on a job. The dilemma is to be resolved, or at least ameliorated, by the teaching of more general subjects in the enhanced and extended vocational schools. This is to qualify the most suitable graduates from vocational schools for admission to the universities. The formal grouping of general education secondary schools, technical vocational schools and intermediate vocational schools (which until now have been separate entities) into a single 'general education and secondary vocational school' (this is the official title; however, these school categories will in future continue to be administered by various ministries and authorities) indicates the intended direction of reform. However, this does not resolve the guidance problem, nor does it bring about true equality of opportunity in gaining access to institutions of higher education. Moreover, it fails to achieve a distinct functional delegation of responsibility among the various types of schools. Instead, the reform plan clearly illustrates how difficult it is radically to restructure traditional institutions according to a new, unified concept. These are institutions which have grown historically into their present forms and are accorded varying degrees of social prestige. As such, they represent varying interests on the part of administration, teachers and parents.

(2) Part of the criticism of schools concerns the traditional organisation of educational content and the teaching methods which are predominantly employed. Or, to use my own formulation, the didactic structure of the Soviet general education school. Here, Soviet educational experts and scholars have long held, in part, highly contrasting opinions. Without going into the details of the didactic controversy, I would like to note here that these are general problems which accompany any sort of educational reform and have comparatively little to do with political and social systems. This is because the controversy revolves around how to keep the material taught in school in line with rapid scientific, technological and social change, at the same time taking youth's altered relationship to conventional school forms into account.

One problem concerns the degree of diversification of courses offered in the upper grade levels. This diversification is necessary better to foster the development of individual abilities and talents. During the 1960s almost every school began offering optional courses to complement the obligatory uniform curriculum. This is not to be confused with the courses offered in designated special schools, such as the type of school which offers extended training in foreign languages from second grade onward, or sports schools. In the reform plan, educational planners continue carefully to explore the process of differentiating curricular content. Still, the underlying principle of basic and mostly standardised school education has not been changed.

Of all the didactic reforms, 'clearing the curriculum of junk' has been accorded the highest priority. With this, the overburdened Soviet student is to be given some relief from the 'rote learning' which has been criticised by the Soviet public for some time. However, it seems more than questionable whether this can actually be achieved if, at the same time, new subjects and courses are also introduced. These include 'Theory of Society', the same in content for all intermediate school types, and 'Introduction to Computer Technology', a course which is still in the planning stages and will eventually be obligatory for all students. The latter is to give proper treatment to 'new technologies'.

These two examples instantly illuminate the two most important goals of the didactic reforms. Firstly, curricula are to be modernised with a view to the 'scientific and technological revolution'. This objective is not to be met simply by establishing a 'computer course'; other school subjects are to be modernised as well. Secondly, the political and ideological content of school lessons is to be stepped up and reinforced. This is seen as part of the overall intensification of Communist education — inside and outside school — which has also been demanded in government decisions. The unchanging goal of education is to shape a 'unified world view' on the basis of philosophical materialism and this has once again been strengthened.

(3) A central element in the proposed educational reform is the expansion of worker training and practical work in general education schools, as well as the reintroduction of vocational education for mass occupations in the upper grades of these schools. This situation existed once before, from 1958–64. It is to be viewed in connection with the structural reforms in technical schools and the greater contribution these are to make to the planned integration of general and vocational 'intermediate education' for all young people. The result is an even stronger orientation of the educational system to employment policies and labour planning than that which already exists in the Soviet planned economy.

The new concept of work instruction and work education, associated, in part, with the intensification of polytechnical work instruction which was initiated in 1977, is based on a four-step linear structure. In the lower grades there is elementary work instruction (three hours per week each year for grades 2–4), while in grades 5–7 this is already to be followed with 'general work education of a polytechnical nature', consisting of four hours per week in each school year. Subsequently, beginning with grade 8, 'education in the mass professions as fits the needs of the national economy'.[4] There are two levels here: until the conclusion of grade 9 (with six hours per week in each school year) productive work (outside of school) is concentrated on, with the goal of trade orientation and a corresponding selection of an appropriate path of further education. Afterwards, in grades 10 and 11 (or 12) of secondary school there is to be, as a rule, full vocational education in a so-called mass occupation. This level consists of eight hours per week each year and is concluded with a finishing examination. Since only a few of these secondary school graduates will be able to attend colleges and

4. In accordance with the general decree 'Concerning the Improvement of Work Instruction, Work Education and Vocational Orientation of Students as well as the Organisation of their Socially-Useful Productive Work', in *Pravda*, 4 May 1984.

universities (this will be the case in the future as well, even though there will be fewer school graduates), this new provision is to ensure that young people aged 17–18 will not enter the labour market untrained after finishing school.

Still, these planned structures of polytechnical and preparatory work training, with vocational education within the eleven-year secondary school casts fresh light on the dilemma, mentioned above, of this kind of school. This is because the planned trade qualifications, which are to be attained simultaneously with matriculation requirements for university studies, are not higher level qualifications. They are instead expressly intended to prepare the student for 'mass occupations' in industry, construction, agriculture, commerce and other service areas. The higher level specialised trade qualifications are to be earned at intermediate technical schools and intermediate trade schools. This reveals the self-contradiction inherent in coupling a higher level general education diploma (qualification for university studies) with lower level occupational qualifications in the eleven-year secondary school. This is not a harmonious pedagogical concept, it is the outgrowth of unresolved problems in Soviet labour planning and an insufficient supply on the labour market of workers for unpopular jobs.

It seems highly questionable whether the planned solution will have the desired success in the long run. Experiences gained during the Khrushchev reform speak against this, although there might now be a better supply of materials and personnel required for giving occupation-orientated work instruction and vocational education to secondary school students than there was then. It is not yet clear what reaction institutions of higher education will have to the reform measures, and no one knows how young people and their parents will go about selecting an appropriate course of education after the ninth grade. The planned upgrading of vocational education schools is intended to alter socially the university's pool of prospective students. In future there are to be less university bound students coming from the 'intelligentsia', a group which is currently overrepresented. Whether this aim can actually be achieved through a devaluation of the 'professionalised' general education secondary school or whether the traditional prestige of university bound general education will carry through in future as well also remains to be seen.

(4) At the XXIV (1971), XXV (1976) and XXVI Party Congress (1981) various 'negative factors' and unsolved problems in the

education of Soviet youth were lamented in bitter and colourful tones. Similar words were heard at the plenary session of the Central Committee in June 1983. Speakers bemoaned the 'political naivete' and 'postponement of maturity for citizenship', the 'parasitic behaviour' and the insufficient willingness of many young people to work. It was also claimed that the class enemy was attempting to exploit the 'special qualities of the youthful psyche' for his own purposes.[5]

The many discrepancies existing between Party-official norms of social coexistence and education, on the one hand, and the concrete social experiences and resultant forms of behaviour which contradict these norms, on the other, have often been identified by teachers, parents, psychologists and even Komsomol functionaries on the basis of individual cases and situations. Novels and short stories, films and other media also devote attention to such themes. The inadequate 'social orientation' of youth is also the subject of empirical academic study and official positions have been taken on this problem. Here it was determined that what was missing was a comprehensive, 'integral theory of education'. Such a theory is seen as necessary for resolving the 'complex tasks of education' confronting schools, families, enterprises and youth organisations.[6]

The range of problems sketched here is of such great importance to Soviet society because the things which are complained about and criticised do not have to do merely with a natural state of tension existing between the generations, with their diverging ideas as to what goals of life are worth attaining. Nor is it simply a matter of mutually exclusive, partly opposing worlds of experience (including youth subcultures). Rather, what is at stake here are basic questions of the regime's ideological identity, of its moral legitimisation and the stability of its rule.

One important aspect which illuminates the problematic role which education plays in the schools can be seen from the following episode. The Party organised a public 'discussion' of the draft proposal for educational reform, during which tenth-grade students from several Moscow schools were also heard. A seventeen-year-old youth said in an interview:

5. Chernenko's speech, printed in *Pravda*, 15 June 1983.
6. See O. Anweiler: 'Das Problem einer "sozialen Orientierung" der Jugend in der sowjetischen Erziehungspolitik' ('The Problem of a "Social Orientation" of Youth in Soviet Educational Policies'), printed in *Osteuropa*, 30/1980, pp. 21–.

The teachers should tell us the truth more. What we hear in the class-room during lessons has nothing to do with what we find afterwards in the real world. For example, they tell us that today's young workers are all full of initiative and are purposeful and active. But when we first started to work at the appliance factory in Moscow, we found out that not all are that way.[7]

These and other noteworthy statements in the official 'Teachers' Journal' were followed by a commentary by the reporter, who maintained that young people insist on the truth and have a highly-pronounced sense of justice.

The contradiction between word and deed, between socialism's official song of praise, written into the curriculum, and the reality 'around the corner', is a contradiction inherent in the system itself and nearly impossible to eradicate. Therefore, state-controlled educational measures cannot adequately deal with the problem. This is why the school is forced to paint a rose-coloured picture of Soviet life and a distorted one of the outside world, even if this places it in growing contradiction to the life experiences of young people and thus destroys its credibility. Those teachers who do their jobs conscientiously are the ones who are most deeply affected by this situation.

Of course, it cannot be doubted that many Soviet theoreticians and practical experts in the area of education do not lack insight into the negative effects of evasive, unrealistic teaching. 'Hushing up inadequacies, painting actual reality in beautiful colours and ignoring all of its current difficulties and contradictions — these things only serve to disorientate young people and to leave them unprepared for the struggle they will be forced to take up against future difficulties.'[8] Nonetheless, strict limits are set to the practical consequences which might result from such theoretical insights. To the regime, the school is first and foremost a place where ideological knowledge is transmitted and where political socialisation is carried out 'without complications'.

In this respect, the new school reform does not offer any changes in the educational system; the answer to existing inadequacies is sought in traditional methods. A new, centralised 'educational programme' is to guarantee a school education which is standardised and lends itself to supervision. The 'unified demands' of various

---

7. *Uchitel'skaya Gazeta*, no. 30, 10 March 1984, p. 2.
8. Quoted from Anweiler (note 6), p. 25.

educators are to be further strengthened and young people's free time is to be better organised. In the school itself, instruction in the social sciences and in military patriotism is to be intensified, as is the battle against ideas which are 'reactionary and hostile to the people'. These instruments are probably not very successful in educating the student to take on an 'active role in life', to quote the standard formula, but they certainly are effective enough as instruments of supervision, insuring the stability of the system. The youth subcultures currently existing in several large Soviet cities are, as a rule, apolitical. And the police know how to deal effectively with other forms of 'deviant behaviour'.

(5) The problem of the non-Russian nationalities in the educational system is a substantial one within the multinational Soviet state. Since 1978 efforts have been substantially increased to improve and broaden obligatory Russian lessons in the general education and trade schools, with the desired goal of all non-Russian graduates attaining a 'fluent command of the language'. This has been underlined in the discussions revolving around the present school reform. The reforms provide for twelve additional hours of Russian per week from grade 2 to grade 12. The goal of all non-Russian citizens being competent in two languages (a goal which the results of the 1979 census show to be remote), is to be reached first of all through school instruction, secondly through the mass media and finally through the use of language in everyday life. This is to occur in areas of mixed nationalities where Russian serves as the official language of communication.

The command of Russian as a 'second mother tongue' would serve to strengthen the professed 'unity of the Soviet people', along with other practical and political purposes. The Russian language serves as a medium of 'internationalist education' in this state of many peoples and also serves to 'cement' the 'political and ideological unity' of the Soviet people. However, we must also not forget that in the predominantly non-Russian and especially non-Slavic regions, the school, like the family, also serves as a factor for maintaining and developing a national consciousness and an independent cultural life. It cannot be doubted that in school education the unifying factor predominates. Nevertheless, the ethnic variety of peoples living in the USSR and the strong cultural traditions of the larger nationalities and their will to preserve their own identities also impose certain limitations on the pressure of political and ideological uniformity. It would be wrong to overestimate the national tensions existing in the Soviet educational system. On the other hand, it would be extremely one-sided to view the 'question of nationality' as having been resolved (as Soviet propaganda claims).

The question formulated in the title of this article concerning the role played by education and training in Soviet society — namely, does it promote stability, or might it potentially lead to crisis? — might be answered by saying that the various existing and partly acknowledged crisis symptoms do not in themselves mean a threat to stability. The Soviet educational system fulfils the role it has been given by the political leadership. It still educates young people adequately enough and prepares them for life in a Communist totalitarian state, just as it has always done. The partial changes planned in the new reform measures are in complete conformity with this line; efficient command of subject matter is to be increased and political loyalty secured. However, the education of the new man, which is still so often invoked in articles in the Party press and in official speeches, has become a pale ritual. A society which has become conservative maintains a conservative-authoritarian style of education. Seen in this way, education is a mere social function. Therefore, the further development of educational and training policies will depend on overall social and political developments.

Propaganda as an Instrument of Power
Paul Roth

One definition of propaganda which is often quoted in academic literature is Lasswell's: 'Propaganda is an attempt to influence the attitudes of large numbers of people. This is done in disputed (controversial) questions in which a particular group has become involved.'[1] If the 'particular group' exercises sole state authority, propaganda usually becomes indoctrination and an instrument of enforcing rule. The distinction between the propaganda which is customary in Western democracies and Soviet propaganda thus lies less in the means and not so much in the goals — although the means and goals of Soviet propaganda have characteristic and unique features. Of greater importance is the fact that in the Soviet Union a 'particular group', that is, the *nomenklatura*, exercises sole authority and employs propaganda as an instrument of control and indoctrination. And no other group is allowed to disseminate propaganda.

The Soviet Concept of Propaganda

In the Soviet Union a theoretical distinction is made between 'propaganda' and 'agitation'. This differentiation can be traced back to G. Plekhanov (1856–1918), was adopted by Lenin and can be found, for example, in the 'Large Soviet Encyclopedia'.[2] It states that propagandist transmits a larger number of ideas to one or several persons. The agitator, in contrast, has one or few ideas and directs them to many persons with the intention of provoking them to do something.

Although Lenin adopted this distinction, he also obscured it. At one time he asserted that the propagandist's main field of activity was the printed word, whereas the agitator worked mostly with the spoken word. Later, he assigned propaganda to magazines and agitation to newspapers. As early as 1898, however, he demanded of

1. Heading 'Propaganda', in: E. Noelle-Neumann, W. Schulz (eds.), *Publizistik*, Frankfurt am Main 1971, p. 305.
2. Bol'shaya sovetskaya entsiklopediya, vol. 1, Moscow 1970, p. 181; vol. 21, Moscow 1975, p. 95.

the party newspaper that it should 'not only be a collective propagandist and collective agitator, but also a collective organiser'.[3] If we add to this the now official translation into Russian of the words 'mass media', the distortion becomes evident. 'Mass media' translates into 'means of mass information and mass propaganda'. Article 52 of the Soviet Constitution permits 'religious cult activities' and 'atheist propaganda'. This means, of course, that it is permissible to engage in atheist agitation and propaganda, but religious communities are not allowed to practise either 'religious propaganda' or 'religious agitation.' If one wishes to adhere to the theoretical distinction, it is at best possible to distinguish between 'Party instruction' (propaganda) and 'mass agitation' (agitation).[4]

However, Soviet 'mass agitation' quite closely matches what we normally call 'propaganda'. And in the West we would even classify most Soviet Party instructions as 'propaganda'. S. Beglov, in his handbook for students of journalism, defines 'propaganda' as follows:

> The dissemination of political, philosophical, scientific, artistic and other ideas in society; in the more restricted sense, political and ideological propaganda with the goal of shaping a certain world view in the masses ... Communist propaganda is a scientifically-based system of intellectual work employed for the dissemination of Marxist-Leninist ideology and politics for the enlightenment, education and organisation of the masses; it is one of the party's instruments in directing the process of revolutionary struggle and the establishment of Socialism and Communism.[5]

According to the Soviet view, the decisive criterion of propaganda is who engages in it, that is, whether it is 'bourgeois' or 'Communist' propaganda.

The Party's Monopoly on Propaganda

The Soviet propaganda machine was not constructed according to a carefully elaborated plan. However, the development and dissemination of propaganda has been firmly established since the October Revolution in 1917. This was a result of the Bolsheviks' claim to

3. Lenin's Works, vol. 5, Berlin (East) 1955–, p. 11.
4. G. Simon, 'Parteischulung und Massenagitation in der Sowjetunion' ('Party Indoctrination and Mass Agitation in the Soviet Union'), in: *Osteuropa* 5/1974, p. 335.
5. S. Beglov, *Vneshnepoliticheskaya propaganda*, Moscow 1980, p. 355.

leadership, which was said to be 'scientifically' based on Marxism-Leninism. The trident of a monopoly on rule, ideology and opinion-making was the political consequence, and propaganda was alloyed with each of the three prongs.

V. Stepakov, in 1967 head of the Central Committee's propaganda section, established in his book *Scientific Fundamentals of Party Propaganda* that 'Vladimir Iliich Lenin saw propaganda as a powerful tool with which the Communist Party could exert influence on the masses every day and could actively influence revolutionary practice and the entire course of social development'.[6] In order to guarantee that the Bolsheviks would retain their monopoly on propaganda, all other groups, organisations and parties were deprived of their right to disseminate propaganda. This began with the Soviet power's first decree on the press (1917), after which the other parties were obliterated, religious communities persecuted and deviants and 'enemies of the people' liquidated. Now that the dissident movement has been muzzled, the Soviet Union is currently making efforts to jam radio broadcasts from abroad. These broadcasts drive holes through their monopoly on public opinion. There can be no equal opportunity for the mass media and the propaganda of the 'bourgeoisie'. On the contrary, it is seen as an 'act of supreme historical justice' to destroy the bourgeoisie along with its media and propaganda. This teaching has remained unchanged since the days of Lenin. It appeared in printed form recently in the German edition of the Soviet magazine 'Socialism: Theory and Practice', published by the *Novosti* press agency. Here, Professor Kovalyov explained the fact that in bourgeois countries Communist parties and their party organs are allowed to exist, whereas their bourgeois equivalent is banned in 'socialist' countries. As Kovalyov sees it, this does not signify a violation of human rights or of the right to equal treatment. He states:

> The bourgeoisie cannot exist without the working class. It cannot 'destroy' the working class, because the latter secures the existence of the bourgeoisie. On the other hand, it is possible for the working class to exist independently of the bourgeoisie. Indeed, the specific precondition of its freedom is the elimination of this parasitic class. In consequence, there can be no sort of 'equality' between the bourgeoisie and the working class. Since it is necessary to eliminate the bourgeoisie in order

6. V. Stepakov, *Partinoi propagande — nauchnye osnovi*, Moscow 1967, p. 82.

to completely liberate the masses and the entire human race, this signifies an act of supreme historical justice.[7]

The loss of the monopoly on ideology and opinion-making would not only mean the loss of the propaganda monopoly but, even more so, a threat to the monopoly of rule. This is commented on in 'The Party and the Means of Mass Propaganda', a brochure published by the Central Committee's Academy of Social Sciences, as follows:

> If the Party leadership underestimates (the mass media), this leads to serious consequences. The events in Czechoslovakia in the year 1968 prove this. At that time the powers wielding mass propaganda, which were in the hand of opportunistic and anti-Socialist elements from the political right, attacked Marxism-Leninism and its most basic tenets of class unity and the press's party nature . . . Mistakes which the Party had made in directing the means of mass information and mass propaganda led revisionists of various colours to demand that the press be made independent of the Party. They said that it (the press) should only be an organ of a collective editorship, an independent social power standing above the party and above its central committee.[8]

Article 6 of the Soviet Constitution (1977) establishes that only the Soviet Communist Party — equipped with the teachings of Marxism-Leninism — is entitled to lead and direct state and society. The monopoly on rule is therefore also anchored in the Constitution. This gives the Party the sole right to utilise propaganda.

Propaganda as an Instrument of Ideology

The main task of Soviet propaganda has been and still is to justify and glorify the political leadership. At the same time — and inseparable from this — propaganda is assigned the task of creating 'new man' by proclaiming the 'science' and 'truth' of Marxism-Leninism. Lenin, at least, still believed that the revolutionary upheaval of the economic base and the political superstructure had created the necessary conditions for an emerging new consciousness, that there would now be a generation of socialists and Communists.

When the Second Party programme was advanced in 1919, Le-

7. S. Kovalyov, 'Wie wir die Menschenrechte verstehen' ('How We Understand Human Rights'), in: *Sozialismus: Theorie und Praxis*, 12/1983, pp. 30f.
8. B. Morozov, *Partiya i sredstva massovoi propagandi*, Moscow 1982, p. 8.

nin's comrades-in-arms, Bukharin and Preobrazhenskii, wrote in their popular explanation of the programme: 'The state propaganda of Communism will, in end effect, serve as a means of annihilating every trace of bourgeois consciousness and will be a mighty weapon for the creation of a new ideology, a new world concept . . .'[9] The propagation of Marxism-Leninism became, in part, the proclamation of a 'doctrine of salvation'. One battled 'religious superstitions', instructed the citizens as to the nature of good and evil, told them who is 'good' and who is 'evil', enlightened them as to the meaning of life and the laws of history, and so on.

D. Suter accurately observes:

> All propaganda is a caricature of the ideology upon which it is based. It extracts a few dogmas from complex ideologies and uses them to forge a few customary mottos . . . Wherever totalitarian ideologies rule, the idea of purge is never far behind. The world view which encompasses all areas of life always and everywhere allows for drawing the distinction between good and evil. But the purpose of this world view is not merely to serve as a road sign. Instead, its purpose is to appeal to revolutionary renewal, to transform ideology's utopia into actual reality.[10]

In the view of the Soviet *nomenklatura*, a 'psychological war' has been in progress since the beginning of the 1970s, conducted by the 'capitalist countries' in order to rob Soviet citizens of their belief in Marxism-Leninism. This has given special importance to the 'intellectual-educational work' of propaganda. General Lieutenant Professor D. Volkogonov writes in his book *The Psychological War* (1983):

> Intellectual-educational work consists of a number of components. Most importantly, life-giving ideas of Marxism-Leninism are to be incorporated into the consciousness of man and Communist convictions and a scientific world view are to be formed on the basis of these convictions . . . Finally, intellectual-educational work requires an uncompromising battle against all things which are foreign, hostile and borrowed, all things which betray themselves as antithetical to our ideology and our morals.[11]

Thus, the propagandist plays his role as a preacher of salvation, a giver of orders, a director of work, an educator and an inquisitor.

9. N. Bukharın, E. Preobrazhenskii, *Das ABC des Kommunismus* ('*The ABC of Communism*'), Hamburg 1923, p. 238.
10. D. Suter, *Rechtsauflösung durch Angst und Schrecken. Zur Dynamik des Terrors in totalitären Systemen*, Berlin 1983, pp. 52, 74.
11. D. Volkogonov, *Psikchologicheskaya voina*, Moscow 1983, p. 256.

The Propaganda Orchestra

If every area of human life is to be covered by politics, propaganda must be omnipresent. The system of total propaganda coverage originated in the Stalin era. Kalnins entitled his book on the Soviet machinery of mass influence 'The Soviet Propaganda State'.[12] The propaganda system is directed by the propaganda section of the Central Committee; this department was mentioned earlier and works on behalf of the Politburo. It includes a number of subdivisions, dealing with the press, radio, television, film, culture, art, etc. For the 'intellectual-educational' work within the armed forces there is a special Central Commitee division, the Main Political Administration. This agency was headed by Army General A. Yepishev.[13]

The guidelines for Soviet journalists have continually demanded that they follow Party directives and at the same time 'form a Marxist-Leninist world view — the foundation of the Communist education of the Soviet citizen'.[14] The mass media, censored and controlled, are divided into bureaucratic-hierarchical pyramics.[15] At the forefront of the 8,172 official newspapers (1981) and 5,195 magazines are the newspaper *Pravda* and the magazine *Kommunist* (earlier entitled '*Bolshevik*'). The words printed in these publications are orders and dogma at the same time.

Information is also included in the propaganda apparatus. In Lenin's words, 'information is agitation by means of facts': information must therefore be selected according to the Party's point of view. The monopoly on information is a part of the monopoly on opinion. The state agency TASS is the supplier and at the same time the filter for information.[16] The State Committee for Television and Radio directs and controls broadcasters.

This listing does not exhaustively portray the means and methods of Soviet propaganda. Added to this are, for example, political instructors, election points, propaganda circles in factories and house groups, wall newspapers, etc. The Soviet citizen does not

12. B. Kalnins, *Der sowjetische Propagandastaat (The Soviet Propaganda State)*, Stockholm 1956.
13. See here A. Epishev. *Ideologicheskaya rabota v vooruzhennykh silakh SSSR* Moscow 1983.
14. *Zhurnalist* 3/1984, p. 44.
15. See here P. Roth, *Sowjetische Medienpolitik. Die kommandierte öffentliche Meinung*, Stuttgart 1982.
16. P. Roth, *SOW-INFORM. Nachrichtenwesen und Informationspolitik der Sowjetunion*, Düsseldorf 1980.

only encounter propaganda on motto-painted banners and posters. Propaganda is also disseminated on postage stamps, paint containers, in the artistic decoration of subway stations, in the form of monumental sculptures and not least during the official processions to the commemorative sites of the Revolution. Of these, the central sacred place is of course the Lenin mausoleum. Just as there is no place which is free of propaganda, so there are no times when propaganda is not heard. The calendar is divided into 'high celebrations' (for example, the October Revolution), memorial days (for example, Lenin's death day) and an endless chain of commemorative days (for example, the day of the chemical worker). Added to this is a never-ending chain of campaigns: for the honour of the Party convention, for the early fulfilment of the Five-Year Plan, against the stationing of American medium-range missiles, to celebrate the harvest, etc.

In 1967, Stepakov, the director of the propaganda section of the Central Committee stated: 'The system of propaganda, as we see it, is like an orchestra in which each instrument has its own special task in accordance with its unique nature. But when heard together, the instruments form a unified and harmonious ensemble.'[17] Thirteen years later, Central Committee Secretary Chernenko spoke to the Central Committee plenary session on 'current problems of ideological and mass-political party work'. He is quoted as saying, among other things, that 'Our entire system of ideological work must function like a well-tuned orchestra, in which each instrument has its own voice and its own part and harmony is attained through skilful conducting . . . The purpose of ideological work is to capture every side of social life and every social grouping and region and to reach every human being.'[18] Neither Stepakov nor Chernenko knew, of course, that the metaphor of a propaganda orchestra was an invention of Goebbels.

Methods of Mastering Conflicts

The monopoly of the *nomenklatura* signifies power and danger at the same time. When propaganda proclaims, promises, predicts or maintains something on behalf of the leadership — with reference

17. V. Stepakov, loc. cit., p. 265.
18. *Izvestiya*, 15 June 1983.

made to Marxism-Leninism — and this turns out to be incorrect, what happens then? Either Marxism-Leninism is unsuitable for making accurate predictions, or the leadership is not able to employ this science. Or was the propaganda simply lying?! If one doubts propaganda, one can also doubt the teaching and the system. It is an especially serious matter when Soviet citizens find out something about events in their own country through foreign radio broadcasts. This is why the leadership is so stubbornly blocking these transmissions.[19] However, I do not wish to devote attention here to the shield erected against information from abroad, but instead to three political-ideological means of settling conflicts.[20] These were introduced by Lenin and Stalin, and are still used to justify actions today. They are: 1. Adapting the teachings; 2. Correcting the past; 3. Attacking the guilty. If, for example, the proclaimed goals do not coincide with the teachings which have been proclaimed heretofore, propagandists then resort to a new interpretation or to a 'further development' of Marxism-Leninism. Careful attention is paid so as not to disturb the appearance of continuity. Stalin's 'socialism in one country', 'Soviet patriotism', the doctrine of 'peaceful coexistence' and 'proletarian internationalism', etc., are examples of how political measures, proclaimed and justified through propaganda, have been reinforced and protected ideologically by altering the teachings which were formerly applicable. This method is very closely related to correcting the past.

Events, persons, statements or programmes which no longer fit current policies or their propagandistic assertions disappear through Orwell's 'memory hole'. This does not include those events which the Soviet citizen has never heard of (for example, the secret adjunct agreement to the 1939 German-Soviet treaty). Trotsky's writings, of course, have disappeared through the memory hole, as has the *ABC of Communism* by Bukharin and Preobrazhenskii (the latter was the Communist catechism for many years).

For several years, Lenin's testament lay in the 'poison cupboard'. When the period of de-Stalinisation arrived, the testament reappeared. Then the well-known Soviet film director M. Romm was obliged to dig up his old Lenin films and cut out all the scenes showing Lenin and Stalin to have been close friends. After Khrush-

19. G. Wettig, *Der Kampf um die freie Nachricht*, Zürich 1977.
20. P. Roth, 'Woher kommen die Feinde der Sowjetmacht? Konfliktbewältigung in der UdSSR', in: *Information für die Truppe* 12/1982, pp. 103–.

chev went into retirement, Brezhnev saw to it that the 'virgin lands campaign' was to be credited not to his predecessor, but to Brezhnev himself. Archivists and librarians in the Soviet Union are constantly busy relegating books, magazines and individual issues and entire annual volumes of newspapers to the 'poison cupboard'. The expatriate author V. Voinovich writes: 'As time passes, even central pieces of Soviet propaganda transform themselves into anti-Soviet propaganda. Simply try today to distribute the speech that Khrushchev gave at the XX Congress of the CPSU. You can count on earning a place in prison or in a psychiatric clinic.'[21] In 1983 the publishing firm of Pahl-Rugenstein in Cologne printed a book containing speeches and articles by General Secretary Andropov. This included a speech he gave in the year 1964.[22] However, no mention was made of the fact that in the German text one-quarter of the speech was missing. Gone were Andropov's crude indictments of China's Communist Party and his praise for Khruschchev, who was sent off into retirement only half a year later.[23] One of the most important Party mottos can be found in Orwell's *1984*: 'He who controls the past controls the future; he who controls the present controls the past.'

The third method was perfected by Stalin. It is based on the fact that to justify itself the Soviet system will always need enemies. If something which has been promised is not attained, the teaching, leadership or propaganda must not be given the blame. One must therefore find scapegoats. Stalin was the first to make use of the term 'enemy of the people'. Since the propaganda assumes that a new, socialist society has meanwhile emerged in the Soviet Union, the main guilty parties must be sought and found in 'capitalist' society. The current defamation campaign against A. Sakharov, who is being portrayed, to all intents and purposes, as an instrument of the American intelligence service, is one of the most recent examples.[24]

21. V. Voinovich, 'Die antisowjetische Propaganda in der Sowjetunion', *Kontinent* 1/1984, p. 51.
22. Text of the speech in: *Pravda*, 23 April 1964.
23. P. Roth, 'Eine Andropov-Rede von 1964 für 1984 zurechtgemacht', *Informationsdienst des katholischen Arbeitskreises für zeitgeschichtliche Fragen*, 125/1984, pp. 62f.
24. An example of this defamation campaign in: N. Jakovlev, 'Die feine Verwandtschaft von Akademiemitglied Sacharow', *Sputnik*, 3/1984, pp. 109f.

Successes and Failures of Propaganda

There have always been private niches in Soviet society, places where scattered groups have held on to a bit of freedom. During the 1920s and 1930s these were to be found mostly in the family, in the peasantry, and in art and religion. The abolition of 'bourgeois' marriage and the emergence of collectivism, 'socialist realism' and the 'Godless movement' have either removed these niches or reduced them in size. Even today, however, they have still not been walled up entirely. More than anything else, religous communities are a thorn in the flesh of the holders of power. They regard cults, holidays and sacraments as a dangerous dissemination of superstition. This is why the 'Society for the Dissemination of Political and Social Knowledge', founded in 1947 (and renamed 'Knowledge' in 1963), continues the work of the 'Godless' association.

Since the second half of the 1950s the Party has also been devoting increased efforts to introducing pseudo-religious rituals which would serve to crowd out 'religious propaganda'. However, as one reads in a Soviet brochure printed in 1982, successes in this area have not been adequate: 'And yet, one currently observes only a few initial steps of this process. New rituals are starting to develop and the necessary conditions are being created for its further perfection.'[25]

Why is it, though, that such niches could not be walled-up? Why have the doubters and dissidents not died out and why has 'new man' not emerged in 'mass form'? In any case, when Stalin died the inheritors of state power knew that Stalinist indoctrination had not been enough. The great 'decline of belief', however, did not begin until after the XX Party Congress, at which Khrushchev (1956) delivered his secret speech on Stalin's 'personality cult'.

As to the effectiveness of Soviet propaganda, not only Western specialists but also former Soviet citizens hold diverging opinions.[26] Their estimates run the gamut from total ineffectiveness to total manipulation. The author Voinovich claims that the Soviet people abhor everything which is praised by Soviet propaganda.[27] The former Soviet journalist L. Vladimirov describes Soviet journalists

25. V. Rudnev, *Obryadi narodnie i obryadi tserkovnie*, Leningrad 1982, p. 148.
26. See G. Simon, 'Die Wirksamkeit der sowjetischen Propaganda', *Berichte des BIOst Köln* 9/1974; G.D. Hollander, *Soviet Political Indoctrination. Development in Mass Media and Propaganda Since Stalin*, New York, Washington, London 1972.
27. V. Voinovich, loc. cit., p. 50.

as decided cynics who see through the propaganda. He admits, however, that even living in the West he still often looks at things in a Soviet way.[28]

M. Voslenskii, himself once a member of the Soviet *nomenklatura* himself, believes that the Soviet intelligentsia is not indoctrinated. Nonetheless, it is politically well versed and sees Marxism-Leninism not as an expression of faith, but as an agreement on linguistic rules.[29] The author and philosopher A. Zinoviev, once a professor in Moscow, portrays the Soviet intelligentsia in his novels as cynical, and at the same time, conforming. He claims that people in the Soviet Union are today generally dissatisfied and that no one believes in Marxism.[30] At the same time, however, he warns that it is futile to hope for a decay in Soviet society and in the power system. He writes:

> and the system of power which encompasses the entire society like a closely-woven net holds fast. And 'the people' are by no means planning its demise, not even its transformation . . . And the lack of belief in Marxism does not weaken it (the government) in any way, for Marxism is an ideology. One does not believe in an ideology; one accepts it.[31]

Zinoviev is also convinced that ideology has left its mark on Soviet citizens. He writes about those who participated in the last emigration, which he calls a 'Soviet' emigration. 'An emigrant from Moscow performs even an anti-Soviet act as though he were doing so on behalf of the Soviet government. He is a Soviet person through and through. Maybe even more so than those who have remained behind in Moscow.'[32] These observations are not nearly as contradictory as they might appear at first glance. What information do Soviet sources offer on this question? One establishes first that Stalin's heirs did not know what their subjects thought or wanted. Stalin had abolished empirical social research. It was brought back to life only slowly and with considerable effort. Since the end of the 1960s the scientifically useful results of opinion research have been available. This empirical research has, however, been increasingly subjected to Party supervision. Only a small portion of the results have been published, the 'tip of the iceberg', as a Soviet researcher

28. L. Vladimirov, *Rossiya bez prikras i umolchanii*, Frankfurt/Main 1969, p. 294.
29. Speech: 'Erziehung, sozialer Aufstieg und Elitebildung im sozialistischen Staat', manuscript of 15 February 1984, p. 7.
30. A. Sinovyev, *Ohne Illusionen*, Zürich 1980, p. 160.
31. A. Sinovyev, loc. cit., p. 112.
32. Sinovyev, p. 158.

assured me. One is led to conclude that the results were disappoint-ing. The same researcher confirmed that Brezhnev's bitter criticism of the mass media and propaganda in a speech given in November 1978 was based on results of opinion sampling which have remained secret.[33]

If one analyses the speeches on the mass media and propaganda given by Suslov, Brezhnev, Andropov and Chernenko since 1978, one encounters harsh criticism of media and propaganda work. The same applies to the two basic Central Committee directives 'Concerning the Further Improvement of Ideological and Political-Educational Work' (1979) and 'Current Questions of Ideological Mass-Political Party Work' (1983).[34]

One cannot expect the holders of state authority to call their own policies or ideology inadequate. They are left only with the logical choice of criticising the inadequacies of their own propaganda and castigating the dangerous influence of 'ideological diversion'. To most Soviet citizens Soviet propaganda is certainly a burdensome but unavoidable phenomenon. The former Soviet propagandist A. Poverennaya tells of how she once gave a speech to Soviet soldiers, who listened without moving. She only later found out that these soldiers were of the Kirghizian nationality and were not able to understand Russian. The army major responsible for the troops calmed the enraged propagandist. He said that not one of those who had listened to the speech had suffered any damage from it, and that now that it had been given, the 'foundation of political education' had been laid.[35]

It is certainly not possible to provide a scientifically reliable answer to the question of how effective Soviet propaganda is. It is quite evident that the propaganda itself is to be blamed less than the 'product' it praises. However, this 'product' consists of several parts. Propaganda's main task is to justify and stabilise *nomenkla-tura* rule. As I see it, although the *nomenklatura* is faced with a number of difficulties, it remains true that the broad mass of people follows its commands and the armed forces march and shoot when ordered to do so. We do not need to go into the question of whether or not this is a Russian trait; in any case, propaganda has been able

33. Texts from the speech in: *'Pravda'*, 28 November 1978.
34. Decree texts: *Kommunist* 7/1979, pp. 10–; *Kommunist* 9/1983, pp. 39–.
35. A. Poverennaya, 'Von der Tribüne abgetreten. Skizzen über die Arbeit eines sowjetischen Propagandisten' ('Stepped Down from the Stands. Sketches on the Work of a Soviet Propagandist'), in: *Kontinent* 1/1984, p. 98.

to make good use of it.

After all, as Soviet citizens often tend to say, Russia was victorious under Soviet rule in the 'Great Patriotic War', whereas the Tsar's Empire crumbled during World War I. In the consciousness that the Soviet Union is one of the world's two superpowers, people there tend to support the leadership's foreign policies and to agree with its assessment of the world political situation.

This consciousness of being a great power also influences the content of ideology. It is no longer Marxism, and the term Marxism-Leninism is also inadequate, even if one considers the Soviet patriotism harnessed by Stalin. Voslenskii states:

> It is not Marxism, but rather the great power chauvinism of the *nomenklatura* which is the central element of official Soviet ideology . . . This ideology guarantees the *nomenklatura* a certain amount of support from the people. The vitality of *nomenklatura* chauvinism rests on the fact that it is less of a lie than are the Marxist and Leninist elements of Soviet ideology.[36]

This great power chauvinism requires an enemy. In the summer of 1957 a group of Soviet journalists took 'soil samplings'; that is, they questioned approximately 800 Soviet citizens from every level of society. One question was: 'Assume that one day all Soviet radio stations reported at once that a nuclear explosion had occurred near Leningrad and had resulted in the deaths of 20,000 people, and that the entire USSR had been placed under atomic alert. What would you believe the cause of this explosion to be?' More than 60 per cent of the workers, farmers, intellectuals and students and 42 per cent of the Party functionaries who were polled responded that they would assume the USA had dropped a bomb.[37] The young man who had seen the results of this poll turned to one of the journalists who had participated in the opinion sample. This journalist explained to him:

> A person cannot personally desire war. We all love peace. Yet at the same time it is possible to believe that your country will definitely be attacked, and this makes you take a position which, to a certain degree, is in favour of war . . . Under these circumstances you will understand that our society affirms every armed action of our government and of the Party,

36. M. Voslenskii, *Nomenklatura*, Vienna, Zürich, Munich, Innsbruck 1980, p. 410.
37. J. Novak, *Uns gehört die Zukunft Genossen*, Bern, Stuttgart, Vienna 1961, pp. 250–.

since we most deeply believe that it is nothing more than a response to imperialism's aggressive intentions.

One might react to this example by saying that it comes from a time when the cold war was only slowly being replaced by the ideology of peaceful coexistence. However, I have not heard that the Soviet population has expressed any reservations over the invasions of Czechoslovakia or Afghanistan — disregarding a few brave dissidents. And to my knowledge, the shooting down of the South Korean airliner was accepted, if not with indifference, at least with the consciousness that a superpower cannot tolerate the intrusion of another power into its airspace.

However, in my assessment the picture looks quite different if one asks whether propaganda has been successful in making ideology the material of beliefs and in educating a new type of man. It was not possible to halt the decline in belief after Stalin's death. The claims of ideology as to the meaning and tasks of life are repeated, but hardly anyone believes them any more.

It would nonetheless be inaccurate to claim that propaganda has been ineffectual in this area. The 'new man' has certainly not been created, but instead a 'two-track thinker', one who no longer reflects society's contradictions but instead takes them for granted. Zinoviev claims that Marxism-Leninism is no longer believed in, 'but year after year, from generation to generation, a certain selective process has been taking place; individuals are emerging who can cope with and live in this social milieu. This means that man is adapting to the milieu, so as to generate such a milieu once again.'[38] These statements are not a full and comprehensive answer to our question. I know that there are millions of believers in the Soviet Union, that the significance of the dissidents cannot be measured by their numbers alone, that Soviet youth is looking for new orientations and that nationalist challenges pose a threat to Moscow's rule, etc. However — in my view — Soviet propaganda has contributed a great deal towards the stability of the system, even if it can no longer mobilise. Propaganda has achieved much less than the holders of power wished and, most of all, it did not succeed in bringing forth a 'new socialist' human being. But it has achieved much more than one would like to see from a Western point of view.

---

38. Sinovyev, p. 80.

From *Brezhnev to Gorbachev*

Ideological Counter-Reformation and Counter-Propaganda

The visible 'decline in belief' after Stalin's death did more than trouble the holders of power; it deeply unsettled them. The proliferation of the 'propaganda orchestra' (that is, the coordination of propaganda work) were not able to halt the decline in belief. Then came the shock of the 'Prague Spring'. Since then the functionaries have been speaking of a 'stepped-up ideological struggle', for which, of course, the 'capitalist' countries are blamed. Since the early 1970s, politicians, philosophers, ideologists and propagandists have been conducting an almost embittered 'ideological counter-reformation'.[39] The methods used are the old ones. Of course, it is now possible secretly to employ the results of opinion polls; this helps in implementing the activities more specifically.

As I have already mentioned, the results do not meet the expectations of the power holders. After the Helsinki Final Accords were signed in 1975, the Western side demanded that concrete acts should now also follow the agreements in Basket 3. The Soviet Union, it is true, had declared before signing that state sovereignty would always take precedence over the flow of information over borders. Nonetheless, they were startled when the West took Basket 3 seriously. Since then a number of conjunctive and simultaneous campaigns have been in progress so as to meet this danger. One campaign has been directed against dissidents in the Soviet Union. They have been condemned, isolated and defamed; it is claimed that they are Soviet citizens acting on behalf of the American intelligence service.

In addition, increased efforts are being made to block 'foreign influence' from the West. Comprehensive jamming of foreign broadcasts was resumed in 1980. The call for the free flow of information is rejected as the West's malicious attempt to 'intervene' in the internal affairs of socialist countries, a 'diversion' and 'psychological war'. It is claimed, at the same time, that the flow of information from East to West is impaired. Associated with this is the 'counter-propaganda', intended for the domestic population. People are warned against allowing themselves to be influenced by 'capitalism' in any form whatsoever. There have been so many publications on this subject that it is no longer possible to establish

39. See H. Dahm, *Der gescheiterte Ausbruch. Entideologisierung und ideologische Gegenreformation in Osteuropa. (1960–1980)*, Baden-Baden 1982.

their numbers.[40] The Soviet citizen is simultaneously assured that there is no such thing as freedom of opinion and freedom of the press in capitalist countries; instead, only manipulation and indoctrination — like the situation described by Orwell in *1984*.[41] With this, 'capitalism' has once again almost taken on the characteristics of a Stalinist vision of the enemy.

The fourth campaign concerns the 'new organisation of world information'. Under the pretext of only wanting to help developing countries to attain their rights and to protect them from 'electronic imperialism', the Soviet Union is offering a socialist model for the 'new organisation of world information'. In the UN and UNESCO the Soviets are demanding that the free flow of information over national borders be condemned. They would prefer instead a provision of international law which would give an individual country the sole right to decide what information may move across frontiers.[42]

There is no indication whatsoever that the Soviet Union is likely to change anything in the function and themes of its propaganda in the near future. In the sphere of foreign propaganda the Soviets will devote greater attention to developing countries and will attempt to ingratiate themselves with peace movements in the West. They will hold fast to the principle which one might formulate by slightly altering the toleration edict of the Peace of Augsburg (1555). That decision proclaimed: *Cuius regio, eius religio*. A Soviet version might be: *Cuius regio, eius propaganda*.

40. See, for example: V. Komarovskii, *Lozh' na eksport. Analiz antisovetskikh aktsii vneshnepoliticheskoi propagandi imperializma*, Moscow 1983.
41. See P. Roth, 'Sowjetische Karikaturen: Massenmedien und Kommunikation in kapitalistischen Staaten', in: *Publizistik* 4/1983, pp. 574–.
42. See P. Roth, 'Die neue Weltinformationsordnung. Argumentation, Zielvorstellung und Vorgehen der UdSSR', *Berichte des BIOst Köln* 44/1982, 17/1983.

Foreign Propaganda
Richard F. Staar

The magnitude of the effort by Moscow to influence target audiences abroad can be seen from estimates of expenditures and personnel involved. A testimony by former CIA deputy director for operations, John McMahon, to a congressional committee indicated that 'given the importance of propaganda and covert action in its foreign policy implementation, the USSR is willing to spend large sums of money on its programmes. Our rough estimate of $3 billion per year is probably a conservative figure.'[1]

If one adds to the foregoing the campaign directed at resident foreigners and visitors within the Soviet Union and Eastern Europe, the totals would increase to half a million persons and about $6 billion. Compared with the entire non-Communist world, the USSR probably spends almost one hundred times more than the former in human and financial resources. Soviet 'public diplomacy' invests a great deal of time and effort in its propaganda campaign, certainly more than any other country on earth. The use of accusations and derogatory terminology, harassment, comprehensive censorship, radio jamming, forgery and general 'disinformation' have all become institutionalised tools of the Soviet Party state.[2]

Central Committee Departments

If anything, the above indicates the importance of propaganda in the eyes of the Politburo, which supervises its dissemination via *agitprop* (agitation and propaganda) operations through the international and foreign departments of the Central Committee. A distinction should be made between Soviet propaganda and

2. Earlier studies include Frederick C. Barghoorn, *Soviet Foreign Propaganda*, Princeton, N.J., 1964 and Lyman B. Kirkpatrick, Jr. and Howland H. Sargeant, *Soviet Political Warfare Techniques*, New York, 1972, pp. 41–82.

agitation.³ The former presents many ideas, primarily through the printed word; the latter uses a single, widely known 'fact' and disseminates it via the spoken word as face-to-face communication. There are two departments in the Central Committee apparatus which deal with foreign Communist parties: one involves relations with ruling movements; the other with non-ruling parties.

The international department, until recently headed by CPSU secretary and candidate Politburo member Boris Ponomarev, maintains liaison with many foreign organisations which are utilised to disseminate Soviet propaganda. Ponomarev, who became head of that department in 1955, frequently publishes on such subjects as Marxist-Leninist theory, Eurocommunism, NATO, American policies, and the worldwide promotion of Soviet interests. In his articles he often presents advice to foreign Communist parties to lead them to 'victory'. In one article, he offered specific guidelines for the consolidation of regimes on the 'path to socialism'.⁴ They must:

— have a revolutionary party guiding society and acting on the basis of scientific socialism;
— strengthen, top to bottom, the organs of democratic power which have been established after eliminating colonial domination;
— build national armed forces, capable of defending the people's gains;
— develop ties with socialist [that is, Communist-ruled] countries, the best and truest friends of independent and freedom-loving states.

The international information department of the Central Committee most likely plays a decisive role in deciding what aspects of Soviet policy to discuss openly and how to present them to various international publics.⁵ Its principal task is to counter the free flow of information generated by the Western media. Soviet officials appear regularly on domestic television programmes and write for the press. They frequently travel to the West, offer propaganda lectures as well as interviews and address meetings of international Communist front organisations. Topics frequently expounded upon include the deployment of US medium-range missiles in

3. 'Agitator's Vocation', *Pravda*, 11 January 1978. See also Baruch Hazan, *Soviet Impregnational Propaganda*, Ann Arbor, 1982.
4. B.N. Ponomarev, 'The Cause of Freedom and Socialism is Invincible', *Problemy mira i sotsializma* 24/1, January 1981, p. 14. His speech to representatives of foreign Communist party newspapers appeared in *Kommunist* 60/17, 1983, pp. 3–19.
5. Elizabeth Teague, 'The Foreign Departments of the Central Committee of the CPSU', *Radio Liberty Research Bulletin*, 27 October 1980, pp. 25–6.

Europe, proposals on arms control and the justification of the Soviet intervention in Afghanistan. The head of the international information department was, until recently, Leonid M. Zamyatin. He had served with the Foreign Ministry since 1946, becoming in 1970 General Director of TASS. Zamyatin held this position until 1978, when he assumed the information department post.[6]

Another unit in the CPSU Central Committee, the foreign [cadres] department, is used as a coordinating centre to inform diplomatic missions from other Communist-ruled states and friendly countries about propaganda lines. Twice a year, on May Day and on the anniversary of the Bolshevik Revolution in November, a list of slogans appears. In effect they represent propaganda 'action directives'. A careful reading of them yields clues as to the general line.[7]

Themes and Typology

The main purpose of Soviet propaganda abroad can be summarised as follows: to present Soviet foreign policy as dedicated to peace and to characterise the Soviet Union as having established the only just society on earth. Foreign propaganda can be classified into three main categories:
— White or non-camouflaged psychological warfare, conducted openly by government and other official organs (Moscow radio, TASS, *Pravda*);
— Grey, emanating from 'independent' organisations and groups (Radio Peace and Progress, international front organisations, friendship societies);
— Black, which is 'a particularly insidious form of ideological diversion, closely combined with terrorist and covert activities', allegedly originating from within target countries (clandestine radio stations, forgeries, disinformation).[8]

6. 'A Biographic Directory of 100 Leading Soviet Officials', *Radio Liberty Research Bulletin*, 10 February 1981, pp. 234–5.

7. Slogans for the 1917 Revolution anniversary appeared in *Pravda*, 16 October 1983, and numbered sixty-one. Only the last twenty deal with foreign policy.

8. Lt General A. Shevchenko, 'An Insidious Weapon', *Krasnaya zvezda*, 18 August 1972. The author was writing about Western propaganda, directed against the USSR, but mirror-imaged what the Soviets themselves do.

Front Organisations

Image projection is largely conducted through the medium of international Communist front organisations, less likely to fall under suspicion of functioning as tools of Moscow than local Communist parties in each country. Officially, fronts do not even adhere to the tenets of Marxism-Leninism, but in practice they are controlled by Communists. According to an authoritative study, the most important groups include the following:[9]

(1) World Peace Council;
(2) World Federation of Trade Unions;
(3) World Federation of Democratic Youth;
(4) International Union of Students;
(5) Women's International Democratic Federation;
(6) International Union of Journalists;
(7) International Association of Democratic Lawyers;
(8) World Federation of Scientific Workers;
(9) International Federation of Resistance Fighters;
(10) International Radio and Television Organisation;
(11) International Institute of Peace;
(12) Christian Peace Conference; and
(13) Afro-Asian People's Solidarity Organisation.

These organisations form a vital link in the world-wide Soviet propaganda network, and the USSR provides them with an estimated subsidy of $63 million per year. They offer a broad range of appeals which attract even non-Communist scholars and scientists who, unwittingly in their pacifist zeal, become exploited by Moscow propagandists. In addition, of course, there exist many friendship societies which perform similar tasks on a bilateral country-to-country basis.

The Soviet Union uses front organisations to promote its ideology by propagandising the membership from foreign countries. The visitor to Moscow may want to see the Tretyakov gallery of Russian art, the largest in that city. During the mid-1970s, it had on display paintings and sketches in a collection entitled, *This is America*. They showed the 'vicious soldiers, the enslaved negroes, the ugly policemen, the sadistic employers, the downtrodden people'. On the

---

9. US Congress, House, *Hearings*, p. 80. All except (9), (10), and (11) are discussed annually in Richard F. Staar, (ed.), *Yearbook on International Communist Affairs*, Stanford. See also Wallace Spaulding, 'International Communist Fronts', *Problems of Communism* 32/2, March–April 1983, pp. 103–5.

other hand, the Soviet citizen is always portrayed 'as the embodiment of every virtue, nobility and generosity'.[10] Such denigration of the United States and idealisation of the USSR are also conducted through international front organisations.

Another duty of the fronts involves formulation of objectives that will coincide with Soviet foreign policy, subtly indoctrinate nonparty members, and then manipulate them into sympathisers. Fronts may also function as a link between political movements that make up a 'national unity' coalition. They support propaganda which directly parallels current Soviet foreign policy, such as the campaign for disarmament, various peace offensives, condemnation of Western imperialism and its alleged economic subjugation of the Third World. 'Their purpose is to spread Soviet propaganda themes and create a false impression of public support for the foreign policies of the Soviet Union.'[11] On their own initiative, front leaders will insist upon 'collaboration' with non-Communist organisations which may correspond superficially to them.

Front Conferences

The most active front organisations are the World Peace Council (WPC), World Federation of Trade Unions (WFTU), World Federation of Democratic Youth (WFDY), and International Union of Students (IUS). An important WPC staged event, the World Parliament of Peoples for Peace reportedly attracted to Bulgaria some 2,260 persons from 134 countries, representing 330 political parties and 137 international organisations. A World Assembly for Peace and Life Against Nuclear War did even better in Czechoslovakia with 2,645 delegates from 140 countries according to the organisers.[12]

Interestingly enough, the WFTU Secretariat did condemn the Soviet occupation of Czechoslovakia, meeting on 21 August 1968 by coincidence at Prague.[13] WFTU held its ninth World Congress

10. Dispatch from Moscow (Canadian Press), 'Hate-US Theme is a Principal One for Soviet Media', *New York Times*, 11 December 1968, p. 45. Five years later, the author saw these same paintings in Moscow during the height of *détente*.
11. US Congress, House, *Hearings*, p. 80.
12. US Department of State, 'The World Peace Council's Peace Assemblies', *Foreign Affairs Note*, Washington, DC, May 1983 discusses the Moscow (1973), Warsaw (1977), Sofia (1980) and Prague (1980) conferences. The World Peace Council also met at Prague in June 1983.
13. Richard F. Staar, (ed.), *1969 Yearbook on International Communist Affairs*, Stanford, 1969, p. 953.

238

ten years later also in that city. Almost 1,000 persons from 126 countries allegedly represented 300 organisations, most of them from the Soviet bloc and the Third World. The Communist-controlled General Confederation of Labour (CGIL) in Italy had announced it would leave WFTU before the congress. At that meeting, a spokesman for the corresponding organisation (CGT) in France made public a decision that no individual from his country would be a candidate for the post of WFTU Secretary General and hinted that the CGT might emulate the CGIL.[14] The WFTU held its tenth World Congress at Havana in February 1982, during which it called for a new international economic order, trade union rights and democratic freedoms (in the West, of course), European security and disarmament, solidarity with Arabs and the peoples of southern Africa, and support for progressive movements in Latin America.[15]

Finally, the WFDY and IUS co-operate in holding world youth festivals which comprise the largest single events sponsored by any front organisation. Most successful to date has been the eleventh consecutive one, held from the end of July to early August 1978 in Havana.[16] Reportedly, attendance totalled about 18,500 delegates from 145 countries. WFDY and IUS meetings echo the same declarations as WPC, that is, they call for 'peace, disarmament, and *détente*' as well as an end to 'imperialist oppression'.

The main assignment of these groups is to produce and disseminate printed propaganda, organise 'popular' support for Soviet foreign policy, convince well-intentioned but politically naïve persons to support CPSU objectives, serve as a non-governmental channel for free or low-cost trips to Eastern Europe or the USSR, and recruit potential Communist party members. Since many of these functions have become known, supplementary techniques had to be devised for influencing world public opinion.

Other Movements

Numerous conferences and international meetings draw together scientists, artists, doctors and academics, ostensibly for open discus-

14. *L'Unita*, 15 March 1978 and *L'Humanite*, 13 April 1978; Rome and Paris, respectively.
15. Staar, *1981 Yearbook*, p. 458; *Flashes from the Trade Unions*, 20 February 1982, published in Prague.
16. *Juventud Rebelde*, 28 July–4 August 1978, Havana.

sion of relevant topics, but in reality to serve as sounding-boards for anti-American and pro-Soviet propaganda.

One such example is the Pugwash movement. Originally established by the industrialist Cyrus Eaton, at the request of Albert Einstein and Bertrand Russell in 1957, its meetings have been attended by hundreds of prominent individuals from the United States, the Soviet Union, Britain, India, France, Mexico, and other countries to a lesser extent. The common denominator is the participants' concern for the future and commitment to the programme statement[17] that 'science must only be used for the good of mankind and never for its destruction'. Recent conferences have been held at Munich, Mexico City, Warsaw, Plovdiv, Venice, Bucharest, and twice in Geneva to oppose the NATO decision on the deployment of Pershing-2 and cruise missiles as well as 'stepping up the struggle against the threat of nuclear war'.[18]

A different series of conferences, restricted to Soviet and American public figures or influential personalities, are the so-called Dartmouth meetings. The eleventh conference was held at Jurmala, Latvia.[19] Bilateral economic relations, the environment and conservation, urgent international problems like disarmament, the immediate establishment of a lasting peace in the Middle East, and European problems were discussed. The Soviet delegation informed American participants about the content of the six-point 'peace programme', advanced at the XXIV Congress of the CPSU.

Georgii Arbatov also attended the most recent Dartmouth Conference, held in April 1983 at Grinnell College in Iowa. Despite a State Department restriction to the effect that the visit should not be used for propaganda purposes, the director of the USA and Canada Institute gave interviews to the Des Moines *Register* and appeared on public television. He also used the opportunity of the supposedly private symposium to lecture in public to more than 1,000 people as well as to speak at a series of breakfast and luncheon meetings.[20]

Another kind of special gathering recently involved the third congress of International Physicians for the Prevention of Nuclear

17. V. Trukhanovskii, 'The Scientists' Duty', *Pravda*, 10 December 1977; see also TASS report, 'Academics Alarm', *Izvestiya*, 16 October 1980.

18. V. Kuznetsov, 'Pugwash Movement', *Izvestiya*, 12 December 1983.

19. *Literaturnaya gazeta*, 20 July 1977.

20. *The Washington Post*, 1 May 1983. The following month, some thirty Soviet delegates appeared in Minneapolis at a conference on 'creating the conditions for peace', sponsored by the Institute for Policy Studies in Washington, DC. A list of American participants appeared in the *Minneapolis Daily American*, 17 May 1983.

War, held in Amsterdam. This organisation, formed in December 1980, claims a membership of more than 50,000 doctors from forty-three countries. The president, Dr. Bernard Lown of Harvard University, said that the purpose of the first conference (held in Virginia in March 1981) had been to increase public awareness of the consequences of a nuclear attack. The Soviet delegation at the Amsterdam meeting included Dr. Yevgenii Chazov, personal cardiologist to Andropov; E.P. Velikhov, a nuclear physicist; and Georgii Arbatov.[21] The presence of the last two men made it clear that the Soviets also use this forum, as they have other international peace and disarmament conferences for propaganda purposes, that is, to promote their image as peacemakers and supporters of disarmament.

Radio Broadcasts

Apart from the front organisations and various specialised conferences at the *élite* level, mentioned already, most Soviet propaganda continues to flood the world via the printed word and radio broadcasts. The major theme, whether it be the Arab-Israeli dispute or southern Africa, is the 'anti-imperialist struggle'. Defensive alliances like NATO as well as co-operative regional organisations, such as the European Economic Community (EEC) or the Association of South-East Asian Nations (ASEAN), remain under constant attack. They supposedly obstruct 'peace-loving' Soviet proposals for security systems in both Europe and Asia.

The USSR devotes more than 2,100 hours per week to foreign radio broadcasts in eighty-two languages. Dissemination of propaganda is enhanced by radio services of other Communist-ruled states. Those in Eastern Europe broadcast about as many total hours per week as the Soviet Union; East Germany (433 hours) is second and Poland (336), third. Kabul radio transmits a total of 38 half-hours per week in Urdu, English, Russian, Arabic, Pushtu, Dari and German. Broadcasts from Cuba total 459 hours per week, with more than half directed at North, Central and South America, with the remainder aimed at countries in the Mediterranean, the Middle East and Western Europe. Moscow also transmits to the United States from Havana in English. South-East Asia is the main

21. *Los Angeles Times*, 23 June 1983.

target of Radio Hanoi, with 301 hours per week.[22]

'Radio Peace and Progress' (RPP), although it has used Radio Moscow transmitters since its establishment in 1964, claims to be independent of the Soviet government. This allows it to assume a more strident tone. Complaints by foreign governments are rejected, even though the station remains under full Soviet control and direction. RPP broadcasts 161 hours per week in fifteen languages and dialects. Its programmes for Latin America are highly inflammatory and anti-United States. In 1981, it quoted a guerrilla as stating that Cuba might intervene militarily in El Salvador.[23] Radio Moscow has not suggested this possibility.

In addition, clandestine stations are operated by exiled Communist party leaders from transmitters in the USSR and Eastern Europe. During 1981, they broadcast a total of some 337 hours. Only two such stations operate from Soviet territory. Radio Ba Yi ('Eight One', for the 1 August 1927 establishment of the Chinese Red Army) first came on the air in early 1979 and is directed toward the armed forces of mainland China. The clandestine station 'National Voice of Iran' has broadcast in Farsi, Kurdish and Azerbaijani from Baku since 1959. It transmitted inflammatory statements prior to the seizure of the US embassy at Tehran. On 7 November 1979, as the world was first learning about the American prisoners, this station continued inciting Iranian mobs to further violence.[24]

Clandestine transmissions to Turkey have continued over *Bizim Radyo* ('Our Radio') since 1958 and 'Voice of the Turkish Communist Party' since 1968 from Magdeburg in East Germany.[25] The Iberian peninsula has in the past been the target of 'Radio Free Portugal' (1962–74) and 'Radio Independent Spain' (1941–75), originating from Romania after the Second World War. *'Deutscher Freiheitssender 904'* and *'Deutscher Soldatensender'* were directed at the Federal Republic of Germany from the so-called (East) German Democratic Republic. Other discontinued stations have included 'Voice of Truth' to Greece (1958–75) and 'Voice of Italian Emigré Workers' (1971–8). A total of seven clandestine transmitters closed

22. USIA, 'Communist International Radio Broadcasting in 1981', *Research Memorandum*, 1 November 1982, Table 1, p. 4. See also Christopher Perzanowski, 'Russia's Radio Putsch', *National Review*, 15 April 1983, pp. 439–40.
23. Department of State, 'Moscow's Radio Peace and Progress', *Foreign Affairs Note*, August 1982, Publication 9292, p. 1.
24. US Congress, House, *Hearings*, p. 79.
25. US Department of State, 'Communist Clandestine Broadcasting', *Foreign Affairs Note*, December 1982, p. 3.

down, after underground Communist parties became legalised in the target countries.

On 20 August 1980, the USSR resumed jamming Voice of America, BBC and *Deutsche Welle* (FRG) transmissions, which had been free from such interference during the preceding several years in accordance with the Final Act signed on 1 August 1975 at Helsinki.[26] This move undoubtedly represented an effort by the USSR to keep news of the strikes and the Solidarity movement in Poland from its own citizens. Jamming of Radio Free Europe and Radio Liberty commenced in 1953 and has continued ever since. Broadcasts to Czechoslovakia and Bulgaria are severely jammed, to Poland less so, to Romania and Hungary not at all since 1963 and 1964, respectively. The USSR employs about 5,000 people and uses an estimated 2,500 transmitters, at a cost of $200 million annually to continue these activities, which openly violate the Helsinki agreement.[27]

The Printed Word

Apart from radio, official government news organisations play an important role in disseminating Soviet propaganda. TASS (Telegraphic Agency of the Soviet Union) has about 200 correspondents in 125 foreign countries. It transmits more than 1,000 air hours of material to all its foreign subscribers daily. The general directorship of TASS since May 1979 has been occupied by Sergei A. Losev, member of the CPSU Central Audit Commission. Losev often travels abroad, appearing on television talk shows, and his articles are printed in Western newspapers and magazines.[28]

Another agency called *Novosti* (News) produces translations and feature articles on a world-wide basis. The chairman is Lev N. Tolkunov, appointed in January 1976. This man completed the Higher Party School and had been a candidate member of the Central Committee since 1966, becoming a full member ten years

26. Board for International Broadcasting, *Seventh Annual Report*, US Government Printing Office, Washington, DC, 1981, p. 1.
27. These jamming trasmitters in the USSR and Eastern Europe cost an estimated quarter of a billion dollars to construct. David Brand, 'Soviets Continue Jamming', *Wall Street Journal*, 14 July 1983.
28. Sh.P. Sanakoev, (ed.), *Voprosy sovetskoi vneshpoliticheskoi propagandy*, Moscow, 1980, pp. 203–204; *US News and World Report*, 30 March 1981, p. 37; John J. Karch, 'USSR', in G.T. Kurian, (ed.), *World Press Encyclopedia*, New York, 1982, pp. 916–17.

later.[29] *Novosti* claims to have connections with 120 foreign publishing houses as well as 140 international and national news agencies. It has reportedly entered into agreements with more than 6,000 foreign periodicals and seventy television companies. Bureaus or correspondents operate in 115 foreign countries, and excerpts from the Soviet press are translated into fifty-six languages. A former director of *Novosti*, Ivan I. Udaltsov, has been identified as a KGB officer who took part in preparing the 1968 invasion of Czechoslovakia. 'An entire division of *Novosti*, known as the Tenth Section, is staffed with KGB men.' In fact, both of these news agencies are virtual centres for undercover subversion and espionage. 'A sizable portion of the Soviet nationals posted abroad as staff members of TASS, Aeroflot, *Novosti* . . . are KGB and GRU officers.'[30]

Novosti material provides the basis for publication abroad of about fifty journals, ten newspapers, and more than 100 press bulletins. The agency claims 4,500 titles and 30 million copies of books or pamphlets appearing with its imprint and distributed each year in fifty-six foreign languages.[31] Many other books are published in non-Communist ruled countries under contract with the Soviet international distribution agency, *Mezhdunarodnaya kniga*. Other titles are sold through normal channels at reduced prices or supplied to jobbers.

In the lesser developed countries, newspapers and journals are easier to circulate than books. Thus more than twenty Soviet periodicals are printed in foreign languages, including *Asia and Africa Today* (two), *Culture and Life* (five), *New Times* (ten), *Soviet Literature* (ten), *Soviet Union* (twenty), and *Soviet Woman* (fourteen languages).

The theoretical and informational journal of Communist and workers' parties is the monthly *World Marxist Review*,[32] with headquarters in Prague. It appears in forty languages and seventy-five national editions, for distribution to 145 countries. Each run allegedly ex-

29. Sanakoev, *Voprosy propagandy*, p. 207; Karch, 'USSR', p. 917; Borys Lewytzkyj and Juliusz Stroynowski, (eds.), *Who's Who in the Socialist Countries*, New York, 1978, p. 627.
30. John Barron, *KGB: The Secret Work of Soviet Secret Agents*, New York, 1974, pp. 15 and 27.
31. One example is Leonid I. Brezhnev, *Istoricheskii rubezh na puti k kommunizmu*, Moscow, 1977. A total of more than 1.5 million copies of this book were published in English, Arabic, Spanish, German, and French translations.
32. Wallace Spaulding, 'World Marxist Review', in: R.F. Staar (ed.), in: *1984 Yearbook on International Communist Affairs*, Stanford, 1984.

ceeds 500,000 copies. Yurii A. Sklyarov, the editor-in-chief, is a candidate for membership of the CPSU Central Committee. A bi-monthly *Information Bulletin* appears in six languages. It provides an additional, and more frequent, outlet for the dissemination of speeches and articles by prominent figures in the world Communist movement.

The weekly *Moskovskie novosti* (Moscow News) has been in existence since 1930. English, French, Spanish, and Arabic translations circulate in 140 countries with a press run of 800,000 copies per editon.[33] This newspaper promotes the Soviet way of life and includes articles on Soviet economic 'successes', Communist peace initiatives, and international relations.

A rather specialised operation is conducted by the Progress Publishing House in Moscow. About 180 translators prepare the works of Lenin, sociopolitical literature and documents from CPSU congresses in forty foreign languages that are sold in twice as many countries.[34] The USSR All-Union Copyright Agency (VAAP) claims to have negotiated more than 1,750 contracts with publishing enterprises in non-Communist ruled states, covering a total of 3,345 titles. For example, a ten-year agreement was signed in 1980 by VAAP and Pergamon Press of London. The latter had already brought out a selection of Brezhnev's *Selected Speeches and Writings on Foreign Affairs*. In an article, the late Party leader explained that his purpose was to 'familiarise [the readers] with our understanding of human rights and their realisation in the Soviet Union'. Pergamon Press also published a volume of Andropov's articles and speeches in English translation.[35]

At times, a country may be the target for propaganda saturation. This is the case with India, where fifty separate Soviet journals or bulletins appear compared with a total of 111 for the remaining ninety-two foreign countries that have diplomatic representation at Delhi. Most Soviet publications are distributed in the capital as well as Bombay, Calcutta and Madras. The journal *Soviet Land* (circulation 550,000 copies throughout India) holds annual essay competitions for the 'Nehru Award', with fifteen prizes that include free trips to the USSR. Five other Soviet periodicals are printed locally in English and sixteen other languages. Of the 150 inexpensive

33. Sanakoev, *Voprosy propagandy*, p. 191.
34. *Bol'shaya sovetskaya entsiklopedia*, 3rd ed., vol. 21, Moscow, 1975, p. 29.
35. L.I. Brezhnev, 'Socialism, Democracy and the Rights of Man', *Kommunist*, 2, January 1981, p. 14; Y.V. Andropov, *Speeches and Writings*, Oxford, 1983, pp. 262.

Soviet technical books, some 40–50 had been adopted by various Indian colleges and universities as texts.

At one time, the three main Soviet publications for Africa were *Rainbow* (Ethiopia), *Polar Star* (East Africa), and *New World* (Nigeria). *Isputnik Digest*[36] in Urdu (Pakistan) and *Soviet Youth* (Egypt) both started in 1969. Soviet embassies print news-sheets, and the mission on Mauritius began a bulletin, called *Soviet News*. The first number of *Soviet Union* in the Thai language appeared in 1971, distributed by the USSR embassy information service. Soviet magazines are also published locally throughout Latin America, e.g. *Enfogue International* (Colombia), *URSS* (Mexico), and the bi-monthly *Indice* (Venezuela).

Aid to Lesser Developed Countries

In addition, certain types of technical assistance are provided to the Third World as a means of establishing influence over the mass media. Radio transmitters and printing presses, training of journalists, and visits by Soviet specialists are written into cultural agreements. These include film and radio material, exchange as a normal part of the aid programme. Such cultural co-operation agreements have been signed by the USSR with twenty-seven African states. Similar treaties have been entered into with Jordan, Lebanon and Iraq. An agreement with the People's Democratic Republic of [South] Yemen provided for the construction of a 200 kW short wave radio transmitter at Aden to reach the entire Arab world. Algeria, Egypt and Syria had also entered into telecommunications' co-operation with the Soviet Union. In 1983, the USSR signed a contract with Grenada to provide the latter with a ground communications station as part of the *Intersputnik* satellite system.[37]

The best publicised example of a Soviet initiative in extending its influence is the Friendship University, founded at Moscow in 1960 and named after Patrice Lumumba. Eleven years later it claimed 700 Africans, 650 Middle-Easterners, 460 South-East Asians, and 802 Latin Americans, among approximately 3,500 enrolled students. In

36. The popular magazine *Sputnik* (published by *Novosti*) is sold in more than 100 countries. It is claimed that each issue appears in more than 200,000 (English), 100,000 (Japanese), 100,000 (French) and 150 (German) copies, respectively. It can be bought also in the Fiji Islands, the Philippines, and Spain.

37. Timothy Ashby, 'Grenada: Soviet Stepping Stone', *Proceedings of the US Naval Institute* 109/12, December 1983, p. 34.

one recent year, diplomas were received by some 80 Asians, 140 Latin Americans, more than 140 Africans and about 100 Soviet citizens. A freshman class of 825 includes 600 foreigners who are reportedly chosen from among 8,000–9,000 applicants.[38]

Those selected receive one or two years of preparatory instruction to fill gaps in their previous schooling and to teach them the Russian language. Six departments open for study include economics and law, history and philosophy, agriculture, medicine, science, and engineering. Students are given free dormitory space plus 80–90 rubles per month for food. It is anticipated that some of the graduates will support Soviet foreign policy through the international Communist front organisations mentioned above. The most useful front is the Afro-Asian Solidarity Organisation which maintains a strong pro-Soviet and anti-colonialist stance.

However, there have been a number of incidents between the Soviet authorities and those attending Lumumba University. One early example of such a conflict became known, when a newspaper in Zambia reported how foreign students had invaded Red Square to protest and demand an investigation concerning the death of a colleague from Ghana.[39] African students were arrested for distributing pamphlets received from the Chinese embassy. Fifteen others from Kenya were expelled, allegedly for political reasons but probably because they had resisted Communist indoctrination. Revolutionaries apprehended in Mexico[40] and insurgents among the radical leftists of Sri Lanka reportedly had received part of their training at Lumumba University.

Future Activities

From the preceding, it is apparent that the geographic thrust of Soviet propaganda during the 1980s will continue to concentrate on the lesser developed countries in Africa, Asia, and Latin America. In the view of Kremlin decision makers, these recently independent states will decide whether or not communism is to be established as *the* socio-political and economic form of organisation over most of

38. Alvin Z. Rubinstein, 'Lumumba University: An Assessment', *Problems of Communism*, November–December 1971, pp. 65–67.
39. *Zambia Daily Mail*, 11 February 1970, Lusaka.
40. J. Barron, *KGB*, pp. 317–25, provides a discussion of activities by former students of Lumumba University in Mexico.

the globe. Hence, the Soviet Union attempts to identify itself with all types of national liberation or separatist movements. *Élites* within the Third World are the target because they decide, in effect, the direction which local developments will take. In this connection, techniques and propaganda themes vary considerably.

Throughout Latin America, the USSR supports any activity by groups which profess anti-American and anti-capitalist beliefs. Moscow has made no secret of its friendly and mutually beneficial ties with Cuba and Nicaragua, attempting to promote their two regimes as models for the region. Soviet propaganda concentrates mainly on the issue of the allegedly 'oppressive' and 'exploitative' policy of US multinational companies. Cuban Communists are predominantly responsible for the dissemination of propaganda in the Western hemisphere. An adapted edition of the *World Marxist Review* (Cuban title, *Revista Internacional*) and a Spanish edition of the journal, *Latinskaya Amerika*, are published by the Soviet Union for wide distribution throughout the region. The Cubans also have a large network of periodicals which they distribute, the weekly edition of the Communist party newspaper *Granma* being by far the most widespread. It appears in Spanish, English, and French with a total circulation of more than 27,000 copies.

Greater variation exists in the Soviet approach to Africa. The Arab states throughout the Maghreb seem more stable than the black ones south of the Sahara. In the latter, Soviet propaganda had expended most of its effort against Portuguese control over its overseas territories of Angola and Mozambique as well as the white-dominated governments of former Rhodesia (now Zimbabwe) and currently South Africa. In addition, approximately 30,000 students from sub-Saharan Africa have been trained in Soviet and East European colleges.[41]

The Middle East and South Asia have become fertile areas for Soviet propaganda, because the USSR has been successful in projecting the image of an ally in the struggle against two American 'puppets': Israel and Pakistan. Roughly two-thirds of the more than 30,000 students from these areas schooled in the Soviet Union and Eastern Europe had come from both Yemens, Lebanon, Iraq, Syria, and (formerly) Egypt.[42] The war between Iran and Iraq has, since

---

41. US Department of State, Bureau of Intelligence and Research, *Soviet and East European Aid to the Third World, 1981*, Washington, DC, February 1983, Publication 9345, Table 12, p. 22.
42. Ibid., p. 23.

1980, posed a slight complication for the USSR. It has remained officially neutral in reporting events. However, the Soviets continue to discredit the United States; criticise the Camp David accords; support the Palestinian people and the PLO as their sole representative and attack Israel's 'expansionism' and 'oppression' in Arab lands.

The most recent Persian Gulf peace proposal, repeated at the XXVI Soviet Party Congress (February–March 1981) called for a nuclear free zone. This apparently had the dual purpose of promoting the USSR as the initiator of peace in a dangerous area of the world, while placing the United States on the defensive. American military co-operation in the Middle East, especially agreements with Oman and Somalia, are described as 'adventurism'.

By contrast, throughout East Asia and the Pacific, the propaganda activities of Moscow exploit cultural relations. A maximum of only about 500 students had been recruited each year, mostly from Burma, Indonesia, and Laos, for education in the Soviet Union or Eastern Europe. Even this number is declining. A trade fair in Malaysia or visits by journalists from the USSR to the Philippines represent limited examples of propaganda opportunities.

The need for Japanese technology to develop Siberia has spurred tourist travel and the frequent exchange of official delegations between the two countries. Thousands of students have graduated from the Russian language programme at the Japanese-Soviet Academy in Tokyo. Moscow's propaganda has been served effectively by Communist-supported campaigns against the security treaty with the United States. A new theme alleges that the American side wants Japan not only to increase its military potential for the fulfilment of certain tasks currently facing the US armed forces in the Far East but also to give economic support for pro-American regimes throughout the region.

The USSR is also attempting to undermine the Association of South-East Asian Nations (ASEAN). It conveys messages to the governments of Indonesia, Malaysia, Singapore, Thailand, the Philippines, and other states in the area, urging them to adopt Soviet proposals for peace. The united stand by ASEAN members against Vietnam and resistance to the Hanoi-installed puppet regime of Heng Samrin in Kampuchea (Cambodia), however, represent attitudes that Moscow finds difficult to combat.

The invasion of Afghanistan and the prolonged presence of Soviet occupation forces has been explained by the USSR as follows: China and the United States have been aiding 'counter-revolutionaries' against the 'legitimate' regime of Babrak Karmal, while Pakistan is being used by imperialists as a 'base for hostile operations'.[43]

Throughout Western Europe, Soviet propaganda themes have concentrated on peace and *détente*. Earlier attacks on the FRG have become muted. As in the case of Japan, the USSR anticipates substantial gains in capital investment (loans) and technology transfer from Bonn. The closer economic and political integration of Western Europe is presented as an obstacle to bilateral trade with the Eastern bloc. The most sustained campaign ever had been waged against Pershing-2 and ground-launched cruise missiles, deployment of which commenced in December 1983 in the FRG, Italy and the United Kingdom.

A special place in Soviet foreign propaganda activities is reserved for the People's Republic of China. Although both countries again exchanged ambassadors, after a four-year hiatus, in October and November 1970, respectively, this has not prevented them from attacking each other in the press and radio as well as at the United Nations. This last forum witnesses Chinese support for Pakistan, whereas the Soviet Union lines up with India. Beijing is accused of discriminating against minorities in Tibet, Sinkiang and Inner Mongolia. Publication of a Chinese atlas in 1979, which laid claim to 600,000 square miles of territory within the Soviet Union, provoked an attack in the official government daily newspaper *Izvestiya*.[44]

The main target of Soviet external propaganda is, of course, the United States. One can imagine the satisfaction in Moscow during the late 1960s and early 1970s when the violence instigated by radicals on college campuses was interpreted by many as the beginning of a revolution which would destroy the hated system. The meaning of words like peace or academic freedom and the 'people' in reality signified coercion and the will of a small minority that used any available means to introduce anarchy. All that Soviet propagandists needed were reports from the American press and television, embellished with some of their own interpretation. Freedom of the press in the West allows for a multitude of printed and

43. *Izvestiya*, 15 January 1981.
44. Cited by R.F. Staar, 'Bear and Dragon in the Third World', *Policy Review* 2/7, winter 1979, p. 97.

spoken criticism of political figures, organisations, society, and government policy which the USSR then cites in articles and speeches.

A news item appearing in the Soviet satirical magazine *Krokodil* stated that: 'In the United States understanding of the word "politician" has long been associated with the word "swindler".' In the next paragraph, the writer claimed that this quotation had come from the *Chicago Tribune* with 'whose opinion, in this particular question, we are in full agreement'.[45] American television programmes have been exploited by Soviet spokesmen. Soviet Minister Vladilen M. Vasev and chargé d'affaires Aleksandr A. Bessmernykh from the Soviet embassy in Washington were interviewed on 'Issues and Answers' as well as 'Face the Nation', respectively. Not since Nikita Khrushchev in 1957 had any Soviet representative been on the latter programme.[46] Reciprocity, of course, does not exist in Moscow.

Disinformation

Examples of prevarication and forgery on the part of the USSR were brought to public attention during congressional hearings in Washington, DC.[47] The Soviet ambassador to Zambia gave that country's President, Kenneth Kaunda, a false warning in May 1978 regarding an alleged American and British plot to overthrow his regime.[48] A former deputy chief of disinformation with the Czechoslovak intelligence service told the US congressional committee about targets of Communist 'black' propaganda. He testified that 'forgeries are the easiest and cheapest form of disinformation'. During one calendar year his unit, which had a staff of twenty-five officers, conducted about 115 actions around the world. Fifty to sixty per cent comprised forgeries, leaked to foreign newspapers and governments.[49]

The most effective forgeries seem to be official-looking documents and personal letters, allegedly written by US government officials. In two cases, the USSR attributed false and misleading

45. *Krokodil*, 2, September 1980, p. 9. See also 'Strange Picture of US that the Kremlin Concocts', *US News and World Report*, 24 January 1983, pp. 31–2.
46. *New York Times*, 13 March 1981.
47. US Congress, House, *Hearings*, p. 246.
48. Ibid., p. 84.
49. Ibid., pp. 7 and 25.

Table 10.1 Soviet expenditure on propaganda in millions of dollars

Budget item	Costs
CPSU international department	100
CPSU international information department	50
Tass	550
Novosti (APN)	500
Pravda	250
Izvestiya	200
New Times and other periodicals	200
Radio Moscow foreign service	700
Press sections in Soviet embassies	50
Clandestine radio stations	100
Communist international front organisations	63
Subsidies to foreign Communist parties	50
KGB's Service 'A'	50
Covert action operations by KGB foreign residencies	100
Support to national liberation fronts	200
Special campaigns (including anti-NATO TNF modernisation campaign)	200
Total:	$3363

Note: The estimate of over three billion dollars per year in Soviet expenditures for propaganda and covert action can be broken down as above, if one only counts proportional costs for foreign as distinct from domestic propaganda, and if other activities of the KGB are considered. The indirect cost, borne by foreign Communist organizations, are not included.

Source: US Congress, House, Permanent Select Committee on Intelligence, 'Soviet Covert Action: The Forgery Offensive', *Hearings* (6 and 19 February 1980), p. 60.

statements directly to the President and Vice-President of the United States. A bogus United States army field manual has surfaced in more than twenty countries. A series of forgeries directed at undermining American relations with Egypt and other Arab states also received wide dissemination. An estimated $100 million went into the Soviet anti-neutron bomb campaign alone and twice that much against the deployment of American theatre nuclear forces in Western Europe.[50]

As suggested earlier, propaganda activities overlap with espionage. The latter involves professionals, who frequently use TASS or *Novosti* as cover. This should not be confused with Western-style

50. Charles A. Sorrels, *Soviet Propaganda Campaign Against NATO*, US Arms Control and Disarmament Agency, Washington, DC, October 1983.

Table 10.2 International Communist front organisations

	Year Founded	Claimed Membership	Headquarters	Number of Affiliates	Countries	Soviet Support
Afro-Asian People's Solidarity Organization	1957	no data	Cairo	87	—	$ 1,260,000
Christian Peace Conference	1958	no data	Prague	48	50	210,000
International Association of Democratic Lawyers	1946	c. 25,000	Brussels	65	80	100,000
International Federation of Resistance Fighters	1951	5,000,000	Vienna	22	—	125,000
International Institute of Peace	1958	no data	Prague	9	—	260,000
International Organisation of Journalists	1946	over 180,000	Prague	111	120	515,000
International Union of Students	1946	over 10,000,000	Prague	117	109	905,000
Women's International Democratic Federation	1945	over 200,000,000	East Berlin	131	116	390,000
World Federation of Democratic Youth	1945	over 150,000,000	Budapest	270	123	1,575,000
World Federation of Scientific Workers	1946	c. 450,000	London	33	70	100,000
World Federation of Trade Unions	1945	c. 260,000,000	Prague	c. 90	81	8,575,000
World Peace Council	1949	no data	Helsinki	142	—	49,380,000
Total:						$63,445,000

Sources: US Congress, House of Representatives, Permanent Select Committee on Intelligence, Subcommittee on Oversight, 'Soviet Covert Action: The Forgery Offensive', *Hearings* (6 and 9 February 1980), pp. 79–80, which also gives a breakdown of Soviet financial support (staff, salaries, administration, travel, publications, conferences, and in-house meetings); Richard F. Staar, (ed.), *1984 Yearbook on International Communist Affairs* (Stanford, 1984), Introduction.

information gathering by an enterprising journalist or foreign correspondent, whose story appears in the press. Soviet professionals are well trained and operate on a career basis. Their reports go directly to the KGB or GRU headquarters in Moscow.

Table 10.3 Communist foreign radio broadcasts (hours per week)

Year	USSR*	Eastern Europe	China
1950	533	412	66
1960	1,015	1,072	687
1970	1,897	1,264	1,591
1980	2,097	2,210	1,374
1981	2,126	2,362	1,318
1982	2,162	1,644**	1,423

Notes: * USSR includes Radio Moscow only and not other stations, like Radio Peace and Progress or 'clandestine' transmitters.
       **Warsaw Pact members only
Source: Board for International Broadcasting, *1983 Annual Report* (Washington, DC, 1983), p. 2; USIA, 'Communist International Radio Broadcasting in 1982', *Research Memorandum* (6 December 1983), Chart 1, p. 2.

Summary of Discussion: Part II

The discussion on political and social conditions in the USSR centred on the scope for action by dissidents, the importance of nationalism and religion to Soviet policy and the role of ideology.

Reinhard Meier's contribution was criticised for overemphasising the stability of the situation. Wolfgang Leonhard commented that in his experience the strength of the Soviet system was always overestimated and too little weight was given to opposing forces. There were many of these, he argued and the values and objectives of the younger generation were different from those of their elders. Dr Meier replied that he had intentionally stressed the factors of cohesion because the usual tendency was to call attention to the regime's difficulties and not to the forces making for consolidation.

How far was the dissident movement connected with the processes of de-Stalinisation and *détente*? According to Gail Lapidus, *détente* had brought about a partial lifting of the information barrier in the Soviet Union, which had made it possible to create a set of information networks.

Cornelia Gerstenmaier replied that the dissident movement should not be linked with *détente*, as it had existed long before. She saw no objection to Western governments intervening by diplomatic means, and she did not think publicity essential. However, this should not mean governments feeling obliged to put obstacles in the way of parallel publicity campaigns conducted by private organisations.

Gerd Ruge regretted that nothing had been said of the part played by the most popular Soviet writers. Such authors as Rasputin and Aitmatov were sometimes acceptable to the regime but could also frequently be dangerous to it. By depicting a world with such values as humanity, decency and justice they were barring off a significant ideological area, and eliminating the possibility of the 'Soviet way of life' taking the place of ideology as a factor of cohesion. Vysotskii's songs were sung everywhere and hundreds of thousands had visited his grave. The government could cut off dissidents from contact with others but could not do away with the great mass of readers. Thus Soviet citizens lived in two worlds: that of ideology and that of real people. The latter world obeyed different rules and had long since discarded the official ideology.

Asked about the administration's 'threshold of tolerance' with regard to literature for the masses and writings by dissidents, Wolfgang Kasack replied that it was determined by literary quality and by whether a work was ignored or taken notice of in the West. A speaker added that the threshold for samizdat was at present rather low; at the same time, the system used samizdat as a safety-valve or lever of social control.

Opening the discussion on tradition, nationalism and the Church, Robert Conquest said that the 'new Russianism' also represented a fight against the Party, especially in its religious aspect. According to Gerhard Simon, the Russian Orthodox Church derived a clear advantage from the latent force of Russianism. On many historical anniversaries the role of the Church had been extolled. This was a change of attitude which the Church could take advantage of for many purposes that would have been quite impossible twenty years ago. Otto Luchterhandt pointed out that the number of Orthodox parishes had decreased since 1965, but that in the last ten years several new parishes had been created.

William Fletcher pointed to the connection between national identity and religion. For many believers [such as Catholics and Muslims] the two were identical. In such people's view, the Russian *élites* were not part of the ethical world.

As regards the part played by nationality in social and political life, Miles Costick said that the main criterion was not nationality but Party loyalty. Disputing this, Gail Lapidus argued that it was a matter of strong emotional import whether, for instance, one more Uzbek or Balt became a member of the Politburo.

Ethnic tensions in the Soviet army were also discussed. The RAND study by Alex Alexeyev had shown, according to Richard F. Staar, that Central Asian recruits were often badly treated, not by their officers but by NCO instructors.

The important thing, said Mrs Lapidus, was not the fact of racial tension in the armed forces but whether, over a longer period, the problem had got more or less serious. A comparison with other multiracial armies would be interesting. The RAND study did not touch on these points, however. When the Soviets said they wished to give the national minorities more opportunities in the army, they had in mind not only senior ranks but also the NCOs.

Ethnic tensions were largely a matter of language. In this connection Gail Lapidus pointed out that Russian language teaching in Central Asia was not to be looked on as Russification but was intended first and foremost to make up for the decline in knowledge of Russian owing to demographic causes. The population lived in a monoglot environment in which Russian was hardly used. The rulers were thus concerned to ensure that young people had a better knowledge of Russian before they were called up for the army.

An extensive discussion on the definition and function of ideology was introduced by Paul Roth, who emphasised the vagueness of the concept. A distinction must be made between the apparatus of justification, on the one hand, and political interpretation on the other. The function of ideology as an interpretation and rule of life displayed considerable weaknesses. Many Soviet books on atheistic themes dealt with such questions as the meaning of life, creation and survival after death.

In reply, two speakers offered definitions of the term 'ideology'. Edward Rozek: 'Ideology is a rationalised absence of logic, used to justify the arbitrary use of power. Communist ideology performs exactly the same function as Nazi ideology.' Oskar Anweiler: 'Ideology is a set of propositions that purport to explain reality and provide citizens with an orientation of values; it serves to determine consciousness and behaviour, and may in certain cases be associated with political sanctions.' Such an analytical definition, the speaker observed, emphasised the functional aspect irrespective of specific content. The main thing was the function of ideology in the educational process. Its content might change, but the function remained.

James Billington commented that ideology served to legitimise the use of power and also played a part in foreign relations. Many members of the political establishment believed in the 'irrevocable process of social revolution'. Thus, ideology could be used to justify Soviet involvement in distant parts of the world in which the old Russian Empire had no interest: for instance Vietnam, Cuba, Africa and even in Afghanistan.

Michel Lesage also emphasised two functions of ideology. On the one hand it was an element of political debate and of the process of political decision-making, while on the other it was a means of forming and controlling men's minds. In the latter sense it was an instrument in the so-called 'ideological struggle'.

Jerry Hough observed that Soviet ideology was also a medium for the discussion of domestic and foreign problems. What often appeared to the West as ritualistic language was indeed a language embodying not one but several rituals. For instance, anyone who used the term 'revolutionary people's democracy' conveyed the idea of socialist orientation and Soviet support, whereas reference to a 'bourgeois democratic dictatorship' implied the reverse. It was, therefore, particularly important to follow Soviet debates and learn how to interpret them. If someone stated that the whole world had a common interest in the stability of the international economic and monetary system, the Soviet public would understand this to mean that the USSR was also interested in the stability of capitalism.

Herman Achminov questioned the view that Soviet ideology was 'dead': it had in fact been revitalised under Chernenko. It made no difference, however, whether one believed the content of the ideology; accordingly he agreed with those who assigned to it a functional role.

Peter Frank considered that the introduction of the concept of 'developed socialism' was a confession of failure in respect of Soviet ideology. There had indeed been a general cultural impoverishment in the Soviet Union. This accounted for the constant appeals to the Russian cultural tradition, which enabled people to work out ethical and moral guidelines for themselves.

Arnold Buchholz put forward an interesting view on the significance of ideology to Soviet intellectuals. All of them had studied the ideology; it served as an orientation and a permanent indication of what had *not* been achieved. As examples he mentioned the standard of Western technology and questions as to the meaning of existence. Ideology was no longer effective as a motive force, so the leadership had created substitute ideologies of patriotism, great-power claims and peace propaganda. However, despite all these, a reform in the Soviet Union could not take place without a solution of ideological problems.

On the subject of propagandising foreign countries it was urged that the West should on no account accede to Soviet demands for the curtailment of broadcasts to the socialist countries. The West, Günther Wagenlehner observed, must be clear as to the political purpose of such broadcasts. There was no doubt how important it was to keep the population of these countries informed, and how effective the broadcasts were.

Paul Roth remarked that events in the Soviet Union were far too little reported in the West.

Was Soviet propaganda really a one-way process, or were congresses of 'front' organisations a double-edged weapon which might have repercussions on the Soviet *élite*? Richard F. Staar thought such repercussions were very slight. It was impossible to influence Soviet functionaries like Arbatov and Zhukov, who did not seem to him intellectually capable of understanding what was really happening in the Soviet Union or the US.

PART III

Political Power

Introduction to Part III: Political Power
Wolfgang Pfeiler

The first priority of the Soviet leadership has at all times been to maintain its political power both internally and externally. Since Lenin's day the principle has been that power must be concentrated in the hands of the Communist Party. Nothing must be allowed to detract from the Party's 'leading role'. Ever since Lenin's time, moreover, political power has been institutionalised in accordance with the principle of 'democratic centralism'. The system admits of no pluralism and no compromise where power is concerned.

In Lenin's time and subsequently, the Western world has endeavoured to come to grips with this system and to understand its structure. For over half a century the Soviet political system has been the object of study by an increasing number of Western institutions and scholars, whose first endeavour was to observe and analyse its internal structure. On the whole it can be said that as a result of this study the functional principles of the system of Soviet rule are today clearly recognised. Even though many details of the system and of current developments are and always have been concealed or at least difficult of access, there is no doubt concerning the leadership principle as such.

There is also basic agreement as to the evaluation of this system. Both in the West and in the East, it is accepted that the Soviet system is incompatible with the values of democratic Western societies.

The political and economic controversy that has also been going on in the West for well over half a century relates to a different point: namely the developmental trends of the Soviet system and the possibilities of influencing it. Ever since Sovietology began there have always been highly divergent expectations in this respect. Since Lenin's day it has been believed, time and again, that the system was on the brink of collapse from internal causes, while some have maintained that such a collapse could only be averted by far-reaching reforms. In the 1950s and 1960s, in particular, a number of experts believed that the Eastern and Western systems might gradually 'converge'. Not a few others, however, took an almost fatalistic view of the unchangeability of the Soviet system. Finally, at all times there has been a small minority who maintained that the

Soviet system would develop dynamically and prove superior to Western models.

While this last expectation is no longer to be met with in the West, the basic argument remains as topical as ever. Hence Part III of the conference was concerned with the structures of the political system, the Party leadership, the succession crisis and the social and political changes in the Party, the political leadership and the bureaucracy. Much attention was devoted to the latter's influence on the state and the economy, and the role of the military within the political system.

In conclusion, the participants examined the basic question around which the whole conference was planned: that of the possibility of changes in the system. The factors making for conservatism and change were analysed and assessed. Are revolutionary changes to be expected in the Soviet Union, or is the political system gradually evolving? Can the leadership 'muddle through' or is it heading for complete stagnation? What are the possibilities and limitations of political reform?.

The answers to these questions, as was no doubt to be expected, were at times controversial and even contradictory. They are still highly topical, not least in view of the measures that have since been adopted by Mikhail Gorbachev, the new General Secretary. It is too soon to say with certainty whether these measures will really succeed in galvanising the system and increasing its efficiency. Some Western observers even think they may on balance have adverse effects, as the fight against corruption and the black market is aimed against the very institutions that make it possible for a rigid system, offering no prospect for the future, to go on functioning at all. Naturally, too, it remains conceivable that an old pattern of Russian history will repeat itself: a few changes are institutionalised from above, after which everything relapses into a state of petrified conservatism.

The papers and discussions on this subject bring clearly into focus the structures and forces that play an important role in the Soviet Union, and which must be understood if we are to form any idea of current developments inside the Soviet empire.

11

The Power Centre

The Kremlin Leadership from Brezhnev to Gorbachev
Christian Schmidt-Häuer

After the fall of Khrushchev, and especially in the last years of the 'old guard', the Soviet Union was the best illustration of Machiavelli's thesis that states maintain themselves by preserving the ideas from which they originated. In Moscow there had long been a growing desire for a leader of a new stamp, in accordance with the truth perceived by Jacob Burckhardt in his *Reflections on History*: 'Great men are necessary to our lives in order that the movement of history may periodically wrest itself free from antiquated forms of life.' The desire positively took on the form of a redemption myth, as the decay of the gerontocrats added ring after ring to the Kremlin tree trunk. Within a mere twenty-eight months, Party and state leaders Leonid Brezhnev, Yurii Andropov and Konstantin Chernenko were successively interred in the Kremlin wall. Many saw their demise as a symbol of the 'antiquated forms of life' of the Eastern superpower.

On 11 March 1985, for the first time in Soviet history, Radio Moscow announced on the same day the death of the Party General Secretary and the name of his successor. Chernenko at seventy-three was the seventh Party chief and the oldest who had ever attained power; now, for the first time since the October Revolution, the leaders chose as the new General Secretary a man who was by far the youngest member of the Politburo. Mikhail Gorbachev, who attained the supreme office at fifty-four, was ten years older than Stalin had been at Lenin's death; but in 1924 the average

age of the Party leaders was only forty-two. Today Gorbachev —
the first Soviet leader too young to have been born under tsarist rule
— is the youngest Party boss in the whole of Soviet-controlled
Europe. He is the first lawyer member of the Politburo since Lenin,
and the only member of that body to have studied two subjects at
university level — though in the case of agricultural economy it was
only a correspondence course.

These facts suffice to show that the assumption of power by
Gorbachev represents a change of generations unprecedented since
Lenin's time. Born in 1931, a year of starvation due directly to
Stalin's autocratic enforcement of the central planning system,
Gorbachev today is endeavouring to correct that system by a more
decentralised form of management. When Germany attacked the
Soviet Union he was ten years of age; when Stalin died he was still a
student. He is thus the first Politburo member too young to have
served at the front, and in his speeches the 'Great Patriotic War' is
reduced to more realistic dimensions. Gorbachev and his generation, who were not even indirectly involved in the Stalinist terror,
have no need to compensate for guilt complexes with reminiscences,
such as are still indulged in by the old guard, of the heroic and epic
struggle against the Nazi invader. The development of the central
planning system, which began with Stalin's fearful human sacrifices
on the altar of industrialisation, to be justified ideologically by the
next generation, is to the younger men no more than a matter of
history, in which they took no part and for which they have no need
to make any personal excuses.

This is the real dividing line between the generations, thanks to
which the way was paved for Gorbachev even before the rush of
mortality from the beginning of 1982, when Suslov, Pelshe, Brezhnev, Andropov, Ustinov and Chernenko all disappeared within a
brief space of time. The change actually set in during the declining
phase of the old-timers. The shaking up of society and the emergence of new forms of public debate were not a product of the
macabre last days of the oligarchs with their petrified dogmas, but
were due to the previous overthrow of taboos by a less inhibited
generation. Thanks to them, economic considerations became more
and more paramount, even in the conduct of foreign affairs. 'Socialism' — Gorbachev declared in December 1984 — 'continues, as in
the past, to influence world developments first and foremost by its
economic policy, by its successes in the socio-economic sphere.'

For such high priests of doctrine as Mikhail Suslov it would have been a confession of total failure to have admitted, even indirectly, that a cardinal feature of Soviet ideology, the collectivisation of agriculture, had been a catastrophic error in the form in which it was carried out. To the younger Soviet *élite* agriculture is no longer a sacred cow, ideologically speaking, but an aspect of the practical problem of reconciling economic efficiency with the buttressing of political power. Significantly, the sharpest and most evident dispute between Chernenko and Gorbachev in 1984 involved two acrimonious conferences on the theme of agriculture.

The pragmatic approach of the new generation — within the bounds of the system, naturally — applies to industry also. The old bureaucracy could only imagine Soviet world power on the basis of an overwhelmingly strong heavy industry. To them tanks, aircraft, cruisers and missiles were the hallmark of progress; consumer goods a mere sop to the masses and a hindrance to the main design. Gorbachev, and especially his advisers in the scientific institutes, on the other hand, are set on putting into practice the ideas proclaimed by the economic theorist Yevgenii Liberman a quarter of a century ago. These involve the planned linking of increased consumption and strengthening of the productive forces, and the promotion of light industry as a stimulant to economic efficiency and a temporary means of rescuing the Soviet people from its desperate state of technological backwardness and launching it into the age of microprocessors.

None of this means that Gorbachev was not also linked with the 'old guard' and even a protégé of important members of the Politburo. His principal patrons were the agricultural expert Fyodor Kulakov, who died in 1978, and the former Party chief Yurii Andropov. There is even some reason to believe that the ambitious politician from Stavropol was befriended for a time by the top ideologist Mikhail Suslov, who died in 1982 and who from 1939 to 1944 was First Party Secretary of the Stavropol regional committee.

Nor should the change of generation mislead us into thinking that the new Kremlin leaders stand for 'liberalisation' in the Western sense of the word. Nothing would be more mistaken than to see Gorbachev as a man who intends to allow greater freedom to dissidents and ordinary citizens. The new General Secretary is a forceful character full of self-assurance. He intends to pursue and develop Andropov's policy so as to create a modern society with a stronger regard for group interests, but this aim must remain subordinate to the firm maintenance of power. Gorbachev's invocation of the NEP — Lenin's economic policy of 1921 permitting private initiative and the leasing and autonomy of enterprises — does not portend any enlargement of civil rights as these are understood in the West. Indeed, it is often forgotten that Lenin's 'New Economic Policy' went hand in hand with intensified political supervision. As a well-known expert said to me in Moscow in the summer of 1985:

> The present leaders want not only more efficient production but more effective control. Of course there will have to be a certain degree of loosening-up. Eighty per cent of the people are basically indifferent, ten per cent are patriots who prefer the old ways, and the other ten per cent are prepared to work for change. If these ten per cent cannot be assured that they will not be punished for criticising, nothing more will happen at the middle and lower levels than a campaign against the cadres who are standing in the way of the new team.

These words give a clear definition of the amount of scope that the change of generation affords to the Party, the Soviet people and the Soviet empire. It is not a situation of radical change, but it certainly represents a new departure after long years of stagnation. If anyone on the sixty-fifth anniversary of the October Revolution — 7 November 1982, three days before Brezhnev's death — had predicted the changes that have since occurred, both in the top leadership and in economic structures, he would have been derided as a hopeless dreamer. How is it that these developments were possible?.

Brezhnev's first ten years, from 1965 to 1975, were the most successful decade of Soviet history from the point of view of economic and social change and achievements in both domestic and foreign affairs. The rate of economic growth was almost 6 per cent *per annum*. The leadership and groupings within the Party were more prepared to find a basis of mutual understanding. After the mid-1970s, however, the upward trend was reversed. The growth in energy production slowed down; agriculture, in spite of huge investments, continued to decline. In certain professions and industries a labour shortage was increasingly felt. To this was added the freezing of supplies to the population in consequence of the arms programme with which Moscow sought to overtake the US lead in defence technology.

The Soviet people's reaction was basically no less 'counter-revolutionary' than that of the Poles in the Solidarity movement of

August 1980. It was expressed, however, in traditional Russian ways. People 'struck' against low wages and meagre supplies by shopping in working hours, while enterprises falsified their output returns. However, as in old Russia, many reacted ambivalently to the conclusions they drew from the shortcomings of the system. As the leadership showed itself less efficient, large sections of the population felt a confused desire for discipline and a strong hand at the helm. This rising *élite* no longer confined themselves to vaguely hoping for a rejuvenation of the leadership, but began to press for the younger generation to take over.

It was Yurii Andropov, for many years head of the KGB, who perceived this mood most clearly. It coincided admirably with the double strategy he had evolved while Brezhnev was still alive, namely to gain power by means of the anti-corruption campaign and thereafter tighten up the system and make it more efficient. Andropov, the coolest and shrewdest member of the Politburo at that time, had long been blocked by Brezhnev's group. Even at the XXVI Party Congress in 1981 he neither delivered a report nor presided over a session. He had no power base of his own with which to combat Brezhnev's clique. The KGB was his instrument, but he could not make open use of it to mobilise the younger generation against the gerontocracy, the experts against the nepotists, and the managers against the bureaucrats. Instead, he loosened the reins of KGB control so as to allow more and more freedom of criticism by the technical institutes and in the media, and in this way increased the pressure of the outside world upon the inner circle — academicians against the Party apparatus, functional experts against functionaries. However, these new outside forces needed a focus for their hopes within the Kremlin, in the shape of disciplined candidates for power who were not discredited and ossified but were representative of the new generation.

This was the role that Gorbachev promptly assumed in Moscow, in close collusion with Andropov. The regional Party boss from Stavropol in the northern Caucasus, who had come to Moscow as late as November 1978 as Central Committee secretary for agriculture, moved into the inner circle of power more rapidly than any similar aspirant before him. In 1980, six months before his fiftieth birthday, Gorbachev became a full member of the Politburo; the average age of its members was at that time 70.1. The aged leaders were out of touch not only with the masses but also with the rising *élite* in the institutions, enterprises and provinces. Gorbachev rapidly set about establishing links with these elements, obtaining information and expert assessments and cautiously introducing suitable hints into his speeches. What, in a nutshell, was the actual common ground between Gorbachev and the rising generation of the *élite* outside the Kremlin? They agreed in rejecting the tradition of accepting actual or potential gains in the international field as a substitute for domestic change. In this respect the co-operation that now began differed from most of the earlier, unsuccessful attempts at reform.

Andropov's position as head of the KGB scarcely fitted him for the role of 'crown prince'. However, he emerged rapidly from the background in two stages, with Gorbachev at his side. Firstly, he gave Brezhnev's preferred candidate, Chernenko, a free hand in his disputes with Andrei Kirilenko, who had for many years been regarded as the designated successor. Then, when the balance tipped in favour of Chernenko, Andropov suddenly attacked him on a new front by starting a campaign against the corruption of Brezhnev and his hangers-on. He brought Kirilenko's supporters on to his own side and finally emerged from the power struggle as a *tertius gaudens*. On 12 October 1982, two days after Brezhnev's death, the Central Committee designated Andropov as the new leader. He consolidated his position with the aid of Kirilenko's following — the latter having by now been thrust from power — and by so doing strengthened Gorbachev's special role. Kirilenko's protégés had belonged to heavy industry, the State Planning Commission and the governmental apparatus of the RSFSR — all bastions of the old system rather than breeding-grounds of economic reform. These former supporters of Kirilenko, being in opposition to Chernenko, loyally supported Andropov and are now solidly behind Gorbachev. However, they were and still are men of probity and enemies of corruption and indiscipline, rather than structural reformers and advocates of initiative at lower levels. This situation helped Gorbachev — who had shown courage and acquired experience in connection with agricultural reforms in the Stavropol region — to become the indispensable chief of staff of the now ailing General Secretary. Even now, again and again it is Gorbachev who sets his sights highest. Former supporters of Kirilenko such as Ryzhkov and Vorotnikov show far less inspiration, at any rate in their public speeches.

When Andropov took over he was already suffering from acute kidney disease, but he tackled with determination the task of reforming Soviet agriculture: performance instead of stagnat on was the watchword. He realised, however, that time would not allow him to carry out reform from the bottom up: all he could do was to make a start at the top. Governing from a sick-bed, his foreign policy ended in stagnation and the erosion of authority in the Eastern bloc, but his personnel policy was of great significance. A few weeks before his death (which took place on 9 February 1984) he brought into the Politburo two opponents of Brezhnev and Chernenko, namely Vitalii Vorotnikov (fifty-seven) and Mikhail Solomentsev (seventy), and also made Yegor Ligachev (sixty-three) a secretary of the Central Committee. Earlier, in November 1982 — immediately after Brezhnev's death — the able Gaidar Aliev from Azerbaijan, aged fifty-nine, had been promoted to the Politburo. At that time also, Nikolai Ryzhkov, aged fifty-three, had been appointed a secretary of the CC with the task of improving the coordination of the economy and pruning the overgrown bureaucracy of the Planning Commission and the ministries.

These changes of personnel were Andropov's most important legacy. He was a transitional leader, but the transition was designed by himself. He built the bridge that enabled a new generation to advance to power over the morass of corruption.

When Andropov died there were two candidates for the office of General Secretary, who could not have been more different. The young and self-confident Mikhail Gorbachev, aged fifty-three gave the impression of competence and stood for a thorough-going reform of the Soviet system, for the enhancement of performance by pressure and incentive, for agricultural experiments and for a new mechanism of economic control. His rival Konstantin Chernenko appeared insecure and incompetent; his age was almost ten years in excess of the average expectation of a male Soviet citizen; he offered a return to peace and quiet, camaraderie and populism on a conservative basis. A majority of the leadership decided in his favour once more. The vote was divided; but Gorbachev's faction, seeing that their chances were still in doubt, did not force a showdown.

In retrospect it can be said that the decision for Chernenko by a narrow margin was a preliminary decision in favour of Gorbachev: a compromise which was a kind of deal between the two generations. Gorbachev was acknowledged as crown prince, and it was guaranteed that the next General Secretary would not perpetuate the gerontocratic system.

271

How was it, even so, that a majority of the Party leaders decided to turn the calendar back fifteen months and appoint a second Brezhnev for a further period of old-style rule? There was a mixture of reasons. The veterans, concerned for privileges and jobs and alarmed at the threat to their protégés in the inflated planning bureaucracy, voted against Andropov's ruthless campaign of 'retirement'. The energetic followers of the late leader must be curbed, and Chernenko, the stolid champion of the *apparat*, was the right man to slow things down. Many senior functionaries still remembered with alarm the experience of Khrushchev's time, when too sudden a change had brought about loss of control and an unpredictable 'thaw' that threatened the planning system.

Chernenko, who had climbed to the top thirty years after Brezhnev, had not proven a match for Andropov and was smeared by the disclosures of corruption among Brezhnev's clique. At the same time, in common with Gorbachev and in opposition to the metal-eaters of the defence lobby, he stood for a higher standard of consumption and general welfare. However, his recipe for this did not go beyond Communist picture book ideas of mass initiative and increased consciousness on the part of workers. The promotion of group interests and incentives in the form of wage differentials seemed to him economically rash and politically suspect.

Such was the background to the tug-of-war between the survivors of Brezhnev's faction, supported by the ministries and the planning bureaucracy, and Andropov's heirs with their KGB backing. Elements of the *apparat* and the old guard did their best to thwart the understanding that Gorbachev would be the next leader. Chernenko, at the point of death, was shown on television voting in the parliamentary elections: the purpose of this macabre scene was to present Viktor Grishin, the Moscow Party chief, in a favourable light as his successor. However, Gorbachev had meanwhile accumulated more power and functions than any 'number two' in the Party, including Mikhail Suslov, had ever possessed. As Gromyko was to disclose on 11 March 1984, Gorbachev at this period took the chair at Politburo meetings whenever Chernenko was absent. As a Central Committee secretary he was responsible for ideology, the Party apparatus, the economy and agriculture: this meant that he superintended the work of six of the other eight secretaries. Grigorii Romanov, long regarded in the West as Gorbachev's strongest rival, was CC secretary responsible for the armaments industry and administrative matters; as such he had under his

272

supervision only one other secretary, Vladimir Dolgikh (heavy industry).

On the day of Chernenko's death (10 March 1984), Gorbachev's opponents once again tried to bring about a change of course. According to the official bulletin, the General Secretary died at 7.20 p.m. Outwardly, business proceeded as before. The Party leaders met at about 10.30 p.m. Of the ten Politburo members three were absent: Shcherbitskii and Vorotnikov (in the US and Yugoslavia respectively) and Kunaev, the Kazakhstan Party chief, who could not get to Moscow in time. Shevardnadze, the Georgian Party chief and a candidate member of the Politburo, was similarly unable to attend. At the meeting Romanov (aged sixty-two) proposed Viktor Grishin (aged seventy) as the new General Secretary, whereupon Gromyko took up the cudgels for Gorbachev. Whoever was now chosen, he declared, must be one who could take the Soviet Union into the next century: if this were not borne in mind, he, Gromyko, might himself become a candidate. Chebrikov, the KGB chairman, also threw his weight behind Gorbachev, pointing to documentary evidence of 'errors' by Grishin as well as the corruption scandals in Moscow and economic misdemeanours by friends of Brezhnev's daughter Galina.

No official statement was issued as to the convocation and outcome of this decisive meeting. It is noteworthy, however, that Gromyko's speech on the following day (11 March), in which he invited the CC plenum to elect Gorbachev, was not published in any Soviet newspaper: it only appeared a week later, in a pamphlet difficult to procure. Gromyko's quite exceptional eulogies made it clear that he, the seventy-six-year-old doyen of Soviet foreign policy, was addressing himself to an appreciable body of opinion which called into question Gorbachev's experience, style of leadership and ideological reliability. As though to dispel doubts concerning the new General Secretary's competence and firmness in foreign affairs, Gromyko declared:

> As a result of my official duties, this has perhaps been somewhat clearer to me than to some other comrades: he [Gorbachev] is capable of perceiving promptly and with good judgement the nature of developments outside our country, in the international field. I have often been surprised by his ability to grasp the essence of a problem quickly and accurately and to draw conclusions that were correct in a Party sense.

With the election of the new General Secretary the opposition of

273

the old stagers in the Politburo seemed to crumble like a mummy exposed to fresh air.

In the past, Soviet Party chiefs had generally taken five years — if they did not die in the meantime — to consolidate their power. Stalin conducted his murky struggle for power against Trotsky, Bukharin and Zinoviev; Khrushchev fought against Beria, Bulganin, Malenkov, Molotov and Kaganovich. Brezhnev had to assert himself against Kozlov, Suslov and Kosygin. Gorbachev, on the other hand, seemed from the outset to be firmly in the saddle and to have trusted followers in all key positions. The extent to which his power was genuine, and the difference between the beginning of his rule and the first steps of his predecessors, may be illustrated by three aspects of his performance to the present: his style *vis-à-vis* the population and Party, the reorganisation of personnel at the highest level in the Kremlin, and changes in the structure of the economy.

Style

Lenin once complained of 'the worst enemy in our Oblomov republic — the Communist who has not learnt to fight bureaucratism but merely hushes it up'. The lack of a sense of initiative, responsibility and discipline on the part of the Russian population and bureaucracy has been found frustrating not only by Gorbachev's Communist predecessors but also by reformist tsars. The latter did not question the principle of autocracy because, while it might be a source of social weakness and torpidity in domestic affairs, it was also a guarantee of national strength and influence in the international field. The Soviet leaders have inherited this outlook. As in tsarist times, the ethnic Russian majority — only just a majority, but a compact one — in the multiracial Soviet state expects any change for the better to be introduced from above.

The first few months of Gorbachev's rule, on the other hand, showed that he is attempting to tackle the problem of the 'Oblomov republic' at both ends. Like Andropov before him, he intends by means of the anti-corruption campaign to impose on the Party and state apparatus the criteria of a society based on performance. He wishes to discipline and hearten the population by encouraging initiative, and thus to bring about changes both from above and from below. History and the present insoluble problems of the Soviet economy suggest that he too will be brought to a standstill before long — caught in the dilemma between independence, which is economically desirable, and private property, which is ideologically suspect; or between initiative, which is encouraged, and spontaneity, which is condemned.

For the time being, however, the Russian peasant's son from the Caucasus has brought life into a lethargic society. As a senior member of the American embassy in Moscow said to me: 'It's like starting a new book. People are turning the pages excitedly. they don't know how the story will go on, but their expectations are still rising — so far. And each group hopes that it will turn out well for them: poets and dissidents, economists and ecologists, nationalists and would-be emigrants.' In the first month or two Muscovites were chiefly engaged in swapping stories about Gorbachev's way of doing things. Like all *nachal'niki* he let it be known that he was going to visit a certain hospital — but then went to a different one, unannounced. Or again: like his predecessors, when he visited factories he spoke to an audience hand-picked by the KGB and the works management. However, unlike earlier times, the organisers — at the ZIL car factory in Moscow, for example — were under orders not to produce mere applauders but ordinary customers with complaints to put forward.

In the early months particularly, what fascinated the Soviet citizen was not what the new General Secretary said but how he said it. A senior dignitary had never before addressed them in a pleasant conversational tone, putting aside his speech notes with their red and green underlining; sometimes with his hands in his pockets, sometimes counting on his fingers to show the audience that a ruble is worth three times as much if it is invested to save energy rather than used on energy production; or building up a new relationship of confidence with pauses, smiles and a quiet tone of voice. In Leningrad, in the middle of May 1985 — leaning casually on the elegant balustrade of the former Smolny Institute for daughters of the nobility, whence Lenin in 1917 had announced the take-over of power by the Bolsheviks — he admonished a group of top officials in an almost chatty tone. while they listened to him with bated breath. In June he made a similar appearance at the metallurgical works in Dnepropetrovsk, a former stronghold of Brezhnev's: making plain what he wanted, but in a moderate tone, urgent but not importunate.

Many Party members looked askance at this unusual publicity campaign conducted from balconies and in the streets and marketplaces, as if the General Secretary of the CPSU were standing for popular election. Among those who disapproved were not only Gorbachev's immediate opponents but all who believed in an omnipotent, inflexible Party and whose object was, as in the past, to govern human beings by decree and not arouse them by means of a dialogue. How — they exclaimed privately — can a Party leader take to the street, and what will become of the Party if it starts asking the people to approve what it is doing? Those who argued thus could invoke the authority of Lenin himself, whose 'vanguard' concept of the Party left no room for populism.

Beyond question, the ZIL workers were delighted with the new style of leadership. However, enthusiasm and charisma have always been a cause of suspicion and alarm to the Soviet *élite*. They can lead to false hopes, they can incite the masses to chaos and anarchy — that is what the tsarist autocracy once feared, and it is still feared by many senior bureaucrats.

It could be seen from the Soviet media how many *agitprop* functionaries were alarmed by Gorbachev's unconventional excursions into the market-place and his disregard for ritual. The programme makers were at pains to tone down his populist and publicist approach. In the TV version of his Leningrad speech Gorbachev could clearly be heard to say 'A worker told me . . .'; *Pravda* replaced this by 'Someone told me . . .' At the 'Discussion on scientific and technical progress' in June 1985 Gorbachev argued that science, education and culture should be given new forms; the newspapers suppressed this statement. Even the KGB, to which Gorbachev can look for support as the heir of its former chief Andropov, does not seem to be of one mind as to the new style. An official in a good position to know told me: 'Some people ask "Where is all this leading to?", while others say "This is the only way."'

Gorbachev's public appearances with their air of spontaneity were in fact not mere 'walkabouts', but part of a carefully laid plan to defeat his opponents. This brings us to the second main aspect of the change of guard at the Kremlin.

The Power Structure at the Top

Gorbachev's three-day visit of inspection to Leningrad, which is by now almost legendary, was of the first importance from the point of view of the power struggle. The old tsarist city was for a long time the headquarters of Gorbachev's rival Grigorii Romanov, its Party chief until 1983, who set an example to all who stood for inflated claims of economic performance and opposition to reform. Vain, narrow-minded and much influenced by the military, Romanov — in clear contrast to Gorbachev — showed no concern, in his industrial policy, for the social interests of the population. The bulk of investment went into heavy industry and defence. Basic research was neglected while light industry, especially textiles, was increasingly starved.

Gorbachev, on his visit to Leningrad, made a special point of inspecting light industrial concerns such as the Bolshevichka clothes factory. He made no mention of Romanov, but let it be clearly understood that the emphasis had been misplaced during the past years under the latter's control. Speaking almost extempore, in a quiet tone — not threatening, but rather pleading for understanding — he declared: 'We all have to change our tune, from workers to ministers, CC secretaries and government leaders . . . Anyone who won't do this must simply clear out, he mustn't stand in our way.' Thus, after only two months in office the new General Secretary announced in quiet tones that his rival was due for a heavy fall. This became clear on 1 July 1985, when the CC plenum, without a word of appreciation of Romanov's services, announced his retirement on health grounds (he was then sixty-two). The allusion was clear: Romanov, who had been much involved in scandal and had supported Grishin instead of Gorbachev for the succession, was also a notorious drunkard, as had been seen on television at the Hungarian Party Congress at the end of March 1985. Such was the final, ostensible cause of his downfall.

In the same way, Gorbachev's public appearances in the Proletarskii district of Moscow and at Hospital No. 53 in mid-April 1985 not only stirred up public morale but also helped to unseat Grishin, the Moscow City Party chief. The visit was a pointed demonstration of how far Brezhnev's former adherent had neglected the social needs of the metropolis. On this occasion, it is true, Grishin put up a successful resistance with the aid of his Moscow mafia, which included the nationalist wing of 'cultural' functionaries: evidently not all the old bastions were ready to fall at the first assault. Gorbachev was also unsuccessful, at the CC plenum of 1 July 1985, in his attempt to oust Tikhonov (aged eighty, and an erstwhile friend of Brezhnev's) from the premiership. Only a few months later, however, his adherent Ryzhkov took over this top-level post.

However, Andrei Gromyko, who for a long time had been closer to Gorbachev than to Tikhonov, then carried out a cunning and well-planned stratagem. On 2 July 1985, after twenty-eight years' service as foreign minister — a world record — he took over the position of Head of State. His successor as foreign minister was, to the world's surprise, Eduard Shevardnadze, aged fifty-seven, at that time Party chief of Georgia and formerly its minister of the interior. A veteran opponent of corruption, the new foreign minister had more than once shown himself to be a man of imagination who had shown skill, courage and determination in quelling nationalist disturbances of various kinds among the Georgian masses. His Caucasian charm was in evidence at the tenth anniversary of the Conference on Security and Cooperation in Europe (CSCE) at Helsinki at the beginning of August 1985, the first occasion for many years when the Soviets scored a victory over the Americans in the field of diplomatic propaganda.

Gorbachev's completely unexpected appointment of Shevardnadze killed several birds with one stone. The office of foreign minister was once more held by a Party man instead of by Gromyko, a professional diplomat who might have a will of his own. The promotion of a Georgian to the Politburo, alongside the Azerbaijani Aliev, meant that another non-Russian representative of the unruly Caucasian nations was associated with the supreme power. Finally, the new foreign minister had no experience whatever of diplomacy, so that Gorbachev could upstage him in the field of foreign affairs. The new Party chief thus demonstrated his intention of having his own way in all matters, whereas most observers had predicted that he would have freedom of movement in domestic affairs but would pursue an inflexible foreign policy under Gromyko's tutelage.

Gorbachev's foreign policy, however, will not be free from constraint. If he is in earnest about reforming the economy and achieves all he has set himself to do, he cannot afford to remain cut off from the West and in a state of confrontation with the US. If essential reserves can only be mobilised by constantly invoking the danger from abroad, instead of by the country's own efforts and by correcting shortcomings in the system, then the new Kremlin leaders, like the old, will have no chance of escaping from the shadows of the past, the hushing up of weaknesses and the permanent denial of realities.

On whom can Gorbachev rely for help; who today are members of the innermost circle of power? The first three men next to the Party leader are those whom he placed in the Politburo in April 1985, less than six weeks after assuming office. These are the CC secretaries Ligachev and Ryzhkov (who in their rapid rise even bypassed the status of candidate member of the Politburo) and the KGB chief Chebrikov. Then come three more high-fliers of recent years: Vorotnikov, Aliev and Shevardnadze. Together with the two veterans, Gromyko and Solomentsev, this makes a total of nine out of thirteen Politburo members. Thus, in the run up to the XXVII Party Congress in February 1986, Gorbachev and his group had a solid majority of nine to three over the 'old guard', consisting of Grishin, Kunaev, and Shcherbitskii.

Yegor Ligachev, aged sixty-five, is the second man in the Party and the chief ideologist. A tough, stern-faced individual, he was fetched by Andropov from the wastes of Siberia in April 1983 to replace Ivan Kapitonov, a follower of Brezhnev's, as head of the important CC department for Party organisational work — the Party's personnel department, as it were. Gorbachev's rapid rise to power is largely the work of this efficient administrator, who was tireless and relentless in weeding out, downgrading and retiring corrupt and incompetent bureaucrats and Brezhnev protégés. A skilled aircraft engineer, he was associated with the reform-minded *élite* from a relatively early date. In 1957, when Khrushchev founded the Siberian department of the Academy of Sciences and caused the now famous town of Akademgorodok to arise amid the Siberian wastes, Ligachev was appointed *raion* Party secretary. In 1961, when he was thirty years of age, Khrushchev brought him to Moscow and made him deputy director of the *agitprop* department of the RSFSR Central Committee. Even critics of the regime to whom I spoke in Moscow remembered that he had expressed decidedly anti-Stalinist views at that time. In 1965, when Brezhnev had to find jobs for his own followers, he removed Ligachev to the oil and gas producing region of Tomsk in western Siberia, where he served for eighteen years as First Party Secretary. There, using relatively flexible methods, Ligachev brought about a considerable improvement in labour discipline and in regional economic structures: Andropov in fact wished to extend Ligachev's Tomsk experiment to the entire Soviet Union.

At first sight there could hardly be a greater difference than that between the present Kremlin chief and his number two. Ligachev, a brawny figure with a mane of strong, bristling grey hair, accustomed to hammer out speeches in a loud, monotonous, guttural tone, pushing out words as though they were stabs with a chisel. They were instructions rather than suggestions: 'There must be a firm tightening of discipline'; 'Shirking will no longer be tolerated'; 'There will be no deviation into market economy and private enterprise.' However, if one looks more closely it becomes clear that the man in the old-fashioned horn-rim spectacles is a very different type from the drab old-timers who surrounded Brezhnev. Ligachev makes a dynamic, purposeful impression, like a man who knows what he is saying and means the greater part of it.

The next man in the new hierarchy is the KGB chief, Viktor Chebrikov. Originally a comrade-in-arms of Brezhnev's from Dnepropetrovsk, he transferred his allegiance to Andropov and Gorbachev: the KGB was Andropov's instrument in the fight against corruption and has so far been the principal support of the new chief. The most important man for the reconstruction (*perestroika*) of the economy proclaimed by Gorbachev is Nikolai Ryzhkov, a Politburo member and CC secretary. He comes from Sverdlovsk, the former power base and political home of Kirilenko. An architect of heavy industry and the defence industry in particular, he is so much of a technocrat as never to have served in the Party apparatus. He was for a long time director of the country's most important industrial complex, Uralmash. His main task since Andropov's time has been to shake up the planning bureaucracy in the ministries and state committees, so as to achieve better coordination and a more effective management of industrial operations.

Vitalii Vorotnikov is an aeronautical engineer and, like Ryzhkov, a former follower of Kirilenko. In 1979, when the latter's fortunes were declining, Vorotnikov, at that time a deputy premier of the RSFSR, was relegated to the Cuban embassy. Andropov brought him back and put him in the front line of the anti-corruption campaign against Brezhnev and Chernenko. By June 1983 he had become premier of the RSFSR. Gaidar Aliev, the last member of the leading group, hails from Azerbaijan in the Caucasus, bordering on Iran. A skilled and ingenious organiser, his chief task is to remedy the disastrous state of the transport system. He was for a long time KGB chief in Azerbaijan, and then First Party Secretary. He made his name by combating the proverbial corruption in that Republic, and won respect not only for his severity but for genuine economic achievement. During his term of office, between 1975 and

1980, the Azerbaijan GNP increased by 47 per cent, while the All-Union average was only 23 per cent.

The question remains to be asked, however, whether the present ruling group is capable not only of proclaiming the need for profitability and the observance of priorities, but also of putting into practice specific structural improvements and developing further ideas of reform. So far little has been heard in public from Ryzhkov, the chief supervisor of the economy, while Vorotnikov, at the outset, used language scarcely differing from that of the old guard. At the middle and lower levels it soon appeared that there was no reserve capacity to be thrown into the battle for reform. The younger generation is indeed more open-minded and ready to experiment. However, the old-style, narrowly based training programmes from technical college to Party university will not produce enough highly qualified cadres in the foreseeable future, yet these are absolutely necessary in the lower term if Gorbachev's reconstruction is to succeed.

Reform of the Economic Structure

Some words by Yegor Ligachev are often quoted as a proof that the younger generation in the Kremlin is doing no more than pour old wine into new bottles. At the end of June 1985, speaking as the Party's chief ideologist to the CC Academy for Social Sciences, he declared that 'revolutionary transformations' would be effected 'without any deviation towards market economy and private enterprise'.

Many observers who judge the system purely by the political yardstick of a liberal economy cannot imagine how any transformation can take place on this basis. They therefore regard it as already evident that Gorbachev will be brought to a standstill, despite his initial enthusiasm, because he does not really want to break down the system: he cannot, they say, give managers more genuine independence and increase the autonomy of large and small concerns, because all this would undermine Party authority and set in motion uncontrollable social changes.

The basic question is, however, whether Gorbachev, with all his proclaiming of ideological dogma, will not be forced to the pragmatic realisation that the Soviet Union is much less endangered by experiments than it would be by a 'complete conversion' (*Pravda*) and a 'profound transformation' (*Novosti*) of its internal structure?

281

If Gorbachev is given credit for seeing this, further questions may arise: Will the planned changes develop a dynamism of their own, and has Gorbachev enough determination to accept the modifications that are forced on the system by practical necessity? From this point of view, four aspects should be examined more closely.

The reformers' position

The new men in the Kremlin are technocrats, loyal to the system, who believe they can repair the mechanism of the Soviet economy. They want to improve the engine's performance, not replace it by a new one: their object is modernisation, not reform in the Western sense. They intend to maintain the hierarchical system of central control, but to tighten up the hierarchy and prune the overgrown bureaucracy. For this purpose the powers of ministries and the state apparatus are being curtailed so as to give scope for Gorbachev's initiatives, designed to enable enterprises, workers' collectives and teams to enjoy reasonable prosperity. That is to say, for central planning to be more efficient it must be assisted by a certain degree of decentralisation, no more and no less.

This, on the face of it, is understandable. In the first place, Gorbachev's generation is under the influence of a past in which over-hasty reforms, from Khrushchev to the Solidarity movement in Poland, led to still greater planning difficulties or to the collapse of Party control. Secondly, to promote private enterprise in a huge empire with a market potential varying enormously from the Baltic to the Caucasus, from a merchant to a bazaar tradition, is a great deal more risky than to do so in a small homogeneous country like Hungary. Thirdly, Gorbachev's team must avoid antagonising the opposition in the bureaucracy and administration, in heavy industry and in some military circles, where the structural changes are already thought to go too far. By and large it can be said that Gorbachev will prefer a rationalised economy administered from the centre, after the GDR model, rather than the Hungarian pattern of increased private initiative and the autonomy of individual enterprises.

This position provides the starting-point for a modified structure of production and incentives, in agriculture and in the development of direct commercial relations between enterprises. The system of teams (*brigady*) working on their own account and their own responsibility is intended to increase material incentives and set new

282

standards of remuneration and bonuses. In order to allow enterprises more freedom of decision, 'the number of centrally fixed planning quotas is to be greatly reduced' (Gorbachev). Enterprises will have wider powers to dispose of various sources of finance and depreciation allowances; extended credits will be available for investment. At the beginning of August the authorities promised that enterprises would be allowed to keep part of their foreign exchange earnings from exports.

Even such changes as these may set things in motion within the Soviet system. This was shown by the 'unloved' but by no means inconsequential reform of 1965, of which Gorbachev's efforts are a continuation. That reform gave enterprises more independence by allowing them to distribute up to 20 per cent of their profits to the work-force by way of bonuses and social benefits. This increased the citizen's purchasing power and his social claims on management. The latter, however, could not and still cannot react flexibly, because the distant ministries assert their authority and their bureaucratic requirements in ignorance of regional conditions and local capacities.

Gorbachev's economic strategy

In his first months of office the new Party leader has asserted his position in a more concrete and precise manner than his predecessors. At the special conference on scientific and technical progress (11 June 1985) he departed in an unprecedented manner from the ritual of ostensible unity between the Party leadership and the state authorities, by sending back to the latter, for revision, the main directives for the new Five-Year Plan. This was a vote of no confidence in the prime minister, Tikhonov, and the chairman of the State Planning Commission, Nikolai Baibakov, also a member of the old guard. In the meantime both of them have been superseded.

Gorbachev would like to scrap the Planning Commission, hitherto a stronghold dedicated to statistics and quotas: 'We must begin at the highest level to put Lenin's idea into practice and transform the Planning Commission into a scientific institution including the best academic economists and leading practical experts.' Gorbachev has already threatened many specialised ministers with redundancy: 'The control apparatus in particular industries must be considerably reduced, cutting out all that is superfluous.'

It remains to be seen whether these strong words will bear fruit

— when, for instance, the four transport ministries are merged into one, or where all the redundant bureaucrats are to be sent to. However, at any rate the new leader has made a significant beginning.

Specific measures

A whole series of these were announced by the Party and government at the beginning of August 1985, continuing the process, begun in 1965, of enlarging the independence of enterprises. Thus, managers are to have wider powers as regards the capital invested in new plant, research and development. Plans for extension and modernisation can be worked out by the enterprises themselves; they require approval by the competent ministries only if the sums required exceed 4 million rubles in the case of heavy industry or 2.5 million elsewhere. The supply of materials, technology and funds for important building and overhauling works is henceforth to be supervised only by the local organs of the State Procurement Committee and not, as formerly, by the Planning Commission in Moscow.

Unused modernisation funds can now be carried forward to the following year to finance major projects. Banks may also use the deferred funds as credits for the modernisation plans of other firms. Another new regulation is that advanced-technology enterprises manufacturing top quality goods may raise their selling price by as much as 30 per cent, while plants whose products are of inferior quality must reduce their prices by degrees. To balance their books they may then draw on the bonus funds up to a maximum of 70 per cent.

This last provision, which places a heavier responsibility on the workers' collectives than on management, illustrates how half-baked some of the new measures are. How is a team to meet its deadlines and quality requirements if certain deliveries are unserviceable or fail to materialise? Generally speaking, however, it can be said that the structural reforms are well adapted to the situation. They are founded on the material bases of independent management created in 1965 and since then cautiously enlarged, namely the so-called incentive funds or reserves to cover bonuses, modernisation and social benefits.

Prospects and limitations of the programme

As a rule — and this is also true of many enterprises in the West — organisational changes are no more than a pretext for evading discussions of substance. However, the restructuring of the Soviet economy has been accompanied by an extensive discussion which began in Andropov's time. An example may show the kind of taboo that is being called into question. According to the orthodox position formulated by Stalin, ever since socialism abolished the private ownership of means of production there have been no social groups with particular economic interests. However, in the present discussion the sociologist Tatyana Zaslavskaya has observed (*Izvestiya*, 31 May 1985) that resistance to the new course comes from 'those people and groups who oppose everything that threatens their own narrow conception of the general interest or their own group concerns'.

On the practical side, Gorbachev's reconstruction is so far only patchwork. However, if he can even partially realise his vague ideal, it will in the long run bring about a far-reaching transformation of Soviet economic structures. This may well have growth-stabilising and performance-increasing effects.

On the other hand, there are major obstacles in the way of Gorbachev's lasting success. Where is the money to be found for investment, to which he attaches prime importance, in engineering, electronics, electrotechnology or biochemistry? Where are cuts to be made if Soviet oil output and the international price of oil continue to fall? (A drop of one dollar per barrel in the price of oil means an annual loss to the Soviets of about $400 billion worth of foreign exchange.)

Gorbachev can rely on his charisma for a limited time only. For two or three years he will be able to sweep the bureaucracy along with him and achieve the annual 4 per cent growth of the economy which he constantly proclaims as his objective. For that length of time he will no doubt remain convinced that his dynamic personality, the exploitation of all reserves and limited structural reforms will generate enough momentum to allow the bases of the Soviet economy to remain unchanged. Afterwards, as growth rates fall off again and Gorbachev's image is impaired, and as the system itself begins recognisably to defeat his aims, he will finally have to confront the crucial decision whether to embark cautiously on a transformation of the principle of central planning itself.

The Hungarian Party leaders never inscribed on their ideological banners what they actually allowed in their pragmatic balancing act. The Soviet leader has a far more difficult problem. However, there is some reason to think that his perception of necessity and determination to succeed may, at decisive moments, prevail over the fear of experiment.

The Leadership Crisis in the Soviet Union
Ernst Kux

All signs indicate that the Soviet Union is now in the first phase of a systemic crisis. To be sure, Soviet leaders admit that 'yes, we do have contradictions as well as difficulties' and that these can result in 'serious collisions'[1] However, they deny emphatically that the Soviet Union and Marxism-Leninism are experiencing a crisis. Such assertions are for them only inventions of 'ideological enemies' attempting to deny the 'unstoppable progress of the socialist system' and divert attention from the 'crisis of capitalism'. The nervous reactions to crisis diagnoses, the admission of existing problems and references to the increasing 'complexity' of political, economic and social developments in the most recent speeches of Soviet leaders all prove that their strongly expressed conviction of constant, smooth progress in the Soviet system corresponds less and less to its reality and can be maintained only with the greatest effort. The hope and promise that 'the present generation of the Soviet people will live under Communism!',[2] which was proclaimed in the third Party programme of the CPSU at the XXII Party Congress in 1961, has proved to be illusory. The planning goal set in that programme — to overtake America in industrial and agricultural production by 1980 and give the Soviet citizen a 'bowl of abundance'[3] — was not achieved and remained at best a distant dream. The collapse of Khrushchev's Party programme inflicted irreparable damage on the infallibility and leadership claims of Soviet ideology. The 'Soviet model' has lost its attractiveness everywhere — in the Third World, among Eurocommunists and even in Eastern Europe. At the end of the 1970s and the beginning of the 1980s, the economic growth of the Soviet Union declined rapidly; one crop failure followed another; social and national tensions increased. The crisis in Poland after 1980 and the occupation of Afghanistan shook the Soviet *imperium*. Moscow's expansive foreign policy suffered reverses on all fronts. *Détente* was replaced by a new freeze in East-West relations, Soviet

1. Y. Andropov, 'The teachings of Marx and several questions of socialist construction in the USSR', *Kommunist*, 10 1983, p. 22.
2. *XXII S"ezd Kommunisticheskoi Partii Sovetskogo Soyuza, stenograficheskii otchet*, III, Moscow 1962, p. 335.
3. Ibid., here I., p. 167.

influence in the Third World declined, the conflict with China was not resolved and tendencies towards greater independence increased within the 'socialist community'. The coincidence of the decline of Marxist-Leninist ideology, economic stagnation, new social problems and foreign policy reverses with a period of weakness in the Kremlin leadership as a result of the frequent changes at the top produced at any rate an extraordinary situation within the Soviet system. In its extent and seriousness this situation is more significant than earlier periods of weakness and transition and must be considered a crisis. Western observers should therefore consider the development and intensification of the crisis or even the development of a 'revolutionary situation' in the Soviet Union, as well as a possible introduction of far-reaching and effective reforms or a continued 'muddling through' along traditional lines to be 'objective possibilities' (according to Max Weber's definition). At present a dispute about these three developmental possibilities and their consequences has begun within the Soviet leadership. The danger of an intensification of 'contradictions' and 'conflicts and collisions' within 'developed socialism' has been realised.

On the one hand, the crisis is understood as the coincidence and accumulation of problems which can be resolved in time with adequate means; on the other hand, it is considered a cataclysm with no solution. Jacob Burckhardt described the great crises of history as a dialectical process in which 'historical power with an extremely high momentary justification' arises and develops its 'earthly forms' such as a constitution, classes, religion, property relationships and social customs; then comes 'resistance of these forms and break, through revolution or gradual decay', and 'in the meantime new forms are created whose external structure will suffer the same fate in time'. According to Burckhardt crises begin when the 'accumulated protest against the past' mixes with the 'dazzling, fantastic forms of the future'.[4] Lenin's view was similar: 'The really great revolutions are born of the contradictions between the old, between everything directed towards assimilation and the use of the old, and the completely abstract striving for something new, which has to be so new that it does not contain a single particle of the old.'[5] Lenin

4. Jakob Burckhardt, *Über das Studium der Geschichte*, text of the 'Weltgeschichtliche Betrachtungen', based on the manuscripts, Munich 1962, pp. 228 f. and 210.
5. V.I. Lenin, 'Lieber weniger, aber besser', *Werke*, vol. XXXIII, Berlin 1962, p. 485.

had developed a crisis theory according to which a 'political crisis' changed into a 'revolutionary situation' in three phases. The 'revolutionary situation' was then followed by the actual revolution. He did not exclude the possibility that the 'revolutionary situation' could subside and be resolved. He also perceived a difference between a 'constitutional and a revolutionary crisis': 'The former can be resolved within the framework of the existing basic laws and political order, while the latter requires breaking these laws and the destruction of the feudal order.' In Lenin's view the crisis begins at the top, with a 'government crisis of the ruling classes' resulting from the 'contradiction between promises, words, paper measures and reality'.[7] The preconditions and components of a 'revolution crisis' were for him 'the impoverishment of the village, a depression in industry, the realisation of the hopelessness of the present political situation and the much praised constitutional way'.[8] However, these developments are not sufficient to ignite a revolution. In Lenin's opinion the decisive, absolutely essential feature of a 'revolutionary situation' was the 'impossibility for the ruling classes to maintain their power unchanged; one crisis or another of the "upper classes", a political crisis of the ruling class'.[9] He described this situation with a simple sentence: 'The lower classes don't want to tolerate the existing situation any longer; the upper classes cannot change it.'[10] In their theory Marx and Lenin took up and developed the main theme of philosophies of history in the nineteenth century, namely the rise and fall of civilisations. They constructed in their Communist Utopia a future society which would not be subject to the cycle of rise and fall because in it the class struggle, which they viewed as the driving force of this process, would no longer exist. Their Utopia would thus be immune to crises and revolutions. History has since shown that all Communist countries have experienced serious crises — the 1921 Kronstadt uprising in Soviet Russia, the strike of East Berlin workers in 1953, the Hungarian Revolution of 1956, the Prague Spring of 1968, the Chinese 'Cultural Revolution' of 1966–76 and the crisis in Poland since 1980.

The shock of events in Poland, the spontaneous rising of the Polish workers and their suppression by a 'Bonapartist coup' both

6. Ibid., here vol. X, p. 533.
7. Ibid., here vol. VIII, p. 496.
8. Ibid., here vol. XV, p. 276.
9. Ibid., here vol. XXI, p. 206.
10. Ibid., here vol. XXXVI, p. 308.

289

of which, according to Marxist-Leninist theory cannot occur under 'real socialism', triggered a discussion in the Soviet Union about the 'deformation of socialism' and the 'contradictions of developed socialism'. In this discussion there have not only been differences of opinion about the causes of such 'negative developments'; various ways have been suggested to avoid or overcome them. Implicitly, this theoretical discussion involves the very relevant question of whether a similar crisis could break out in other 'socialist countries', including the Soviet Union, and how this should be prevented. As early as 1981 Chernenko, with an eye to Poland, warned of the 'danger of social tensions and political and socio-economic crises',[11] which could arise as a result of 'an incomplete and late analysis' or 'disregarding the social interests of some class or group' in Soviet society. The 'bitter lessons' of the events in Poland had shown him 'that the political situation can develop a crisis character', that the 'greatest danger for the party is its alienation from the worker and peasant masses' and that it would disappear if it lost touch with them.[12] He warned against assuming that 'the vanguard role of the Communist Party is guaranteed from the very beginning and forever'. Similarly, Andropov considered it possible that 'under certain circumstances the contradictions in Socialism could lead to serious collisions'.[13] He admitted that 'in politics one has to pay for mistakes. If the Communist Party loses its leading role, the danger will arise that the country could slip into a bourgeois reformist development. The ties between the party and the people will be lost, and in the resulting vacuum pretenders to the role of the defenders of the interests of the working masses will emerge.'[14] This insight into 'mistakes' and 'problems' and the fear of dangers and possible conflicts was obviously not only due to the crisis in Poland. It was intensified by the political and economic stagnation in the last phase of Brezhnev's rule. Andropov indirectly criticised this situation in April 1982 with the remark that 'Lenin's teachings do not permit stagnation'.[15] After being elected Brezhnev's successor as General Secretary in November 1982, Andropov tried to overcome the

11. K.U. Chernenko, 'Concerning several questions about party work in the period of developed socialism', *Kommunist* 10 1981, p. 11.
12. Chernenko, 'An important question for the entire party', *Voprosi Istorii KPSS*, 2 1982, p. 5.
13. *Kommunist*, 3 1983, p. 22.
14. Speech at the Central Committee plenum of 15 June 1983, *Pravda*, 16 June 1983.
15. *Pravda*, 23 April 1982.

stagnation and bring about 'change'. With astonishing frankness the new Party leader exposed 'unsolved problems of yesterday' in the Soviet system and observed without the usual glossing over that 'the tasks set at the last party congress have by no means been fulfilled'.[16] He thus rejected Brezhnev's assertion at the XXVI Party Congress in 1981 that 'the goals set by the last party congress have by and large been achieved'.[17] Andropov justified his criticism by pointing out that 'the search for ways to fulfil the new tasks was frequently not sufficiently energetic; often only half-hearted measures were taken and the accumulated inertia was not overcome quickly enough'. In his speeches to the plenary sessions of the Central Committee in November 1982 and June and December 1983, in his talks with Moscow workers and Party veterans and in his fundamental article on Marx in the Party magazine *Kommunist* (no. 3, 1983) Andropov presented a comprehensive catalogue of errors in the Soviet economy: Plan targets were often not fulfilled, the change to intensive production was proceeding too slowly, the 'practical application of the achievements of science and technology' left much to be desired; raw materials, goods and capital were being wasted; agriculture was backward, the supply of essential goods for the population was inadequate. As causes Andropov mentioned 'deviations from the norms and demands of economic life' and the continuing 'forces of inertia and old habits'. Even worse, as Andropov had to point out, the Party itself was no longer functioning properly. Decisions of the Central Committee and orders from above were not being carried out at lower levels. Party organs were dominated by 'bureaucratism', and corruption was becoming a habit among functionaries. Even the 'most valuable treasure' of the Party, Marxist-Leninist ideology, was no longer adequate for the tasks of providing the leadership with a correct 'scientific' policy and persuading and mobilising the masses. This 'gap between word and deed' has persisted since Andropov's death, and 'the society in which we live and work has not been adequately examined from a theoretical point of view', which 'is the reason why we are sometimes forced to act in an irrational way, so to speak empirically, by trial and error'.[18] These admissions of 'mistakes' and 'unfulfilled

16. Meeting with party veterans in the Central Committee of the CPSU, *Neues Deutschland*, 18 August 1983.
17. L. Brezhnev, 'Rechenschaftsbericht des Zentralkomitees an den XXVI. Parteitag der KPdSU', Moscow 1981, p. 3.
18. *Pravda*, 16 June 1983.

tasks' add up to a picture of a deep, pervasive crisis in the Soviet system, although Andropov denied the existence of such a situation. At any rate, he realised that speedy and radical changes were indispensable in all areas if the 'failings' were to be overcome and socialism perfected. For this reason, he demanded 'deep, quantitative changes of the productive forces and a corresponding perfecting of production conditions' accompanied by 'changes in the consciousness of the people and in all forms of the social superstructure', which had become an 'objective necessity'.[19] Andropov demanded quick results, knowing that continued hesitation would only make a critical situation worse. In his eyes the first task was 'to put what we have in order', and he began a campaign to 'strengthen party, state and work discipline as well as organisation and responsibility'. He also envisioned 'changes in planning and direction as well as in the mechanism of the economy'. He began a purge of old, corrupt functionaries and replaced them with younger Party and government cadres. Andropov's intention was by no means to introduce real reforms, such as free market elements and a decentralisation of the economy, or an opening in the direction of 'pluralism', which he completely rejected. He was concerned rather with reorganising and modernising the existing system to transform it into a 'smoothly functioning, well-tuned mechanism'. In a word, Andropov's plans for change were intended to make the vertical structure of Party rule more effective and thus make possible better order in and supervision of Soviet society as a whole. As a result of the measures he introduced, a certain improvement became apparent at the end of 1983. In a speech read in his absence at the December plenary session of the Central Committee, which became his testament, Andropov asserted that 'the most important thing now is to maintain the pace and the generally positive attitude and develop the positive processes even more actively'.[20] On 9 February 1984 Andropov died. His initiatives in Soviet domestic and foreign policy, which even before his death had been slowed by his illness and his long absence as well as by the resistance of the establishment, became bogged down. The Andropov era, which had begun with many initiatives and much promise, may be regarded as an interim of only fifteen months or as a decisive turning point, but it left the Soviet Union in an insecure and uncertain condition. The

19. Ibid.
20. *Pravda*, 27 December 1983.

cumbersome and rigid Soviet system, a giant with feet of clay, had hardly been set in motion with considerable effort when it ground to a halt again.

The two rapid changes at the helm of the Soviet Communist Party led to a leadership crisis unprecedented in the previous turbulent history of Party rule with its numerous internal conflicts. Earlier, Soviet leaders had boasted of the strength and stability of their governments compared to the Western democracies with their frequent changes of administration. The long physical and mental decline of the aged Brezhnev and Andropov's increasing incapacity, which could be covered up only with difficulty, gave rise to doubts in the Soviet Union and abroad about the permanence and ability to function of the Soviet system. The alleged advantages in the Communist system of the concentration of power in the hands of one person or an oligarchy (or gerontocracy) are offset by the inherent weakness resulting from the lack, due to ideological and political factors, of any institutionalised system of leadership change and succession. 'Charismatic systems of rule', of which, according to Max Weber Communism is one, 'know neither a form nor an orderly procedure for the installation or removal' of political leaders. The 'selection of the right individuals' takes place not in a free election, but in a 'struggle for leadership'. The successor is chosen by the most powerful followers of the previous leader and receives the obligatory acclamation of the ruled.[21] Although neither Andropov nor Chernenko can be regarded as 'charismatic leaders' in the proper sense of the word, their rise to the top was accompanied by a struggle for power; their elections took place within the small circle of the Politburo, and they received the unanimous applause of the Central Committee and their subjects. Like earlier Party leaders, both met the only condition for election: simultaneous membership of the Politburo and the Central Committee. The two successions in November 1982 and February 1984 clearly exposed the limitations of this selection procedure and the inscrutable and unpredictable nature of the Soviet power structure, which is suited neither to the reality of a modern industrial society nor to the requirements of the nuclear age. Whereas in the Soviet Union and the rest of the world Andropov's rise to power had caused many people to expect that the experienced KGB chief would prove to be a 'strong man' and

21. Max Weber, *Grundrisse der Sozialökonomie*, III, Tübingen 1947, pp. 75f and 141 ff.

bring about a 'change', the election of Chernenko as his successor raised doubts as to whether, apart from questions of age and health, he possessed sufficient firmness and ability to lead the Soviet Union in a difficult period. Chernenko, whom Brezhnev had chosen as his successor, had lost the struggle for succession to Andropov in 1982 and had been practically written off as a man to be reckoned with thereafter. The fact that he was able nevertheless to follow his rival as leader of the Soviet Union signified a victory of the 'old guard' and the continuation of the gerontocracy in the Kremlin, which was anything but inspiring. At any rate, the 'Brezhnevists', whose power and privileges had been reduced by Andropov, had now in the person of Chernenko their own man at the head of the Party, and they expected him to protect their privileges and continue with Brezhnev's policies. After this change of leadership fundamental differences of opinion emerged about the future course of the Party and the continuation of the 'change' which Andropov had begun. These differences became clear in the election speeches of the twelve Politburo members, the six candidate members and the five Central Committee secretaries before the elections to the Supreme Soviet between 9 February and 2 March 1984. The members of the 'collective leadership' declared unanimously their support for 'continuity in the domestic and foreign policy of the CPSU', but whereas some understood this to mean retaining and continuing the 'stability' of the Brezhnev era, others demanded a continuation and acceleration of the changes begun under Andropov. When he was elected General Secretary, Chernenko defined 'continuity' as 'moving forward but also preserving everything that has already been achieved'.[22] For this purpose it was necessary 'to evaluate our accomplishments realistically, without exaggerating, but also without belittling them'. Chernenko expressed his basically conservative attitude clearly in the warning: 'That is the way things have been until now, and that is the way they will remain!' In his election speech in Moscow on 2 March, Chernenko did advocate the 'strengthening of order, organisation and discipline', the 'perfecting of the direction of the economy and the reorganisation of the economic mechanism' and 'stable and dynamic economic growth'; he proclaimed the slogan: 'Armed with experience, from correct ideas to bold deeds.'[23] However, in contrast to the energy and

22. Speech at the special plenary session of the Central Committee on 13 February 1983, *Pravda*, 14 February 1983. Italics by author.
23. *Pravda*, 3 March 1984.

initiative demonstrated by Andropov after he assumed power, his successor was following a cautious course and, as he has said, was guided by the Russian proverb: 'Measure seven times and cut once.' The younger Politburo members, such as Gorbachev, Romanov, Vorotnikov and the new Central Committee secretaries Ligachev and Ryzhkov strongly disagreed with this attitude. In their election speeches they demanded a continuation of change and renewal. They attributed the successes achieved in 1983 to Andropov personally and were committed to the continuation of the policies he had introduced. They were not satisfied with 'maintaining what has been achieved', as Chernenko and his followers advocated, but demanded that change be accelerated. Presumably this demand was also motivated by the strong desire of the 'young guard' to take power. The youngest member of the Politburo, the fifty-three-year-old Gorbachev, who apparently assumed the duties of Second Secretary, presented himself in his election speech in Stavropol on 29 February as a protagonist of Andropov's policies and, indirectly, as a challenger to Chernenko. For Gorbachev the 'necessary securing of continuity' consisted precisely in 'strengthening and developing positive tendencies and consolidating and increasing everything new and progressive which has entered the life of our society in recent months'.[24] He described the main political tasks as 'strengthening Bolshevik objectivity, which concentrates on practical results at work, the improvement of the leadership style of the Party and all activities of the state and economic apparatus so that individuals at all levels in the organisational chain develop initiative and know and fulfil their duties'. In the economy he demanded 'the acceleration of the development of our economy and the improvement of efficiency' as well as 'the basic reorientation of the production processes of our society to concentrate on improving the well-being of our people'. The experience of the past year had shown that 'we have to work more efficiently if we want to achieve a better life and fully satisfy our material and spiritual needs. There is no other way and there will not be one'. For Gorbachev a decisive task was the training and promotion of cadres of individuals who 'think and act in a modern way'; he criticised 'satisfaction with what has been achieved' and demanded 'an atmosphere of action and not of loud talk'. Is it possible to imagine a greater contrast than that between Chernen-

---

24. *Izvestiya*, 1 March 1984.

ko's defence of 'everything achieved until now' and Gorbachev's support of 'everything new and progressive'? The different standpoints and goals of the outgoing General Secretary and Gorbachev, who was twenty years younger, became clearer at the Union conference on problems of the agro-industrial complex in Moscow on 26 March. In his opening speech Chernenko praised the successes of the Food Programme introduced by Brezhnev in May 1982 and urged the carrying out of the resolutions of the XXVI Party Congress (1981) and its economic strategy for the 1980s. This meant a continuation of the Brezhnev course.[25] Gorbachev, on the other hand, who has been responsible for agricultural matters in the Politburo since 1979 and had actually shown conspicuously little enthusiasm for the Food Programme, expressed his dissatisfaction with the general state of Soviet agriculture and its previous achievements, which according to his statistics had fallen far short of plan targets.[26] He referred to the inadequate levels of grain and food production, criticised 'serious shortcomings of the kolkhozes, regions and ministries' and demanded a 'sober evaluation of successes and mistakes. In his view, 'wishes' could not provide 'solutions to the fundamental problems of our development'. Rather, it was necessary to 'make the work of the direction of our economy more dynamic and determined, consolidate and intensify everything new and progressive' and overcome 'immobility and clinging to old ways'. Gorbachev announced that the Party would continue along the path of 'courageous and innovative solutions', for 'indeed, we have no other way'. The 'acceleration of economic development and the intensification of the total production of our society' was 'vital' because it was made necessary by 'objective factors', among which he listed the 'competition of the two social systems, the well-known demographic features of the present phase of development, the increasingly complex geological conditions in mining and the limited possibilities for capital investment'. Gorbachev's enumeration of these 'objective factors' was also a list of the main causes of the present crisis in the Soviet Union. He summed up his analysis by observing that 'we stand at the beginning; we still have a long way to go. The most important tasks are yet to come'.

25. *Pravda*, 27 March 1984.
26. Gorbachev, 'Report on the tasks of the Party, Soviet and economic organs responsible for increasing the efficiency of agriculture', Radio Moscow, 26 March 1984; BBC Summary of World Broadcasts, SU 7603. C/1f. Important parts of Gorbachev's speech are not included in the summary in *Pravda*, 27 March 1984.

The Soviet leadership must now decide whether to continue the 'old course' or look for a 'new way'. The 'sometimes difficult struggle of the new against the old', which according to Chernenko 'can be found in every social organism', even in Soviet society[28] and which according to Burckhardt or Lenin is the cause of crises or 'really great revolutions' is presently taking place within the Party leadership. The different attitudes and suggestions — on the one hand the continuation or restoration advocated by Chernenko, the 'old way' of the Brezhnev era and the XXVI Party Congress, and on the other hand Gorbachev's demands for 'courageous and innovative solutions' such as have not been heard for a long time in the statements of Politburo members, show the conflict within the present 'collective leadership' between the followers of Brezhnev and those of Andropov, between the 'conservatives' and the 'modernists'. The power struggle between the 'old guard' and the 'Young Turks' has centred around the question of who will succeed Andropov and Chernenko, and is related to the inevitable generational change in the Kremlin. Of course we know nothing about the internal developments behind the Kremlin walls, and the answer to the question 'who — whom?' can at best be only speculative. Facts, however, such as the frequent changes of leaders within a short period, the high average age of Politburo and government members, the inevitable rise of a younger generation, and the public differences about the direction and pace of future development have been clear signs and evidence of a leadership crisis in the Soviet Union. This crisis is related not only to the composition of the 'collective leadership', the high average of its members and the necessary generational change; its real cause is the obvious indecision about the course to be taken. In the internal disputes, which also involve collisions of different power interests, the main questions are whether the Soviet Union has entered a crisis and, if it has, what the causes of the crisis are and how it can be overcome. The Party leadership faces the fundamental decision of whether to continue with the previous course, which has proved unable to resolve the problems which have developed in the Soviet system and will probably only lead to new and greater difficulties and conflicts, or to introduce radical reforms, which would change the existing

27. *Kommunist*, 3 1983, p. 31.
28. Speech at the plenary session of the Central Committee, 'Aktuelle Fragen der ideologischen und massenpolitischen Arbeit der Partei', *Neues Deutschland*, 15 June 1983.

system and thereby possibly 'weaken the leading role of the Communist Party' (as Andropov feared). Marxist-Leninist theory cannot provide the Soviet leaders with a clear and certain answer to the question of whether one decision or the other will help overcome or will aggravate the enormous problems of the Soviet empire. In the Soviet Union a situation has arisen in which the main feature of a crisis recognised and described by Lenin is becoming increasingly visible, namely the 'political crisis' in which it could become impossible for the ruling class 'to maintain its power unchanged'.

12

The Party

Social Change in the Soviet Union and the Social Structure of the CPSU
Boris Meissner

The domestic political difficulties of the Soviet Union, which have increased since the XXVI Party Congress in 1981, are not only of an economic nature. They are mainly caused by the fact that the existing one-party system, in which totalitarian traits predominate, is, because of its centralist-bureaucratic power structure, neither in a position to significantly advance the modernisation process nor to contribute to a satisfactory solution to the most important problems facing Soviet society. These problems are caused, on the one hand, by numerous contradictions which are evident in the development of the Soviet Union and, on the other hand, by the effects of profound social changes.

At the XXVI Party Congress Brezhnev announced that during the 1970s 'differences between all classes and social groups of Soviet society' had become smaller. He even put forward the ideologically questionable assertion that this development justified the assumption that the 'classless society' would be achieved 'primarily within the historical framework of mature socialism'; this meant within the stage of 'developed socialism', which, in the Soviet view, only the Soviet Union has reached.

This disappearance of class differences of which Brezhnev spoke has been only partial and insignificant. On the contrary, differences within Soviet society and its various component groups have become even more pronounced. This process has been greatly furthered by continuing urbanisation, expanding industrialisation (which

299

has particularly affected the Asian regions of the Soviet Union) and the rising educational level of the population.

From 1965 to 1983 the urban population of the Soviet Union rose from 120.7 m. (52 per cent) to 174.6 m. (64.4 per cent). The rural population declined from 108.9 m. (47 per cent) to 96.6 m. (35.6 per cent). The percentage of persons employed in agriculture is still very high, compared to Western industrial societies (1982: 22.6 per cent contrasting with 2–12 per cent in the West).

Soviet society has undergone profound changes in recent decades. These can best be understood if the social structure of the Soviet Union is analysed in terms of its main social groups and their individual components and strata. Only when these have been described precisely will an examination of particular interest or opinion groups prove useful. Because of the one-party system, these groups have a different character than their counterparts in pluralistic Western democracies. Detailed analysis will concentrate on the overlapping groups of Soviet salaried non-worker employees, the intelligentsia and the bureaucracy.

In considering the social structure of the Soviet Union, Soviet sociology bases its analysis on a formal division of society into three parts. In addition to the workers and the kolkhoz farmers, who are considered classes for ideological reasons, a third social group is distinguished which is referred to sometimes as the 'intelligentsia', and sometimes as 'salaried non-worker employees'.

The terms 'worker' and 'non-worker employee' are more formal catagories than 'intelligentsia'.

Members of the intelligentsia are primarily non-worker employees. If, however, they have worker jobs, which is mainly the case with engineers and technicians, they are classified as workers.

In the strict sense of the word, the intelligentsia includes only graduates of universities and middle-level technical colleges, who are classified as 'specialists'. They cannot be equated with intellectuals in the Western sense.

Several Soviet sociologists, for example Semionov, make a distinction that is very important for our examination, between a scientific-cultural and a technical-economic intelligentsia. At the XXV Party Congress in 1976 Brezhnev based his remarks about the social structure of the CPSU on these two component groups of the intelligentsia.

Other Soviet sociologists attempt to blur this important distinction with the collective term 'scientific-technical intelligentsia' and

300

thus to stress the uniform character of the Soviet intelligentsia. They have achieved the generally uncritical acceptance of this term in the West.

After Stalin's planned economic 'revolution from above', the members of the 'new intelligentsia', which was at first mainly a technical intelligentsia, were simply classified as non-worker employees. The main sociological distinction between such employees and workers was that the former usually performed mental and not physical work. Since the census of 1959, a distinction has been made between specialists who belong to the intelligentsia and non-specialists, including, in addition to clerical and service workers, unskilled employees. For Rutkevich and other Soviet sociologists the essential difference is the degree of difficulty of the mental work involved.

Developments in recent years show that generally the employee share of the population has grown in urban and rural areas, whereas the number of workers has risen only in the countryside. Soviet statisticians have attempted to cover up this development by classifying part of the non-worker employees as workers. The number of kolkhoz farmers continued to decline as a result of urbanisation.

Today, most of the non-worker employees belong to the 'intelligentsia'. This means that they are primarily specialists with considerable education. Their numbers grew, between 1965 and 1983, from 12.1 m. to 31.0 m. The number of specialists with a university education grew from 4.9 m. (40 per cent) to 13.0 m. (41.9 per cent); the number of specialists with middle-level technical education from 7.2 m. (60 per cent) to 18 m. (58.1 per cent). Among the specialists with a university education the number of women increased from 2.5 m. (51 per cent) to 6.9 m. (53.1 per cent) and among specialists with middle-level technical education from 4.4 m. (61.1 per cent) to 11.5 m. (63.9 per cent). Altogether, 18.3 m. women were specialists (59 per cent of the total).

The high percentage of women is especially remarkable when one considers the fact that only a quarter of Party members were women and that there were no women in the Kremlin leadership.

While the number of university-trained engineers among the specialists increased from 1.6 m. to 4.9 m. between 1965 and 1980 and the number of graduate agronomists rose from 0.3 m. to 0.6 m. during the same period, the number of graduate economists expanded from 0.3 m. to 1.1 m., the number of jurists from 0.1 to 0.2 m., of doctors from 0.5 m. to 0.9 m. and of educationalists from 1.9

301

m. to 3.8 m. It is striking that university-trained economists, despite their large numbers, are not represented among the highest echelons of the Party leadership.

The total number of workers and non-worker employees increased, between 1965 and 1982, from 76.9 m. to 115.2 m., the share of employees rising from 27.3 per cent to 70.2 per cent. It is worth noting that specialists with university and middle-level technical training, the intelligentsia, who are mostly classified as non-worker employees, accounted for 26.9 per cent in 1982, as compared with only 15.7 per cent in 1965. It is also important to note here that the number of university graduates among the total number of workers and non-worker employees increased from 6.4 per cent to 11.3 per cent, 42 per cent of all specialists in 1982.

To slow the rush to the universities, the new educational reform places particular emphasis on helping pupils to acquire professional qualifications as early as possible and giving as many as possible further training in technical colleges.

Among the intelligentsia in the broader sense, a term which in addition to the 'practical' professions also includes intellectuals who are not 'specialists', one must distinguish, between the two groups already mentioned, the technical and the scientific-cultural intelligentsia, also called the 'creative intelligentsia' in the Soviet Union. In both groups, in which the share of university graduates increased by the same percentage, a growing differentiation can be observed. The same is true among workers and to a lesser extent among kolkhoz farmers. Social differences have increased, not only between university graduates and those of middle-level technical colleges, but also between highly skilled workers and the mass of the working class. This development has not, as Brezhnev claimed, strengthened the 'leading role of the working class' but has rather reinforced the dominant social position of the university-trained groups of the intelligentsia and the already present beginnings of a 'worker aristocracy'. In addition to an upper class, which not only includes elements of the various power elites, those sections of the middle strata of Soviet society are thus becoming more important and are gradually merging to form a middle class, a kind of 'state bourgeoisie'.

The above figures clearly show that the social structure of the Soviet Union is becoming more like that of the more advanced countries among the socialist states of Eastern Europe.

In view of this development, the distinction between both large sections of the intelligentsia and their relationship with the ndividual parts of the bureaucracy acquires a special significan:e. The bureaucracy, which is part of the non-worker employee group, overlaps with the intelligentsia but is not completely identical with it. This is also true of the political-administrative burea⎤cracy, which actually exercises political power and which, like the economic bureaucracy, is recruited primarily from the technical intelligentsia. It also applies equally to the Party and state bureaucracy.

The term *nomenklatura*, which Professor Voslensky has made popular in the West, can be helpful in identifying the individual component parts of the bureaucracy. However, one must remember that in the Soviet Union, because of the system of state socialism, there are several *nomenklatury*. Among them that of the Ccmmunist Party is especially important politically. All non-worker employees are listed in the *nomenklatura* of 9 September 1967. In terms of work classification it distinguishes between leaders, specialists in a functional sense and technical personnel, who perform the actual work. Among the employees, those who have secure positions and are thus described as officials (*dolzhostnye litsa*) have a special place. It is significant that they are mentioned several times and, for the first time, in the Soviet Constitution of 1977. The position given such officials by Soviet labour and administrative law is decisi/e. In Soviet labour law a distinction is made between managemen⊤ personnel (*rukovodyashchii sostav*), popularly called '*nachalstvo*' and 'operative personnel' (*operativnyi sostav*). These subordinate '*apparachiki*' include primarily non-worker employees who in terms of their function must be considered specialists but who are different from specialists with university degrees.

The administrative division of officials can be seen in their position in Soviet constitutional and administrative law. In this respect only 'state service' or 'cadres of the administrative apparatus' are mentioned. However, it is clear from the literature that the corresponding regulations also apply to positions in social organisat ons, especially in the Party. The key question in the organisation of this group is, therefore, whether an official may exercise power in the name of the state. This produces a division of 'representatives of the state power (*predstaviteli vlasti*) and 'functional co-workers' (*funktsional'nye rabotniki*).

Depending on the formal structure of the *nomenklatura* in question, the bureaucracy constitutes a larger or smaller group among the non-worker employees. The different sizes of the respective bureaucratic groups result in a pyramid-like structure which, from the base to the top, has the following levels:

(1) 'Management-administrative personnel' (*administrativno-upravlencheskii personal*).

In its broadest sense this bureaucracy includes, according to the official Soviet statistics of 1959, almost 5.6 m. people, or 28 per cent of the 19.7 m. non-worker employees at that time.

(2) The 'leading cadres' (*rukovodyashchie kadry*).

This group includes all political and economic managers. In 1959, according to Semionov, it consisted of about 2.4 m. people; according to Rutkevich-Filippov, 2.7 m. At that time the 'cadre bureaucracy' included c. 11.7–31.2 per cent of all non-worker employees.

The size of the management personnel group (*rukovodyashchii sostav*) is greater than that of the 'leading cadres' because it includes the scientific-cultural area. The different composition of the management personnel group can be seen in the two indexes which were appended to the decree of the Presidium of the Supreme Soviet of 20 May 1974.

(3) The 'representatives of the state power' (*predstaviteli vlasti*).

This group is composed of the leadership cadres authorised to exercise state power and includes the corresponding leading Party functionaries. In 1959 this political-administrative bureaucracy, whose composition is shown by the basic *nomenklatura* (*osnovnaya nomenklatura*) and the register and control *nomenklatura* (*uchet-nokontrol'naya nomenklatura*) of the CPSU, consisted of about 700,000 people. At present the number is probably almost one million.

(4) The senior bureaucracy.

This group includes about 400,000 Party and state functionaries who occupy positions of power listed in the two Party *nomenklatura* at the Union and Union Republic level.

Here the occupants of positions of authority listed in the 'basic *nomenklatura*' are the most numerous. These positions are filled directly by the responsible Party organs, whereas in the case of positions in the register and control *nomenklatura*, which includes mostly state positions, only their consent is required for individual appointments.

The core of the senior bureaucracy, as the top layer of the administrative and political bureaucracy, is formed by the small political *élite*, which includes members of the Central Committee and the Central Control Commission (in so far as they are top Party or state functionaries) as well as a number of other full-time Party functionaries.

In addition to the bureaucracy, the military is a powerful grouping within the formal category of non-worker employees, which also includes most university-trained specialists who only have social management functions and non-specialists who perform auxiliary functions.

The power *élite* consists of the senior bureaucracy and the senior officer corps. A certain counter-weight is formed by the economic managers (part of the 'leading cadres') and a top-level group of the technical intelligentsia, as well as by a prestige *élite* consisting of scientists, writers and artists (representatives of the scientific-cultural intelligentsia).

The superior position of the senior bureaucracy is a consequence of the hierarchical structure of the Soviet one-party state, which is itself a result of the totalitarian one-party rule and related structural elements established on the basis of state socialism.

As the senior bureaucracy consists to a considerable degree of members of the technical intelligentsia, who are primarily university-trained engineers, a certain amount of overlapping occurs. The relationship of the senior bureaucrats with the prestige *élite* is characterised by more tension than their relationship with the economic managers. This has become especially clear in recent years in the conflicts with dissidents, who belong mainly to the scientific-cultural intelligentsia.

The unlimited power of the senior bureaucracy results from the fact that the monopoly of power, information, organisation and planning claimed by the Party lies in its hands. The greater, though very limited, political influence of the economic managers compared to that of the prestige *élite* is due to the fact that most of them come from the technical intelligentsia, as well as to their partial merging with the senior bureaucracy. The effects of this are strongest within the 'military-industrial complex'. The great majority of members of the Politburo are, in their professional training, engineering graduates of universities; several are university-trained agronomists. Only a minority belongs to the scientific-cultural intelligentsia. Gorbachev has degrees in agronomy and law. This makes him the first jurist in the Politburo since Lenin. Although Chernenko was neither an engineer nor a jurist, he completed studies at a teacher training college.

In the ruling senior bureaucracy as a whole, one must distinguish between the Party and state bureaucracies. This distinction, which is bridged in the careers of many top functionaries by a zig-zag course, is due to the fact that the Party functionaries are primarily responsible for informing the country about and supervising the execution of basic political decisions made by Party organs, whereas state functionaries, who are also responsible for the economy, are in charge of operative administration.

Khrushchev attempted to expand the power of the Party bureaucracy. The effect of his administrative reforms, however, was to make the entire bureaucracy uncertain and insecure. After his fall, Kosygin's economic reforms were intended to create a better sociological equilibrium between the two bureaucratic groups. The main result was to make the ministerial bureaucracy more important. In this way, the stability of the 'collective leadership' was indeed increased, but overall the system developed a greater bureaucratic rigidity. Kosygin's attempts to continue the reforms begun in 1965 were as unsuccessful as Brezhnev's plans for a comprehensive administrative reform. With his campaign against corruption, cliques and inefficiency and his introduction of limited reforms, Andropov attempted to break through the rigid bureaucratic structure and reduce domestic political inertia. Given Chernenko's benevolent attitude towards the cadres and his power base in the Party and the government bureaucracy, there had until recently been a danger that the bureaucracy, which Andropov had alarmed with his campaign, would fall back into its old lethargy and that a complete generational change in the senior bureaucracy would be delayed once again.

The social structure of the CPSU corresponds to the class structure of Soviet society and the estate-like organisation it requires. The original small, tightly disciplined party of mostly intellectual professional revolutionaries with a strong proletarian element has become a mass Party, with 18.1 m. members on 1 January 1983, whose cadres consist of bureaucratic politicians. Under Brezhnev an effort was made to draw more workers into the Party in order to prevent an imbalance of non-worker employees and thus of the intelligentsia. Brezhnev's successors have also supported such a policy. The results, which can be seen in the following table, are deceptive as members of the intelligentsia who occupy positions classified as worker jobs are considered, from a sociological point of view, to be workers.

That these figures do not reflect the actual share of the intelligent-

Table 12.1 The social composition of the CPSU, in millions

'Class'	1966	1971	1976	1981	1983
Workers	4.7	5.8	6.5	7.6	8.0
Peasants (kolkhoz farmers)	2.0	2.2	2.2	2.2	2.2
Non-worker employees (intelligentsia and others)	5.7	6.4	6.2	7.7	7.9
	12.4	14.4	15.6	17.5	18.1

The social composition of the CPSU (per cent)

'Class'	1966	1971	1976	1981	1983
Workers	37.8	40.1	41.6	43.4	44.1
Peasants (kolkhoz farmers)	16.2	15.1	13.9	12.8	12.4
Non-worker employees (intelligentsia and others)	46.0	44.8	44.5	43.8	43.5
	100	100	100	100	100

sia (in the narrow sense of the word) in the Party membership can be seen in the growing proportion of 'specialists' and also in the educational level of Party members.

Table 12.2 The intelligentsia (specialists) membership of the CPSU

	in millions	per cent of all Party members
1966	4.4	35.6
1971	5.9	41.1
1977	7.9	51.3
1981	9.2	53.0

New figures are not available, but the actual share of Communists with university or middle-level technical degrees has probably continued to grow, as Brezhnev explained at the XXVI Party

Table 12.3 Membership of the Central Committee and the Central Control Commission divided according to function (absolute numbers)

Function	Members of the Central Committee		Candidate members of the CC		Members of the CCC	
	1976	1981	1976	1981	1976	1981
Party	128	143	51	50	19	8
State and economy	93	95	40	46	25	29
Trade unions and co-operatives	3	5	4	4	2	4
Komsomol	1	1	1	—	1	1
Military	19	22	10	13	5	4
State police	1	4	4	1	1	—
Judiciary and prosecuting attorneys	2	2	1	1	—	—
Ideology, culture and science	15	16	16	15	10	10
Foreign service	15	15	4	6	5	4
Workers, lower-placed employees and peasants (Kolkhoz farmers)	10	16	8	13	14	13
Other	—	—	—	2	3	2
	287	319	139	151	85	75

Congress in 1981 that the 'influx of representatives of the intelligentsia into the Party continues'. The percentage of specialists with a university education has especially increased; in 1977 their share was already 2.6 per cent.

Of the share of the non-worker employee intelligentsia, which according to the formal class structure amounted to 44 per cent of the entire Party in 1976, 20 per cent belonged to the technical and 24 per cent to the scientific-cultural intelligentsia and the military.

Classified according to educational level, 72.1 per cent of all Communists had passed the equivalent of A-Level examinations in 1981; 28 per cent of these had university degrees and 2.2 per cent had attended a university without earning a diploma. Therefore, it can be assumed that in reality more than 60 per cent of Party members belong to the intelligentsia. From a purely quantitative

Table 12.4 Membership of the Central Committee and the Central Control Commission divided according to function (per cent)

Function	Members of the Central Committee		Candidate members of the CC		Members of the CCC	
	1976	1981	1976	1981	1976	1981
Party	44.6	44.8	36.7	33.1	22.4	10.7
State and economy	32.4	29.8	28.8	30.4	29.4	38.7
Trade unions and co-operatives	1.1	1.6	2.9	2.7	2.3	5.3
Komsomol	0.3	0.3	0.7	—	1.2	1.3
Military	6.6	6.9	7.2	8.6	5.9	5.3
State police	0.3	1.3	2.9	0.7	1.2	—
Judiciary and prosecuting attorneys	0.7	0.6	0.7	0.7	—	—
Ideology, culture and science	5.2	5.0	11.5	9.9	11.8	13.3
Foreign service	5.2	4.7	2.9	4.0	5.9	5.3
Workers, lower placed employees and peasants (Kolkhoz farmers)	3.5	5.0	5.7	8.6	16.5	17.3
Other	—	—	—	1.3	3.5	2.7
Difference	0.1	—	—	—	—	0.1
	100	100	100	100	100	100

point of view there can, therefore, be no question of a 'leading role of the working class' in the CPSU.

While the majority of Party members clearly belong to the intelligentsia, the Party leadership is dominated by the senior bureaucracy. In 1981 its share of full members of the Central Committee was 83.7 per cent divided more or less equally between Party and state bureaucracies. The next strongest group was the military with 7.2 per cent. The two groups of the intelligentsia, in so far as they did not occupy positions of power, had a share of 4.1 per cent, whereas 5 per cent of the members were workers and peasants (kolkhoz farmers).

In this table the entire Politburo, including Politburo members with state functions, is included under Party. The area 'state and economy' includes primarily state functionaries and only a few economic managers. The classification 'ideology, culture and science' includes primarily Party and state functionaries responsible for this area and only a few members of the prestige *élite*.

The composition of the Party leadership shows that it consists primarily of representatives of the interests of the ruling senior bureaucracy. The 'dictatorship of the proletariat' has become allegedly a 'state of the entire people', which in fact represents a system of rule dominated by the 'dictatorship of the bureaucracy'.

This statement does not mean that the bureaucracy in general or the senior bureaucracy in particular forms a monolithic unit. Different sub-bureaucracies are responsible for individual areas. It is also necessary to distinguish not only between the different institutional and professional groups and their positions in the various levels of administration but also between their special positions in the autocratic-totalitarian power structure and their access to those who have real power. In this respect, the question of whether a monocratic or an oligarchic element predominates in the Kremlin leadership is especially important.

Nationality also plays a special role in a multinational state like the Soviet Union. The CPSU is primarily a Russian Party. The share of Great Russians in the Party as a whole was 60 per cent in 1981, although they comprised only 52.4 per cent of the total population in 1979, in reality even less. Of the Central Committee members, 68.3 per cent were Great Russians. The next strongest groups were the Ukrainians with 14.1 per cent and the White Russians with 2.2 per cent. These two groups, however, have a higher share of the total population. Demographic changes, which can be observed in the high population growth rates of the Islamic peoples and groups, particularly the Turkic peoples of the USSR, are not reflected in the Party leadership.

With the fall of Khrushchev, the last 'controls from above' on the senior bureaucracy as well as the uncertainty about its own position in the Soviet power structure disappeared. Given the totalitarian character of the Soviet one-party state, there could be no such thing as 'control from below'. In this respect it is possible to speak sociologically of absolute bureaucratic rule since Khrushchev's fall. In addition to the increasing divisions within the bureaucracy itself, however, several other factors stand in the way of a consolidation of bureaucratic power. Firstly, the power of the military in comparison with that of the political-administrative bureaucracy has increased. Within the Soviet power elite the senior officer corps has acquired greater political influence relative to that of the senior bureaucracy. Other groups and classes in Soviet society have also gained more influence and self-confidence. At the same time, the pressure from the younger generations has increased. This is true not only of the higher ranks of the intelligentsia but also of the skilled workers. Because of this, reform efforts, as they were expressed in the 'Novosibirsk study' in 1983, have also become more numerous. Their gradual realisation would involve corresponding restrictions on the unlimited power of the ruling senior bureaucracy.

At the present time a thorough reform of the existing economic and social system in the Soviet Union — and thus more freedom safeguarded by laws — is advocated primarily from among members of the scientific-cultural intelligentsia. However, these demands are also supported by representatives of the technical intelligentsia and the 'enlightened bureaucracy'. The present situation in the Soviet Union is reminiscent of the time of Nicholas I, before the beginning of the reforms in the nineteenth century, when there were also 'enlightened bureaucrats' who were guided by the realisation that the existing system and the Empire as a whole could only survive with the help of certain reforms.

Under the rule of the bureaucracy the scientific-cultural intelligentsia suffers much more than does the technical intelligentsia. For this reason it is not surprising that the former group is the primary social basis of the forces of reform. Whereas the senior bureaucracy is interested in maintaining the totalitarian form of one Party rule, the advocates of reform within the intelligentsia seek to promote developments which could lead to a freer (though still authoritarian) one Party system and ultimately to a constitutional form of one-party power under the rule of law. If the reformers within the intelligentsia have not made much progress in this direction so far, this is due to their not having succeeded in establishing close contacts with the workers.

Bureaucracy in Party and State
Gyula Józsa

The Leading Role of the Party and the Function of the Party Apparatus as an Instrument of Power

The phenomenon of growing bureaucracy, the predominance of the executive branch in its relations with the legislative in modern democracies with free economies, is well known. This phenomenon results from the fact that more and more social and other services are entrusted to or demanded from the modern state. In the case of the Soviet bureaucracy and especially the administrative organs of Party and state, one might gain the impression that under the system of 'real socialism' bureaucracies are essentially the same as those in Western democracies.

This is an assumption which has been much discussed since the 1960s in connection with the 'convergence theory' and with comparative studies of the two systems. It has caused many observers to develop illusions about the short and medium-term ability of the Soviet system to change. Some who based their analyses on such assumptions made the mistake of ignoring or underestimating the basically different functions of bureaucracy under the two systems. This difference is to be found at the macro-level, for the problems of administration at the microlevel (e.g. in a refinery or a community) are similar in some respects under both systems.

To describe the basic difference, using Max Weber's catagories, one can say that whereas in modern democracies bureaucracies are 'purpose' orientated (and regulated, controlled and corrected accordingly), the essence of the bureaucracies in the Soviet Union is their 'value' orientation. They are subordinated to the control of a parallel bureaucracy, the Party apparatus. 'Controlling the controllers' is the exclusive right of the central Party organisation. The 'values' which have determined the orientation of Soviet bureaucracies by the CPSU since they were created under Lenin have remained basically the same: namely the maintaining and expansion of power. Economic, social and other 'goals' are merely secondary. They serve to maintain and expand the system according to a 'chiliastic' ideology. Such a bureaucratic orientation can be considered 'ideocratic'.

How do the Party and state apparatuses function at present? What problems in their mutual relations are important for Soviet foreign policy? In the short space available here only a few aspects of these extremely complicated questions can be examined. I must also formulate my observations as theses and assume a knowledge of the roles and functions of both these pillars of the Soviet system on the part of my readers.

In connection with the relevance of domestic political developments to Soviet foreign policy, the question of the condition of the back-bone of the system, i.e. the Party, is of major importance. The Party leads, and its leadership role is actually expanding, as Party members and the Soviet people are told daily. What is meant by the leadership function of the Party? Certainly not that its present 18 million members participate in the leadership according to democratic rules. The leading role of the Party must be understood as the primary role of the Party apparatus in the Soviet system.[1]

The Party apparatus and the strictly centralised, hierarchically structured, constantly active central and regional Party organs, in which full-time officials control and direct the entire state, economic and social bureaucracies, are identical. The number of persons employed in these central and regional Party organs can only be estimated. At present it is about 500,000. The Party apparatus, especially the central apparatus, with its Central Committee departments, secretariat and Politburo at the top, functions, as is well known, not only as a control and direction mechanism but also as the main decision-making authority of the system.

Clearly, important social changes have led to corresponding changes in the composition and behaviour of the Party apparatus, but this has not altered its basic function. Certainly, the apparatus is not what the formal Party constitution and Party literature claim — a mere instrument. Rather, the reverse is true. The Party is a cadre reserve and school under the control of the apparatus, which assigns individuals by means of the *nomenklatura* system to various functions within the bureaucracies. Only the lower levels of the apparatus serve as instruments in the hands of the higher levels. However, with regard to parallel bureaucracies, the state administration for example, the basic control and supervisory function remains.

1. Gyula Józsa, 'Die Herrschaftsfunktion des Parteiapparats der KPdSU', in Meissner, Brunner, Löwenthal, (eds.), *Einparteisystem und bürokratische Herrschaft in der Sowjetunion*, Cologne, 1978, pp. 171 ff.

The Party Apparatus and the Problem of Succession

The foundations of the power of the Party apparatus were laid under Lenin. However, the creator and creature of the apparatus in its present form was Stalin, who, however, also terrorised it with the help of his private secretariat. Lenin, never General Secretary, based his power more on the government apparatus, but, because of the respect in which he was held, his authority was seldom questioned at the higher levels of the Party. After Stalin had eliminated his opponents with the help of the Party apparatus, he established his own absolute dictatorship through his 'secret', 'special', or 'private' secretariat, which he personally supervised and which represented an apparatus within the Party apparatus. However, the latter continued to function smoothly as the back-bone of the system even when Stalin purged it and, in his position as General Secretary and head of the Soviet government, began to depend more on the state apparatus at the beginning of the 1940s. However, if A. Avtorkhanov's hypothesis of a 'conspiracy' against Stalin (around 1952) involving Beria, Malenkov and Khrushchev should turn out to be the true story of events leading up to his death, then his neglect of certain sections of the Party apparatus (his private secretariat) had fateful consequences for him, too.[2] Khrushchev consolidated his victory over his rivals by rehabilitating the Party apparatus decimated by Stalin and gaining control of it. In June 1957 he was saved by the regional secretaries, who formed and still form the most homogeneous group within the Central Committee. In 1964 he was deposed because he had endangered the interests not only of the Party apparatus but also of the military (and the state and economic bureaucracy) by constant reorganisations and the introduction of a rotation system for Party cadres.

Brezhnev learned the lessons of history well. By his policy of 'regard for cadres' he won the support of broad sections of the Party apparatus. The policy led ultimately to gerontocracy and to political inertia, not only in the central but also in the regional Party apparatus. Strangely enough, this development was offset by the considerable foreign policy successes of the Brezhnev era. It seems that the gerontocratic tendency affected the Party apparatuses of the border Republics much less than the central and regional Party bureaucracies of the RSFSR. The stagnation in cadres (and in the

2. A. Avtorkhanov, *Zagadka smerti Stalina*, Frankfurt/M, 1976.

country at large) during Brezhnev's last years concealed certain developments which affected the central as well as the regional Party apparatus and most parts of the bureaucratic structure: the increasing corruption, the lack of initiative and the inability to achieve self-renewal. Only certain sections of the central Party bureaucracy and the state bureaucracy which showed more initiative and efficiency did not conform to this pattern — the Central Committee departments concerned with foreign policy, the 'military-industrial complex' and the KGB.

In November 1982 something remarkable happened. For the first time, the post of General Secretary fell to someone who had had little to do with the Party apparatus for fifteen years and who had received more attention abroad than at home. As V. A. Afanasev, the chief editor of *Pravda*, told Japanese journalists, Yurii Andropov was elected General Secretary by a 'responsible and honest' majority of the Politburo.[3] This majority preferred Andropov to Brezhnev's candidate, Chernenko, and instructed him to secure order and discipline in the country in view of the increasingly dangerous international situation.

Contrary to the highly successful propaganda abroad with regard to Andropov's 'liberal' and 'reformist' tendencies and quite apart from whatever his long-term plans were, his speeches and actions proved only one thing: His main aim was to restore order and discipline as instructed. He initiated a purge which affected all apparatuses, with the exception of the military-industrial complex. The Central Committee and the regional Party apparatus were especially affected by personnel changes. The first official act of Andropov's successor, Chernenko, was to let the Party cadres know that he intended to continue with Brezhnev's cadre policy.

In view of this resolution of the succession question, the hypothesis seems plausible that in November 1982 the Politburo made its decisions without any special consideration of the lower ranks of the Party apparatus and the Central Committee and that in February 1984 a solution was found which, if it had turned out differently, would possibly have encountered resistance in the Central Committee. The largest and most influential bloc within the Central Committee was composed of party *apparatchiki*.

Three references to the role and function of the Party apparatus in the succession question provide a basis for the following theses:

3. *Neue Zürcher Zeitung*, 19 November 1982.

(1) In power struggles within the Soviet leadership those persons usually win who have the support of the Party apparatus or exercise control over it.

(2) Any innovation or reform of the system can be realised only in so far as the Party apparatus accepts it. Examples are Hungary (1956, 1968), Poland (1980–1), Czechoslovakia (1968–9) and even the Soviet Union under Khrushchev.

(3) Any serious crisis in the system is preceded by a division and crisis within the Party apparatus, for example in Hungary in 1956.

These theses relating to the role and function of the Party apparatus in the succession question as well as in potential and actual changes or even reforms of the system can be reduced to the basic principle that the predominance of the Party apparatus over other pillars of the Soviet system has not been shaken or essentially changed. If Andropov had remained in power longer, we could perhaps have expected other possibilities.

The Real Condition of the Party Apparatus at the Death of Yurii Andropov

Before considering the question of the relationship between the Party and state apparatuses, it seems important to take a brief look at the actual condition of the former. We want to consider especially the twenty Central Committee departments (the 'super ministries' of the Party) and the local and regional secretaries (the 'provincial princes').

In Brezhnev's last years some curious new departments, which all indicated increasing difficulties or even conflicts within the secretariat or the Politburo, were created in the Central Committee apparatus.

In Brezhnev's last years three new Central Committee departments were established: The department for international information (led by L. Zamyatin and the former ambassador in Bonn, V. Falin), the citizens' complaints department (B. Yakovlev) and the department of agricultural machine production (I. Sakhnyuk). The creation of the first two departments, presumably on Chernenko's initiative, indicates on the one hand that Brezhnev and Chernenko were increasingly dissatisfied with the work of M. Suslov (who died in January 1982). On the other hand, it was an indirect criticism of official information channels, including the KGB. It was above all

Chernenko who, under the impression of events in Poland, was seriously worried about the fact that the Party leaders lacked reliable information on the mood of broad segments of the population.[5] The establishment of a new agricultural supervisory agency within the central Party organisation suggests that since the 1970s there had been differences of opinion and uncertainty about what should be done to improve the situation of Soviet agriculture, which had been administered to death.

Organisational as well as personnel changes in the Central Committee apparatus have great political significance. They are more important than those in the state apparatus, for the Central Committee apparatus is the 'inner sanctum' of the system. For this reason the public is kept more ignorant of goings on there than of those in the state and economic bureaucracy. The 3000–4000 Party officials and employees who work in the Central Committee apparatus control all state and social organs as well as the regional Party apparatus. In addition, the most important decisions of the Central Committee secretariat and the Politburo are prepared and in some cases presumably even anticipated in the Central Committee apparatus.

Under Andropov the Central Committee apparatus was subjected to a thorough shake up. Almost half of the departments, nine altogether, received new directors. During his short period in office, about two dozen new deputy department directors appeared, not all of whom have been identified with specific departments.[6]

The removal of I. Kapitonov as head of the cadres department (spring 1983) and his shunting into the supervisory area of the consumer goods industry seems especially significant. Ye. Ligachev, the new cadre head, and his new people from the cadres department were especially active in the provinces during the purge. The agricultural department was also made responsible for the foodstuffs industry; the department of planning and finance was remodelled into the economy department. We can only attempt to guess the long-term administrative intentions behind these measures. The short-term intentions were clear: the Party machine had to be set in motion. Whether in addition a long-term change in the function of the Party apparatus is planned — in the direction of coordinating with the functions of the state and military apparatuses or even the

4. 'Sowjetunion 1982/83', *Jahresbericht des BIOst*, Munich, 1983, pp. 39 f.
5. Ibid., p. 46.
6. *Le Courrier des Pays de l'Est*, no. 282, March 1984, p. 7.

security agencies — is difficult to determine.

Now to the regional Party apparatus: Of the 159 local and regional secretaries, the 'provincial princes' or 'prefects', thirty-five (more than 20 per cent) were removed.[7] The majority were disciplined, downgraded or pensioned off. The Politburo formally thanked only a few of them for their work. It can be assumed that these measures greatly alarmed the provincial Party leaders.

The Problem of the Relations between the Party Apparatus and the State Bureaucracy

During Andropov's short time in office there were also significant personnel changes within the state administration. It is estimated that some 20–25 per cent of the ministers and state committee chairmen in Moscow were removed. The extensive personnel changes in the diplomatic corps were little noticed, although they were of great significance for Soviet foreign policy. The huge bureaucratic structure represented by the state apparatus cannot be described in detail here.[8] When Andropov came to power there were thirty-three all-Union and Union-Republic agencies; that means sixty-four ministries, twenty state committees, four central agencies belonging to the Council of Ministers (e.g. Cosbank) and one or two dozen central agencies subordinate to the Council of Ministers. In decreasing number, agencies and authorities corresponding to these 120 are found in the fifteen Union Republics and the twenty autonomous republics.

The state apparatus is constantly expanding. The number of ministries increased by forty-seven between 1965 and 1972, the number of state committees by eight. Under Andropov (1983) two additional state committees were created (for security in the nuclear energy industry and for international tourism).[9]

The swollen state apparatus and its inertia have been criticised constantly, without any effective measures being taken to remedy the situation. In June 1983 Andropov pointed out that the number of *apparatchiki* could be reduced without endangering efficiency.

---

7. Ibid.
8. See D.J.R. Scott, *Russian Political Institutions*, (4th ed.), London, 1969; B. Meissner, *Das Verhältnis von Partei und Staat im Sowjetsystem*, Opladen, 1982; M. S. Smirtyukov, *Sovetskii gosudarstvennyi apparat upravleniya*, Moscow, 1982.
9. B. Meissner, *Sowjetische Kurskorrekturen*, Osnabrück, 1984, p. 55.

Considering Khrushchev's experience in this regard, Andropov showed courage, if not cockiness, with his programme.

The expansion of the state apparatus and the economic bureaucracy also worried Andropov's successor. Chernenko too introduced a programme to reduce the number of bureaucrats. Although he attempted to achieve a revival and a certain rationalisation of the cumbersome apparatus, he did not pursue this goal at the expense of the Party apparatus, nor did he resort primarily to disciplinary measures, as did his predecessor.

As the thesis of the predominance of the Party apparatus was especially emphasised at the beginning of this paper, the question may be asked whether the apparatus can push through anything it desires. Well, it can't. The relationship between the Party apparatus and the state and economic bureaucracy clearly reveals that the instruments the Party has created are becoming increasingly cumbersome and that the leadership is having serious difficulties in dealing with them. The state apparatus is able to resist innovation stubbornly.

'The party leads, the state administers'

Since Lenin this principle has been elaborated, nuanced and varied innumerable times and has been adhered to by the Party apparatus, even though this has involved increasing difficulties. After Khrushchev's fall the branches of the Party with a natural scientific orientation together with the ministerial structure were re-established and a hard struggle began to bring the state and economic bureaucracy more effectively under Party control.

Party organisations within the state administrative organs were granted the right of supervision of the state ministerial bureaucracy after 1971 and were urged to make use of this power. Since 1973 the Party leadership has been reorganising the state and economic administrations with the aim of replacing the main administrations of the branch ministries (*glavki*) with industrial organisations in charge of keeping the books.[10] They are intended to manage production organisations and individual enterprises and thus weaken the ministerial bureaucracy by assuming some of its responsibilities. After ten years this plan has still not been completely realised, in

10. B. Meissner, 'Die Reform der sowjetischen Industrieverwaltung in ihrer rechtlichen und politischen Bedeutung', *Kurzinformationen des BIOst*, 8 July 1977.

part because of the resistance of the state bureaucracy.

An outward sign of the silent struggle between the government and the Party was the developing conflict between Breszhnev and Kosygin. By means of the new Constitution (1977) Brezhnev was able to make the prime minister or the Council of Ministers responsible to the head of government (i.e. Brezhnev) or the Presidium of the Supreme Soviet. This was supposedly an enhancement of the status of the Soviet's organs. However, as the same person now held the offices of Party leader and head of government, this was in reality a demonstration of the authority of the Party. Kosygin did his duty with obvious reluctance and, whenever possible, sent his first deputy to report. Shortly before his death (near the end of 1980) he angered Brezhnev (and the Party apparatus) by submitting his resignation from the Politburo not at a plenary session of the Central Committee (which was actually responsible for such matters) but at a session of the Supreme Soviet.

One has the impression that since 1981 the Party leaders have been racking their brains about how to overcome the inertia of the state and economic bureaucracy by means of new administrative measures. In 1981 Brezhnev announced that the Soviet Union wanted to learn from the experiences of the fraternal socialist countries. The commission studying these experiences was led by the then head of Gosplan, Baibakov. In this case, Brezhnev was probably asking for trouble. At any rate, nothing was heard from the commission even under the supposedly reform-minded Andropov.

Department egoism and the difficulty of coordinating and harmonising the work of official agencies (vedomstvennost' and stykovka)

Even in *Pravda* one can find telling examples of department egoism, for example, agriculture is administered to death, kolkhoz chairmen are kept from attending to their actual tasks every year by hundreds of decrees, ordinances and reports. In his own words, the director of the agro-industrial association in the area of Orenburg has to study about a hundred pages of official instructions every day.[11] To illustrate the pitfalls of the Soviet bureaucracy with one example, at the regional level there are about a dozen agencies which supervise agricultural enterprises and provide services for agriculture. Usually

11. *Sovetskaya Rossiya*, 25 March 1984.

they belong to different ministries. The main concern of all these agencies and administrative organs is to fulfil their plan goals. For example, it can happen that the kolkhoz director who needs a screw for a combine is forced to have the machine completely overhauled so that the repair shop can meet its plan goals.

One has the impression that department orientation is gradually affecting the Party itself, that elements of this kind of thinking are becoming visible there, too. Brezhnev warned of this danger as early as the Party Congress of 1981.

To resolve the problem of authority conflicts and to harmonise the work of the state and economic apparatus, interdepartmental administrative organs were created in the highest planning agencies, the Presidium of the Council of Ministers and in several territorial production combines. As early as 1976 Brezhnev spoke of the necessity of 'creating a system for the direction of groups of identical and related (administrative) branches'. No progress has been made in this matter since then.[12] In agriculture, for example, the RAPO (District Agricultural Production Organisation) was to take care of difficulties at the district level. To support the agricultural sector, new 'agricultural departments' have been created everywhere since 1982, even in district Party committees. In Hungary ministries are being combined and large administrative units dissolved; in the Soviet Union new official agencies are produced continuously.

The problem of separating political from executive-management functions

The danger of *podmena* as the phenomenon is called, was emphasised by Andropov and Chernenko. This term refers to the tendency of Party officials to interfere directly in matters of state and economic administration on an executive level by using the authority of their Party positions. Party members have been warned not to do this, on the grounds that confusing their tasks with those of the state apparatus will endanger the Party's political leadership function. Immediately after his election, Chernenko appealed directly to the Party apparatus[13] and demanded that Party committees confine themselves to political leadership, exercising control of the

12. B. Meissner, '*Sowjetische Kurskorrekturen* . . . ', p. 58.
13. *Pravda*, 30 March 1984.

parallel bureaucracies primarily through cadre policy.

Recently, the tendency of the Party apparatus to interfere increasingly in the affairs of the state and economic administration has become obvious. Keeping political and executive functions separate is becoming more and more difficult. The Penza regional committee received 1,270 inquiries about current economic problems and only 22 about cadres policy or ideological decisions in 1983.[14] If this tendency cannot be stopped, the possibility that the primacy of the political function of the Party might be 'undermined' cannot be excluded.

The insistence on the leadership function of the Party has two possible meanings: the Party claims always to be right because the Party apparatus has more rights than any other group. If correct instructions are not carried out properly, the state and economic bureaucracy can always be blamed. Its whipping-boy function was especially evident in Kosygin's last years.

Another possibility is for the Party apparatus to confine itself to the most important political tasks, largely withdraw from matters which are the concerns of the state and economic bureaucracy and leave a broad area for practical competence, economic and administrative rationality, real initiative, experiments and even risk taking. In Hungary such a change in the behaviour of the Party apparatus led to the reform of 1968, but the shock effect of 1956 was a necessary factor in this. The Soviet Union has not yet experienced such a crisis.

The events in Poland probably did have a shock effect on the Soviet leadership, but the answer of the majority of the Politburo to the challenge of new NATO armaments to offset Soviet increases and the prospect of a crisis *à la* Poland was the election of Andropov and a pledge to guarantee 'law and order'.

Chernenko was especially worried about the crisis in Poland. He even committed the ideological mistake of warning of a possible similar crisis occuring in the Soviet Union if the Party apparatus should fail to pay attention to the expectations and wishes of the masses and the various social groups. It seems highly improbable that the apparatus under his leadership was prepared to make the same or similar concessions as were made in Hungary.

14. Ibid.

Signs of a growing awareness of problems

The view that the Soviet leadership is increasingly concerned about the swollen bureaucracy is supported by surprising figures recently published in the Soviet press: The annual 'turnover' of documents and papers in a medium-sized combined economic enterprise or organisation is about 30,000 items. Of these, only 7 per cent are kept for reference; the remaining 93 per cent are superfluous pieces of paper. Ten per cent of all persons employed in Soviet industry are administrators.[15] The forms filled out by machine in a medium-sized enterprise fill from fifty to sixty files a month. Reduction of administrative personnel at the lower bureaucratic levels is usually neutralised by increases at the higher ones.[16] From 1975 to 1983 the number of administrative personnel in the Soviet Union grew by three million. The Ministry of Building Materials alone employs 160,000 'administrators', but office personnel amount on average to only 3.8 per cent of all personnel for the country as a whole.[17]

The problem of excessive bureaucracy (as well as possible solutions) are occasionally discussed in Soviet journals. This did not begin under Andropov.[18] The relevance of such problems to Soviet foreign policy lies in the fact that the Party oligarchy has not yet shown a readiness really to confront growing domestic problems, which would require restraining its instinctive tendency to expand its power at home and abroad. If at some future date not only a 'law and order' policy but also real reforms should be introduced in the Soviet Union, it could then be assumed that the period of aggressiveness and deliberately inflamed war psychosis had come to an end.

15. *Pravda*, 26 December 1983.
16. *Pravda*, 31 March 1984.
17. *Isvestiya*, 13 May 1984; *BPA-Ostinformationen*, 17 May 1984, p. 17.
18. See the reform project of B.P. Kurashvili in *Sovetskoe gosudarstvo i pravo*, 6/1982, p. 38 ff. and the bibliography of similar essays in the same periodical, 6/1984, p. 128 ff.

13

Bureaucracy and the Military

Bureaucracy in State and Economy
Robert Baraz

There is in fact very little information about the Soviet government and economic bureaucracy. Apart from the statistical data, there is some Western literature on the *nomenklatura*, but we lack systematic studies on the bureaucracy overall. Indeed, even in the Soviet literature the bureaucracy as such is not much discussed. Nowhere among Soviet heroes does one find a bureaucrat; one may find an astronaut or an agronomist, but the bureaucrat is an un-hero even in the Soviet Union, despite the fact that there are so many of them and they are so important in Soviet life. We may in time get some more data from the very ambitious Soviet interview project, as it reveals more sociological information about the Soviet Union.

Again, one is really talking about a very imprecisely defined subject. Even in Western industrialised countries one talks of such things as 'co-operate' or 'business' bureaucracy. In the Soviet Union, where many things which would obviously be recognised as private organisations in the West are really part of the regime, it becomes very difficult to sort out where the margin or borderline of the bureaucracy may be. I will not try to impose a formal definition on the subject now, but simply confess right at the outset that I am aware how hazy the term is.

I would like to focus on three factors which tend to shape the Soviet bureaucracy and which are, perhaps, less obvious.

One I would put under the general category of measures of effectiveness. In effect, this is looking at the economists' problem of indices from a sociological standpoint. What is it that the system is going to reward or not? In the economic field everybody, I suppose, has collected his favourite anecdotes. There is the now quite old story of the factory, whose index for production of light bulbs was wattage; they discovered that by making 200 watt light bulbs they had much better indices for productivity. The shipping tanks filled with water to make up the index for moving freight is another such example.

As a general matter, I would argue that a Soviet bureaucrat is much more likely to be rewarded for steady performance than for innovation or taking risks. Unusual success is not going to be rewarded as handsomely or as certainly as failure to do the established and defined job. Putting it the simplest way, one cannot get rich in the USSR by inventing the hula-hoop or the Apple computer. There is a widespread tendency in the bureaucracy to avoid taking decisions for which one might later be blamed. The Soviet bureaucracy is by and large better equipped to muddle through than to originate or to plan.

Another characteristic of the Soviet bureaucracy which has struck me — and here I am thinking more of senior officials like those of the *nomenklatura* — is the absence of career mobility or alternative career structures. A Soviet bureaucrat has little chance of moving from one career into another. One can think of some exceptions: people have moved from the Central Committee into journalism, or from the Party into diplomatic assignments; things are not totally immobile. Most Soviet bureaucrats, however, make their careers within one ministry. Furthermore, if one looks at the Council of Ministers, it becomes obvious that once someone gets to be a minister he is likely to stay there forever. Gromyko was a sort of quintessential example; so far as I know, he had been foreign minister longer than anybody else has ever been foreign minister of any country.

To the extent that senior officials do not go back to their private businesses or their law practices they tend to have very high standards of professionalism. The Soviet bureaucrat tends to be highly skilled in the particular business in which he is engaged; he will have had his portfolio much longer. There are, of course, cross-cutting implications of this.

On the one hand, these are people who do not forget the old ways. They do not forget the reasons for existing policy and are less likely to make any drastic changes. They will make changes, of course, but they will tend to make them incrementally, rather carefully, and in the context of the previous policy. On the other hand, this is a bureaucracy which has an amazing capacity to avoid bothering the boss. It runs smoothly. One is struck, if one contemplates the amount of time that Khrushchev could spend travelling, the very short workdays of Brezhnev in his declining years, or the limitations on Andropov when he was obviously very seriously ill, how well the machinery could run along with so little direction from the very top.

A third topic is generational change. Certainly, when one looked at some of the very elderly men on the Council of Ministers recently, one realised that there was going to be change. But in the Soviet bureaucracy generational change is likely to be slow in having an effect. The filters through which people have to pass as they rise up the system will tend to weed out the mavericks, those who are too original, and it will be the more conventional individuals who will have what Weber would have called the best life chances. Also, incidentally, one has to caution against the assumption that reformers are going to be liberals. This correlation tends to be true of people who will cultivate the society of foreign visitors. Nevertheless, the tendency of Andropov towards combining authoritarianism and reform, a combination which has a tradition in Russian history, should be taken as a caution against assuming that people who might want to reform the economy are necessarily going to be moving in the direction of democracy or political liberalism.

One had the impression that Andropov would have relied more on the government bureaucracy, because of its technical expertise and competence, and that Chernenko was more inclined to look to the support of the Party bureaucracy and to its propaganda and indoctrination function. In one speech, Chernenko alluded to the need for the Party not to exceed its brief and become involved in minor detail. This seems to me to be pretty standard Party rhetoric.

The Party bureaucracy is likely to be an important element for continuity in future policy. This is not to say that change will be impossible. Certainly there will be change, but to the extent that the bureaucracy is part of the process, these changes are likely to be introduced slowly and by degrees.

Only if there is more in the way of alternative career structures will one be entitled to optimism about economic reform. Only if we begin to see more bureaucrats developing a pattern of greater career mobility and being allowed opportunities to innovate.

In foreign affairs one might expect the tendency to be for policy to develop along more or less familiar lines; that is, tending towards incrementalism rather than moving in great leaps and bounds. I have observed over the years that when Moscow makes its annual show-case disarmament proposal at the UN, one is more startled by the ingenious way with which the old material has been reworked than by the novelty of the proposals.

The Role of the Military
Amnon Sella

This paper sets out to examine whether and under what circumstances the growth of the Soviet armed forces was reflected in the shaping of Soviet policy. The main thrust of the argument is that although the prestige of the military has certainly grown over the years, that it now consumes a greater part of the GNP and that it must be consulted on many major national issues, the ultimate decision still lies with the political state organs. Furthermore, military representation on these organs has definitely grown over time but the military say in decision — making is still quite limited. This examination purports to show that military representation on some of the major state organs is functional, i.e. designed to serve high policy purposes rather than strictly military ones.

It is sometimes argued that the military may intervene in internal politics when there is a vacuum in the political leadership, or when the government can no longer rule. Despite a lingering feeling in the West that the Soviet leadership has been in crisis for a very long time, despite a growing uneasiness in the West in the face of what seems to amount to a nationalistic sentiment in the USSR, there have been no substantial signs that the military might intervene in the affairs of the government in an illegal way.

The article will examine briefly two cases: the war in Lebanon and the destruction of KAL-007 in order to show that the system may function even when there is a malaise at the top.

The Arms Race Conspiracy

The balance of terror is basically a game for two played on a global scale and aided by many smaller games in regional theatres. The chief actors or perhaps one should say, culprits, in this game are to be found in political, military and economic circles. No matter how talented, reckless, or responsible these people are, their game involves us all in ever growing risks and ever mounting costs. It is worthwhile mentioning that one of the main themes of Ronald Reagan's first presidential campaign had been that the Soviet Union was investing a huge amount of money in defence and that the rate of growth of this investment was about 6 per cent a year. This estimate, like so many others, was based on the findings of the CIA and it gave a great boost to the man who claimed that under the presidency of Jimmy Carter the US was lagging behind the USSR and that the US ought to do something about it. About a year ago the CIA came out with a new report to the effect that the earlier one had been based on a gross error and that according to some new findings it was now clear that the USSR rate of growth in defence investment over the eight years from 1976 to 1984, had actually been only about 2 per cent. Still, one would try in vain to trace the impact of this revelation in American official military, political, or economic writings.

In the rich crop of Soviet writings concerning the American military threat one would come up time and again against analysis, interpretation and estimates of American investment in defence. The general tenor of these writings, naturally, is that the Soviet Union is a peace loving country, that it does not have any aggressive designs against its neighbours; on the contrary, it is precisely because of American ill intentions that the arms race is still raging. It should not come as a surprise to us that a great deal of these expressions are propounded by the military. Not only are they more proficient in this particular subject (in the Soviet Union and elsewhere) but they are also the interested party in the Soviet Union as well as in the West.[1] In other words, we are faced here by the arms race conspiracy. On the one hand, both superpowers feel threatened; on the other hand, belittling one's own efforts and exaggerating the efforts of the other party exacerbates the arms race. If the military can persuade the political leadership that the other party is getting stronger more resources will be put at its disposal. The more resources there are, the greater the prestige and the significance of the military and the greater the stake of the politicians who set store by them. Unfortunately, as has already been mentioned above, the balance of terror is a game for two. When the military of one side succeeds in getting some extra money for defence on the grounds that otherwise it could not guarantee the defence of the homeland, the military of the other side feels insecure and the game starts all over again. 'But they are Communists', they cry in the

---

1. Col. Gen. Nikolai Chervov, 'American military budget and Washington's "peacefulness"', *Soviet Weekly*, 17 March 1984; Marshal Kulikov, *Sovetskaya Rossiya*, 23 February 1984; Stephen E. Ambrose & Jones Alden Barker Jr. (eds.), *The Military and American Society*, London, 1972 pp. 62–3.

West; 'but they are Imperialists' they shriek in the USSR. The aim of this exercise was not to equate East and West but to point out the mechanism of the conspiracy between the military and the political establishment. Of course the West must arm against the threat from the East, but that is exactly the way they feel in the East. Security and threat are most unfortunate twin concepts; one is in the hands of the military, the other in the hands of the political leadership. In a country like the USSR which suffers from a long tradition of 'siege complex' compounded by a strong departmentalism it is to be expected that the need for security will enhance the feeling of threat.

Apparently, then, one way in which the military may influence the politicians is by emphasizing the threat. It should be remembered of course that intelligence, the collation of information, its processing and selection is strictly in the hands of the military. By subtle manipulation of information and evaluation military intelligence is capable of influencing the decisions of the politicians. Indeed, the final decision in many countries, including the USSR, is in the hands of the politicians. There are not too many representatives of the military in Soviet political, state organs.[2]

Correlation Between Military Function and Political Significance

The role of the military is to defend the borders of the country, or to use the Soviet parlance, the borders of 'the homeland'. One way of assessing whether or not the military adheres to this stricture is to analyse military participation and involvement in internal politics. The Soviet armed forces have never had anything to do with internal politics in the Soviet Union unless they have been either victims of the system under the reign of terror, or subject to the political supervision of the Party, or the control of the security organs of the state. That does not mean that the Soviet armed forces are apolitical; on the contrary, their politicisation is probably the best guarantee that they will stay loyal to the state and imbued with the spirit of true communism. The Party was involved with the armed forces from the very inception of the Red Army. No doubt, the founders of this army were experts in undermining and subverting military organisations. They founded their new army on the wreckage of the

2. T.J. Colton, *Commissars, Commanders and Civilian Authority*, Cambridge (Mass.), 1979, p. 253; *Soviet Constitution*, 1977, clause 121/14.

old imperial one that they themselves had helped to destroy.

The new army had gone through a long process of experimentation with a system of dual command; that is a military, professional commander under the supervision of a commissar. The history of the dual command in the Red Army is well-known and documented and there is no need to repeat it here; however, it is worth mentioning that there were three periods in the history of the Soviet command: (1) The period of domination by the commissar; (2) The period of struggle between professional commander and commissar; (3) The period of symbiosis. The last period began after the end of the Second World War. The role of the Party is not only being upheld today; also the political officer in the forces has come to play many functions that in other armies are carried out by social workers or by members of the clergy. However, there is little novelty in the fact that the Party's position in the Soviet army is so strong; the novelty lies in the political functions that are assigned by the state to military personnel. It has already been mentioned that there are not very many officers in political positions in the USSR. It is therefore very interesting to analyse the reasons why some officers do find their way into the non-military state organs.

The Soviet Far East has been a problem for the government from the very beginning. It is not surprising then that, with no original solutions to old problems, the new regime had to revert to old solutions — namely to divide the command over the huge theatre of activities into sections or military districts. When this arrangement was not good enough the Soviet High Command emulated its predecessor and bestowed great authority upon the Far Eastern command. One should remember the autonomy that Blyukher enjoyed for a while, the free hand given to Zhukov when he dealt with the Japanese sixth army during the incident that went down in Soviet annals as the War at Khalkhin-Gol, in order to appreciate the extent of the problem. In a book published recently it was stated that

> throughout the 1970s the Soviet build-up in the Far East has attracted wide attention. However, perhaps the most significant development in the overall strategic posture of Soviet forces East of the Urals was the establishment in late December 1978 of a major theatre of command in the Far East, probably comprising the Far East, Transbaikal and Siberian Military Districts under the overall command of Army General V.I. Petrov. . . . Speculation regarding the Far East Theatre was sparked off

initially by a report in the Soviet Press that L.I. Brezhnev, in his capacity as Chairman of the Supreme Defence council, had received Petrov and a number of other senior officers on their appointment to new duties. . . . A Chinese report in early 1979 stating that Petrov is commanding in the Far East, while vague, was supported by Petrov's subsequent election in March 1979 to the Supreme Soviet of the USSR for the Lenin District of Irkutsk (Siberian Military District).[3]

The sequence of events was that a talented officer who had already proven his ability in another theatre was sent to the Far East at a time of crisis. An entire new command was given to General Petrov, a great responsibility and an enormous sphere of authority. Upon assuming command he and some of his officers were given an audience by Brezhnev as a token of his new status and a few months later Petrov was also elected to the Supreme Soviet of the USSR. His election was, of course, partially in recognition of his new status as a commander of a huge area to which the Soviet government attaches great significance, and partly a symbol of the subordination of the military to the state. In the Supreme Soviet, General Petrov can hardly be expected to be a spokesman for the armed forces.

There have been changes in the military representation in the state organs, but these were more of a qualitative nature than a quantitative one. At the XVI Party Congress in 1930 there were five military representatives among 137 members of the central Party organs (3.64 per cent). After the XVII Party Congress of 1934 their number increased to eight out of 139 (5.75 per cent). At the XVIII Party Congress of 1939, when there was a need to compensate the military after the purges and in the face of the German threat, the number of military representatives in the central Party organs grew again to fifteen out of 139 (10.79 per cent). Subsequently, there were twenty at the XX Congress (1956), thirty-one at the XXII (1961), thirty-three at the XXIII (1966) and thirty-three at the XXVI Party Congress in 1981.

However, the point I want to stress is that when there was a pressing need, the political leadership decided to co-opt or allow the election of military personalities to central state and Party organs. That was the case in 1939 when the Soviet Union started to brace itself for the possibility of war, and the same happened in 1978–9 in

3. J. Erickson, Lynn Hansen, Amnon Sella, Ivan Volgyes, James Westwood, Richard Woff, *Organizing for War: The Soviet Military Establishment Viewed Through the Prism of the Military District*, The Center for Strategic Technology, The Texas Engineering Experiment Station, The Texas A&M University System.

the teeth of growing tensions in the Far East. By brandishing military personalities at the top the Soviet leadership achieves several goals: it cements the ties between the military and the state; it highlights the loyalty of the armed forces to the state; last but not least, it pays a tribute to the Generals to whom it entrusts its security.

Nevertheless, one cannot leave this argument without attending to the problem of the highest organs, namely: the Supreme Commander-in-Chief of the Soviet armed forces, the Defence Council and the Military-Industrial Commission. The C.-in-C has always been a civilian, that is excluding the period from 1924 to 1941 when the position fell into abeyance, a default for which the Red Army paid dearly at the beginning of the German onslaught. In the nuclear age it was absolutely impossible to leave this post vacant and although we cannot ascertain the fact it seems more than likely that the General Secretary of the Communist Party assumes the post of C.-in-C automatically, together with his political office. There is, of course, the problem of making the nomination public. Certainly, there are many problems involved here. If there is a struggle at the top an early publication gives an obvious advantage to the nominee; on the other hand, the publication is not made for either internal or external consumption, it is done for both. Thus, we must assume that sometimes the struggle at the top is so intense that this critical nomination is postponed, or that only a limited group of people is notified of the fact until after the dispute at the top is over, or else that there are other ways and means to let the military know who is their new C.-in-C, that we in the West are not aware of.

The problem of the Defence Council had been properly regulated under the Constitution of 1977. Clause 119 of the Constitution states that the Supreme Soviet, in a joint meeting of the two houses elects the Presidium of the Supreme Soviet. Clause 121/14 states that the Presidium establishes the Defence Council, deliberates on its composition and nominates and changes the High Command. In short, the Defence Council, the chairman of which is the General Secretary of the Communist Party, is subordinated to a political rather than to a military organ. Certainly, in such a secretive body many manipulations are possible, but then this is generally the case. Suffice it to say that the machinery is there at the service of the General Secretary if he wanted to use it. There should be no doubting that in an emergency, say a nuclear alert, a decision will be taken by a small group of people, in close consultation with the military. In peacetime, however, the ceremonial fanfare of military nomination calls for a larger body of decision-making, say the Presidium, as is stated in the Constitution.

The Military-Industrial Commission directs military production and the whole complex of R&D. Very little is known about this body, but from the little that is known it seems that this key organ of research, design and production, is headed by a deputy chairman of the Council of Ministers, i.e. not a military man.[4] On the one hand, then, the increase in military representation on the higher state organs has been quite modest, perhaps less than expected in a country as centralised as the USSR. On the other hand, there has been no noticeable slackness in the control of the Party (the state to all intents and purposes) over the military.

The Military and the Crisis of Leadership

There have been six transitions of power since 1917 but what a difference between them! During the Stalin period it was inconceivable that the Soviet Union would be able to function without a dictator. Indeed, many a theory was written to the effect that 'The Gods Are Athirst' (to borrow Isaac Deutscher's expression), that there is something inherent in the Soviet regime which compels it to kill its prominent figures. However, in due course the leaders learned how to preserve themselves, and how to settle their differences without bloodshed. It is still a cruel game at the top of the Soviet pyramid, there is still no public supervision of the government and a change of guard is still decided high at the top among the elect, but it is a far cry from the Stalin outrages. Furthermore, it seems as though the transition from one ruler to the next has become smoother. It is noteworthy that there is no clause in the Constitution to help the leaders regulate the transition. The end result, i.e. the fact that there is an agreed leader after such a short spell is a feat of politics all of its own. It means that the Soviet leaders have learned, perhaps the hard way, the art of political negotiation, the art of give and take. If these assumptions are correct, there is hardly any call for military intervention in internal politics, which usually occurs when there is a vacuum in the leader-

4. R. Amann & J. Cooper, *Industrial Innovation in the Soviet Union*, New Haven (Conn.), 1982, p. 298.

ship resulting in anarchy in the country.

Nevertheless, it is probable that in a lingering leadership crisis like the recent one the process of decision-making may be affected. Throughout the period of crisis, starting with the noticeable deterioration in Brezhnev's health, one can think of several major decisions taken by the Soviet leadership: the invasion of Afghanistan, the invasion of Lebanon and the destruction of the Korean airliner KAL-007. The common denominator of all these are the following: they all occurred during the period of the crisis of leadership; they all involved decisions of a military nature. There are, of course, many differences between these events. In the first place, Afghanistan is close to the Soviet border and Lebanon may be considered only within the outer defence perimeter. Secondly, the decision regarding the invasion of Afghanistan was taken after long preparation as a Soviet initiative. The decision regarding the war in Lebanon was taken outside Soviet frontiers and the Russians could respond by a deed or by default. The case of the Korean airliner was altogether different from the above-mentioned points of view. It was a definite emergency, well covered both by regulations and by international law, on the face of it within the jurisdiction of the military. Still, we have had three different outcomes from the same country, the same system, the same apparatus of government. Should we, then, attribute the differences to the crisis of leadership? Can we be sure that the decision to invade Afghanistan had been taken by the military because by the time of decision Brezhnev was already physically too weak to object? It is true that General I.G. Pavlovskii had gone to Afghanistan in mid-1979, together with General Yepishev. Their assessment was apparently far too optimistic and it may well be that General Pavlovskii was replaced by General Petrov as a result, but would it all have been different had Brezhnev been in better shape? Then, again, supposing the military had been foolhardy in the train of decisions which led the USSR astray in the case of Afghanistan, why then was the military so cautious in the case of Lebanon? Finally, why were the armed forces left to fend for themselves in the case of the Korean airliner?

As it is plain that the military had been involved in all three cases one must look for other explanations. The military have always been and are still today an organ of the state. They are consulted in matters that concern them and they must be in a position to give the political leadership adequate answers to problems of foreign policy which pertain to the security of the State. There are three basic considerations regarding the question of Soviet military intervention in a foreign country:

(1) What would be the reaction of the USA?

(2) What would be the response of the government and the people?

(3) Are the armed forces capable of carrying out the job in hand?

Strictly speaking, the military is called upon to answer only the third question. This is, of course, a somewhat schematic answer to a very complicated problem, yet it provides us perhaps with a better explanation to the riddles of Soviet behaviour in Afghanistan and Lebanon. In the case of Afghanistan the military had overestimated the tactical performance of the troops that were first sent in. However, the political assessment of the possible American reactions proved to be accurate, while the political assessment of the co-operation of the Afghan people was utterly wrong. The USA did not, indeed could not do anything about the invasion while the Soviet troops have improved their performance enormously, a not unfamiliar phenomenon with armies in general and with the Soviet armed forces in particular. As far as the political situation inside Afghanistan is concerned, it is not very likely that the Afghans would change their heart regarding the invaders, but as to who is better equipped to sustain losses for a prolonged period one should withhold one's judgement.

The major differences between the cases of Afghanistan and Lebanon have already been indicated above, yet it goes without saying that the military must have been deeply involved in both cases. Let us now examine the case of Lebanon in the light of the above-mentioned three considerations. The USA had shown great interest in Lebanon from early on (one should bear in mind the involvement of the Marines in 1958). It was an interest in the country, in containing Soviet influence and in Israel. There were forces inside Lebanon that could perhaps help Soviet expeditionary forces; however, the PLO and the Syrian forces were too weak to withstand the Israeli forces. The Soviet advisers knew that only too well — after all they themselves had equipped and trained these forces. To put it bluntly, according to the Soviet Field Regulations an offensive force must have an advantage of four or five to one over its opponent. Under the circumstances that had developed in Lebanon at the time, this would have meant sending in about twenty Soviet divisions. There is no need to develop this argument any further.

Evidently, in that case as in the previous one the problem was not solely that of the crisis in the leadership, but partly, perhaps mainly, considerations of high policy amongst which military ones are most prominent. It was only natural that immediately after the truce between Syria and Israel, high-ranking Soviet officers were rushed to Syria for fact finding and to sort out the many problems emanating from the less than satisfactory performance of both troops and equipment. The Soviet doctrine and training methods for Third World countries also left much to be desired. There could be no doubt that a great deal of military activity was taking place in Syria after the end of hostilities between the two countries. Moreover, in the political manoeuvres and in the military reconstruction of Syria after the war the Russians demonstrated their usual caution: they were not prepared to commit their troops to any far-reaching action of a strategic nature, and they built a formidable anti-aircraft belt in Syria, incorporating in it (for the first time in the history of the Arab-Israeli conflict) some elements of a deterrent nature, namely, SA-5s and SS-21s, yet by and large it is still a defensive system.

The case of the Korean airliner is the only one of the three in which one may trace some faults in the communications between the military at the periphery of the Soviet Union and the centre in Moscow. One possible reason for the lack of clarity in the Soviet chain of command was the reorganisation of the air force and air defence which had started at the end of the 1970s. For instance, the National Air Defence Command, fighter regiments of Frontal Aviation and Ground Forces, AA guns and missiles have been unified. The organisation of the PVO *(Protivo-Vozdushnaya Oborona Strany)* was transformed from a national command with subordinate air defence districts to a series of theatre commands under the Commander-in-Chief of the local TVD.[5] It seems that in 1979 Colonel-General Kirsanov assumed command of the Far East Theatre. In December 1982 Kirsanov was promoted to the rank of Marshal and three weeks after the destruction of the plane Kirsanov signed an article detailing the tragic events. The aeroplane, then, strayed into Soviet airspace when the air force command was still in the process of reorganisation. Some confused statements of Soviet officers were not so much the result of a guilty conscience but more of embarrassment because the chain of events leading to the order to destroy the airliner revealed some dangerous vulnerabilities in command, control and communications within the Soviet command

5. Mark Urban, 'Re-organization of the Soviet Air Force', *Armed Forces*, June, 1983, p. 207.

and between the military command and the civilian authorities. Amongst the many officers who were interviewed, wrote articles and gave statements there was one conspicuous sphinx, C.-in-C Air Defence and deputy minister of defence Marshal Koldunov. A paper in West Germany was of the opinion that the order to destroy the plane had been given by General Gudkov, who is in fact the Commander of the Naval Air Forces of the Pacific Fleet. It is more plausible that the order was given by the Deputy C.-in-C Far East who is also the commander of the air defence forces in the area. Be that as it may, the result demonstrated the complexity of the command chain in a most sensitive area which is subordinate to three organisations, all in charge of air defence.

The upshot of this argument is that for security reasons as well as for organisational considerations the military was granted wide authority in the Soviet Far East; that while the process of implementing these reorganisations was in the making, the Far East command was called upon to cope with an emergency and did not prove itself up to the mark. The military were left to fend for themselves because in an impossible situation it seemed easier to attribute the failure to factors of security than to political-international reasons, although there was no lack of these too.

Current Events and Conclusions

In the early part of 1984 many prominent military personalities gave expression to their views about the current situation. It so happened that these opinions were given vent to at the same time as yet another transition in the Soviet leadership, when Andropov died and Chernenko replaced him. Thus one could watch Marshal Ogarkov on television on 23 February talking, amongst other topics, about the high standard of education of Soviet servicemen; one could read in *Pravda* (29 February 1984) an article by Marshal Ustinov about the problems of the Soviet economy; General Yepishev published an article in *Izvestiya* about the significance of the Soviet armed forces and about the importance of the elections; *Krasnaya Zvezda* (25 February 1984) reported a meeting opened by General Yepishev, in which Marshal Ustinov addressed a gathering of Party functionaries at the Ministry of Defence. As one of the ways to assess military participation in political life is by quantifying public appearances, one might have surmised that there had been a revolutionary change in military involvement. As a matter of fact, on analysis, all these appearances took place around traditional occasions (23 February, for example, is Army Day and just before elections to the Soviet).

In conclusion, the Soviet system is apparently stable and although the prestige of the armed forces has been enhanced, owing to the growing feeling of threat in the USSR, and to the military's growing share in the GNP, they are still no more than an organ of state. Major decisions are taken in civilian, or at least in state organs in which military personalities are represented as a tiny minority.

Those military personalities who were elected to the highest state organs were elected because their functions demanded their presence there, or because their responsibility in assignments went far beyond their rank or formal authority. Last, but not least, military personalities on the whole confined their public utterances to military affairs or to an agreed upon topical issue of the day, like the threat of 'American Imperialism' or the dangers of cruise and Pershing-2 missiles in Europe. The role of the military in the Soviet Union has grown but that fact does not seem to change the nature of Soviet foreign policy decisions.

14

Reform in the Political System: Limits and Possibilities

Forces for Change
Wolfgang Leonhard

The security of the Western democracies depends not only on the military strength of NATO or the possibility of reaching agreements on arms control with the present leadership of the Soviet Union (or other Soviet bloc countries) but also decisively on whether and to what extent systems such as that prevailing in the Soviet Union can 'open' themselves, carry out reforms and respect human rights.

All developments in the Soviet Union which lead to a turning away from bureaucratic–dictatorial centralism promise an opening of Soviet society and the expansion of democratic freedoms and social rights reflect socio-economic necessities as well as the wishes and hopes of large parts of the population.

Reform of the Soviet political system is, however, a precondition for an improvement in East–West relations. The realisation of reforms, more freedom and greater liberalisation offer the possibility of overcoming the present difficulties and frequent set-backs threatening East–West relations and open the way to a relaxation of tensions.

Here a number of questions have to be asked:
I. To what extent are such reforms of the Soviet system possible?
II. What social and political forces support reform?
III. What conditions would make the realisation of such reforms easier?

IV. What conclusions should the Western democracies draw from the answers to these first three questions?

Are Political Reforms of the Soviet System Possible?

Doubts are frequently expressed about the possibilities of reform within the Soviet system (and the systems of other Soviet bloc countries), usually in the form of two arguments:

(1) 'All previous attempts have failed.' The possibility of a reform of the political system is denied with the assertion that the regime would never permit such reforms and all earlier attempts in this direction — Hungary in 1956, Czechoslovakia in 1968 and Poland in 1980–1 failed; one has to accept the regime in the Soviet Union (and the other Soviet bloc countries) as they are. At most, some improvements involving minimal change will be introduced by the leadership, but no real reform of the system can be expected.

This objection overlooks two facts:

(a) In spite of the failures mentioned above, the Soviet leadership has had gradually to accept the increasing efforts of the East European countries to achieve autonomy and independence.

(b) History shows that attempts to reform a given system are seldom successful immediately. Usually, repeated attempts are necessary before such reforms can be realised.

(2) 'The lack of a democratic tradition in Russia.' In Russia there has never been a democratic political tradition; liberalisation and reform of the present political system are therefore completely inconceivable.

Russian history does contain fewer democratic traditions than that of many other European countries; but this certainly does not mean that democratic developments in future are impossible.

The Soviet Union is an industrial state; large segments of its population are well educated and possess extensive, often painful political experiences. The majority of Soviet citizens are persons of the younger generation whose views have been formed by developments since the death of Stalin. The official state ideology (Marxism-Leninism) is hardly an important factor in their lives; they have completely different values and models.

The authority and legitimacy of the system are increasingly questioned. The hopes during the de-Stalinisation period, the fall of Khrushchev in October 1964, the period of authoritarian restoration under Brezhnev, the development of an intellectual opposition (the dissident movement) with manuscripts passed from hand to hand and the widespread hopes for political reform have left their mark on the thinking and critical judgement of Soviet citizens.

Moreover, the samizdat writings make clear how much Soviet citizens think about the system and a possible liberalisation in their country.

Reform of the Political System: Preconditions and Socio-political Forces

The possibility of political reform in the Soviet system depends on:

(a) the extent of contradictions and conflicts within the system;

(b) the strength of social and political groups which support political reforms; and

(c) conditions which would make a breakthrough of efforts to achieve such political reforms of the system possible or easier.

Contradictions and conflicts in the Soviet system today

In spite of its apparently 'monolithic unity', the present Soviet system is by no means stable. The deep conflict between new social forces and the tasks of an emerging modern industrial society on the one hand and the obsolete, outmoded, bureaucratic–dictatorial system on the other are becoming increasingly obvious.

These contradictions are primarily visible in the following areas:

(1) The bureaucratic-centralistic economic system hinders the economic and technological development of the country and has resulted in a serious, long-term crisis in Soviet agriculture. Far-reaching reforms in industry and agriculture in the form of decentralisation and a dramatic reduction of bureaucratic planning, direction and controls are necessary if the Soviet Union is to overcome its agricultural crisis and not fall hopelessly behind the West in economic and technological development. However, economic reforms are hardly possible without a certain political and cultural liberalisation.

(2) The Russification policy of the Soviet leadership (in a country where fewer than 52 per cent of the people are Russians) has led to increasing national contradictions and to stronger ethnic self-awareness among the non-Russian nationalities. This requires a

turning away from Russification and the introduction of a policy of equal rights among the peoples of the Soviet Union.

(3) The Soviet state ideology, Marxism-Leninism, once a source of inspiration and motivation, now receives only lip service. The ideological and psychological vacuum is obvious. The clearly reduced influence of ideology makes it necessary to permit other philosophies and even to conduct a dialogue with systems advocating other values and goals.

(4) Social contradictions in the Soviet Union are becoming more pronounced. This is especially true of dissatisfaction resulting from the inadequate food supply situation, the one-sided emphasis on heavy and armaments industries, which results in a neglect of consumer goods production, and the social privileges of the *nomenklatura* functionaries. The increasing number of strikes and attempts to organise independent trade unions in the Soviet Union indicate a growing dissatisfaction with the social situation and more self-confidence among industrial workers. Important changes in the area of social policy and a recognition of independent trade unions in the Soviet Union cannot be avoided in the long term.

(5) The inability of the regime to guarantee the supply of food and consumer goods for the population has resulted in the development of a 'second economy', including private business activity and a growing number of private 'underground factories', which produce urgently needed goods of the desired quality. In spite of strong measures to suppress it, all the efforts to eliminate this second economy have failed.

It is not 'speculators' or 'black marketeers' who are involved in this second economy, but a new social class with extensive connections to the highest circles of the Party and state bureaucracy. The legalisation of the second economy in the Soviet Union can hardly be avoided in the long term.

(6) The administrative machinery of the regime, created by Stalin to carry out the industrialisation of this once economically backward country, long ago lost its social function. It now exhibits a growing number of parasitic traits: career mindedness, nepotism and, above all, corruption. The entire *nomenklatura* system is in deep crisis, and the symptoms of degeneration in the administrative organs are proof that a thorough reorganisation of the political system is necessary.

The forces of social and political reform

The contradictions mentioned above have produced different socio-political forces in the Soviet Union which (even though they differ in strength and form) are interested in promoting political reform of the system.

(1) Part of the scientific-technical intelligentsia as well as some economic functionaries support far-reaching economic reforms, such as decentralisation and more independence for enterprises and lower economic organs.

(2) Some of the increasingly self-confident industrial workers are demanding that they be allowed to become an independent political force and express their interests through independent trade unions.

(3) Among the non-Russian peoples efforts are increasing to achieve stronger representation in the national government as well as greater autonomy and independence in some areas.

(4) Part of the younger generation, which is becoming more important, is tired of the constant stream of Soviet propaganda; Soviet young people often have other values and goals and are ready and able to try new directions.

(5) Among religious groups, churches and communities many people are resisting the official atheism and demanding freedom of religion and conscience.

(6) The 'representatives of the second economy', suppressed by the regime, who produce and provide urgently needed consumer goods and services for the population, are demanding a legalisation of their economic activities.

(7) Performing and other artists, who enjoy great respect among the population, are urging creative freedom and the elimination of humiliating censorship and are also supporting the advocates of freedom and social justice.

(8) The number of active champions of human rights is indeed relatively small and their opportunities to exert direct influence are limited by constant persecution. The human rights movement is, however, an expression of widespread demands for democratic conditions and freer development and could be of great importance as a crystallisation point at the beginning of processes of change.

Under What Conditions is Political Reform of the Soviet System Possible?

Political reform of the system depends not only on the extent of contradictions within it and the presence of social and political forces which support the liberalisation and 'opening' of Soviet society.

The concrete social and political conditions which make a breakthrough of these forces possible are decisive. In this respect the coincidence of 'pressure from below' and serious disagreements in the leadership has proved to be an important precondition.

The 'pressure from below'

The history of Soviet Communism has shown repeatedly that relaxation of control, concessions to the population, reforms and liberalisation are as a rule granted only as a result of economic necessities and in the face of growing political dissatisfaction among the masses (pressure from below).

Under difficult conditions, economic and political objective necessities, which could seriously endanger the regime, Soviet leaders change course quickly and are prepared to make concessions to their own people. However, as soon as the situation has stabilised and they feel safe again, repression at home becomes more severe and expansionist tendencies in foreign policy more pronounced. Examples are the New Economic Policy (1921–7), the situation in the first years of World War II (1941–3) and the de-Stalinisation period (1953–7).

One can, therefore, conclude that the probability of political reform in the Soviet Union will increase:

(a) the more the present *nomenklatura* system is forced to accept economic reforms as a result of objective economic necessities;

(b) the less it is able to divert the attention of the population from internal problems and compensate for domestic difficulties by foreign policy successes;

(c) the more pressure from the population strengthens the position of reformist forces and tendencies in the government apparatus and the leadership.

Disagreements within the Leading Groups of the Regime

The enormous government machinery of the Soviet Union is not so uniform as it once was. Among the pillars of the regime — the Party, the state administration, the army and the security service (KGB) — there are occasionally considerable differences of opinion; and within one and the same organisation, factions also develop with different and sometimes even opposing views.

The effects of such tendencies are especially clear in the following areas:

(a) In economic policy a struggle is taking place between those who hope to overcome the backwardness of the Soviet Union by stricter labour discipline and those who support a reform of the completely outmoded bureaucratic system of central economic planning.

(b) In investment policy there are differences between the advocates of heavy and armaments industries and the proponents of an expansion of consumer goods production. Moreover, there are also conflicting views regarding necessary investment in agriculture.

(c) Nationalities policy is marked by differences of opinion between supporters of increased Russification and those who want to stress the multinational character of the Soviet Union.

(d) In foreign policy there are the 'globalists', who want to continue an active foreign policy all over the world, and other groups who consider this policy 'adventurist' and too expensive and want to replace it with a limited continental policy in Europe and Asia.

(e) With regard to the Western powers, some groups in the Soviet leadership advocate more and closer relations — primarily for technological and economic reasons, whereas others, for political reasons, stress the view of the West as the 'enemy' and push for an offensive foreign policy. Such differences are usually not serious in normal times. In difficult situations, however, they can lead to far-reaching conflicts, even to a polarisation of the higher *nomenklatura* functionaries.

Under these conditions, the functionaries form two large groups. On the one hand there are those who advocate even more repression and who believe that they can divert the population from the difficulties in the Soviet system with the help of alleged internal and external enemies and strengthen the system and their own power by an artificially induced conflict psychosis.

On the other hand, a 'modern' wing is developing, characterised by attempts to provide certain carefully measured and controlled reforms and to eliminate the most 'extreme' systemic contradictions in the hope of achieving an increase in economic activity and an improvement in the supply situation. Examples of such polarisation were visible in, among other things, the introduction of the 'new course' in the GDR (spring 1953), in the spring and summer of 1956 in Hungary (the reform group around Imre Nagy and authoritarian Stalinists around Rakosi) and before and during the Prague Spring in Czechoslovakia in 1968. In the Soviet Union, too, there were similar polarisations in the years of de-Stalinisation (1953–8); they could be seen in the numerous succession problems following the deaths of Brezhnev (November 1982), Andropov (February 1984) and Chernenko (March 1985). The previous development of Communist systems has shown that pressure from below leads to disagreements in the power structure, which makes reform of the system possible or at least easier. This could also be the case in future reforms of the Soviet system.

Conclusions for Western Policy towards Eastern Europe and the Soviet Union

Western governments should not ignore domestic political developments and the possibility of political reforms in the Soviet Union in their attempts to understand developments there. Western policy towards the Soviet Union cannot be limited to reactions to measures taken by the present Soviet leadership; it must not lose sight of long-term developments and should take into account possible effects of conflicts, crises and changes.

As a rule, domestic political changes in the Soviet Union have an effect on East-West relations. The more the Soviet Union moves away from its present bureaucratic-dictatorial regime, the more modern, pluralistic, flexible and moderate it becomes, the greater are the chances for a successful *détente*. And conversely, a hardening of the repressive domestic political character of the regime is usually accompanied by a harder line towards the West.

A liberalisation of the political system depends on internal factors and cannot be forced upon the Soviet Union. It is, however, possible and necessary for the Western democracies to pursue a policy which does not make the work of Soviet supporters of internal reform more difficult and, if possible, makes it easier to influence the process of liberalisation in a positive sense. Such a policy could consist, among other things, of the following:

(a) a clear distinction in all official statements about the Soviet Union between the leadership on the one hand and the Soviet population on the other. This corresponds to reality and would be received with thanks by many Soviet citizens who dislike being constantly lumped together with the Kremlin leadership;

(b) public expressions of solidarity with representatives of the human rights movement in the Soviet Union by private Western organisations and institutions.

Contrary to a widespread view, such expressions of solidarity do not hurt dissidents but actually help and protect them against persecution or, if they are in prison, lead to improvements in their prison conditions.

Public honours, such as the awarding of the Nobel Peace Prize to Sakharov in 1975 and Lech Walesa in 1983, are examples of such positive efforts; they should be intensified and expanded by proclamations of solidarity with and awarding of prizes and honours to less well-known representatives of the human rights movement. Greater recognition and distribution of the writings of the Soviet human rights movement would also be useful.

(c) repeated demands, above all from private organisations that the Soviet Union abide by agreements signed and ratified by the Soviet leadership itself, such as the United Nations agreements on civil and political rights and the declaration of the Conference on Security and Co-operation in Europe in Helsinki (1975) and Madrid (1983). Soviet ratification gives the Western democracies the right to insist that the Soviet Union respect these agreements and to point out its failure to do so.

One such violation of ratified agreements is the Soviet jamming of Western radio broadcasts since August 1980. This jamming represents a violation of obligations assumed by the Soviet leadership, and the Western democracies have a right to demand that it be stopped.

(d) a strengthening and expansion of Western radio broadcasts for the population of the Soviet Union. Broadcasts such as those of Radio Liberty, the Voice of America, BBC London and the Voice of Germany represent the only source of information for many interested Soviet citizens. BBC London and the Voice of Germany broadcast exclusively in Russian; an expansion of the broadcasts to include Ukrainian, Estonian, Latvian and Lithuanian (all European peoples) would be appropriate. Efforts of the Soviet leadership to stop the reception of such free broadcasts in the name of a so-called 'new world information order' must be opposed vigorously.

(e) In addition to taking into consideration the differences mentioned above between the Soviet leadership and the population, it is important in the present period of struggle for the succession to understand divisions within the Soviet leading class and to react appropriately to them.

This kind of Western firmness should make clear to the 'hawks' in the Kremlin the limitations of their power and the danger of further expansionist steps. On the other hand it seems advisable to encourage the moderate, realistic and modern forces within the leading groups of Soviet society by flexibility, understanding and a readiness to negotiate and to offer them the possibility of improved East-West relations.

All of these and other measures are intended to serve the goal of supporting, at least indirectly, the forces of future political reform in relations with the official leadership. The opening of Soviet society, respect for human rights and political reforms of the Soviet system are by no means purely the internal affairs of the Soviet Union; rather they are at the same time the decisive preconditions for smoothing the way to real *détente*, for creating possibilities of expanding East-West relations beyond negotiations with the Soviet leadership and gradually establishing good relations between the peoples of East and West through the political reform of the Soviet system.

Change in the Soviet Political System
Robert F. Byrnes

The political systems of all societies possess strengths and weaknesses, some inherent in the nature of man, some structural, some temporary and minor, some the price of progress as achievements strain old institutions and practices and create new tensions, some the consequences of reluctance to revise hallowed procedures, some the results of developments beyond the boundaries of the society. In short, change is everywhere the law of life.

The Need for Change

The problems Soviet rulers face when they contemplate changes that will preserve the system's fundamental character and at the same time make it more efficient, productive, and responsive are even more complicated than those which Western peoples confront. In part, this reflects the achievements of the Brezhnev years, the transformation of an essentially underdeveloped country into a truly global power. In a sense, the Soviet Union must now pay penalties for progress or at least revise the system to ensure stability on a new plateau. As Toynbee wrote, nothing fails like success.

It appears to me that the Soviet Union is approaching a time of decision similar to that of the mid-1920s, when its leaders discussed the policies which should succeed NEP. The issues are also cumulative, converging, interrelated, and vital.

(1) The most important of these is the slowing rate of growth of the highly centralized, complex economy and the stringencies and difficult decisions this raises concerning the allocation of resources, choices which affect every part of the political system.

(2) A second is the need to repair the infrastructure. The discussion in this book has illuminated these requirements, visible and invisible, from transport and housing to demographic trends, health care, education and civic morale to the continuing silence of Russian culture. As in an earlier period of Russian history, we encounter a swollen state and a spent society.

(3) The third is the inherent, growing instability of Eastern Europe which the Soviets consider an essential part of their system.

351

Poland plays the central role it has often played within the Russian constellation and in Russian and Soviet relations with the West. In effect, it constitutes a cancer that the Soviets may freeze into a temporary remission, but for which even a miraculous economic renaissance would provide no solution.

(4) The fourth is the requirement that the Soviet Union somehow keep abreast of the rapid scientific, technical, economic, and intellectual developments in the shrinking world. They can obtain certain access to this vital knowledge only by maintaining friendly relations with the West, but they can acquire and use this information only by introducing foreign injections into a body politic they seek to isolate. In this age of information, in which knowledge is the most important product, preserving an authoritarian system and an isolated society is becoming increasingly difficult. In nineteenth century terms, the Soviets seek a fire that will not burn.

The Limitations upon Change

(1) The nature of these problems, their interrelationship, and the way any effort to introduce innovations for *any* of these issues would reverberate throughout the system constitute a most important limitation upon change.

(2) The second fundamental limitation is the nature of the Soviet system and the refusal of those in power, supported by the millions who benefit from Soviet rule, to weaken centralised control over all aspects of Soviet life. Basically, the system is immobile, frozen, and resistant to change: central control and direction are vital for Communist rule, and significant changes would undermine the system. In short, the Soviet Union has reinforced Bagehot's 'cake of custom'.

Thus, changing the allocation of resources is a delicate issue because it is so tightly related to the character of the system and to potential quarrels among leaders, and because the immediate interests of central institutions and élites are so engaged. Bureaucratic opposition to innovation and relaxing familiar controls is entrenched. In addition, significant changes would encourage pressure for innovation in Eastern Europe that would threaten stability, especially in Poland.

Similarly, tinkering or introducing palliatives would have little effect in Poland, but honouring the 1980 agreements is unthinkable because it would excite Polish appetites for sweeping changes and threaten the Soviet position in Poland and throughout Eastern Europe. Decentralising the Polish economy or liberalising the production and sale of consumer goods would unleash forces now seething and signal pressures for comparable changes elsewhere in Eastern Europe and in the Soviet Union itself. In short, as earlier, Poland constitutes a limitation upon efforts to introduce change into the Soviet Union.

(3) The third fundamental limitation on the clear primacy of foreign policy in an unsettled world full of both hazards and opportunities. Soviet military power and foreign policy give the system its legitimacy and therefore receive priority over change.

The Possibilities of Change

Brezhnev, Andropov, and Chernenko have carefully selected and monitored the new leaders who will one day emerge into power. So far as one can tell, these fifty and sixty-year olds share the values of those who chose and trained them, they embrace and benefit from the Communist system, and they view the world in much the same way as their elders did. They are probably eager to rule. They seem aware of the grave character of Soviet problems and more eager to 'get the country going' than their elders have been. Under Chernenko, and after him, the debate over policy choices may sharpen. Candidates jostling for place and power may advocate changes they believe are needed to advance the interests of their bureaucratic or territorial constituencies or simply to amass personal power. Policy disagreements may arise within the leadership, and some candidates may adopt demagogic postures for change to strengthen their positions. No one can forecast whether or when such debates or disagreements will become acute or how the leadership will resolve them. However, the problems are such that intense concerns are likely to break through and that some members of the elite will advocate significant changes. Our discussions have made clear that foreign observers are not able to determine whether the new leaders will have the authority, resolution and skill necessary to carry through important innovations, but certainly early action seems unlikely because of the limitations upon change I have noted and because a Communist leader needs time to consolidate his position and create a lasting loyal coalition.

353

Soviet problems, the character of the system, the primacy of military authority (which is likely to grow) and the central role of foreign policy suggest that far-reaching changes within a decade are unlikely, even though numbers of the elite may recognise the need for such innovations. Chernenko and his successors will almost certainly talk a good deal about massive reforms, and their public relations abroad may persuade some foreign observers that the Soviet system is gradually mellowing and moderating. However, they are likely to concentrate upon law and order, labour discipline, Soviet nationalism, negative incentives and cultural isolation. In short, muddling through, or muddling down, is most probable, with a somewhat more effective and increased repression. At the same time, Chernenko's successors may combine this disciplinary approach with some economic experiments, especially in agriculture, by increasing the size of private plots, emphasising the family unit and 'links' within the collective farm, stressing productivity awards and allowing private service shops in the cities. Such an approach would delay fundamental decisions until the 1990s and leave the Soviet Union a strong state but one of ever declining power and attraction.

The probable effect upon the Soviet foreign policies which emerge from this tinkering or muddling through, or from a failure to introduce significant innovations, will depend to some degree upon the wisdom, resolution, and co-operation of the Western states as they will upon the Soviet rulers.

Chances and Limits of Political Reforms
Robert R. Conquest

The reasons for 'reform' in the USSR seem obvious to all of us in the West. The obstacles are equally obvious, and we seem agreed that political and economic reform are not really divisible. Other writers in this volume have dealt with the malign roles of inertia, interest, institutions, ideology; I would like to consider ideology, but in a rather different sense from the way Dr Kux has dealt with it. I do not feel that ideology in the sense of a Marxist 'science' is really quite the heart of the matter. It is true that there is an essentially ideological point which Dr Amann rightly stressed, that you must not have commodity relations, that socialism is almost defined by the absence of commodity relations, that this is the *raison d'être* of the regime. They are allowing peripheral bits of marketing, yes, but any economic change central to the system seems to be impossible — so long as it does not go into one of the final crises of which Dr Kux has written.

However, generally speaking I think the word ideology is a misleading one regarding most of the motivations of the Soviet leadership. After all, the formal beliefs are the ones they share with Dubček and Mao and Berlinguer and so on. The problem goes deeper than that; their mind-set, their way of looking at things is not simply a matter of intellectual belief, as 'ideology' implies, but soaked into their bones: not so much the formal content of Marxism, but — apart from the basic principle of commodity and so on — the central political attitude involved in the teachings of Leninism which, I think, can be summed up in four main points.

Firstly, it is a way of seeing the world which is in the strictest sense dogmatic: a final world-philosophy and political philosophy, a science of society, have been discovered. It is a closed system of thought and, as Solzhenitsyn puts it, 'the primitive refusal to compromise is elevated into a theoretical principle and regarded as a pinnacle of orthodoxy'.

Secondly, political leaders and political considerations generally are on a higher and a more comprehensive plane than all other elements of society and empowered to make the final decisions in all fields. They have not lately made decisions in biology, but they used to, remember.

Thirdly, and most importantly, it is based on a view of history and of the world in general that sees struggles and clashes as the essential mode of political and all other actions — the '*kto kogo*' of Lenin. Everything is a struggle in which there is a winner and a loser. And this, I think, is not merely as between political systems but also as between themselves. Moreover, the Soviets have a long practice of putting this into operation, which has generated an attitude so ingrained as to be practically automatic.

Finally, of course, the dogma's claim is universal, applicable to the whole world; all other political orders are in principle illegitimate, including other Communist political orders like Dubček's and Mao's, and subject, also in principle, to total suppression — just as their ideas are subject to total suppression within the Soviet Union.

During the Stalin period a political-psychological process of unnatural selection produced a species with these characteristics deeply ingrained. Chernenko joined the Party in 1931, the same year as Gromyko, Ustinov in 1927, Ponomarev goes back to 1919, but that is rather a special case, though for Westerners who go to the Soviet Union he is the man they are likely to meet.

As to the eventual generational change, Gorbachev joined the Party within Stalin's lifetime, just. And the next leadership are in any case not the forward-looking characters to be found among the younger Soviet generation; they are the nasty little Komsomol secretaries from the universities, the narks and general troublemakers. It is notable that all the dissidents regard the coming generation of rulers as worse than their predecessors. Sakharov says so, Ginzburg says it, Siniavsky says it, Roy Medvedev says it and Nadezhda Mandelshtam said it before she died.

Western academics are often wrong on such matters. They know a great deal about political 'systems', but have little of the imagination needed to get themselves into the skins of the Soviet or, indeed, other leaders. It was the novelists, Orwell and Koestler, who knew much more about Stalin's Russia than the stars of sociology, Beatrice and Sydney Webb. Condé complained that French historians did not understand him, men of the same culture, because, he says, 'these rascals make us behave as they would have done in the same circumstances'. When I am talking to peace groups and so on, I try to get them to avoid this trap, to use their imaginations, to envisage the *apparatchik*, by saying 'don't think of some abstract administrator, think of J.R. Ewing, from the film *Dallas*', and this does strike home. One can envisage J.R. Ewing, — even a J.R. Ewing who is a good bit nastier and brought up in a large community of J.R. Ewings who think behaving like J.R. Ewing is a good thing.

As a result of the Soviet mind-set we get this huge arms program we have written about and the internal economic, and in particular, the agricultural crisis. From our point of view, of course, we want Soviet reform in the sense that we want them to disarm, so that we can disarm. Thus our interests are very much in favour of political reform of a fairly radical nature. I always think that concern with human rights in the Soviet Union should not be based on ethical grounds, but simply on the grounds of the Helsinki agreement — that such developments are essential to peace, for the obvious reason that if they are imprisoning democrats and Christians in the USSR, then that shows what they would do to us if they could get their hands on us. Psychological disarmament, as Koestler argued forty years ago, is more basic than military disarmament.

I am, however, pessimistic about such change for a variety of reasons. In the short run, you cannot turn your nuclear submarines into ploughshares very quickly. I am not an economist, but my impression would be that it would take a good many years to cut the arms investment down from 16 per cent (or whatever it is) even to say 10 per cent and use the funds to ease the economic crisis. However, if it is going to take three or four years, why not (if one is a Soviet leader) just say, yes, we will do it, start vaguely on it and wait for the next elections in the West? I fear, that that is the sort of future we may be in for. One might respond that all Western governments are going to behave with absolute rationality over the next five to ten years. Well, perhaps.

In internal politics, to turn again to the agricultural problem, it seems to me that there is adequate investment; it is the system that does not work rather than a mere matter of investment. Soviet agriculture faces three possibilities, which could be raised in other contexts as well, three main solutions (or configurations of them). To put it crudely, there is United States grain; there is reform of a pretty radical nature; and there is Stalinism. Because, as Khrushchev said, how did they manage on two billion *puds* in Stalin's time and now they need three and a half; and Khrushchev's answer was, you damned well managed on two billion *puds* under Stalin, he could make you tighten your belts. You may, of course, say that Stalinism cannot be reimposed. I would not agree with that, not because I think it is very probable, but because I think that anything can happen in the Soviet Union. Major changes in the past have been put through by rulers against their own *apparat*: both the emancipation of the serfs and Peter the Great's reforms; and, to a less successful degree, the reforms of Stolypin and of Khrushchev.

I would also agree with those who have argued that a real crisis of the regime is quite possible. And in that context, I think it is worth adding something to what has been written about the military in the course of this volume. Although I would agree with most contributors, that the army is presently under full political control, if a crisis of the regime occurs quite a different situation might ensue. One might easily envisage a military coup, not necessarily one led by the general staff. Coups have been made by small groups of colonels. In a really critical situation anything can happen. The attempted coup in Bulgaria in 1963 was organised by a group of officers, including the commander of the Sofia garrison. They were going to come into the Central Committee with guns and say, 'elect the following politburo . . .'. It would have been 'constitutional', in fact. Thus, you can arrange coups in all sorts of ways. This is not to say that such developments are probable, but at least they are possible. Meanwhile, the political struggle is bound to take place over the agricultural issue, and to a certain extent over other issues, including that of armaments. However, I think we ought to add a little more about the Russianism issue which was spoken of earlier in the previous debate. The *Nash sovremennik* type of phenomenon is not, I think, as suggested earlier, entirely a fad of the intellectuals. The Glazunov exhibitions with all those tsars and saints and things (though without the pictures showing Solzhenitsyn in his prison uniform and so forth) were attended by several hundred thousand people, and the visitors book, which is available in the West, shows this deep Russianism, not simply by intellectuals longing to go to the village and look at birch trees, but by engineers and all sorts of people. It is very deeply rooted, and I do not think that because there is a nostalgic element to it, that deprives it of its power. A major contest is now going on, which has already affected the factional struggle within the Party, for control of this Russianism. Suslov evidently saw this and supported Glazunov and the writers, and Andropov opposed them. But in any case either the Party takes over the new Russianism in some way, or else a new and implicitly anti-Communist national feeling will emerge in Russia as well as on the periphery. Any truly adequate concession to this Russian feeling would itself be a sort of major amendment, a sort of reform, possibly a reform in the direction of autocracy.

On one last point I would like to take issue with Wolfgang Leonhard, and that is his parallels with Eastern Europe. The Soviet Party is not like the East European parties. (Hungary can perhaps be regarded as the Socialist bloc's private plot, it is a special case.) But there are no liberals in the Dubček sense on the Central Committee of the CPSU and there have not been any, unless you count Tvardovskii for a brief period in the 1950.

We have heard about the social and intellectual climate tending to reform, and this is true. My personal feeling about the perfectly sound arguments on the social and other intellectual pressures is this: Stalin had heard about Marx's boiler which blows up when the pressure gets too high, so he built a boiler with walls so thick that the pressures can be contained. This boiler still exists, unfortunately. I do not think a crisis in the regime is impossible by any means, but I think we are not quite there yet. I hope we w ll reach that point at some time.

Summary of Discussion: Part III

The last part of the conference at which these papers were presented concluded with a full and lively discussion on relations between the political and military leaders in the USSR and the possibilities of a change in the system.

What influence do the military have on major political decisions by the Politburo? Contributors gave sharply divergent answers to this important question. Some argued that military influence on Soviet policy had increased considerably since Brezhnev's time; a majority, however, disputed this view and stressed the extent of political control over the armed forces. In many cases the same facts were interpreted in a completely opposite sense, e.g. marshal Ogarkov's press conference after the shooting-down of the Korean airliner.

Members of the former school of thought maintained that the army leaders sought to have a voice in many political and economic matters and were in a good position to assert their claim. According to Ernst Kux, the military cadres had been radically rejuvenated in recent years.

Günther Wagenlehner thought the importance of the military in the Soviet Union had increased tremendously in the last twenty years. There were many signs of this: for instance, the pre- and post-military training of half the population, the shooting-down of the Korean plane and the ostentatious award of decorations; also the recent interference with traffic to and from Berlin.

Richard Staar also mentioned the SALT talks, where the Soviet military representatives had asked the Americans not to give any military information to the civilian delegates.

All other contributors believed, on the contrary, that the political leaders exercised basic control over the military.

As Bernd Nielsen-Stokkeby put it, Mao's old principle that 'it is the Party that gives orders to shoot' had not been abandoned in any Communist country. The Party could not afford any risk of Bonapartism.

Wolfgang Pfeiler declared that it was impossible to understand the nature of the Soviet system if the military were thought of as playing an active part in the decision-making process. The Soviets agreed with Clausewitz as to the primacy of politics over the

military. The political leaders' permanent control was institutionalised in the three ways denoted by the terms 'Main Political Administration', 'Party work', and 'Third Department of the KGB'. The
military machine was thus an arm of Soviet policy. The truth was
not that the Soviet Union had become more militaristic, but that it
was CPSU policy to place greater emphasis on military aspects.

Peter Frank observed that the military had always taken care, in
public statements anyway, to acknowledge the Party's leading role.
The minister of defence was to be seen as representing the Party to
the military and not vice versa. The fact that the military took a
prominent part in discussions did not mean that they wished to
interfere in government matters. Dr Frank cited the often-repeated
statement of the political leaders to the armed forces: 'You will get
everything necessary'. The wording should be carefully noted: it
was not the same as 'we will give you all you need'. The implication
was that the political leaders reserved to themselves the decision as
to the allocation of resources.

Michael Checinski pointed out that all Soviet military personnel
were instructed from the first day onwards that their function was
simply to execute the orders of the political leadership in the
military sphere.

The fact that the military were more in evidence than previously
in connection with the shooting down of the Korean airliner was
explained by Christian Schmidt-Häuer and others as signifying that
the military were made to 'take the rap' for that incident.

Participants who maintained the theory of the absolute priority
of politics conceded, however, that owing to the advance of technology the political leaders had to rely more on the expert knowledge of the military. Hence the latter's role from a purely technical
and advisory point of view was more important than formerly.

The concluding discussion then centred on the possibilities of a
change in the Soviet system, and the limitations on any such change.

Most participants were sceptical of Wolfgang Leonhard's central
thesis that the Soviet system was going through an existential crisis
that would lead to reform. It was asked why the crisis perceived by
Leonhard and Kux was evidently not recognised by the Soviet
leaders, although they had much more information at their disposal
than Western observers.

Herman Achminov pointed out that crisis-type phenomena such
as those described by Leonhard had also occurred in the past; there
was no qualitative change. The main issue still was whether there

would be a transition to a market economy and how this could be achieved in practice. The key question was what the Central Committee would decide.

Christian Schmidt-Häuer, adapting a phrase of Leopold Ranke's, stated that the Soviet Union was coming to an end but would not cease to exist for a long time yet. The problem of internal backwardness and compensatory action in the foreign sphere had existed in tsarist times. From that point of view the Soviet Union still had huge reserves of social and political stability, including Russian nationalism.

Michael Checinski agreed that any possibilities of change in the Soviet Union were long-term only. Developments in the satellite states might in the long run help to bring about change in the Soviet Union also.

John Hardt thought that the chief source of Soviet stability was the link between Russian nationalism and the Communist Party. William Stearman on the other hand regarded the stability of the bureaucracy as an indication of the strength of the system and its ability to withstand crises.

Robert Byrnes thought that important changes, crises or an actual collapse were unlikely because, despite the shortcomings of the system, a large number of Soviet citizens regarded it with a high degree of satisfaction.

Concluding the discussion on stability, Ernst Kux observed that the Soviet Union was not crisis-proof because it was Communist but because the government, with its apparatus of controls, saw to it that no crisis could break out. There was no revolutionary organisation and no revolutionary leader, and therefore he too saw no prospect of an 'assault on the Winter Palace'. There were other possibilities, however, including many that no historian, political scientist or Sovietologist could at present foresee.

Christian Schmidt-Häuer agreed with Wolfgang Leonhard's view that attempts to legalise the 'alternative economy' were connected with the leaders' desire for personal wealth; but he did not think this would lead to commercialisation or decentralisation. It must not be overlooked that centralism was a powerful instrument of political domination. Decentralisation on a large scale would at once bring up the problem of the multinational state. Economic decentralisation was bound to lead to political decentralisation. For this reason Miles Costick predicted that the Soviet Union would adhere to the system of a centralised economy. Computerisation would not alter this. Reforms were possible, but doubtless only within the system.

Wolfgang Leonhard replied that a fully developed new economic policy would lead to the abandonment of centralisation in the economy and would have repercussions in cultural and social matters and in foreign policy. A commercial attitude would introduce categories of profitability and would benefit the ordinary citizen. He would like to see a democratisation *à la* Sakharov.

Ortwin Lowack suggested that the processes envisaged by Leonhard might come about if energy prices sank further and if the Soviet Union's imperialist policy in the Third World continued to be unsuccessful.

Boris Meissner suggested another line of development that might bring about reform. In terms of the Marxist theory of crises there was a deep rift between productive forces and production conditions in the Soviet Union. The former had gone on developing, while the economic mechanism was forty years old. In these circumstances some of the leaders felt a keen desire for change. The question was whether those who wanted change as a means to greater stability were prepared to accept restrictions on their own power. The step from a totalitarian to a freer type of authoritarian system had not yet been taken; but experience showed that a single-party state was quite capable of undergoing change. This, however, was bound to involve some loosening of the absolute power of the bureaucracy.

Disagreement was expressed with Leonhard's view that the present corruption in the Soviet Union was something qualitatively new, that new socio-economic forces were at work and would have to be reckoned with in the future. It was pointed out that corruption had also been rife in old Russia. Michael Checirski even thought that the Soviet leaders did not want to do away with it, because without corruption the system could not work at all.

Botho Kirsch introduced the topic of external as opposed to domestic factors of change. In his view the greatest external obstacle to reform was the East–West conflict and the existence of nuclear weapons. This conferred a stability on the regime that had never before existed in modern times. In Russian history the most favourable time for reforms had always been in the aftermath of an external defeat. Today this was precluded by the nuclear stalemate. However, the external factors of stability might, if rightly used by the West, have a destabilising effect, if the Soviet Union were to suffer reverses in the field of foreign policy.

Claus-Dieter Kernig observed that no one knew in what way a nuclear power could 'export' a domestic crisis. Little enough study had been devoted to the theory of revolution in traditional states, and none at all to the problem in relation to a nuclear power.

The possibilities of the West influencing Soviet policy were touched on rather lightly. Edward Rozek wished that a new George Kennan would write an article on the sources of Soviet behaviour. Such an article, like its predecessor, would have to enquire how Western foreign policy could affect the domestic policy of the Soviet Union. Ernst Kux recalled that Western hopes of bringing about a 'convergence' by economic co-operation with the Soviet Union have not only been disappointed but had had the reverse effect: Moscow had used the input from the West to prevent reform.

Claus-Dieter Kernig placed the emphasis somewhat differently. Soviet backwardness, in his view, was a mark of future strength: the complex West was more vulnerable than the primitive USSR. Our policy should therefore be to make the Soviet Union more modern and thus more vulnerable.

Finally, Robert Conquest expressed a decided view as to the possibility of bringing political influence to bear on the Soviet Union. The main object was to make the Soviet arms build-up economically unprofitable. This was an argument for economic reform and for a two-way disarmament agreement. The right signals must also be conveyed to Moscow. The Russians should be made to understand that the US wanted mutually balanced disarmament, but also that the West did not trust them. This last point should be made, if only so as not to mislead the Western public.

PART IV

Summary and Concluding Remarks

Summary and Concluding Remarks
Hans-Joachim Veen

The third German-American conference was organised around the question: In what direction is the Soviet Union developing? — the importance of internal developments for Soviet foreign policy. In the search for answers to this question, we asked a great deal of our participants; the programme of thirty-six lectures was ambitious and extremely demanding. However, I believe that we succeeded in providing an extraordinarily many-faceted picture of the complex internal situation of the Soviet Union. The spectrum could hardly have been broader. All important areas, factors of internal development and changes of domestic crisis tendencies were discussed.

Our interest was centred primarily on those developments which are or could become important for the scope of action and possibilities open to the Soviet leadership in foreign policy.

I believe that I can say that we came very close to the original goal. I should now like to try briefly to summarise several important conclusions of the conference, although my summary will necessarily be rough and incomplete.

The first part of the conference was concerned with development tendencies of the Soviet economy. Mrs Ruban described the consumer goods sector and the mediocre supply situation of the population. Professor Wädekin showed that the limits of extensive agriculture have been reached. Improvements seem possible. Not the least important reason for this is that so many mistakes have been made in Soviet agriculture that things can only get better. In the private sector, on the other hand, only a moderate increase in production can be expected. Production unit-costs will continue to rise. For the foreseeable future the Soviet Union will still have to import grain, although in decreasing quantities.

The rather extensive possibilities of the Soviet Union in the energy field provided the background for our energy discussion. Dr Bethkenhagen reminded us of the grossly mistaken predictions made by well-known Western institutions about Soviet oil production in the past. The Soviet Union has now become the largest oil and gas producer in the world, and the development prospects for coal are also quite favourable. Professor Campbell stressed, however, that the costs of future investment in the energy sector will be disproportionately high. More than one-fifth of all investments in the next five years will have to be made in the energy sector. All three of our contributors to the energy discussion agreed that Soviet dependence on Western technology will remain small in this sector. They did not agree, however, on the question of how the favourable energy situation will affect the scope of action of the Soviet Union in foreign policy, that is, the development of Soviet political influence abroad. Dr Bethkenhagen referred above all to the burden on the Soviet economy resulting from the energy requirements of the Soviet Union's East European allies. On the other hand, he agreed with Professor Campbell that the Soviet need to export energy to obtain hard currency also placed customers in a strong position.

In contrast, Dr Pfeiler developed the thesis that Moscow could exploit even more the energy dependence of its CMEA partners for political and economic purposes. Moreover, the large energy reserves of the USSR will increase at least its defensive power potential in the world in the long term.

Dr Nötzold described the negative effects of the Soviet system on the whole area of technological innovation. Although the Soviet Union spends more money on and employs more people in science and research than any other country, it lags far behind in scientific productivity and investment ability. Basic improvements can probably not be expected here because of the limitations imposed by the system. Professor Checinski stressed the very close links between the armaments sector and the Soviet economy as a whole. The discussion showed, however, that opinions differed greatly in the question of the efficiency of the armaments industry and its share of the total economy. Our contributors agreed, however, that in future, too, the USSR will be able to keep pace with the USA in armaments.

Professor Levcik maintained, unlike Dr Bethkenhagen, that in regard to Eastern Europe, the terms of trade have greatly improved in favour of the Soviet Union. However, the Soviet Union has not succeeded in achieving a greater international integration of CMEA. The two main obstacles in this respect are the 'radial' bloc structure created by the USSR after the war and the lack of real prices. Dr. Schröder described the improved financial and credit situation of the Soviet Union. Although the 'umbrella theory' has not proved to be correct, Moscow is still considered a good business partner. For this reason, Western sanctions directed against the Soviet Union have affected it least of all.

Professor Kernig developed a model of the Soviet technology development process and its feedback. Using this model as a base, he was able to show that the real problems of the Soviet Union are not in technology or in technology imports, but are due to a lack of innovation and the Soviet inability to mass produce high-tech products. This has resulted in a problematic situation for Western states in that the high point of Soviet military power has coincided with a low point of economic development. If the Soviet Union were refused Western technology, it would concentrate even more on its military forces.

Dr Costick was, however, of the opinion that the present military strength of the Soviet Union is based to a considerable degree on the acquisition of Western technology and that almost all modern Soviet weapons systems have been made possible only by the use of technology imports from the West. For this reason, the Western countries have to work together to stop technology leaks. In the discussion of this view there were several objections. For example, it was asserted that the volume of Soviet technology imports has not been especially large, nor have Moscow's expectations regarding the performance of imported technology been fulfilled. The fear was expressed repeatedly that the implementation of Dr Costick's proposals could endanger several basic values of Western societies.

There were strong differences of opinion regarding the possibilities and limitations of a reform of the Soviet economic system. Professor Hardt considered it quite possible that the new Soviet leaders could decide to undertake reforms in order to increase their political power. He also considered market economy tendencies and decentralisation possible, which could be offset by a centralisation of planning at a high level and be kept within controllable limits. Dr Höhmann, however, was much more cautious in his expectations. At present, he maintained, there is no majority in the Soviet political leadership in favour of tendencies toward a 'socialist market economy', such as those on which the well-known Novosibirsk Study was based. For this reason, only limited reforms can be expected. And that has indeed been the tendency under Chernenko. Professor Amann's view of the situation was similar: On the one hand, the Soviet leaders see the necessity of economic reforms; on the other hand, the political resistance to such reforms is strong. The CPSU is afraid of the political risks any reform of the Soviet economic system would involve.

The papers on socio-cultural developments complemented each

369

other very well. All participants agreed that Marxist-Leninist ideology has lost its earlier leading role as the main political and social motivating force in Soviet society.

Dr Meier observed on the basis of his own experience that the Soviet population lacks any understanding of pluralistic structures. As a result, no fundamental political opposition has developed in the population at large.

Professor Lapidus showed the difficulties the political leadership has with its complicated nationalities problems. These problems are particularly serious in the army because the growing number of non-Russian recruits has led to increasing communications problems. She pointed out, however, that the leadership has been successful in its efforts to find solutions to the nationalities problems. The best example of this is the co-opting of non-Russian elites into the central power apparatus.

Dr Simon expanded this topic by analysing the specific situations in the individual Soviet Republics. He stressed above all that the decline of Marxist-Leninist ideology has been offset by stronger Russian nationalism.

Professor Treadgold and Dr Luchterhandt pointed out that the decline of ideology has also led to a revival of religious interest. They made clear that religiousness and non-Russian nationalism are mutually reinforcing. Generally, however, religion is a social and spiritual rather than a political force. The Russian Orthodox Church especially exercises an integrating influence in this regard.

Professor Billington examined primarily the ethical aspect of Soviet society. He spoke of a 'human energy crisis' of the system and pointed out that a new morality is developing among the younger generation.

In the analysis of the Soviet system of power the main question was whether or to what extent the political role of the military has expanded. The great majority of our discussion participants were of the opinion that the Soviet military continues to be subordinate to the political leadership. Although the prestige of the armed forces has grown, according to Dr Sella, their political influence remains extremely small.

Professor Meissner analysed the social conflict caused by the influence of the bureaucracy, which is opposed to reforms which the scientific intelligentsia would like to see realised. Dr Józsa emphasised even more than Professor Meissner the importance of centralism and the related inertia of the Soviet system. Professor

Baraz also underlined the fact that, in view of the bureaucratic structure, only gradual changes are possible. Dr Schmidt-Häuer provided in this regard an analysis of the Kremlin leadership in which he described in detail the most important trends. In his opinion the significance of the change from Andropov to Chernenko lay in the fact that those groups had the last word in the CPSU who wanted to achieve stability primarily through stagnation. Gorbachev's election as General Secretary, in contrast, represented a change of generations unexampled since Lenin's time. Dr Schmidt-Häuer expressed some optimism with respect to future growth and overall performance.

Following the papers on the Soviet power system the corresponding instruments were examined. Whereas Ambassador Staar concerned himself in the beginning with the foreign propaganda of the USSR, Professor Roth described primarily the influence of propaganda on the stabilisation of the political system. Dr Rupnik advanced the thesis that the political leadership has now faced the problem of the clearly reduced appeal of the official ideology. The symptoms of ideological erosion are to be combated with strengthened ideological education and the new Party programme.

Great efforts are being made to improve the existing situation by using the educational system, as Professor Anweiler showed. Soviet young people are still not being prepared for the reality in which they later have to live. The gap between the official ideology and their actual experiences is more obvious than ever.

The next part of the conference was devoted to the subject of oppositional movements in the Soviet Union. Using the example of a number of Soviet writers who have emigrated to Germany, Professor Kasack analysed the situation with regard to Soviet literature. He concluded that a really good Soviet writer is almost forced to join the opposition. In her lecture, Mrs Gerstenmaier attempted to counter the disinformation campaign which had characterised the late General Secretary of the CPSU, Andropov, as a liberal. She showed how, especially in the relatively short period of Andropov's regime, the legal position of dissidents had worsened.

The last part of the conference was concerned with the possibilities and limitations of systematic reform in the Soviet Union. Here especially, Professor Leonhard's paper encountered the criticism of a number of other conference participants. He had argued that in the Soviet Union the functionaries as a class are increasingly

371

forming an alliance with the second underground economy without which the system can no longer exist today. This alliance will, he maintained, lead to considerable changes in the Soviet Union in the direction of economic liberalisation and pragmatism, which could stabilise the system in the long term. For the West it is important, according to Professor Leonhard, to isolate the 'hawks' in Moscow by encouraging those moderate forces interested in change.

Professor Byrnes did not perceive such tendencies in the Soviet Union. He agreed that changes are necessary but considered them at the same time rather improbable. Not the least important reason why the structure of the system is so rigid is that the great majority of functionaries are interested in maintaining the status quo. For this reason only a 'muddling through' and a series of experiments can be expected.

Professor Kux pointed to the beginnings of a systemic crisis in the Soviet Union. He argued that even if one describes Soviet society in Marxist-Leninist categories, the unavoidable conclusion is that the possibility of a revolutionary situation cannot be excluded, for the crisis of the system is primarily a crisis of the 'ruling class'. The present situation in the Soviet Union is characterised by a conflict between former Brezhnev supporters and those of Andropov. Chernenko's election as General Secretary meant that the 'Brezhnevists' returned to power. The election of Gorbachev, however, means the political end of this clientele and a takeover by Andropov's adherents.

In the last paper of the conference Professor Conquest emphasised, as did Professor Byrnes and the majority of discussion participants, that no basic changes can be expected in the Soviet Union over the next decade. Of course, there are a number of possible developments (a return to Stalinism, reforms from above, a serious crisis of the regime, a military coup), but the probability of such developments is extremely small.

If we now ask what the main conclusions of the conference are, we should mention above all the following points:

Almost all contributors who expressed any opinion in this question agreed that the Soviet Union has an extremely conservative economic and political system at present. True, there are forces working for a modernisation and attempting to overcome the immobility of the system, but they are weak and can achieve little against the forces of inertia. It is a society in which routine work is rewarded, but not innovative behaviour which might improve the performance of the system. The most important reason for this immobility is that the preservation of the power of the ruling functionary class still has absolute priority. Changes are possible only in so far as they do not endanger the power of the political leadership and the *nomenklatura*. The primacy of politics, and that means maintaining the political power of the ruling class, dominates the entire system.

Some other questions which have recently attracted attention in Western countries have been more or less discounted at this conference. Among them are the occasional rumours about profound Soviet economic crises, raw materials and energy problems and the excessive importance attached to the questions of national minorities and religion in Soviet society. The majority of the contributors were of the opinion that serious crises will probably not develop in these areas in the foreseeable future. At the same time, it seems remarkable that all analysts maintain that the official Marxist-Leninist ideology has lost its force as a motivating factor in Soviet society. Nevertheless, that ideology will remain indispensable as a means of legitimising the power monopoly of the CPSU and the totalitarian rule of the *nomenklatura*. In the Soviet Union itself the official ideology has in reality been replaced by a kind of patriotic belief in authority in a largely closed society. In Soviet conduct abroad it has been succeeded by imperialist and militarist great power claims.

Only a few contributors diagnosed a crisis situation which could lead to collapse in the Soviet Union. The number who expected a liberalisation was even smaller. The majority expected rather a continuation of inertia with relatively small adjustments.

It is interesting that it was primarily European participants who considered either a systemic crisis or extensive changes possible. The American contributors were generally more cautious. While not excluding the possibility of far-reaching changes in the Soviet Union it was considered that they were rather improbable. However, the conference undoubtedly made an important contribution to an understanding of the Soviet Union and its current structural problems. It also helped American and European experts to a better understanding of each other.

Notes on the Contributors

Amann, Ronald
Born 1943 in England. Studied Social and Political Science. Director of the Centre for Russian and East-European Studies, University of Birmingham. Main field of interest: Political aspects of the economic reforms in the Soviet Union.

Anweiler, Oskar
Born 1925 in Rawitsch. Professor of Education, Ruhruniversität Bochum. Member of the academic directorate of the Bundesinstitut für ostwissenschaftliche und internationale Studien and of the Ostkolleg of the Bundeszentrale für politische Bildung. Vice-President of the Deutsche Gesellschaft für Osteuropakunde; President of the International Committee for Soviet and East European Studies. Since 1977 on the editorial board of the *Slavic and European Education Review*.

Baraz, Robert
Born 1929 in New York. Studied at Rutgers and Harvard Universities; worked as journalist. Since 1957 in the State Department, Bureau of Research and Intelligence. Main field of interest: Soviet Union and East Europe.

Bethkenhagen, Jochen
Born 1945 in Friedersdorf n. Berlin. Studied Economics at the Free University of Berlin. Since 1970 fellow of the Deutsches Institut für Wirtschaftsforschung (DIW), Berlin, division German Democratic Republic and Eastern industrial countries. Main areas: Trade of the Federal Republic with Eastern bloc countries; energy and economy in the Rat für gegenseitige Wirtschaftshilfe (RGW).

Billington, James H.
Born 1929 in Pennsylvania. Professor of History. Studied at the Universities of Princeton, Oxford and Harvard; 1961–4 Visiting Professor in Moscow and Leningrad. Director of the Woodrow Wilson Center, Washington, DC. Main field of interest: Russian history, political culture of the USSR.

Byrnes, Robert F.
Born 1917 in New York. Studied at Harvard University; Distinguished Professor of History, Director of Russian and East European Studies and of International Affairs, 1959–67, Indiana University, Bloomington. Main

field of interest: Eastern Europe, USSR.

Campbell, Robert W.
Born 1926 in Kansas. Studied at the Universities of Kansas and Harvard. Professor of Economics, University of Indiana, Bloomington. Main field of interest: Soviet resources.

Checinski, Michael
Professor at the Hebrew University, Jerusalem, Soviet and East European Research Center. 1947–67, in the Polish Army. Lecturer at the Military Academy of Warsaw. Main field of interest: Soviet and Polish military policy.

Conquest, Robert R.
Born 1917 in England. Studied at the Universities of Grenoble and Oxford. Former member of the British UN delegation and lecturer at the London School of Economics. PEN prize winner in 1945. Senior Research Fellow, Hoover Institution, Stanford. Main field of interest: Communism, USSR.

Costick, Miles M.
Studied at the Universities of Graz, Chicago and Freiburg. President of the Institute of Strategic Trade, Washington, DC; National Security Consultant, US Government.

Gerstenmaier, Cornelia I.
Born 1943 in Berlin. Read East European History, Philosophy and Slavonic Studies at the Universities of Bonn, Fribourg and Moscow. Since 1978 chief editor of *Kontinent*. Main field of interest: Soviet culture.

Hardt, John P.
Born 1922 in Seattle, Washington. Studied in Seattle and at Columbia University. Professor of Economics, Associate Director for the Senior Specialists in Soviet Economics, Congressional Research Service and George Washington University.

Heck, Bruno
Born 1917 in Aalen. Studied Catholic Theology and Classical Philosophy at Tübingen University. 1952–58 Secretary General of the CDU in Bonn; 1957–76 Member of the Deutscher Bundestag. 1962–8 Bundesminister for Family and Youth; 1966–71 General Secretary of the CDU. Since 1968 President of the Konrad-Adenauer-Stiftung.

Höhmann, Hans Hermann
Born 1933 in Kassel. Studied Economics and East European History at the Universities of Marburg, Berlin and Frankfurt. Official economics adviser at the Bundesinstitut für ostwissenschaftliche und internationale Studien, Cologne; lecturer at the University of Cologne. Main field of interest: Soviet and East European economy, comparative systems analysis.

Józsa, Gyula
Born 1936 in Hungary. Studied East European History and Political Science at the Universities of Budapest, Innsbruck and Leuven. Official adviser at the Bundesinstitut für ostwissenschaftliche und internationale

Studien, Cologne. Main field of interest: Soviet domestic policies.

Kasack, Wolfgang
Born 1927 in Potsdam. Professor and Director of the Slawisches Institut of Cologne University. Member of the executive board of the Deutsche Gesellschaft für Osteuropakunde. 1958–60 chief interpreter at the German Embassy in Moscow. 1974–9 chairman of the Association of University Teachers in Slavonic Studies.

Kernig, Claus-Dieter
Born 1927 in Berlin. Studied Philosophy and Political Science at Freiburg University. Since 1974 Professor of Political Science at Trier University; editor of the comparative encyclopedia *Sowjetsystem und demokratische Gesellschaft*.

Kux, Ernst
Born 1925. Professor at the University of St Gallen; an editor at *Neue Zürcher Zeitung*.

Lapidus, Gail
Born in New York. Studied Political Science at Radcliffe and Harvard. Professor of Political Science and Director of the Center for Soviet and East European Studies at the University of California, Berkeley. Main field of interest: Soviet Union (social policies, the nationalities question).

Leonhard, Wolfgang
Born 1921 in Vienna. Professor of History, Yale University. 1942–3 at the School of the Comintern Ufa/USSR. Main field of interest: Communism (cadres, ideology).

Levcik, Friedrich
Born 1915 in Prague. Honorary Professor at Vienna University. Since 1978 Director of the Vienna Institut für Wirtschaftsvergleiche. Formerly Director of the Czech Academy of Science as well as head of division of the UNO Commission for the European economy.

Luchterhandt, Otto
Born 1943. Studied Law, Economics, Slavonic and East European History at the Universities of Freiburg, Bonn and Cologne. Assistant Professor at the Institut für Ostrecht at Cologne University. 1980, awarded the prize of the Deutsche Gesellschaft für Osteuropakunde.

Meier, Reinhard
Born 1945 in Uetikon, Lake Zurich. Studied German Literature and Philology and Journalism at Zurich University. 1972–4 editor of the *Argentinisches Tageblatt* in Buenos Aires, extensive travelling throughout South America and political reporting for various Swiss newspapers. 1974–9, correspondent of the *Neue Zürcher Zeitung* in Moscow, since then in Bonn.

Meissner, Boris
Born 1915 in Pleskau. Professor and Director of the Institut für Ostrecht at Cologne University. 1961–71, founding chairman and member of the

directorate of the Bundesinstitut für ostwissenschaftliche und internationale Studien, Cologne; 1959–82, member of the academic directorate of the Ostkolleg of the Bundeszentrale für politische Bildung, Cologne. Member of the editorial board of *Sowjetsystem und demokratische Gesellschaft*.

Nötzold, Jürgen

Born 1936 in Zwickau. Studied Political Science and Economics at the Universities of Munich, Göttingen, Wilhelmshaven and Berlin. Fellow of the Forschungsinstitut für Internationale Politik und Sicherheit of the Stiftung Wissenschaft und Politik, Ebenhausen. Main field of interest: East–West relations and politics and economics in the Rat für gegenseitige Wirtschaftshilfe (RGW).

Pfeiler, Wolfgang

Born 1931 in Erfurt. Studied Political Science, History and Communication at Bonn University. Fellow of the Research Institute of the Konrad-Adenauer-Stiftung, division 'Internationale und Sicherheitspolitik'. University lecturer (*Privatdozent*) in Political Science at Bonn University. Editor of *Beiträge zur Konfliktforschung*. Main field of interest: USSR, East–West relations.

Roth, Paul

Born 1925 in Berlin. Studied Philosophy, Theology, History, Psychology and Journalism at the Universities of Berlin, Erlangen, Frankfurt and Munich. Has lived in the USSR for thirteen years. Main field of interest: Soviet media policies.

Ruban, Maria-Elisabeth

Born 1919 in Leipzig. Studied Russian and English at Heidelberg University and Economics in Berlin. Fellow of the Osteuropa-Institut at the Freie Universität, Berlin. Since 1961 Fellow of the Deutsches Institut für Wirtschaftsforschung, Berlin-Dahlem, division GDR and Eastern industrial countries. Main field of interest: Soviet economy, especially questions of living standard and social policies.

Rupnik, Jacques

Born 1950. Studied Political Science at the Universities of Paris and Harvard. Since 1982 Lecturer at the Foundation Nationale des Sciences Politiques; previously East European section of the BBC World Service. Main field of interest: Eastern Europe, Communist parties, relations within the Eastern bloc.

Schmidt-Häuer, Christian

Born 1938 in Hanover. Political correspondent of *Die Zeit*; since 1970 East European correspondent of *Die Zeit*.

Schröder, Klaus

Born 1943 in Holstein. Studied Economics at the Universities of Kiel and Berlin. Fellow of the Stiftung Wissenschaft und Politik, Ebenhausen. Main field of interest: Economy in the Soviet Union and Eastern Europe.

Notes on the Contributors

Sella, Amnon
Born 1934 in Israel. Studied Russian, International Relations, University of Edinburgh, Department of Politics. Member of the Senate of the Hebrew University, Jerusalem. Main field of interest: Soviet military policies.

Simon, Gerhard
Born 1937 in Pommern. Since 1968 adviser at the Bundesinstitut für ostwissenschaftliche Studien, Cologne. Lecturer at Cologne University. Read History and Slavonic Studies at the Universities of Hamburg, Göttingen and Indiana, Bloomington. Main field of interest: The nationalities question and Soviet contemporary history.

Staar, Richard F.
Born 1923 in Warsaw. Studied Political Science at the Universities of Yale and Michigan. Ambassador, Professor of Political Science, Senior Fellow, Hoover Institution, Stanford. Main field of interest: Communism in Eastern Europe and USSR.

Treadgold, Donald W.
Born 1922 in Oregon. Studied History at the Universities of Oregon, Harvard and Oxford. Research Professor at the Academy of Science in Moscow in 1965. Professor of History and Chairman of Russian and East European Studies at the University of Washington in Seattle, Washington. Main field of interest: Communism in USSR, China and Eastern Europe.

Veen, Hans-Joachim
Born 1944 in Strasburg. Studied Political Science, Law and History at the Universities of Hamburg and Freiburg. Until 1976 Assistant Professor at Freiburg University, since 1978 deputy, since 1983 Director of the Research Institute of the Konrad-Adenauer-Stiftung.

Wädekin, Karl-Eugen
Born 1921 in Wörishofen. Professor at Giessen University, Zentrum für kontinentale Agrar- und Wirtschaftsforschung. Member of the editorial board of *Osteuropa*. Main field of interest: Soviet agriculture.